FINANCIAL MANAGEMENT FOR NOT-FOR-PROFIT ORGANIZATIONS

FINANCIAL MANAGEMENT FOR NOT-FOR-PROFIT ORGANIZATIONS

Ronald Braswell
Florida State University

Karen Fortin
University of Miami

Jerome S. Osteryoung
Florida State University

John Wiley & Sons
New York   Chichester   Brisbane   Toronto   Singapore

Copyright © 1984, by John Wiley & Sons, Inc.

All rights reserved. Published simultaneously in Canada.

Reproduction or translation of any part of
this work beyond that permitted by Sections
107 and 108 of the 1976 United States Copyright
Act without the permission of the copyright
owner is unlawful. Requests for permission
or further information should be addressed to
the Permissions Department, John Wiley & Sons.

Library of Congress Cataloging in Publication Data:

ISBN 0-471-84214-1

Printed in the United States of America

10 9 8 7 6 5 4 3 2 1

CONTENTS

PREFACE

The role of not-for-profit organizations in our economy is prominent and is expanding at a rapid rate. Parelleling this increased role is an increased emphasis on financial management. Competent financial management is necessary for the efficient and effective operation of not-for-profit organizations as well as for profit-oriented organizations. Financial decision-making techniques for profit-oriented firms have been presented in numerous books. Financial decision making for not-for-profit organizations, however, has generally been ignored. This book remedies this situation by presenting analytical concepts and techniques which can be used by not-for-profit organizations to improve their financial decision making.

This text focuses upon the key concepts and applications relevant to decisiom making for the majority of not-for-profit organizations. Many of the tools and techniques developed for profit-oriented firms are directly applicable to not-for-profit organizations. Other techniques are applicable only after modification in order to take into consideration the special characteristics of not-for-profit organizations. Still other techniques used by profit-oriented firms are not applicable at all for not-for-profit organizations. Descriptive material is included where necessary; however, the overriding emphasis is on analytical concepts to improve financial decision making within not-for-profit organizations. The tools and techniques are illustrated using examples drawn from representative not-for-profit organizations.

Financial Management for Not-for-Profit Organizations provides the flexibility to be used in a variety of settings. The book can be used as a basic text in undergraduate and graduate financial management for not-for-profit organizations courses in either business, public administration, economics, government, or urban and regional planning curriculums. No prior courses in business or finance are necessary, only a basic knowledge of algebra and statistics is needed. Since all of the material necessary for understanding the basic concepts is included, the book can also be used in seminars and professional training programs that emphasize the application of financial theory to problem solving for not-for-profit organizations. Furthermore, the book should serve as a valuable reference to financial managers and administrators at all levels within not-for-profit organizations.

We wish to acknowledge and express our appreciation to the many people who assisted in the preparation of this book. The students, both past and present, of our various courses owed a debt of gratitude for their comments and suggestions which have certainly improved the contents of this book. A special thank-you goes to the several typists at our various institutions for typing and retyping portions of the many drafts of the manuscript for this book. The helpful comments and criticisms of our colleagues who have reviewed various drafts of the manuscript are greatly appreciated. Any remaining mistakes or omissions are, of course, the authors' responsibility.

And last, but certainly not least, we wish to thank our families for their patience, indulgence, understanding, encouragement, and love during the preparation of this manuscript. Their lives were disrupted too long by the "need to work on the book."

AN OVERVIEW OF FINANCIAL MANAGEMENT FOR NOT-FOR-PROFIT ORGANIZATIONS

The role of not-for-profit organizations in our economy has become increasingly prominent over the last several decades. Not-for-profit organizations presently account for 20 percent of our national income. Over the past twenty years, the not-for-profit sector has expanded at about twice the rate of national income.[1] Changes in the size and complexity of not-for-profit organizations in response to the dramatically increased demand for services, combined with economic factors which have accelerated the costs of providing services, have drawn attention to the need for improved financial management methods for not-for-profit organizations.

In distinguishing the public sector of the economy, the terms not-for-profit and nonprofit are often confused. This book separates the public sector into two components--the nonprofit and the governmental components; these subsectors together form the not-for-profit sector of the economy. The governmental subsector is made up of the various federal, state, and local governments, as well as public school systems and a wide variety of special governmental districts. Nonprofit organizations are those local, regional, and national organizations which operate as tax-exempt,[2] voluntary associations pursuing the public good. Nonprofit organizations, then, are the nongovernmental services institutions.

They are a diverse mix of independent organizations numbering approximately six million in the United States.[3] Other than their service orientation, many nonprofit organizations appear to have little in common in terms of objectives, activities, constituencies, and operational policies. For example, the Ford Foundation operates with broad multiple objectives and constituencies, and employs a large professional staff. On the other hand, a community church operates with fewer objectives and a smaller constituency, and is run almost entirely by volunteers.

The nonprofit sector is important to the economy in terms of both jobs and income. Peter Drucker comments that nonprofit organizations have grown so large that they now employ more people than the combined federal, state, and local governments.[4] Drucker also observes that many of these service institutions now pay salaries that are comparable to government and all but the top executive positions in private industry.

The government, the second component of the not-for-profit sector, is also a large and important element in our national economy. There were 79,913 governmental units operating in the United States at the beginning of 1977. An array of governmental units by types and level is provided in Table 1.1.

TABLE 1.1
Number of Types of Governmental Units, 1977

Type of government	Number	Percentage of total
Federal government	1	–
State governments	50	0.06%
Counties	3,042	3.81
Municipalities	18,862	23.60
Townships	16,822	21.05
Local school districts	15,174	18.99
Special districts	25,962	32.49
Total	79,913	100.00%

Source: Bureau of Census, Department of Commerce, 1977 Census of Governments, Volume 1, Governmental Organization, G(77) (1) (1), p. 1.

Local school districts and special districts account for just over one-half of the governmental units. Municipalities and townships comprise almost 45 percent of the total number of organizations, while less than 4 percent of the total number of organizations are represented by the federal, state, and county governments. The average number of governmental units per state varies from 6,620 in Illinois to 1 in Hawaii, as shown in Figure 1.1.

The impact of government is seen everywhere. Governments provide a variety of services from national defense to garbage collection. Local governments provide basic domestic goods and services such as police protection, fire protection, water and sewer services, and garbage disposal. Municipal expenditures, amounting to $71.2 billion in 1976-1977, are broken down by functional categories in Figure 1.2. Figure 1.3 shows the functional breakdown of the $41.4 billion expenditures by county governments in 1976-1977. In 1978, total expenditures for all governmental units amounted to over $760 billion. These expenditures were made in order to protect, serve, educate, aid, employ, transport, advise, inspect, subsidize, regulate, and govern us.[5]

Financial management in the public sector has increasingly aroused the attention of the citizenry. President Ronald Reagan was elected on campaign promises to reduce the size of the federal budget and federal income taxes. High taxes, among other factors, resulted in the approval of Proposition 13 in California.[6] The financial difficulties of New York City, Cleveland, and other large urban cities have highlighted the need for improved financial management. For example, the New York City financial crisis in 1974-1975, brought about by years of financing current deficits with long-term debt, resulted in a complete loss of confidence in the municipal bond market. The Securities and Exchange Commission, after investigating the crisis, denounced the abuse of the accounting system and inadequate financial management and control.[7] Other local and state governments are now faced with financial crises and a public which no longer accepts the decisions of governmental bodies without question. As these trends continue, financial management of governmental units will have to be increasingly responsive to the public's demand for accountability and adequate financial control.

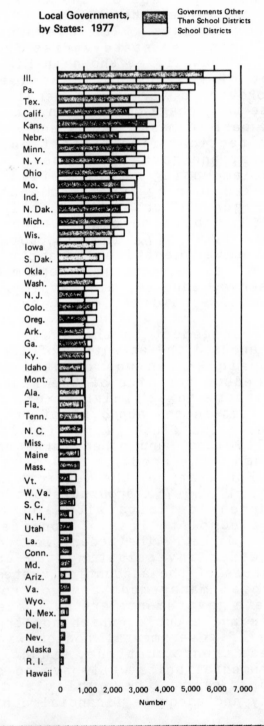

Figure 1.1   Number of Government Units per State

Source: Department of Commerce, Bureau of Census, 1977 Census of Governments, Volume 1, Governmental Organizations, p. 20.

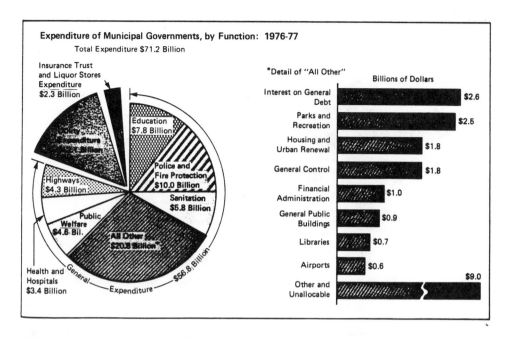

Figure 1.2 Expenditure of Municipal Governments, by Function: 1976-1977

Source: Department of Commerce, Bureau of Census, 1977 Census of Governments, Volume 2, Municipal Finances, p. 9.

UNIQUENESS OF NOT-FOR-PROFIT ORGANIZATIONS

Having examined some statistics on the size and scope of not-for-profit organizations, an examination of their distinguishing characteristics is in order.

The "not-for-profit" classification is far too broad to provide immediate insight into the appropriate methods of management which should be applied to this heterogeneous array of enterprises. The Internal Revenue Service uses 293 code numbers to classify nonprofit organizations for tax-exempt purposes because of their diversity.[8] For example, a cancer research institute has little in common with a cemetery association, except for the nonprofit classification. The governmental sector includes everything from the huge federal bureaucracy to small local districts and townships. To complicate matters, many not-for-profit enterprises are very similar to profit-seeking firms. Managing a large mutual life-insurance company,[9] for example, is similar to running a large stock insurance company.

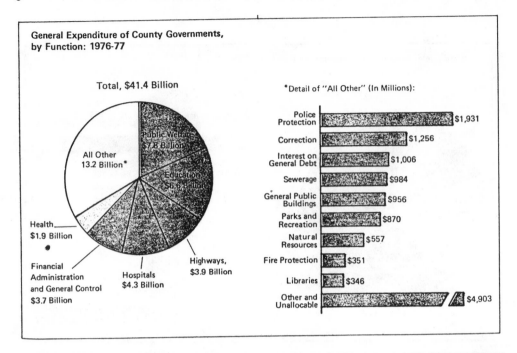

General Expenditure of County Governments, by Function: 1976-77

Total, $41.4 Billion

Public Welfare $7.8 Billion

Education $8.8 Billion

All Other 13.2 Billion*

Health $1.9 Billion

Financial Administration and General Control $3.7 Billion

Hospitals $4.3 Billion

Highways, $3.9 Billion

*Detail of "All Other" (In Millions):

Police Protection	$1,931
Correction	$1,256
Interest on General Debt	$1,006
Sewerage	$984
General Public Buildings	$956
Parks and Recreation	$870
Natural Resources	$557
Fire Protection	$351
Libraries	$346
Other and Unallocable	$4,903

FIGURE 1.3 General Expenditure of County Governments, by Function: 1976-1977.

Source: Department of Commerce Bureau of Census. 1977 Census of Governments, Volume 2, Municipal Finances, p. 7.

To help understand the not-for-profit organization, the key economic and management features which affect their decision processes must first be examined. Decision making may be defined as "the job of selecting a particular course of action from among various alternatives."[10] Differences in decision making between profit-oriented firms and not-for-profit organizations, to the extent that they exist, stem from differences in their mission; i.e., providers of services rather than products, and the operating alternatives available. Robert N. Anthony and Regina E. Herzlinger identified seven characteristics of not-for-profit organizations which affect the decision-making process relative to profit-motivated organizations:

1. The absence of the profit measure.
2. The tendency to be service organizations.
3. The absence of a strong marketplace role.
4. The dominance of professionals.
5. Differences in ownership.
6. Their tendency to be political organizations.
7. A tradition of inadequate management controls.[11]

Profit Measures

The profit measure is a very useful tool for the profit-oriented firm. Since its dominant objective is to earn a satisfactory return, the profit measure provides the criterion for choosing among alternative actions. The profit measure also provides a means of analyzing alternative proposals. The analyst and the decision maker can address such questions as: "Is the proposal likely to produce a satisfactory level of profits or not?"[12] The best manager is the one who performs best on balance over a combination of separate activities, as reflected in the profit measure. Finally, the profit measure permits a comparison of the performance of heterogeneous operations not possible with any other measure. For example, the results of a department store can be compared with the results of a paper mill by one measure--profit.

The absence of a measure corresponding to profit makes the financial management function in a not-for-profit organization more difficult than in a business firm. An organization's effectiveness is measured by the extent that its outputs accomplish its objectives. Efficiency is measured by the relationship between organizational inputs and outputs. Profit provides an overall measure of effectiveness and efficiency for a profit-oriented firm. The output of a not-for-profit organization, however, is often a service which is intangible and difficult to measure. A few services have basic service units, such as the kilowatt hour in the case of an electric utility, which are well defined physically. Other areas may find it almost impossible to define a single basic service unit. For example, the basic service units for police protection, fire protection, and urban transportation are poorly defined. The quality of output is even more difficult to measure and is often a value judgment. The judgment of the suppliers of services may be at odds with the judgment of the consumers of the services.

In addition, many not-for-profit organizations have multiple objectives, and there may be no feasible way to combine the varied outputs into a single measure of overall effectiveness. "The absence of a satisfactory, single, overall measure of performance that is comparable to the profit measure is the most serious management control problem in a nonprofit organization."[13] In addition, there is often no way of estimating the relationship between inputs and outputs. For example, "Would the addition of another fireman increase the value of fire protection by an amount that exceeds the cost of the fireman?"

It is difficult to measure performance in not-for-profit organizations since their primary goal is to render service, not to make a profit. Consequently, even when revenues and expenditures can be measured, they do not provide a measure of the organization's primary objective. In fact, a surplus of revenues over expenditures in a not-for-profit organization is often looked on with great disfavor. Surpluses in local governments have often been a factor in the election of new administrations.

The difficulty in quantifying output has led to the development of surrogate measures of effectiveness. These surrogate measures, however, usually focus on resources consumed and, as such, are not really a measure of services provided. For example, man hours expended per household by a municipality to collect garbage in a certain area may be compared with man hours expended by a profit-oriented collection service. This surrogate, however, does not measure the amount nor the quality of service provided.

Service Organizations

The majority of not-for-profit organizations provide intangible services rather than tangible goods. This presents special problems to the financial management of such organizations. Service cannot be stored in inventory, awaiting demand. If the personnel and facilities are not available at the time demanded, then the services are denied the user. In addition, many not-for-profit organizations must provide services regardless of whether the person is able to pay for the service or not. A hospital cannot deny emergency service to a patient because he is a bad credit risk, nor can a municipality deny police or fire protection to a citizen who is delinquent in the payment of taxes. As a result, most not-for-profit organizations have a more difficult time in collecting revenues and controlling costs than a profit-oriented firm.

Market Forces

The market dictates the conditions and limits by which most profit-oriented firms operate. A company cannot survive unless it meets the performance level of its competition, nor can it supply a product or service not demanded by the market. Each consumer is attempting to satisfy his own needs in accordance with his purchasing power. The composite demand of millions of individual consumers, along with the decisions of the various producers of the product or service, determines what it produces.[14] The "voting" mechanism is the price system which indicates the willingness and ability to pay given prices for particular goods.

In contrast, not-for-profit organizations must decide what services to offer without the benefit of market information to determine the community's preferences for their services. The governing body of the not-for-profit organization must plan expenditures and services for the forthcoming year based on the budget and judgment of the demand for the service. Also, most not-for-profit organizations lack the powerful incentive provided by competition to endorse the wise use of resources. In fact, government often discourages competition through the imposition of regulations and other controls, considering competition an unnecessary duplication of effort. Ultimately, of course, the not-for-profit organization cannot survive unless the needs of its constituents are met. The contributors of resources to not-for-profit organizations will withdraw their support, or the voters will elect new public officials.

Professionals

A number of not-for-profit organizations are dominated by professionals—doctors in hospitals, professors in colleges, scientists in research laboratories, to name a few. These professionals play a major role in the policy decisions of their organizations. The dominance of professionals has several implications for the financial management of such organizations. The evaluation of professionals is geared toward criteria established by the profession rather than the efficient use of resources. Factors which motivate professionals are often inconsistent with good resource utilization. Success is measured by the perceptions of professional colleagues rather than by meeting objective financial standards. Consequently, the professional is faced with a dual set of standards, those imposed by the organization and those imposed by professional colleagues. Professional quality is often of utmost consideration and all other considerations are secondary. The financial implications of decisions are given little weight.

Ownership and Political Organizations

Many not-for-profit organizations, such as state and local governments, labor organizations, business associations, and nonprofit membership organizations, are very politically oriented. They are responsible to the membership, electorate, or legislative body representing the electorate. The necessity for re-election, public visibility, external pressures, or legislative restriction, may override financial and economic considerations in coming to a decision.

Inadequate Management Controls

"Nonprofit organizations have been slow to adopt 20th century accounting and management control concepts and practices."[15] Many are still operating in the 19th century with its emphasis on fiduciary accounting. The major purpose of accounting then was to keep track of funds entrusted to an organization to ensure their honest use. The broader function of providing useful information to interested outside parties and the management of the organization was missing.

The modern concepts and techniques generally used by business--the accrual concept, cost accounting, standard costing and variance analysis, breakeven analysis, and responsibility accounting are generally not used by not-for-profit organizations. Although many not-for-profit organizations are making improvements, others are a long way from achieving adequate management control.

FINANCIAL MANAGEMENT OF NOT-FOR-PROFIT ORGANIZATIONS

The financial management of not-for-profit organizations involves the acquisition, allocation, and

spending control of financial resources and the
financing of assets in order to provide services
demanded by a segment of the public. Figure 1.4
shows a typical organizational structure for a municipality's finance department. The divisional names
may differ, but the functions and duties of the
finance department will be similar.[16]

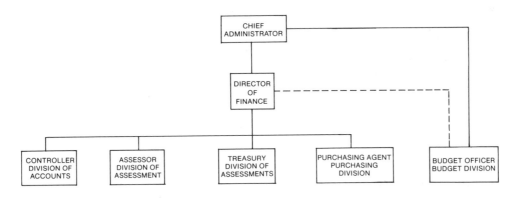

**FIGURE 1.4 Typical Organization for a Municipal
Finance Department.**

NOTE: The dashed line between the director of
finance and budget office indicates that the budget
officer is often primarily responsible to the chief
administrator, but is physically located in the
finance department to prevent a duplication of
records.

Source: Based on Figure 12.1 in Robert Lamb and Stephen P.
Rappaport, Municipal Bonds: The Comprehensive Review of Tax-
Exempt Securities and Public Finance (New York: McGraw-Hill
Book Company, 1980), p. 242.

Director of Finance
● Supervises all finance activities
● Advises Chief Administrator in fiscal policy
● Manages retirement and other city investments
● Handles debt administration
● Makes interim and annual financial reports

Controller--Division of Accounts
● Preaudits all purchase orders, receipts, and
  disbursements

- Prepares payrolls
- Prepares and issues all checks
- Keeps general accounting records
- Maintains or supervises cost accounts
- Bills property and other taxes, special assessments, and other service charges
- Maintains inventory records of all municipal property

Assessor--Division of Assessments

- Makes studies of property values for assessment purposes
- Prepares and maintains property maps and records
- Assesses property for taxation
- Prepares assessment rolls
- Spreads special assessments for local improvements

Treasurer--Treasury Division

- Collects all taxes, special assessments, utility bills, and other revenues
- Issues licenses
- Administers tax sales
- Maintains custody of all city funds
- Disburses city funds on proper vouchers or warrants

Purchasing Agent--Purchasing Division

- Purchases all materials, supplies, and equipment for city departments
- Establishes standards and prepares specifications
- Tests and inspects materials and supplies purchased by the city
- Maintains warehouses and stores system
- Administers city's insurance program

Budget Officer--Budget Division

- Makes departmental work measurements studies for development and administration of the budget system
- Assembles budget estimates and assists Chief Administrator in preparing budget document
- Acts as agent of the Chief Administrator in controlling the administration of the budget
- Conducts studies relative to improvements in administrative organizations and procedures

To gain perspective on the organizations, a representative sample of financial statements for such organizations is presented for examination. Tables 1.2 and 1.3 contain comparative financial statements of ten not-for-profit organizations.[17]   The particular sample was chosen to represent different types of not-for-profit organizations. The sample includes a social services organization, a medical complex, a voluntary health organization, a research organization, a municipality of approximately 5,000 persons, a nonprofit organization with a focus on conservation, a symphony, a church, and a youth organization.

Several observations regarding the comparative balance sheets and income statements are in order. The comparative balances sheets of Table 1.2 reveal that the fundamental accounting equation differs from that of a business firm. In business firms, the equation is assets = liabilities + equity; in the not-for-profit organizations of Table 1.2, the equation is assets = liabilities + funds. Not-for-profit organizations have no ownership or equity claims as found in the typical business. Instead, the not-for-profit organization has a source of financing vaguely defined as "funds." Funds are either provided by contributors who have no subsequent claims against the assets of the organization or are generated by organization operations.

Not-for-profit organizations are not concerned with making a profit. Instead, the emphasis is on accountability and stewardship. Gifts or funds restricted for specific purposes are segregated and their receipt and disposition are reported separately. This separate reporting of assets according to specified purposes is called fund accounting, a system of accounting used by most not-for-profit organizations. For example, a family donates $50,000 to a university to conduct research into the causes of cancer. The $50,000 transaction would be included as part of a special or restricted fund for that stipulated purpose. Since the various funds for each organization in Table 1.2 were aggregated, the significance of restricted funds cannot be seen. The table is useful, however, for comparing the relative composition of the assets and liabilities.

Table 1.2

Relative Composition of Balance Sheets of Not-for-Profit Organizations

Assets and Financing	Goodwill Industries	Hollywood Presbyterian Hospital	Muscular Dystrophy	Museum Modern Art	Rand	Rosemont, Illinois (General Fund)	Sierra Club	Southern California Symphony	Van Nuys Baptist Church	Young Life Campaign
	(1)	(2)	(3)	(4)	(5)	(6)	(7)	(8)	(9)	(10)
Cash	2.7%	0.1%	7.5%	0.8%	1.2%	10.2%	1.1%	3.5%	(-0.6%)	4.6%
Short-term investments	6.5	11.5	53.4	46.7	0	6.6	40.0	81.0	0.2	11.9
Accounts receivable	1.8	12.2	0	1.9	17.3	8.8	19.8	7.1	0.2	15.0
Notes receivable	1.5	0	0	0	0	0	0	0	0	0
Due from subsidiaries or govt. agencies	0	0	10.8	0	6.8	2.2	0	0	0	0
Inventory	6.5	1.0	0	1.6	0	0	23.2	0	0	2.3
Long-term investments	0	0	4.2	0.3	0	0	0	0	3.5	0
Net fixed assets	80.7	73.6	22.3	47.8	44.5	70.5	0	4.8	94.2	64.8
Other assets	0.3	1.6	1.8	0.9	30.2	1.7	15.9	3.6	2.5	1.8
Total assets	100.0%	100.0%	100.0%	100.0%	100.0%	100.0%	100.0%	100.0%	100.0%	100.0%
Accounts payable	2.1%	5.3%	2.4%	1.6%	7.4%	2.1%	31.9%	5.7%	0.8%	7.6%
Borrowing	4.1	51.9	0	0.6	13.5	46.6	33.5	0	39.9	6.6
Other liabilities	4.5	13.8	37.9	3.5	26.3	7.6	23.3	26.4	5.9	3.6
Funds	89.4	29.1	59.7	94.3	52.8	43.7	11.3	67.9	53.4	82.1
Total financing	100.0%	100.0%	100.0%	100.0%	100.0%	100.0%	100.0%	100.0%	100.0%	99.9%
Size of total assets & financing (in thousands)	$5,207	$30,541	$20,519	$38,471	$15,573	$15,712	$1,421	$6,295	$5,749	$11,387
Date of statement	12/74	6/74	3/74	6/74	6/74	12/77	9/74	6/74	12/74	9/74

Source: Thomas E. Copeland and Keith V. Smith, "An Overview of Nonprofit Organizations," Journal of Economics and Business (Winter 1978), pp. 148-149 and Preliminary Official Statement, Village of Rosemont, Cook County, Illinois, $19,000,000 O'Hare International Coliseum Revenue Bonds, Series 1978.

Table 1.3

Composition of Income Statements of Not-for-Profit
Organizations As A Percentage of Total Revenue

	Goodwill Industries (1)	Hollywood Presbyterian Hospital (2)	Muscular Dystrophy (3)	Modern Museum Art (4)	Rand (5)	Rosemont Illinois (6)	Sierra Club (7)	Southern California Symphony (8)	Van Nuys Baptist Church (9)	Young Life Campaign (10)
Operating revenues	92.6%	98.8%	0%	48.7%	91.4%	80.0%	42.8%	69.1%	30.1%	31.1%
Contributions	6.0	0	98.6	31.8	0	0	52.2	27.4	69.0	68.6
Government transfers	0	0	0	4.6	0	4.3	0	2.6	0	0
Endowment income	1.3	1.2	1.7	13.4	0.4	1.7	3.7	0.9	0.9	0.6
Other revenues	0.2	0	(0.3)	1.5	8.2	13.3	1.2	0	0	(0.3)
Size of total revenues (in thousands)	$4,600	$17,309	$24,806	$7,007	$33,124	$4,058	$4,431	$5,399	$2,386	$9,700
Operating expenses	100.5%	92.3%	99.3%	119.3%	99.1%	60.1%	98.4%	97.9%	86.8%	105.2%
Debt retirements	0.4	1.3	0	1.8	0.7	21.5	.4	0	12.3	0
Other expenses	0	4.2	0	0	0	7.1	1.9	0	0	0.1
Net gain (loss) (% of revenues)	(0.8%)	2.1%	0.7%	21.1%	0.2%	11.3%	(0.8%)	2.1%	0.9%	(0.53%)
Size of total expenses (in thousands)	$4,638	$16,950	$24,628	$8,484	$33,124	$3,600	$4,467	$5,287	$2,364	$10,212
Date of statement	12/74	6/74	3/74	6/74	6/74	12/77	9/74	6/74	12/74	9/74

Source: Thomas E. Copeland and Keith V. Smith, "An Overview of Nonprofit Organizations," Journal of Economics and Business (Winter 1978), pp. 148-149 and Preliminary Official Statement, Village of Rosemont, Cook County, Illinois, $19,000,000 O'Hare International Coliseum Revenue Bonds, Series 1978.

Table 1.2 reveals a considerable diversity among the composition of assets and liabilities in not-for-profit organizations. Cash ranged from a negative 0.6 percent of total assets for the church to 10.2 percent for the municipality. The symphony has 81 percent of its total assets in short-term investments, while the research organization and church have only negligible amounts of short-term investments. Five of the ten organizations have no inventories. Accounts receivable represent more than 12 percent of total assets for four of the organizations. Fixed assets vary from zero for the conservationist organization to over 94 percent for the church. On the financing side of the balance sheet, borrowing accounts for over 50 percent of the financing of the hospital and none of the financing for the voluntary health organization. Funds represent from 11 percent (conservationist) to over 94 percent (museum) of total financing.

Table 1.3 shows the relative percentages of revenue and expenses for the ten not-for-profit organizations. Operating revenues are derived by selling goods and services directly to consumers, by contributions from the public, or by taxing citizens. Almost all of the hospital revenues are from operations, while none of the voluntary health organization's revenues are from operations. Contributions from individuals and groups account for over 98 percent of the revenues of the voluntary health organization but none of the revenues for the hospital, research organization, and municipality. Governmental transfers or subsidies from federal, state, and local governments account for only a small proportion of total revenues for three of the ten organizations. Interest and dividend income from endowments accounts for 13 percent and approximately 4 percent of total revenue for the museum and conservationist organizations, respectively. The greatest proportion of expenditures for all ten organizations was used to provide goods and services. Expenditures exceeded revenues for four of the organizations. The excess of expenditures over revenues resulted in decreases in fund balances, which is analogous to a reduction in equity or net worth for a business firm.

As discussed earlier, not-for-profit organizations exist primarily to render a service, rather

than to earn a profit. Although "service" is more
vague and difficult to measure than "profit," financial management tools and techniques are valuable
aids in achieving the objective of providing the
best possible service within the available resources. The tools of financial management provide
the manager of a not-for-profit organization with a
framework for making better decisions. The value of
financial management for not-for-profit organizations can be demonstrated by a few examples.

Financial management techniques--such as net present value analysis or benefit-cost analysis--can be
used to determine the cost implications of various
investment and financing alternatives. As discussed
in detail in Chapter 12, a university could use
these techniques to decide between the construction
of a new central air conditioning facility for all
buildings on its campus or keeping its present decentralized system. A municipality could use the
techniques to determine whether it should lease or
purchase police vehicles. Admittedly, cost may not
be the only factor to be considered in making such
decisions, as other noneconomic factors may be very
important; however, to make the best decision, the
management of a not-for-profit organization must be
aware of the cost implications of various alternatives. The use of appropriate financial-management
techniques can lead to such an awareness.

The not-for-profit enterprise can also minimize
its investment in accounts receivable and inventories by the use of other financial-management
tools and techniques such as: pro forma cash budgeting, cash-management techniques, accounts receivable, and economic order quantity models. Minimiza-
tion of investment in these assets will allow the
enterprise to provide its services at lower cost.
Additionally, well-planned budgets and cost reports
allow the not-for-profit enterprise to better control its internal operations. Cost determination
and adequate planning are vital to the success of
the not-for-profit organization in the long run.

PLAN OF THIS BOOK

This book presents a framework for financial-
management decisions within the not-for-profit or-

ganization. Competent financial management is essential to both not-for-profit and profit-oriented
organizations. Financial decision-making techniques
for profit-oriented firms have been presented in
numerous books. There is, however, a lack of consideration of financial decision-making techniques for
not-for-profit organizations. This book is intended
to remedy this deficiency by presenting a variety of
analytical concepts which may be used by the majority of not-for-profit organizations to improve their
financial decision making.

Many of the tools and techniques developed for
profit-oriented firms are directly applicable to
not-for-profit organizations. For example, the
management of current assets and current liabilities, where liquidity is of prime concern, is similar for both types of organizations. Other techniques are applicable after certain modifications to
take into consideration the special characteristics
of not-for-profit organizations. Major differences
exist, however, between the profit and not-for-
profit sectors in the factors which influence long-
term financial decisions.[18] The maximization of
stockholders' wealth leads to appropriate criteria
for making long-term investments and for establishing the mix between debt and equity for profit-
oriented firms. Not-for-profit organizations do not
have a profitability or wealth maximization motive,
nor do they have the equivalent of equity or ownership claims. Consequently, the standard procedures
used by business firms are not necessarily applicable.

Analytical tools and techniques which may be used
by the majority of not-for-profit organizations are
stressed in this book. Because of the wide diversity in not-for-profit organizations, examples are
drawn from various representative not-for-profit
organizations. For example, a municipality is used
in Chapter 7 to illustrate cash-management techniques rather than a church since cash represented
10.2 percent of total assets, as shown in Table 1.2,
while it was only 0.6 percent of total assets for
the church.

The book is divided into five major parts. Part
I provides the introduction to financial management
for the not-for-profit organization. An overview
and accounting concepts are presented in this section. Various tools and techniques for financial
analysis, planning, and control are covered in Part
II. The chapters contained in Part III provide a

framework for the management of working capital. This part of the book is concerned with investment in assets which will be converted into cash within one year and with the manner in which these assets are financed.

The appropriate investment in long-term assets is discussed in the three chapters comprising Part IV. This part includes a presentation of the time value of money, capital budgeting, cost-benefit analysis, and the definition of appropriate discount rates. The final part is concerned with long-term financing of not-for-profit organizations. Various methods of financing are discussed with emphasis placed on the use of long-term bonds. The final chapter in this section discusses methods to improve efficiency and effectiveness in debt management.

QUESTIONS

1. What are some of the characteristics of not-for-profit organizations?

2. What purpose does a profit measure serve in profit-oriented firms?

3. What factors complicate performance measures for not-for-profit organizations?

4. Who makes "product" decisions within not-for-profit organizations?

5. What is a major factor in the existence of inadequate management control in not-for-profit organizations?

6. How does the balance sheet of a not-for-profit organization differ from that of a profit-oriented firm?

7. What is the primary emphasis of the accounting function in a not-for-profit organization?

ENDNOTES

1. Robert N. Anthony and Regina E. Herzlinger, Management Control in Nonprofit Organizations (Homewood, Ill.: Richard D. Irwin, Inc., 1975), p. 8.

2. Tax-exempt under Internal Revenue Code 501(c) (3) through 501(c) (18) and 501(d).
3. Peter F. Drucker, "Managing the 'Third Sector'," Wall Street Journal (October 3, 1978).
4. Ibid.
5. Department of Commerce, Bureau of Census, 1977 Census of Governments, Volume 1, Government Organizations, p. 1.
6. Frank Levy, "On Understanding Proposition 13," Public Interest (Summer 1978).
7. Robert Lamb and Stephen P. Rappaport, Municipal Bonds: The Comprehensive Review of Tax-Exempt Securities and Public Finance (New York: McGraw-Hill Book Co., 1980), p. 281.
8. William E. Newman and Harvey W. Wallender, III, "Managing Not-for-Profit Enterprises," Academy of Management Review (January 1978), pp. 29-31.
9. A mutual insurance company is an association formed for the benefit of the policyholders. Any excess of revenues over expenses, after providing for reserves, is used to reduce premiums. A stock insurance company seeks to earn a profit for its shareholders.
10. Daniel A. Wren and Dan Voich, Jr., Principles of Management and Behavior (New York: 1976), p. 9.
11. Anthony and Herzlinger, p. 34.
12. Ibid., p. 36.
13. Ibid., p. 35.
14. William H. Anderson, Financing Modern Government (Boston: Houghton Mufflin Co., 1973), pp. 2-3.
15. Anthony and Herzlinger, p. 53.
16. Lamb and Rappaport, p. 242.
17. Except for the Village of Rosemont, Illinois, this sample is from: Thomas E. Copeland and Keith V. Smith, "An Overview of Nonprofit Organizations," Journal of Economics and Business (Winter 1978), p. 147.
18. Copeland and Smith, p. 154.

2

ACCOUNTING FOR NOT-FOR-PROFIT ORGANIZATIONS

INTRODUCTION TO FUND ACCOUNTING

The term "not-for-profit" is used to define many types of organizations which have as a common characteristic an absence of the profit motive. In accounting for not-for-profit organizations, the accounting practices are generally divided into two distinct categories--government accounting and accounting for other types of not-for-profit organizations. Governmental accounting deals with governmental units, such as city, county, or state governments or one of their subdivisions, while not-for-profit accounting deals with accounting for all other types of not-for-profit organizations, such as hospitals, universities, fraternal societies, and churches. Though there are numerous differences, there are certain similarities in the reporting practices of these two types of not-for-profit organizations. The major similarity is their use of the fund as the basic reporting unit.

The fund is defined as:

> ... an independent fiscal and accounting entity with a self-balancing set of accounts recording cash and/or other resources together with all related liabilities, obligations, reserves, and equities which are segregated for the purpose of

carrying on specific activities or attaining
certain objectives in accordance with special regulations, restrictions, or limitations.[1]

The use of the fund as the basic reporting
entity, however, is confusing to most accountants
and financial managers who have dealt primarily with
the financial statements and reporting requirements
of the profit-oriented commercial enterprise. The
commercial enterprise is a singular reporting
entity. One set of the accounting records is kept,
and from these records are prepared a single set of
financial statements, the income statement, balance
sheet, statement of retained earnings, and a statement of changes in financial position. Under the
fund theory of accounting for not-for-profit organizations, the entity itself is not the basic
reporting unit; each of the funds within the entity
itself is a basic reporting unit. A great deal of
confusion may develop because one not-for-profit
entity may have hundreds or even thousands of separate funds. Each of these funds then has its own
set of accounting records and prepares a set of
financial statements appropriate for that fund.

Until recently, providing any kind of summary
data for the various funds was openly discouraged.
Even now, summary information is recommended rather
than required. Comprehensive consolidated statements combining results for all funds may not be
presented. Thus, the user of financial statements
may have to wade through volumes of individual funds
statements to determine the overall financial pic-
ture of the not-for-profit organization. Not only
is this time-consuming, but it would be an
impossible task for someone without adequate background in the peculiarities of fund accounting.

The remaining parts of this chapter provide an
introduction to fund accounting practices for several types of not-for-profit entities for which
accounting practices have been somewhat
standardized. Two organizations have tried to standardize accounting practices for not-for-profit
firms: the American Institute of Certified Public
Accountants (AICPA) through its Industry Audit
Guides, and the Municipal Financial Officers
Association which has specifically addressed
accounting practices in governmental bodies. There
are several discrepancies in the accounting practices prescribed by these two groups. The financial

manager who is dependent upon accounting information
must be prepared to deal with a variety of possible
accounting alternatives in extracting the data necessary for decision making.

There are many accounting practices and terms
which are peculiar to not-for-profit entities using
the fund theory of accounting. Since each entity
may also have a number of different funds for different purposes, the accounting practices between
funds of the same entity may also be quite
different.

Entire texts and courses are devoted to not-for-
profit accounting. This chapter serves as no more
than an introduction to the practices and funds
encountered in not-for-profit accounting. There are
several practices which are peculiar to fund accounting, such as the encumbrance system and the
recording of the budget in the accounting records,
which will be introduced briefly. Then, the funds
used in accounting for governments, hospitals, universities, health organizations, and other not-for-
profit entities will be discussed.

Basis of Accounting in Not-For-Profit Organizations

The basis of the accounting system in a not-for-
profit organization will generally fall into one of
three categories--full accrual, modified accrual,
and cash basis. Not all funds, however, within one
not-for-profit organization will use the same basis;
i.e., one type of fund may use the full-accrual
basis and another type of fund may use the modified-
accrual basis within the same organization. Further
complicating the understanding of the accounting
system is that the details of practice of the modified-accrual basis of accounting may also vary between types of not-for-profit organizations. For
example, the special revenue fund of a municipality
and the restricted current fund of a university
perform substantially similar functions but their
particular accounting practices, though both are
defined as modified accrual, are quite different.

The most commonly encountered basis of accounting
in not-for-profit organizations is the modified-
accrual basis rather than the full-accrual basis.
The major difference between full accrual and modified accrual lies in the timing of recognition of
revenue and expense items. First, under the modified-accrual basis of accounting, many revenues will

not be recognized until actually received. This is
particularly true of certain taxes and fees collected by municipalities. These are not thought to
be "subject to accrual" and are recognized on a cash
basis only. Property taxes, on the other hand, are
normally accrued with appropriate allowances for
uncollectable taxes. Second, since not-for-profit
organizations normally do not charge directly for
services rendered, there is no basis for matching
the expense of providing services with revenues
generated. Thus, in several types of funds the term
expenditure replaces expense since expense implies
use of this matching principle. In addition, expenditures are not necessarily recognized only when
resources are consumed. In the modified-accrual
basis used for fund accounting, expenditures are
often recorded when resources are acquired. Thus,
when supplies are purchased, an expenditure is recognized even though those supplies may remain in an
inventory for some time and the acquisition of fixed
assets may be recognized as a current expenditure.

Certain funds and certain types of not-for-profit
organizations will use full-accrual accounting,
however. If a governmental entity carries on an
activity designed to be self-supporting, the fund
used to account for that activity should follow the
full-accrual basis. Similarly, a not-for-profit
hospital derives a major portion of its revenue from
services to patients. The accounting practices of
hospitals then generally follow full-accrual principles in their various funds. While many persons
would like to see full-accrual accounting for all
not-for-profit organizations, the modified-accrual
basis is firmly entrenched in the major funds of
most of these entities and it is unlikely there will
be major changes in the near future.

Though not a recommended basis of accounting,
many small not-for-profit organizations follow the
cash basis of accounting. In addition, some trust
funds of larger organizations may also follow a cash
basis of accounting. Under this method of accounting, revenue and expenditures (expenses) are recognized in the accounting records only when the cash
is received or disbursed. This method of accounting
has all the drawbacks encountered when it is used in
the profit-oriented firm; i.e., manipulation of
recognition of revenues and expenditures by delaying
or speeding up the receipt and disbursement of cash.
It is for this reason that it is generally not an
acceptable method of accounting. However, it is a

simple method which does not require an extensive accounting background. As such, it is often used by the smaller not-for-profit organization on the basis of expediency.

Recording the Budget

In many not-for-profit organizations, the formal budget adopted for a period is a limiting factor on the amount of resources that may be expended. While it is a misconception, it is felt that the formal recognition of the budget in the accounting records aids in controlling these expenditures. When the budget is recorded in a fund, an estimated revenues account is debited, an appropriations (the estimated expenditures) account is credited, and the balancing entry is either a debit or credit to the budgetary fund balance.

> **Example:** Platt City's estimated total revenues are $450,000 and approved expenditures of $460,000 for its 19X2 budget; these are recorded formally in the accounting records as:
>
> Estimated revenues--control $450,000
> Budgetary fund balance   10,000
>   Appropriations--control $460,000
>
> The excess of appropriations over estimated revenues requires a debit entry to the budgetary fund balance.

When the budget is recorded in the above man-ner, it must be reversed when the closing entries are recorded for the fund. Thus, the closing entry would be:

Appropriations--control $460,000
    Estimated revenues--control $450,000
    Budgetary fund balance   10,000

Actual revenues and expenditures are then closed to the fund balance account in a manner similar to that of normal accounting practice. For example, if Platt City's actual revenues and expenditures were $483,000 and $469,000, respectively, the closing entry would be:

```
Revenues--control                    $483,000
     Appropriations--control                    $469,000
     Fund balance                                 14,000
```

Under fund accounting practices for governmental units prior to the issuance of Statement: <u>Governmental Accounting and Financial Reporting Principles</u> by the Municipal Finance Officers Association, the balancing budgetary entry was treated as a direct increase or decrease in the fund balance in the following manner:

```
Estimated revenues               $450,000
Fund balance                       10,000
     Appropriations                            $460,000
```

When the budget was recorded in this manner, a somewhat different closing procedure was required at the end of the accounting period. If actual revenues and expenditures equalled those estimated in the budget no adjustment would be required for the fund balance at the end of the period. The only adjustments required in the fund balance at the end of the period would be for differences between actual and estimated revenues and expenditures. For Platt City with actual revenues of $483,000 and expenditures of $469,000, the closing entries would be:

```
Revenues                         $483,000
     Estimated revenues                      $450,000
     Fund balance                               33,000

Appropriations                   $460,000
Fund balance                        9,000
     Expenditures                            $469,000
```

Note that the above entries are <u>closing</u> entries. The actual revenues would have been recorded originally as credit entries and the expenditures as debit entries. In this closing procedure, the closing entries only adjust the fund balance for differences between actual and anticipated revenues and expenses. While this procedure has been superseded, it may still be encountered quite often in practice.

The Encumbrance System

Another accounting procedure encountered in some not-for-profit organizations is the formal accounting recognition of commitments to expend resources in the future. Theoretically, the purpose of the encumbrance system is to provide, through the subsidiary ledgers, a running tally comparing appropriations to expenditures and commitments for expenditures (encumbrances), providing the control mechanism to ensure that authorized appropriations are not exceeded. The encumbrances would be recorded in the accounts in the following manner:

> **Example:** Platt City issued purchase orders for stationery and supplies in an amount estimated as $2,500. The entry would be:

Encumbrance--control $2,500
    Fund balance reserved
        for encumbrances $2,500

When the supplies are received, the <u>actual</u> cost of the supplies is recorded as an expenditure, even though this amount may be different from the estimated amount encumbered; the related encumbrance, however, is reversed at its original amount.

> **Example:** When Platt received the supplies, the actual bill was $2,450, requiring the following entry:

Expenditure--control $2,450
    Cash or vouchers payable $2,450

Fund balance reserved
    for encumbrances $2,500
        Encumbrances $2,500

If properly monitored, this system does provide some measure of control for total expenditures and commitments. In addition, when actual expenditures vary from those encumbered by substantial amounts, the management should be alerted to investigate other possible sources of supply or alternative purchasing procedures.

Depreciation Expense

In fund accounting practice, fixed assets are generally recorded in separate funds rather than in the fund used to account for the day-to-day operating revenues and expenditures of the organization. While fixed assets facilitate the daily operations, they are not considered to be a resource available for current operations to pay for such things as salaries and supplies; hence, their placement in a separate fund. In addition, most not-for-profit organizations do not attempt to match revenues and expenses and, as a result, it is felt the recording of depreciation on fixed assets serves no purpose. The only type of not-for-profit organizations which consistently records depreciation on fixed assets is hospitals. Hospitals generally record depreciation expense in the same manner as in commercial accounting because they are often reimbursed by third parties on the basis of full cost of operations and their client orientation provides a greater correspondence between revenues and expenses than in other types of not-for-profit organizations. Other not-for-profit organizations may record depreciation expense under two common circumstances. First, depreciation may be recorded in those funds or for those operations which are to be self-supporting. Second, if the not-for-profit entity desires to set aside resources for replacement of existing plant assets it may recognize depreciation expense with a corresponding transfer of assets to a fund for replacement of plant.

Interfund Transfers

One of the most frustrating elements of fund accounting, which has made the preparation of comprehensive consolidated financial statements somewhat more complex for the not-for-profit organization, is the accounting treatment of interfund transfers. Since there may be numerous funds for one entity, there are many instances where resources may be transferred between funds. When these fund transfers are made, the transfer may be treated in one of several ways. First, the most recent recommendation for governmental units is to treat the interfund transfer as an other financial use in the transferring fund with the recipient fund recognizing an other financial source. However, prior municipal practice often had the transferring fund recognizing an expenditure while the recipient fund recognized a revenue. In other instances, however, the transfer would be treated by the transferring fund as a reduction in the fund balance while the recipient fund recognized it as an increase in the fund balance. There is also a great deal of inconsistency in the recording of interfund transfers in other types of not-for-profit organizations. Thus, someone interested in aggregating the financial data of several funds must be aware that revenues and expenditures may be overstated due to the existence of interfund transfers.

Accounting For Governmental Units

There are two primary sources of information on the accounting practices for governmental units. One is Audits of State and Local Governmental Units, an audit guide, issued by AICPA; the other is Statement 1: Governmental Accounting and Financial Reporting Principles, issued by the National Council on Governmental Accounting. These two sources are in relative agreement on accounting principles and Statement 1 includes recognition of the desirability of the governmental unit preparing financial data in accordance with generally accepted accounting principles (GAAP).[2]

Eight types of funds, broken down into three categories and two account groups, are prescribed for state and local governments. The first category of funds is the governmental-type funds and includes five funds: the general fund, the special revenue fund, the special assessment fund, the capital projects funds, and the debt service fund. There are two proprietary funds--the enterprise fund and the internal service agency fund. The last category of funds is the fiduciary funds and includes trust and agency funds such as the expendable and nonexpendable trust funds and pension trusts. The two account groups, the long-term-debt account group, and the general-fixed-asset account group are unique to fund accounting and have no counterpart in commercial accounting. The five governmental funds generally follow the modified-accrual basis of accounting. The two proprietary funds are supposed to be self-supporting funds and generally follow full-

accrual accounting procedures. The basis of accounting for the trust and agency funds follows the
purpose for which the fund was established and may
be either the accrual, modified accrual, or possibly
even a cash basis.

The two account groups, long-term debt and general-fixed-asset account groups, are not used to
record transactions, as are the other funds. These
account groups serve the purpose of inventorying or
cataloging long-term debt and fixed assets. Thus,
someone interested in the maturity value of the
long-term debt undertaken by a municipality could
look at the items in the long-term-debt account
group.

The General Fund

The general fund uses the modified-accrual basis
of accounting and is used to account for the normal
operations of the municipality which are not properly accounted for within one of the other funds.
The budget is normally recorded as shown previously,
the encumbrance system is generally used, and many
of the general fund revenues are not recorded until
actually received. Property taxes are consistently
accrued; i.e., when the property taxes are levied
against the taxpayers, the revenue is recorded along
with the associated accounts receivable. Expenditures are recorded when made and no attempt is made
to match revenues and expenses, as is done in commercial accounting. In addition, a transfer of
funds from the general fund to one of the other
funds usually results in the recognition of an other
financial use of funds in the general fund and an
other financial source in the other fund even though
it was originally recorded as a revenue in the
general fund and will be a subsequent expenditure in
the other fund. Thus, the same funds may be recognized as a revenue in one fund and another financial
source in another. Failure to understand the exact
nature of revenues and expenditures and other financial sources and uses of funds may lead one to
believe total resources coming into and going out
from the entity are greater than they actually are.

The Special Assessment Fund

Capital improvements such as street lighting or sidewalks, which are undertaken for and financed primarily by the users they benefit, are accounted for in a special assessment fund. All transactions relating to construction and financing are accounted for within this fund until the project is complete and debts discharged. Since the assessments may usually be paid over a period of time which extends well past the construction period, the special assessment fund generally issues and accounts for any debt undertaken to pay for the project as completed.

The Special Revenue Fund

The special revenue fund is used to account for the resources earmarked for specific purposes rather than general operations; i.e., if ten mills of the tax levy are specifically assessed for operation of the local library, these funds and the operations of the library would constitute a special revenue fund. The accounting procedures in a special revenue fund closely parallel those of the general fund.

Capital Projects Fund

The capital projects fund is used to account for the construction of assets to be used for general operations of the municipality. The capital projects fund will not account for assets constructed by special assessment funds nor for enterprise fund assets. The capital projects fund receives its revenue from general obligation bonds or from transfers from other funds. The recording of budgets is optional but the encumbrance system is used.

The Debt Service Fund

The debt service fund is used to account for the payment of principal and interest on long-term debt which is a general obligation of the municipality. Debt issued by the special assessment or the enterprise funds will generally be accounted for within their own funds, however. The debt service fund receives its revenues either from other funds or from interest on investments made with these funds. The major peculiarity in accounting procedure in the debt service fund is that the principal amount owed is not recorded until the maturity of the debt. Since total debt is catalogued within the long-term debt group account, a credit to term bonds payable is unnecessary until maturity.

The Enterprise Fund

The enterprise fund is designed to account for the operations of a governmental unit which is primarily self-supporting. The enterprise fund serves the public and derives its resources from charges to the users. The accounting in the enterprise fund most closely resembles that of commercial accounting, even to the use of retained earnings and contributed capital accounts rather than the "fund balance" account. Since it is to be self-supporting, depreciation of assets should be recorded and full-accrual accounting should be used.

Internal Service Agency Fund

Centralized service facilities, such as computer facilities and motor pools which serve other governmental units, primarily are accounted for in an internal service agency fund. This fund, like the enterprise fund, should be self-supporting and requires the use of full-accrual accounting, including the recording of depreciation.

Trust and Agency Funds

Trust and agency funds are used to account for resources held temporarily by the governmental unit and which will be transmitted to other recipients at a later date or for nonexpendable trust assets. Such things as the portion of sales taxes collected by the state, which will be returned to local governmental units and pension trust funds, fall into this category. The accounting in these funds follows usual procedures for trust funds.

The Long-Term-Debt and the General-Fixed-Asset Account Groups

There is nothing similar to either of these group accounts in commercial accounting. They are catalog accounts--the long-term-debt account group simply lists in debit and credit format the amounts to be provided or the amounts available (debits) to pay the principal of long-term debt (credits); the fixed-assets account group lists assets at their cost as debits with an investment in fixed assets from the appropriate fund as the credit. Only debt not properly accounted for elsewhere, such as debt issued by the special assessment and enterprise funds, is catalogued in the debt service fund. Similarly, when assets are properly accounted for in the enterprise, intragovernmental service agency, or trust funds, they are not catalogued in the fixed-asset account group.

No transactions are recorded in either of these account groups. Thus, while debt principal is cata-logued in the long-term-debt group, all payments of principal and interest are in fact made out of the debt service fund. Similarly, the existence of the fixed-asset account group effectively prevents de-preciation of the general assets of the governmental organization. Assets are simply catalogued in this fund when purchased by another fund--that fund re-cording an expenditure. When the asset is sold, the original entry in the fixed-asset group account is reversed and the appropriate fund records another financial source of funds in the amount of the sale price. No depreciation is recorded during the asset's useful life and no gains or losses are recorded on the disposition of the assets.

College and University Funds and Accounting Procedures

Other nonprofit organizations such as colleges, universities, hospitals, health care agencies, clubs, and churches follow fund accounting practices similar to those of governmental units. The major differences are found in the types of funds set up by these organizations and the specific purpose served by each type of fund due to the nature of the organization.

Accounting practices for colleges and universi-ties are covered in two publications: the College

and <u>University</u> <u>Business</u> <u>Administration</u> of the
<u>National Association of College and University</u>
<u>Business Officers</u>; and the <u>Audits</u> <u>of</u> <u>Colleges</u> <u>and</u>
<u>Universities</u> of the AICPA. While there are more
differences between these two statements than between the two authoritative statements for governmental bodies, these differences are beyond the
scope of this text and are not relevant to a basic
familiarity with college and university fund accounting.

College and universities use six types of funds:
a current fund, loan funds, endowment funds, annuity
and life-income funds, plant funds, and agency or
custodian funds. Several of these funds are similar
to governmental funds and/or to funds of other not-
for-profit organizations, but serve the specific
purposes of a college and may vary in the detail of
their operations.

Current Fund

The college or university current fund is similar
to the governmental general fund and accounts for
resources available for current operations and is
the only college fund in which revenues and expenditures are recognized. It is, however, a dual fund
in that the current fund is subdivided into restricted and nonrestricted funds. The unrestricted current fund of a college generally recognizes revenues
and expenditures on an accrual basis. As a result,
transfers to and from the unrestricted current fund
are treated as either mandatory transfers in or out,
for required transfers, or additions or reductions
in the fund balance for discretionary transfers. In
addition, since several of the auxiliary services of
a university are self-supporting, but are not accounted for in separate funds, depreciation may be
recorded in the current fund and resources transferred to the plant fund for replacement.

The restricted portion of the current fund is
used to account for resources available for specific
current operations. The unusual feature of this
fund is the method in which it recognizes revenues,
the receipt of resources. When resources are contributed to the fund, the appropriate asset account
is debited and the fund balance is increased
directly. When the resources are spent, expenditures are recognized; but revenues are then also
recognized to the extent of expenditures. Thus,

revenues always equal expenditures in the restricted current fund.

> **Example:** The State Central University received $20,000 from an alumnus for library books on January 2, 198X. On January 18, $7,000 of books were purchased. The receipt of the money is recorded in the restricted current fund as:

Cash	$20,000	
Fund balance		$20,000

The purchase of the books requires the following entry:

Expenditure	$7,000	
Cash		$7,000
Fund balance	$7,000	
Revenue		$7,000

The restricted current fund balance always shows the amount of resources still available for the specified purpose.

Endowment Funds

Endowment funds are used to account for resources donated to the university, which have been restricted as to their use by the donor for a limited or indefinite period of time. Pure endowment funds are funds which must be maintained indefinitely. Term endowment funds are restricted for a specified time period. After this term expires, however, all or part of the principal may be expended for operations. In addition to endowments set up by outside donors, the governing board of the institution may establish quasi-endowment funds which restrict the use of board-designated assets for specific purposes. Endowment funds recognize increases or decreases in assets as changes in the fund balance directly rather than as revenues or expenditures.

Each endowment should be accounted for in its own specific endowment fund to maintain the integrity of the restrictions on principal and income. Invest-

ments, however, are often made by pooling the resources of several funds in order to benefit from
economies of scale and professional investment management. Problems do arise in accounting for the
allocation of income and capital gains resulting
from these pooled investments and each fund must
agree to the basis of allocation, such as market
value at date contributed, prior to establishing a
workable pooling arrangement.

Loan Funds

Loan funds of colleges and universities are types
of funds usually found in no other type of not-for-
profit organization. The purpose of the loan fund
is to account for resources available to faculty,
students, and staff on a loan basis. The loan fund
is designed to be a self-supporting fund but, again,
increases and decreases in assets are recorded as
increases or decreases in the fund balance rather
than as revenues and expenditures.

Annuity and Life-Income Funds

Annuity and life-income funds are similar in some
respects to endowment funds. Resources are donated
to the institution by an outside donor. However,
the trust agreement specifies that payments are to
be made to the donor or someone designated by the
donor from the fund either for a specified period
(annuity) or for the person's lifetime. At the end
of that time, the resources remaining in the fund
revert to the general use of the university or for
other specified purposes.

Plant Fund

The plant fund of the college or university is
generally not a single fund but is a group of up to
four funds, each with a specific purpose. The four
subgroups are the investment in plant fund, the
unexpended plant fund, the plant fund for renewals
and replacements, and the plant fund for retirement
of indebtedness.

The investment in plant fund is used to account
for all plant assets, except those properly account-

ed for in the endowment or annuity funds, as well as
any related liabilities. This one fund serves a
function similar to that of both the general-fixed-
asset and long-term-debt account groups in a governmental unit. The unexpended plant fund accounts
for resources which are to be used to acquire fixed
plant and equipment in the future. The plant fund
for renewal and replacement is used to account for
funds which are used for maintenance of plant and
equipment. The plant fund for retirement of indebtedness is similar to the governmental debt service
fund. It is used to account for resources which
will eventually be used to pay interest and principal on debt.

Agency or Custodian Funds

Agency or custodian funds are simple fiduciary
funds used to account for resources for which the
university has custody, but which belong to another
organization. An example would be student fees
collected for the student government operations.
Since none of the funds belong to the university,
the asset balance must equal the liabilities to
other parties and there is no fund balance.

HOSPITAL FUNDS AND ACCOUNTING PROCEDURES

Of all not-for-profit organizations, hospital
accounting procedures most nearly resemble those of
commercial enterprises. Many of the services provided patients are paid for by third parties; e.g.,
Medicare, Medicaid, and Blue Cross. These third
parties often pay for many services on the basis of
cost. This has led to well-developed accounting
procedures which reflect the required cost data.
Two organizations, again, have been involved in
setting accounting standards for hospitals, the
American Hospital Association through its Chart of
Accounts for Hospitals and the AICPA in its Hospital
Audit Guide. They recommend essentially the same
accounting procedures for hospitals, except that the
American Hospital Associations Chart of Accounts for
Hospitals recommends carrying long-term investments
in securities and plant, property, and equipment at
current value rather than historical cost.
Hospitals generally follow full-accrual accounting
practices, including depreciation of fixed assets,

presented in fund accounting format.

The types of funds recommended for hospitals are an unrestricted fund which is the general or operating fund, specific purpose funds, endowment funds, and a fund for plant replacement and expansion. Several of these funds are similar in nature to those of governmental units or colleges but the unrestricted fund includes a much broader range of transactions than those normally encountered in an operating fund.

The Unrestricted Fund

The hospital unrestricted fund is used to account for almost all its day-to-day operations, including nursing and professional services, fiscal services, and administrative services. An unusual feature of hospital accounting is the accounting for donated service as both a revenue and expense. This facilitates comparison of operating data between hospitals with varying amounts of donated services. Hospitals also account for their plant property and equipment in the unrestricted fund. This facilitates the recording of depreciation on fixed assets for determination of full costs. Since there is a separate fund for plant replacement and expansion, however, there are many interfund transfers between this and the unrestricted fund. Resources earmarked for eventual plant replacement will be transferred to the plant replacement and expansion fund from the unrestricted fund; when the fixed assets are acquired the resources will be returned to the unrestricted fund and the acquisition accounted for in that fund.

Specific Purpose Funds

Donor-restricted resources which are to be used for specified purposes are accounted for in a specific purpose fund. This fund operates in much the same manner as the governmental special revenue fund and the restricted portion of a college's current fund. Assets in this fund must be donated by outside sources. Assets designated for specific purposes by the hospital board are accounted for in the unrestricted fund. One peculiarity in accounting procedures for this fund is that revenues are first recorded in the unrestricted fund and then trans-

ferred to this fund; disbursements require a transfer to the unrestricted fund with the actual recognition of the expenditure in that fund.

Plant Expansion and Replacement Fund

Since plant assets are accounted for in the unrestricted fund, hospitals do not have elaborate plant
funds. The plant expansion and replacement fund is
used to account for assets donated by outsiders and
set aside by management for the purpose of replacing
or adding to existing assets. When plant assets are
acquired with these resources, they are first transferred to the unrestricted fund, with actual acquisition recognized through that fund.

Endowment Funds

Endowment funds for hospitals are essentially the
same as those of universities. They may be permanent or term endowments with the primary accounting
concern the maintenance of the endowment fund according to the donor's wishes. Resources of this
fund are not spent directly from this fund, either;
they are first transferred to either the unrestricted or specific purpose fund when they become available for use. The consistent transfer of funds to
the unrestricted fund prior to expenditure has one
benefit. The operating statement of the unrestricted fund contains summary information on all the
revenues and expenditures of the hospital.

HEALTH AND WELFARE ORGANIZATIONS

In spite of the existence of several documents
outlining accounting practices which should be followed by health and welfare organizations, there are
greater variances in their accounting practices than
in any other type of not-for-profit organization for
which standards exist. Both the National Health
Council and National Welfare Assembly in its
Standards of Accounting and Financial Reporting for
Voluntary Health and Welfare Organizations and the
AICPA in its Audits of Voluntary Health and Welfare
Organizations have attempted to standardize accounting practices under the fund theory of accounting;
however, failure to achieve consistency in practice

must be attributed in part to the wide variance in operating purposes exhibited by organizations classified as health and welfare organizations. While one hospital exhibits many of the same characteristics as another, the Salvation Army performs totally different functions than the American Cancer Society.

Recommended accounting procedures for health and welfare organizations follow most closely those prescribed for hospitals. The recommended funds are the current unrestricted fund; the current restricted fund; the land, building, and equipment fund; the endowment fund; the custodian fund; and the annuity fund. The endowment, custodian, and annuity funds serve the same purpose as their counterparts in hospitals and universities and a description of their purposes will not be repeated.

The Current Unrestricted Fund

The current unrestricted fund is the operating fund for the health and welfare organization; it is used to account for the day-to-day operations of the organization. However, many of these organizations carry on two types of activities: one is the program(s) for which the organization exists, such as cancer research, and the other is the activity of raising funds to support that program(s). The accounting records should be set up in a manner which carefully separates expenditures for these two types of activities.

While full-accrual accounting is recommended for health and welfare organizations, many variations are found in practice. It is not recommended, however, that fixed assets be accounted for within the unrestricted fund. Rather, they are accounted for in the land, building, and equipment fund. Thus, depreciation on fixed assets is normally not recorded in the unrestricted fund unless it is funded by a transfer of resources to the land, building, and equipment fund. And, unlike hospitals, the value of donated services are excluded from the accounting records.

The Current Restricted Fund

Resources from outside donors, which are earmarked for specific current purposes, are accounted for in the current restricted fund. Board-designated assets set aside for specific purposes are accounted for in the current unrestricted fund as appropriations of the fund balance rather than in this fund. While the current restricted fund is similar in purpose to the hospital special purpose fund, accounting procedures differ. Revenues and expenditures are recorded directly in this fund without interfund transfers to and from the unrestricted fund; thus summary operating data of the organization are contained in the financial statements for both the restricted and unrestricted funds.

The Land, Building, and Equipment Fund

The land, building, and equipment fund is a singular fund which is used to account for the fixed assets of the health and welfare organization, assets contributed for the acquisition of fixed assets, and any debt related to the fixed assets. The AICPA Audits of Health and Welfare Organizations in recommending full-accrual accounting procedures includes a recommendation for depreciation on fixed assets similar to that of hospitals. The National Health Council and National Social Welfare Assembly standards did not include a general provision for depreciation. Since these recommendations preceded the AICPA's by ten years, the change to depreciation accounting has not been universal.

OTHER NOT-FOR-PROFIT ORGANIZATIONS

Accounting standards for other not-for-profit organizations have not been well defined. Fund accounting procedures, however, have been accepted by most accountants as a proper method of accounting in not-for-profit organizations. There is not universal acceptance of full-accrual accounting since the matching of revenues to expenses is impossible for many types of not-for-profit entities. The alternative to full accrual, however, is modified accrual rather than cash basis. The cash basis is subject to the same type of manipulation that can occur in profit-oriented enterprises; yet, it may be found in many organizations because of its simplicity. It also must be noted that for many small clubs and organizations with relatively few resources there is little to warrant extensive accrual accounting procedures. The differences between cash and accrual basis are minimal and the statements of these organizations are seldom subject to rigid auditing procedures.

For many not-for-profit organizations, the only fund that is necessary is some type of general or operating fund. This fund can be used to account for all the activities that the smaller or limited organizations will engage in. Beyond this fund, however, the accounting requirements should be based on the needs and purpose of the organization. There are several types of special purpose funds that may be necessary. First, some form of restricted fund may be needed to account for donated resources which are available for current specific purposes. Second, donors may contribute resources on a permanent or term endowment basis, requiring a separate endowment fund. While it complicates depreciation procedures, most not-for-profit organizations that possess substantial fixed assets will establish a separate fund to account for them and for any related debt. In addition to these funds, the not-for-profit organization may need agency or annuity funds. The major consideration should be accurate reporting for the entity within the fund accounting framework. Thus, the accounting system should be based on common sense to facilitate the organization's purposes.

Financial Statements of Not-For-Profit Organizations

Since the basic reporting entity for most not-for-profit organizations is the fund, each fund will prepare a set of statements appropriate to its purpose. In general, those funds that report revenues and expenditures or expenses prepare a statement, similar to an income statement, which reports on revenues and expenditures. In addition, this statement may also include budget data as well as actual data for the current period for a direct comparison of the planned performance to actual results. All funds and account groups prepare a balance sheet which details the assets, liabilities, and fund equity for the particular fund or account group. Most funds prepare a statement of changes in the fund balance which includes details of increases or decreases in the fund balances from operations, interfund transfers, or from other outside sources. If the fund is a proprietary-type fund, then the fund would prepare a statement of changes in retained earnings. A few funds may also prepare a statement of changes in financial position, which is a statement almost identical to that prepared for the commercial enterprise and would be appropriate for those funds with accounting practices similar to those of commercial enterprises.

In addition to the individual statements of the various funds, aggregate data may also be prepared for the various types of not-for-profit organizations. Governmental units may prepare general purpose financial reports which include:

1. Combined balance sheets for all the various fund types and account groups

2. Combined statements of revenues, expenditures, and changes in fund balance (budgeted vs. actual) for the general and special revenue funds

3. Combined statement of revenues, expenditures, and changes in fund balances for all governmental-type funds and expendable trust funds

4. Combined statement of revenues, expenses, and changes in retained earnings or fund balances for the proprietary-type funds and the nonexpendable and pension trust funds

5. Combined statement of changes in financial position for the proprietary-type funds and the nonexpendable and pension trust funds

In addition, the governmental unit may also prepare comprehensive annual reports which include not only the general purpose financial reports but provide aggregate data for each particular type of fund.

Universities, hospitals, and health and welfare organizations also provide some aggregate data in addition to individual fund data. Universities generally prepare a statement of current funds revenues, expenditures, and other changes which combines data from the restricted and unrestricted current funds. In addition a balance sheet and a statement of changes in fund balance will be prepared which combines data for all funds. Hospitals generally

prepare a statement of revenues and expenses for the
unrestricted fund, a combined balance sheet for all
funds, a combined statement of changes in fund balance for all funds, and a statement of changes in
financial position for the unrestricted fund.

Health and welfare organizations generally prepare three financial statements--a statement of
support, revenues, and expenses and changes in fund
balances; a balance sheet; and a statement of func-
tional expenses. Each of these statements may be
prepared for the individual funds with aggregate
totals presented for all funds. Two unusual features are found in these statements: First, support
is separated from revenues since it represents the
charitable contributions of the general public and,
second, expenses are reported by the individual
programs within the organization in a separate
statement in addition to the data provided in the
statement of support revenues and expenses and
changes in fund balances.

Legal Compliance

Various forms of not-for-profit organizations
from governmental units to the smallest club may be
subject to some form of reporting requirements imposed externally. Organizations which receive support from the federal government are required to
report in a specified manner. State legislatures
may require that reporting practices for the state
operations follow a certain format. Chartering
bodies may require annual reports on a specific
basis. These required reporting practices may conflict with what constitutes good accounting practice. When this conflict arises, the person in
charge of accounting should maintain the accounting
records in a manner which facilitates preparation of
all necessary information. Reporting should follow
good accounting procedures first; then, however,
additional supporting schedules can be prepared
which meet the reporting requirements of governing
bodies.

SUMMARY

This chapter presented a brief introduction to
accounting practices often followed in fund accounting for not-for-profit organizations. Among these

were the encumbrance system, the entering of budgets
into the formal accounting records, and depreciation
practices.   The various funds for four specific
types of not-for-profit organizations--governmental
units, colleges and universities, hospitals, and
health and welfare organizations--were described
briefly.   While there are many similarities between
funds of the various organizations, the details of
operations are inconsistent and can be a great
source of confusion to one not thoroughly familiar
with these details. Since the financial manager
must often extract information from the accounting
records, an understanding of the accounting practices of the particular organization should be
acquired.

QUESTIONS

1. Define fund, the basic reporting unit of the
   not-for-profit organization.

2. Why does the system of fund accounting often
   confuse someone familiar only with the
   statements of a profit-oriented firm?

3. What two organizations have attempted to
   standardize fund accounting practices?

4. Why is the term <u>expenditure</u> used in fund accounting rather than <u>expense?</u>

5. What types of funds use full-accrual accounting?

6. What basis of accounting is most commonly
   encountered in not-for-profit organizations and
   how is it distinguished?

7. Why is depreciation seldom recorded in not-for-
   profit organizations?

8. How has the recommended treatment of interfund
   transfers for governmental entities changed
   recently?

9. What are the two primary sources of information
   on accounting practice for governmental units?

10. What types of funds are recommended for
    governmental units? Briefly describe each of
    their functions.

11. What purposes do the long-term-debt and general-fixed-asset account groups serve?

12. What types of funds are recommended for college and university accounting? Briefly describe each.

13. What types of funds are recommended for hospital accounting? Briefly describe each.

14. What are the primary sources of information on accounting practices for colleges and universities, hospitals, and health and welfare organizations?

15. How does accounting for health and welfare organizations differ from that for hospitals?

16. What types of financial statements do not-for-profit organizations prepare?

ENDNOTES

1. National Committee on Governmental Accounting, Governmental Accounting, Auditing, and Financial Reporting (Chicago: Municipal Finance Officers Association of the United States and Canada, 1968), pp. 6-7.
2. The National Council on Governmental Accounting, Statement 1: Governmental Accounting and Financial Reporting Principles (Chicago: Municipal Finance Officers Association of the U.S. and Canada, 1979), pp. 4-5.

3

CONTROL SYSTEMS

INTRODUCTION

In the private sector, the "bottom line" or net income or loss for an enterprise provides the ultimate control. Companies which consistently fail to make a profit simply do not survive. The area of managerial accounting is devoted to the various concepts, procedures, and practices of the firm's internal reporting system which are designed to monitor the operations of the firm on a day-to-day basis so that the objective of profitability, revenues exceeding costs, is achieved. In general, private sector revenues are controlled by the interaction of the firm with the market place. Price and quantity of goods or services sold are entwined. Private enterprise cannot force someone to purchase a good or service at a price he does not wish to pay. The inability to indiscriminately raise revenues is one of the greatest incentives to establishing and maintaining elaborate control systems within the private sector. This same incentive often does not exist within the not-for-profit organization. Property taxes may be levied at a rate determined by the amount of revenue which must be generated. The federal government increases the national debt if revenues fail to meet expenditures. Hospital rates are based on the costs of operation. Fund drive objectives are often based on the budgeted costs of the programs they support. In other words, rather than the limitations on revenues necessitating the limitations on costs which exist in private enterprise, often the public sector first determines its costs and then raises its revenues accordingly. As a result, there has been little incentive to establish elaborate cost control systems in not-for-profit organizations. Yet, with today's inflation and Proposition 13 type movements, control systems are becoming a necessity for the not-for-profit entity.

PURPOSE OF A CONTROL SYSTEM

Ideally, the purpose of any control system should be to ensure the maximum effectiveness and efficiency of all enterprise inputs in achieving its goals and objectives. While the private sector often has goals and objectives other than that of maintaining profitability, this goal is common to all profit-oriented firms. No such common goal binds the not-for-profit sector. The not-for-profit firm often translates its goal of providing service to the public to one of providing service at any cost. With some major exceptions, there is often no relationship between the services provided and the revenues generated to support these services. What relationship exists between the taxes imposed by the federal government on the taxpayer and the benefits received through revenue sharing? Even in our cities, is there any direct relationship between property taxes paid by one individual and the services received? Thus, in the not-for-profit enterprise we often have an important factor missing in establishing a control system--a relationship between the goods or services provided and revenue generation. In other words, the profit motive almost automatically leads to some type of control system--even a primitive one. Without this motive, some other basis must be found for control.

The Budget

The budget is the main vehicle for control within any form of organization. "Budgeting is an essential element of the financial planning, control, and

evaluation process of governments. Every governmental unit should prepare a comprehensive budget
covering all governmental, proprietary, and fiduciary funds for each annual fiscal period."[1] Almost
all not-for-profit organizations prepare some form
of budget either because of formal legal requirements or as requirements of their charters, by-laws,
or board of directors. These budgets may take several forms, but two essential elements of these
budgets are the estimation of available revenues and
of the costs to provide the services for which the
organization exists. Once the budget has been
adopted or approved, it is often incorporated within
the accounting system as a means of control. A
running total is kept of actual expenditures and
commitments for expenditures against the total
amount of money that has been allocated for these
expenditures. This is done, particularly in governmental units, because legally total expenditures in
an area may not exceed the total provided in the
budget. The emphasis of control in these situations
has been not to exceed budgeted amounts. Little
attention has been paid to how effective the expenditures have been in achieving the objectives of the
organization. Many not-for-profit organizations can
simply cease providing particular services for a
period of time if the budget is exceeded. In the
1980 budget crunch, one Wisconsin school district
simply abandoned an entire summer school program
rather than exceed its annual budget. Alternatively, the not-for-profit organization can seek approval to exceed its budget in the current period under
the assumption that additional revenues will be
raised in subsequent periods to cover the deficit.
The lack of relationship between revenues and expenditures permits these situations to exist along with
the emphasis on cost control of absolute amounts
rather than cost control based on cost effectiveness.

Goals versus Objectives

The not-for-profit organization must consider how
effectively dollars are spent. Are the dollars
spent doing the best job they could in providing
organization services? This question is not easily
answered, however. How do we operationalize the
measurement of cost effectiveness? The first step
in any formal control system for a not-for-profit

organization is to explicitly recognize the goals of the organization. These goals cannot be stated in broad terms, however; they must be stated in clear, precise terms which are understood by management and which can be communicated to the people carrying out the services. A university cannot control costs based on the broad goal of quality education. A goal of quality education as evidenced by a faculty-student ratio of 1 to 25 per course provides specific guidance for cost control. Department chairmen can then use estimated class enrollments from pre-registration to provide sufficient teachers to staff the required number of sections of a course so that there is one section for every 25 students.

In order to facilitate control in a nonprofit organization, it may be helpful to think of goals and objectives as two different things. In the private sector, profit-oriented firms always have at least that one goal of profit to focus on. In not-for-profit organizations, the goal of some form of service to a group or groups of people is the goal. A goal then can be thought of as a broad statement of purpose in a nonprofit organization. For example, a hospital in a small community could have as its goal providing a broad range of general hospital care for the community. A school district has the goal of providing education for the children and young adults in a community. A church could have the broad goal of providing spiritual guidance for all members and others with an interest in that particular denomination within a town or other geographic area.

The specific goals of service need to be explicitly understood by those charged with the operation of an organization. We are all familiar with the term bureaucratic red tape. One of the major difficulties in governmental units is the failure to keep sight of the goals of service; an employee may become so caught up in the administrative detail required to provide the services that completion of all the paperwork becomes the goal rather than providing the service.

However, goals must also be refined to understandable and operational objectives. The hospital with a goal of general medical care could proceed in several different directions depending upon individual definitions of what constitutes general medical care. One administrator may feel that no hospital without a coronary care unit can meet general needs; yet another may feel this is a critical specialty better suited to a larger hospital complex. Thus, goals must be refined. The refinement of goals into specific statements may be thought of formally as the organization objectives. Objectives provide the basis for implementing the goals of the organization. Objectives must be specific. They must provide the guidance necessary to fulfill the goals of the organization. Thus, the hospital may specify its objectives in establishing the goal of general hospital care as:

1. staffing a 24-hour emergency care center
2. maintaining a 10-bed maternity ward and neonatal nursery
3. maintaining facilities for 100 hospital beds which can provide pediatric, general medical, surgical, and geriatric care
4. establishing a four-bed intensive care unit
5. provide a surgical unit with one delivery room, two general operating rooms, and one combination delivery-operating room
6. the hospital will maintain complete laboratory and x-ray facilities as well as a pharmacy. A study is to be undertaken on the advisability of staffing these on a 24-hour basis
7. no facilities are to be provided for long-term care of drug and alcohol addiction and mental illness

While the above does not cover all areas that would have to be considered in establishing the objectives of a community hospital, the necessity of specifying objectives in some detail should be clear. There can be little or no control over whether an organization is effectively meeting goals if those goals are not stated in a manner which facilitates understanding for control.

The Control Structure

In order to carry out the objectives of the not-for-profit entity, it must carry on certain organized activities. To control these activities so that resources are used wisely, care should be exercised in the organization of these activities. One of the ways to organize these activities is through the recognition of specific programs which are designed to meet the organization objectives. The effectiveness of a program can be analyzed using stated objectives as one measure of comparison. The designation of programs is a useful control tool for upper-level management. For lower-level managers, programs may be subdivided into units called responsibility centers over which the middle manager exercises control. A program, if sufficiently small in scope, may also constitute a responsibility center. Normally, however, there will be several responsibility centers for a single program. In addition, activities performed by one responsibility center may be used by several programs. This arrangement complicates the control procedure, but may provide the most efficient utilization of resources.

Program Structures

If the objectives, both for recurring and nonrecurring activities of the organization were always explicitly understood, the program to meet these objectives would have a solid basis. Ideally, all objectives should be stated in quantifiable terms rather than as qualitative objectives for an effective control system. "To increase church membership" is a qualitative objective which can take on more quantitative characteristics by redefining the objective to something similar to "increasing the church membership by 10 percent over the next year." Once this goal is stated, a controlled program or programs can be developed which are designed to meet this goal. One such program could be the formation of a visitation committee to personally contact all persons who have visited the church within the last two years but who have not joined. At various intervals during the contact year, the names of persons visited by members of the visitation committee can be tabulated and a check made to see who has joined the church. While this example is very simple, it shows the elements of the program control system:

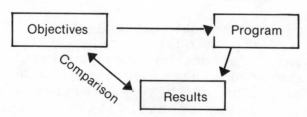

This quantitative objective provides the most useful tool for comparison of the results of the program. Unfortunately, not all goals can be quantified so easily. If the church has as one of its objectives increasing the spiritual awareness of the teenage members of the church, there may be no specific way of quantifying this objective since spiritual awareness is not a measurable quantity. A control system need not be abandoned. If we cannot measure results directly for comparison to objectives, then it is necessary to use some form of "means" surrogate. If the church decides to establish a teen group which combines fun, friendship, and some serious bible study, then the number of teens attracted to the programs and the programs' growth may serve as a surrogate measure of spiritual awareness.

The need for very specific objectives can also be seen from the community hospital previously illustrated. One objective was the staffing of a 24-hour emergency facility. Emergency care could be viewed as a program of the hospital which must be implemented and a control system developed. While at first glance this objective may seem adequate, numerous problems arise. How many persons are going to staff this facility? Will there always be a doctor present? Will it be staffed by nurses with doctors simply "on call"? If possible, these questions should be answered prior to establishing the program. Statistical information from other hospitals may help in designing the program. If statistics at other hospitals show that most emergencies occur in the late afternoons and evenings and on weekends, then the emergency room should be most heavily staffed at those times. Whether the program should include full-time physicians, doctors-on-call, or some type of coverage by the staff doctors may then depend on the resources available.

Responsibility Structure

A responsibility center may be defined as an area of activity which is under the direction of a single manager. If a program is small, it may be a responsibility center. In larger organizations, however, many responsibility centers exist to carry out their various programs. In profit-oriented firms, the responsibility centers are built in building-block fashion from the smallest area of activity to top-level managers. The plan of responsibility centers looks very much like a detailed organization chart.

In the nonprofit organization, the responsibility centers should be defined in a manner which enhances the attainment of organization programs and objectives.

When well-defined programs exist, the designation of responsibility centers may be relatively simple and provide a very effective control mechanism. If a city has a garbage collection service, areas of responsibility may be those shown in Figure 3.1. In

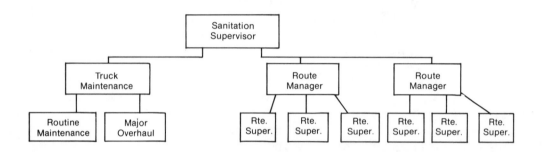

Figure 3.1

this structure, each route supervisor has a crew of men and trucks which collect garbage from a geographic area. The route managers supervise several route supervisors and all report to the sanitation supervisor. Truck maintenance is divided into routine and major repair since there are enough trucks to be maintained to warrant that type structure. If there were fewer trucks, then truck maintenance may be a singular responsibility center. In this type of unit, there is little overlap in the activities of each of the responsibility centers. The control system may readily follow the responsibility centers with the entire garbage-collection system the object of program control.

Many programs may have overlapping responsibility centers which complicate the control structure. The local welfare agency may administer both the aid to dependent children and food stamp programs. Costs of administering each of the programs must be collected separately; yet many persons receiving aid to dependent children receive food stamp assistance as well. In order to operate most efficiently, the social workers working with families receiving aid to dependent children should be able to complete all the necessary paper work for the issuance of food stamps. In order to collect food stamp program administration costs, some form of allocation must

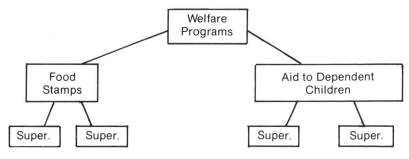

Figure 3.2

be made by the social workers handling the combined services. These allocations require judgment and may not accurately reflect the resources spent on each function. If, however, the emphasis is placed on accurate cost collection, then the functions should be separated. This would then require handling of an aid to dependent children-food stamp family by two social workers. The two workers would probably collect much of the same information, resulting in a waste of resources. In setting up a control system for programs with overlapping activities, consideration must be given to necessary allocation of costs. However, when allocations are made, they are usually made on some arbitrary basis and, in analyzing these costs for control purposes, their arbitrary nature must not be forgotten. It must also be remembered that a responsibility structure which provides better control may waste resources by duplication of services. Alternatively, if the control system is totally ineffective because of multiple overlaps in activity areas, more resources may be wasted through this lack of control. It may prove more efficient in the long run in this case to redesign the activities along program lines for effective cost control.

ACCOUNT CLASSIFICATIONS

The usefulness of a control structure based on individual responsibility centers, ultimately building to program control, may seem very logical; yet, the implementation of such a program takes substantial effort and cooperation on the part of the accounting department. Since the analysis of costs incurred by the responsibility center or the program are the primary objective of the control system, an extensive accounting system which permits the classification of the costs incurred by responsibility centers is necessary. In many governmental units, budgeting and cost collection must be organized by a numbered account classification system which permits identification of the program and type of cost, facilitating the establishment of a control system. If the existing accounting system does not permit a breakdown of costs by responsibility center, then the accounting system must be changed or the concept of control by responsibility center abandoned. Again, this is a management decision which must weigh the possible benefits of the control system against the increased accounting costs. In analyzing the benefits of establishing an accounting system for control purposes and its costs, the capital budgeting techniques presented in the later chapters of this text may be used for the decision process.

Efficiency versus Effectiveness in a Control System

Control of operations has two quite distinct elements--effectiveness and efficiency. If unlimited resources are available to operate a program, an effective program could almost always be established. Thus, in staffing the emergency room of a hospital, one doctor and four nurses could be available twenty-four hours a day, seven days a week with an additional staff of one doctor and two nurses at peak hours. While this program might be effective in providing immediate emergency attention in a small community hospital for anything short of a major disaster, it is akin to the "killing of a fly with a sledge hammer."

Program control should aim at assessing two areas--effectiveness and efficiency. Effectiveness deals with the question of meeting stated objectives. Efficiency considers the costs of meeting those objectives. For most not-for-profit organizations there must be a consideration of both elements and often trade-offs must be made between effectiveness and efficiency. It is simply not efficient to have one doctor and four nurses sitting idle during six hours of an eight-hour shift when on an average only sixteen hours of actual work are performed by the five staff members during that period. If only two nurses staff the facility continuously, with a doctor on call at all times, most emergency situations could be handled within twenty minutes of admittance. While this program is less effective, it provides a tremendous improvement in efficient utilization of resources.

Efficiency can be explained in a more definitive manner--the one most of us recognize in the profit-oriented sector--the ratio of outputs to inputs. Is the organization getting the most return from the resources being consumed? Whether we're talking about the hospital emergency room or city garbage collection, the objective of any program control system is to ensure the efficient use of resources in providing a satisfactory level of service. Both elements are important, but combining them in a control system is not an easy task. Both effectiveness and efficiency are comparative terms in themselves. What are the absolutes against which they are to be measured? In most cases, no absolutes exist. If the emergency room of one hospital handles each emergency situation within 15 minutes of admission at a cost of $200 per admission, while a second handles each emergency within 25 minutes at a cost of $125 per admission, then the first is more effective but less efficient than the second. If all else is equal in the comparison, it would be a management decision to change operations in the first hospital to make it more efficient by cutting back on costs. However, in making comparisons between operations, "all else may not be equal." Costs allocated to the emergency room may differ among hospitals. Hospital one may be a small hospital with few emergencies, while hospital two may be a large metropolitan emergency center which benefits from economies of scale. Thus, in making judgments of effectiveness and efficiency by comparison, consideration must be given to the fact that no two facilities will be identical. This does not, however, negate the usefulness of the comparisons since similar facilities can usually be found for comparative purposes.

Input-Output Analysis for Control

The traditional profit-oriented measure of efficiency is the ratio of outputs to inputs. Outputs are the dollars of revenue generated by the sale of goods and services, while inputs are the dollar measure of all the direct and indirect costs which are required to generate the output. In many of the client-oriented, not-for-profit organizations where there is a relationship between the revenues generated and services provided, such as a hospital or university, this measure of efficiency may be quite useful but it is of little value in those not-for-profit firms in which revenues are unrelated to services provided. In these organizations some form of surrogate measure for output must be developed and used.

Relevant Input Data

The purpose of establishing a control system by programs and responsibility centers is to provide a framework for the collection and analysis of inputs. The question then arises, "What input data are relevant for a control system?" If the efficiency of the manager in charge of a responsibility center is to be assessed using input data, then the type of input data collected is critical. The concept of controllable and noncontrollable costs provides an answer to this problem. Controllable costs are those costs which are directly affected by the manager within the period of time considered. Similarly, uncontrollable costs are those over which the manager has no influence.

There are two diverse opinions on what costs should be included as input measures for a responsibility center. One theory states that only controllable costs should be included since the manager has no influence on uncontrollable costs and should not be held responsible for them. The other view states that all costs should be included since the manager should be aware of all costs to the organization. Whichever view is chosen, the costs should be kept separate; controllable costs should not be mingled with noncontrollable costs. Any evaluation based on inputs over which the manager had no control may only prove to be dysfunctional, even though it may be valid to have the manager aware of total costs.

The designation of controllable and uncontrollable costs requires consideration since the dividing line is often vague. Three criteria have been established for assigning costs of a responsibility center:

1. If the person has authority over both the acquisition and the use of the service, he should be charged with the cost of such services.
2. If the person can significantly influence the amount of cost through his own action, he may be charged with such costs.

3. Even if the person cannot significantly influence
   the amount of cost through his own direct action,
   he may be charged with those elements with which
   the management desires him to be concerned so
   that he will help to influence those who are
   responsible.[2]

In the not-for-profit service organization, personnel costs are controllable and should be charged
directly to the supervisors and managers in the
responsibility structure. Materials consumed are
generally considered controllable costs. Difficulty
arises in assessing responsibility for indirect
costs such as rent, heat, light, and depreciation,
if applicable. For a period of time, the tempera-
ture to be maintained in public buildings was specified by the federal government. In that respect, a
specified level of heating and air conditioning was
removed from management control; yet, it was the
managers' responsibility to see that these specified
levels were maintained. If two responsibility centers share facilities, how should the rent or depreciation expense as well as utilities be apportioned
between them? Theoretically, neither responsibility
center manager may have had any control over the
physical facilities they occupy. The rent or purchase price (and subsequent depreciation policy) are
determined by upper-division management and these
costs should be considered uncontrollable and omitted from their evaluation. Alternatively, however,
an allocation basis such as square footage could be
used to divide these costs as well as those for
utilities. The arbitrary nature of these allocation
procedures must then be recognized in the evaluation
process.

In administering the responsibility center control concept, a spirit of cooperation and a free
flow of information must exist between the various
levels of management. Since the budget will probably remain a major control device within the not-for-
profit organization, input from all levels of management in budget preparation should be encouraged.
The manager must feel he is an integral part of the
organization and must understand its goals. When
any type of evaluative control system is used, the
manager must believe that the system is reasonable
and fair; otherwise some managers will find ways of
operating which are designed solely to "beat the
system."

Output Data

The costs of operation, or input data, may usually be determined for almost any type of not-for-profit organization. While some problems arise in assigning costs to responsibility centers and programs, particularly in assigning costs of jointly shared facilities or services of responsibility centers, the problem can be solved by the concept of controllable and noncontrollable costs or by the use of a reasonable basis for allocation. The measurement of output for the not-for-profit organizations is much more complex and difficult.

The output of the private enterprise is its revenue. The major problem in this type of firm in measuring efficiency as a ratio of output to input is assigning revenues to subunits. In practice, revenues generally can be attributed to major operating areas only. Some other form of efficiency measure must be found for the smaller subunits of operation. Efficiency measures for subunits usually take the form of a cost measure per unit of output. (Note that when an activity is used to measure output, the ratio of output to input is usually inverted and stated as cost per unit of output.)

In the public sector, the problem is compounded by the lack of relationship between the revenue and costs. Thus, for many not-for-profit organizations any dollar-based output/input ratio is meaningless. In these instances it is essential to develop some other form of output measure; again, this usually takes the form of an activity measure such as costs per student in a school system, costs per student credit/hour for a university, daily patient costs for a hospital, costs per passenger mile for a public transportation system, cost per residence for garbage collection, and so on.

In order to develop these efficiency measures, a reasonable activity unit must be found. Some activity units may seem fairly straightforward. A social service agency which serves a particular type of client may find it convenient to use the number of clients serviced as the activity measure. A stenographic pool could use the number of acceptable typed pages as an activity unit. A visiting nurses association could use the number of visits made. Other organizations may perform such a variety of services using the same people that a singular activity unit may not be feasible. A small city government may employ several clerical persons who send out tax bills and collect money for taxes and various licenses, as well as perform the more usual clerical tasks of typing and filing. One output activity measure may be difficult to develop and the development of several may be impractical as the additional record keeping required may offset any benefit of control.

There are several other problems which can be encountered in output measures. First, many not-for-profit organizations must be available to provide service even when no one desires to use the service. A telephone hotline service must have operators available even when no one calls. Any type of efficiency measure based on number of calls handled will penalize operators who handle slow shifts. Thus, efficiency measures must consider the level of demand for services. Given equal service demands, a valid comparison of efficiency may be made. Another consideration, however, is that quality service may be less efficient. One hotline operator may handle calls very quickly and achieve a high efficiency rating based on calls handled; yet the operator may fail to provide as extensive counseling or referral information as the caller needs. Thus, another operator may be less efficient but provide more effective counseling. In this type of situation where the callers remain anonymous, it may be impossible to accurately assess either effectiveness or efficiency.

The problem of measuring efficiency when there are variations in service demand can be somewhat alleviated by extending the time periods of measurement to encompass a wide variation in service demand. For example, the cost of running the hotline on a cost per call basis may vary widely between time of day, days of the week, or even particular times of the year; yet over a period of a year, the cost per call may provide an accurate measure for comparison to another similar service. It must be remembered that efficiency and effectiveness measures are comparative in nature; when comparisons are made, the conditions under which the units operate must be similar for a valid comparison. When differences in operations exist, the comparisons must allow for them.

There is another problem in output measures which plague certain not-for-profit organizations--the indirect output. If traffic lights are installed at an intersection, the object is to prevent accidents. The number of accidents prevented as an output can

only be estimated from some other data--not measured
directly. Development of immunizations for various
diseases has proceeded on the basis of estimated
number of illnesses and/or deaths prevented. Any
analysis of outputs based on estimated occurrences
prevented should be combined with an analysis of how
the numbers for prevented occurrences were derived.

One final problem which is also found in the not-
for-profit organization is that some activities may
be carried on for long periods with no measurable
output. An enormous amount of cancer research is
being conducted today. How does one measure the
efficiency of any one particular research effort in
conquering this disease? If a breakthrough in the
search for a cure or immunization for cancer is
found, then the research is extolled. Yet years of
totally unproductive results may have been necessary
to achieve even the smallest step. Here again,
long-run benefits of a cancer cure, both in allevii-
ating human suffering and actual costs of treatment
and lost productivity, are weighed against research
costs in establishing and continuing the research
efforts. However, it is impossible to establish any
overall efficiency measures for the project. This
does not preclude using control systems for areas
within the research project. In developing output
measures for not-for-profit organizations, management must be aware that relevant measures may not be
possible for all areas of activity, but inability to
develop output measures in some areas should not
lead to abandonment of the entire control system.

Analysis of Data

The development of input-output data for not-for-
profit organizations requires time and resources
and, as a result, should be used effectively to
improve operations. Since efficiency and effectiveness are comparative terms, the data should be used
to compare activities of one unit to a similar unit.
These comparisons must be made with deliberation,
however, since units are rarely identical.

Comparisons may be made on several bases. One of
the most common comparisons is made based on total
costs of programs or activity units. The total cost
of garbage collection or a social service agency is
usually available from accounting data and may be
used for comparison purposes. When looking at total
costs, however, the units compared must be substan-

tially similar in size and scope to provide a valid comparison. The inability to make these total cost comparisons on substantially similar units is the primary reason comparisons are usually made on a cost per unit activity basis. Even on this basis, however, comparisons must be made only after an evaluation of the data for certain critical factors:

1. Are the cost data collected for the similar units similar? If one unit includes only the costs of materials and personnel, while another includes charges for facilities as well, costs are not comparable.
2. Are the conditions under which the costs were collected and activities conducted similar? For example, comparisons made between units with cyclical activities should be made for comparable cycles or for longer periods which include a broad range of cycles.

Comparisons of similar activities can then be made between individuals, between groups or units, or between entire programs. One of the most useful comparisons for control purposes is to compare unit costs of a nonprofit organization with a similar activity carried out in a profit-oriented firm. Garbage collection is often carried out by governmental units and by private garbage services. Since the private garbage service must operate at a profit in a competitive environment, a greater incentive for cost control often exists and greater efficiency is often assumed. If the public system is operating at costs similar to those of the private firm, then the operation is probably reasonably efficient.

If operating data for comparable activities are not available, must any form of analysis of efficiency be abandoned? While comparisons offer a firmer foundation for assessing efficiency, experienced managers should be able to use total costs or cost per activity unit as raw data to assess their reasonableness. For example, a three-person typing pool produces only 60 to 70 typed pages of copy per day on an average and often hires temporary help. The manager from past experience knows that a reasonable typist should be able to type 4 to 5 pages per hour over an eight-hour day or approximately 34 pages per day. Three typists should average at least 100 pages per day. Thus the manager should be alerted to investigate whether the people are poorly qualified, are failing to work efficiently, or are typing data which in fact require substantially more than the average amount of time.

In many situations it may be advantageous to have outsiders review the efficiency of operations. It must always be kept in mind, however, that outside assessments may be relatively expensive and should be undertaken in those areas where the expected long-run benefits of increased efficiency outweigh the costs. Another option for efficiency assessment is the management or operational audit conducted by public accounting firms. This type of audit is usually conducted along with the audit of financial statements and is discussed in the following section.

Audits of Not-For-Profit Organizations

When auditing of not-for-profit organizations is mentioned, the normal reaction is to think of compliance of financial statements with generally accepted accounting principles and the requirements of other governing bodies. In 1973, however, the U.S. Comptroller General issued the booklet, Standards for Audit of Governmental Organizations, Programs, Activities and Functions, which listed three audit functions:

1. Financial and compliance--determines (a) whether financial operations are properly conducted, (b) whether the financial reports of an audited entity are presented fairly, and (c) whether the entity has complied with applicable laws and regulations.
2. Economy and efficiency--determines whether the entity is managing or utilizing its resources (personnel, property, space, and so forth) in an economical and efficient manner and the causes of any inefficiencies or uneconomical practices, including inadequacies in management information systems, administrative procedures, or organizational structure.
3. Program results--determines whether the desired results or benefits are being achieved, whether the objectives established by the legislature or other authorizing body are met, and whether the agency has considered alternatives which might yield desired results at a lower cost.[3]

The traditional financial audit encompasses only the first objective. While the importance of this aspect of the audit function should not be ignored, due to the nonprofit nature of the organization, the other two objectives take on added significance.

In the private sector, audits are designed to assure the current or prospective investor that the financial statements fairly present the financial operations and position of the firm so that this investor may rely on them in making his investment decision. These results then summarize the efficiency of the firm in the net income figure. The nonprofit organizations's results of operations generally take the form of a comparison of budgeted revenues and expenditures to the actual revenues and expenditures. If the budgeted and actual data coincide, then the organization is generally considered to have performed well. Nothing in this type of financial reporting, however, leads to an assessment of the efficiency of its operations. Thus, objectives 2 and 3 of the audit function should be the area in which most not-for-profit organizations could benefit.

When the objectives of an audit are to assess efficiency and program results, the audit is termed either a management or operational audit. This type of audit is substantially different than the financial audit and should be conducted by persons skilled in this function. Assessing the adequacy of the financial accounting records is entirely different than assessing the adequacy of personnel and programs in meeting the objectives of the organization efficiently. Failure on the part of the auditors to appreciate the sensitive nature of the operational audit may spell failure for them. Fortunately, the importance of the operational audit is receiving increased emphasis in the private sector. Thus most larger public accounting firms have experience in and provide training for operational audits. When conducted with care, the operational audit can often demonstrate that improvements can be made in the future operations of the organization and thereby serve a useful purpose.

SUMMARY

The purpose of the control system in a not-for-profit organization is to assess its efficiency and effectiveness in meeting the stated goals and objectives of the organization. In order to operate efficiently, however, goals and objectives must be stated explicitly and understood by those who manage the organization. The organization structure can facilitate the control system if it is organized along program lines and responsibility centers. This structure provides the framework for assessing the effectiveness of the inputs in achieving the outputs. In the not-for-profit firm, inputs are the costs of operation. Outputs are usually measured as units of activity rather than as revenue generated. Efficiency, then, is usually assessed by comparing the cost per unit of activity of one operating unit to that of another similar unit. When cost comparisons cannot be obtained, experienced managers may have to judge efficiency on an absolute basis; alternatively, outside consultants, such as auditors who conduct a management audit, may be brought in to conduct studies of operations and make suggestions for improvements. Regardless of the method of analysis chosen, a control system should be implemented in all or part of the nonprofit organization to ensure operating efficiency.

QUESTIONS

1. What is the purpose of a control system?

2. What difficulties are encountered in establishing a control system within a not-for-profit organization?

3. Why do budgets often fail to provide adequate control in not-for-profit organizations?

4. How are goals and objectives distinguished within the text?

5. What are the basic elements of a program control system?

6. Why are surrogate measures of effectiveness often required in not-for-profit organizations?

7. What is a responsibility center and how does it fit into a control structure?

8. How does the accounting system complement a system of responsibility accounting?

9. Distinguish between efficiency and effectiveness. Why is this important in not-for-profit organizations?

10. Distinguish between controllable and noncontrollable costs as related to responsibility centers.

11. What are some examples of controllable costs generally encountered in not-for-profit organizations?

12. What difficulties are encountered in determining output measures for not-for-profit organizations?

13. How may the efficiency and effectiveness of a not-for-profit organization be assessed?

14. What purposes may audits of not-for-profit organizations serve if there is no report to shareholders as in profit-oriented firms?

ENDNOTES

1. The National Council of Governmental Accounting, Statement I: Governmental Accounting and Financial Reporting Principles (Chicago: Municipal Finance Officers Association of the U.S. and Canada, 1979), p. 13.
2. "Report of Committee on Cost Concepts and Standards," Accounting Review (April 1956), p. 189.
3. Comptroller General of the United States, Standards for Audit of Governmental Organizations, Programs, Activities and Functions (Washington, D.C.: U.S. Government Printing Office, 1973), pp. 1-2.

4

BUDGETING SYSTEMS

INTRODUCTION

One of the essential ingredients to successful management in any type of organization is the development of plans for ongoing operations and the effective implementation of those plans. Few profit-oriented organizations can survive if there is no systematic plan of operations to coordinate the various activities within the firm. In the not-for-profit organization, some form of managerial planning tool is also absolutely essential to ensure that the activities of the organization meet its service objectives. The primary planning tool in the not-for-profit organization is the budget. The budget is the formal statement of expected resources and proposed expenditures. In most governmental units, the budget is considered so important that it may be a legally binding document which absolutely limits the expenditures of the government. In most other not-for-profit organizations the budget requires formal approval of a governing body such as the board of directors or trustees. As the major organizational planning tool, and the document which may also form the primary basis for control within the organization, the budget must be given thorough consideration.

The budget should form the backbone of the comprehensive plan of operation for the not-for-profit organization. When it does, its preparation requires a number of steps beyond budget preparation. First, the broad goals of the organization must be specified. These broad goals must then be translated into more specific objectives. These goals and objectives should then give rise to a long-range plan of operation in broad terms and the short-range plan or operating budget for the current cycle. Once the budget is prepared, it should provide the basis for a systematic performance review and other necessary follow-up procedures. These steps provide the framework for managing the not-for-profit organization and, when properly developed and applied, foster effective and flexible management through a continuous communication and feedback process.

NATURE OF THE BUDGETING PROCESS

There may be several types of budgets prepared by an organization but they have one common element-- the budget is expressed in monetary terms. The operating budget expresses in monetary terms the planned activities of the organization for a specified time period, usually one year. The cash budget is a statement of anticipated cash receipts and disbursements, again for a specified time period. However, for adequate cash management the focus of the cash budget may be shorter periods--quarters, months, or even days. The capital budget details planned capital expenditures generally for time periods well in excess of one year, usually three to ten years, depending on the organization. While all three types of budgets are important, the operating budget is the primary focus of the following discussion; brief discussions of the cash and capital budgets are included at the end of the chapter, however.

The Operating Budget Cycle

In order to prepare a timely budget, the efforts of a number of people in the not-for-profit organization generally must be coordinated. This coordination will be facilitated if one person or a small committee oversees budget preparation.

In a large not-for-profit organization, there may

be a budget officer whose primary responsibility is preparation and monitoring of the budget process. In other organizations, the chief executive officer, the controller, or the financial manager may perform the functions of the budget officer. If a committee oversees the budget, it should be small and the members should come from the operating managers and/or the board of directors.

The budget cycle encompasses a number of separate steps. First, the budget for the current period must be reviewed. The actual preparation of the budget requires the development of a set of guidelines which can be disseminated to those who take part in the process. The budget review period should be used to develop these guidelines, to determine which existing programs need to be expanded or contracted, and which programs are to be added or terminated. Once the operating policies and budget guidelines have been developed, the budget officer must present a detailed set of instructions for budget preparation to each area involved. These instructions should include not only a statement of the fiscal policy and general guidelines to be followed, but should also include such things as the timetable for completion, detailed worksheets for estimation of all budget requests, and forms which facilitate the aggregation and presentation of all budget requests in the final format required for that particular organization. All of this material should be presented with sufficient lead time to facilitate thoughtful and accurate preparation.

It is critical to this budget-preparation process that each area be made aware of any major policy changes which affect their operations as well as any changes in revenue projections, workloads, or pricing policies. Without a complete and accurate understanding of the level of future operations and expected revenue and expense adjustments prior to budget preparation, the process is unnecessarily complicated and prolonged. This type of information should be given to each area manager prior to or coincident with the budget-preparation instructions issued by the budget officer.

The next step in the process is the submission of all budget requests to the budget officer. These requests are then put together to form the total budget which the budget officer must then review. It is generally the responsibility of the budget officer to see that a balanced budget exists. The central review process is the mechanism by which this is carried out. If the budget is not balanced, or an unacceptable deficit exists, the budget requests must be adjusted. Once the necessary modifications are made, the rough draft of the formal budget document is prepared.

Again, budget preparation is often simplified by the informal negotiation process that takes place within the formal budget procedure. When a free flow of information exists between the area managers preparing budget elements and both the budget officer and organization executives, the budget draft may need little revision. If area managers understand operating policies and objectives, they can more accurately translate them to budget items. In addition, when the budget officer and upper management are more fully aware of the problems of area managers, they may be less inclined to make changes in budget items and they may be able to offer suggestions on improving operations prior to preparation of the formal budget.

If there is a chief executive officer of the organization other than the budget officer, then a second budget review will normally take place. Since the budget officer has had to make decisions regarding budgeted amounts in order to present a balanced budget, the second review process gives those whose initial budgets have been modified an opportunity to appeal decisions of the budget officer. Often the executive officer holds meetings with the department heads and budget officer to give each an opportunity to explain his or her position. Following this, final budget modifications must be made.

The final budget document is then ready for completion. The document must contain a summary of revenues, usually by major sources, a summary of expenditures by program or other useful categories, a summary of major changes from the prior year's budget, and the logic behind the recommendations for the coming period.

In addition to these formal steps that take place within the organization, it may be legally required or desirable to hold some type of open public forum on the budget document to obtain input from the citizens, contributors, or beneficiaries of the organization's services. Local taxpayers certainly should have the right to express their concern for rising taxes. They may prefer a cut in the level of services rather than large tax increases. Failure to solicit or heed taxpayer opinion can only in-

crease the probability of taxpayer revolt. Many
other not-for-profit organizations are facing increased costs and reduced revenues requiring service
cut-backs. Certain services may be cut more easily
than others. Unless the service priorities of the
service beneficiaries are determined, suboptimum use
of the available revenues may result.

Once all the informal, formal, and public
hearings on the budget document are held, final
adjustments are made and the budget is readied for
final approval. For governmental units this is
usually a legislative body or, for other organizations, the board of directors or trustees. The
formal adoption of the budget may be a rather per-
functory process or it may entail several information and formal hearings, depending upon the not-
for-profit organization. Again, sufficient time
must be allotted between the presentation of the
formal budget and the beginning of the fiscal period
to which it applies to allow for necessary delibera-
tions of the body charged with formal approval.

From the above steps in the budget cycle, it can
readily be seen that the entire process may take
several months to complete. The advantage of having
one person in charge of budget preparation is that
he may continually monitor the steps in the budget
preparation so that the process moves smoothly
toward completion. In addition, with prior experience in this area, he may offer a great deal of
assistance to the various managers in the swift
completion of their budget proposals. While some
not-for-profit organizations may continue to function without formal budget approval for a period of
time, certain organizations (governmental units, in
particular), may be threatened with a shutdown of
operations if budget approval does not come before
the beginning of the fiscal period. Thus, timely
budget approval is critical to their existence.

PREPARATION OF THE BUDGET

The actual preparation of the budget requires a
two-way flow of information. The management of the
organization must first develop and communicate
guidelines for budget preparation to all levels of
the organization. In the profit-oriented enterprise, one essential guideline is the expected level
of sales (and the estimated revenue), which controls
the level of operation of the firm. In the nonpro-

fit organization, other guidelines must be developed since service provided and revenues raised are frequently unrelated to one another. Thus, guidelines often take a form which does not necessarily lead to efficient use of resources such as "costs should not exceed last year's by more than the rate of inflation." When a guideline of this nature is issued, however, several dangers exist. Will anyone examine prior years' expenditures to see if they were necessary? Given a percent allowable increase such as the rate of inflation, will any request be made for less than the full amount of the increase? And the most common abuse is that this type of guideline encourages spending all of the current year's resources or there is the risk of having the budget reduced the following year.

Other guidelines such as overall reductions in expenditures are becoming more common. Changing economic conditions, which have produced inordinate increases in fuel and utility costs, may require one set of guidelines to an area with a high dependence on fuel and other set to an area relatively unaffected by these changes. Another budgeting technique examined briefly in a later section is zero-base budgeting. The guideline tacit in zero-base budgeting is that no cost is a given, but that each cost, each year, must be justified.

When revenue is unrelated to costs, guidelines expressed in nonmonetary, service-related terms may prove more useful in guiding budget preparation. In client-oriented organizations, budget guidelines could be based on the number of clients served and the breakdown of type of service generally provided clients. Other organizations may base budgets on the number of hours of operations and estimated traffic during these hours. Nonmonetary guidelines are often difficult to develop for all areas, however; thus, both monetary and nonmonetary guidelines may be combined where appropriate in the budget guideline document providing the maximum amount of guidance.

Besides guidelines for costs and/or operations, guidelines must also be issued on the format and timing of the budget. Program directors may be directed to prepare their budgets to meet program objectives, but they need some type of formal procedure to carry this out. Costs should be collected in a manner consistent with those of prior years to facilitate comparison. In addition, area costs should be broken down into unit costs where feasible and some form of cost per unit of output should be developed; these steps facilitate not only analysis at the budget stage but comparisons of actual versus planned performance.

Once the guidelines have been developed by the budget officer, they must be communicated to the managers, so that budget preparation can begin. The actual budget preparation requires the involvement of each level of management. The guidelines must be communicated to each manager from upper to lower level. When a manager has a well-defined responsibility center the budgeting process is facilitated.

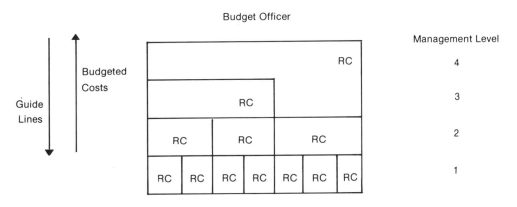

Figure 4.1   Budget Process

Figure 4.1 is a simplified schematic of the budgeting process. The guidelines first are transmitted from level-4 management through the pyramid to level 1. Following that, level-1 responsibility center managers prepare the budgets for their area of responsibility. Level-2 managers receive the budget from level-1 managers for review, consolidation, and addition of level-2 costs. The two level-2 managers submit their budgets to the level-3 manager for the same type of analysis and adjustment and the level-3 and remaining level-2 manager then submit their budgets to the level-4 manager for final review and consolidation. It should also be noted that any revisions should follow the same downward and upward paths; i.e., the level-4 manager should not go directly to the level-1 manager for a revision but should work through levels 3 and 2 managers. In this way, the same types of revisions should be avoided in future years.

In some organizations, it may be possible to include in the guidelines passed to lower-level managers an estimate of the resources available to them for their operations, on which they can then budget their costs. In not-for-profit firms, however, the availability of resources for a particular area is often based on a judgment allocation. Even in client-oriented not-for-profit firms, the amount of resources to be made available to smaller responsibility centers which serve a program are made on the basis of arbitrary allocations. Whether these allocated figures are made available to lower-level managers must be an upper-management or budget-officer decision, since it is their ultimate responsibility to put the entire budget together, matching revenues and costs.

Forecasting Financial Resources

For most profit-oriented firms, estimated revenues less desired profit provides the limitation on costs for the budget period. Thus, the starting point for the development of all the budget figures is estimated revenues. In addition, each budget period is treated separately, so that any excess profits earned in the preceding period remain in that period rather than carrying over to subsequent periods to offset either reduced revenues or increased costs. It is also true that, for this type of firm, the revenue generation process is tied directly to the sales of goods and services. The estimated revenue for the not-for-profit firm differs from that of the profit-oriented firm in two important ways. First, the revenues of many not-for-profit firms have no direct relationship to the services provided. Second, since the firm is to be nonprofit, the excess of revenues over expenditures in any period should be available in the next period since the objective in any one period is to have an equality between revenues and expenditures. Finally, a third difference often arises in the budgeting process--rather than the estimation of revenues limiting expenditures, necessary program expenditures may be estimated first and revenues raised accordingly. While this is not true of all governmental units, property taxes are often levied on this basis; e.g., the school district determines the amount of resources it needs based on its costs of operation. Using total assessed valuation of the

property in the school district, a mill levy is
determined for each dollar of assessed valuation.
The property taxes earmarked for schools vary then
as their costs of operation vary.   In addition,
hospitals often have allowable patient charges for
services determined by elaborate cost allocation
formulas.   The United Fund members submit their
budget requirements prior to the annual fund drive.
In each of these cases, costs have some impact on
the determination of revenues. While this budgeting
process may require several iterations (i.e., required revenues as determined from aggregate costs
are deemed infeasible, the budgets are returned for
reconsideration, new costs are aggregated, a second
round of budget trimming takes place), finally the
budget requests are finalized and the budget approved.

Many not-for-profit organizations or some portion
of them, however, operate and prepare their budgets
in the more traditional manner and first estimate
available revenues.   There may be legal limits on
the amount of taxes or tax increases that can occur
in a period which necessitate this.   Other not-for-
profit organizations may operate in a somewhat competitive environment which in fact limits their
revenue; e.g., one golf club may be able to charge
slightly more for membership than another because of
its name or prestige, but major differences in membership fees are tolerated only on the basis of
services offered.   One club may provide a 27-hole
course, dining, swimming, tennis, and other athletic
facilities, while another may have only an 18-hole
course and limited clubhouse facilities.   The latter's membership fee will have to be much lower than
the former to attract members.

Primary and Secondary Resources

Most not-for-profit organizations have one or
more revenue sources which provide the bulk of their
available resources. For convenience, these are
called the primary sources, while smaller or nonrecurring amounts from varied sources are termed secondary sources.

In estimating primary revenues, the actual
sources are easily identified. A city's primary
source will generally be the property taxes; a hospital's primary source is patient revenue from
either the patients themselves or from third-party

reimbursements. A church's primary source is the weekly offerings or tithes of the members. A university may have several primary sources, such as tuition and room and board fees. These sources of revenue are not easily overlooked. Therefore, more time may be spent on the accuracy of these estimated revenues.

Historical data may be very useful in developing accurate estimates of available resources. A university needs to know how many students will actually register for courses to estimate tuition revenue. Yet more freshmen are generally accepted than will actually register and a number of students from prior years fail to return. Statistical data from prior years can be used to predict the actual number of students enrolling for the coming term and their tuition revenue. Organizations which depend on voluntary contributions can use past trends to estimate expected revenue. Hospitals develop estimates of daily patient costs; average hospital occupancy rates for the period can be used to determine total revenues derived therefrom.

There is, however, one danger in using past data to estimate current revenues. Changes may have occurred which affect the accuracy of the past data. A city which estimates property tax revenue from assessed property valuations must be sure that these assessments include all property added to or deleted from the property tax rolls. The revenue from state income taxes must be adjusted for changing economic conditions. If there has been widespread unemployment in a particular period, revenues from not only income but sales taxes will need adjustment from historical trends. Thus, while locating the primary revenue sources is simple, accuracy of estimates may require skill and judgment.

Secondary sources which are small in nature should be estimated with some concern for accuracy, but elaborate procedures for estimation are not warranted since their impact on the total budget is relatively small. In many instances, an educated guesstimate will suffice. There are, however, several areas which should be considered in greater detail.

First, many not-for-profit organizations have both temporary investments and long-term investments in endowment and annuity-type funds. The question always needs to be asked if these investments are earning their maximum return. In addition, cash often sits unnecessarily idle in several checking accounts rather than being consolidated and invested either in savings accounts or in readily marketable securities.

Prior-year surpluses provide a nonrecurring revenue source for some organizations. Excessive budget surpluses can cause several types of problems. In membership-type organizations, the members may question whether the level of services could have been improved. In governmental units supported by taxes, taxpayers may experience increased resentment at paying taxes when large surpluses exist. While the control system should aim at preventing the waste of resources simply to avoid year-end surpluses, surpluses should not remain unexpended for indefinite periods. The surpluses should be used to provide an increased level of services or a reduction in required revenues as soon as practical.

Revenue Sources

When revenues fail to cover estimated costs, the first reaction is often to cut costs by cutting services so that they do not exceed estimated revenues. Another method of balancing the budget is to increase revenues by raising taxes or fees or having special fund drives. Another method of raising revenues is often overlooked, however; there may be other sources of secondary revenues which have gone untapped. Cities may often overlook revenue-sharing or grant programs from the state or federal government. A college may have never developed a matching gifts program for its fund-raising campaigns. Governmental units may be empowered to levy certain taxes or fees, such as dog licenses, but never have done so. A health organization may undertake estate planning seminars which point out the tax advantages of various forms of programs of giving which encourage people to establish endowment and annuity funds. The budget officer should undertake a study of applicable laws of the governmental unit or study the operations of other types of not-for-profit organizations to see that all legitimate sources of revenue are being pursued. This should not wait, however, until budget deficits exist, but should be an ongoing search, especially with the ever-changing laws and government programs which can be a source of revenue for the not-for-profit organization.

Forecasting Expenditures

The accurate forecasting of departmental expenditures is a difficult but necessary task in the not-for-profit organization. Often a comparison of budgeted versus actual expenditures is the primary method of assessing the effectiveness of a manager. Thus, it is in a manager's self-interest to present estimated expenditures which he foresees will not be exceeded, rather than a "cut-to-the-bone" budget. In addition, in order to forestall future budget cuts, the manager may devise ways to make expenditures approach budgeted amounts if a surplus develops; e.g., a school district may order supplies for the coming year out of the current year's budget so that the supplies-budget surplus is exhausted. Budget preparation often degenerates to a cat and mouse game; i.e., the manager knows the budget requests are always cut by 10 percent; therefore his budget requests are for 111 percent of what he believes he will actually need. Then, when the 10 percent cut is made, he has exactly the budgeted amount he desired originally.

Each manager however, must realize that he is competing for a limited amount of resources. Budget requests should be accompanied by a systematic justification for the funds requested based on an analysis of the efficiency of the department; changes in the level of program activity, in particular, require a demonstration of the necessity for added expenditures for personnel and operating equipment and supplies, or, if the program is cut, a reduction of expenditures should also result. It is also helpful to final budget preparation if the manager specifies priorities in budgeted amounts since this facilitates budget adjustments with a minimum of disagreement.

Organization of Expenditures

While revenue sources may be fairly limited, the breadth of expenditures is normally extensive. It usually facilitates budget preparation if expenditures are grouped into the categories of wages and salaries, supplies, operating expenses, and capital equipment. In many types of not-for-profit organizations, elaborate systems of account classifications are used to organize and categorize the expenditures by responsibility centers and programs.

Codes of from six to fourteen digits are used to identify the expenditure by unit, fund, responsibility center, and type. The use of budget codes which correspond to the accounting codes for expenditures also facilitates collection and comparison of actual expenditures during the fiscal period to budgeted amounts.

Wage and Salary Expenditures

For many not-for-profit organizations, the personnel costs constitute a major portion of current operating expenditures. Productivity among personnel is an area which needs constant monitoring since wages and salaries have such a major impact on the total budget.

In order to determine the personnel budget, the personnel requirements must be established based on program objectives. The personnel requirements should be specified not only by number of persons but by job classification as well. Once these are specified, total personnel costs can be estimated by multiplying the number of persons in each classification by their salaries and summing over all positions. Consideration in the budget should also be given to overtime pay or temporary help at peak operating seasons as well as any necessary shift differentials. At the final rounds of budget preparation, compensation for members of the board of directors or trustees and/or any regulating commissions should also be included.

The budget practices of the particular type of organization should dictate additional budget requirements. In governmental budgets, it is common practice to include a salary-vacancy factor. If positions remain unfilled or are filled at lower than budgeted salaries, a salary-vacancy factor is created and should reduce overall budgeted expenditures for salaries. In hospitals, it is common practice to include both as a revenue and an expenditure the value of donated services. These amounts then should be included in budget estimates, again to facilitate comparison between actual and estimated revenues and expenditures.

Operating Expenditures

While all expenditures technically are operating expenditures, a narrower definition helps categorize the not-for-profit organization's expenditures for budgeting purposes. Organization expenditures then are defined as expenditures other than those for personnel services, supplies, and capital outlays. When supplies expenditures are small, they too are often included in the operating expenditures category but they are not included here in order to facilitate the distinction between supplies and capital expenditures.

Operating expenditures include such things as gas and electric utility bills, telephone expense, reproduction costs, postage, and vehicle maintenance. While personnel expenditures may be estimated in a fairly straightforward and consistent manner, the estimation of operating expenses may require several different bases. A number of expenditures such as postage, reproduction, and vehicle maintenance may bear a direct relationship to the number of persons employed or the number of clients or members to be served; others, such as utilities, vary according to the space used or number of hours of operation. The following chapter includes a discussion of direct, variable, and semivariable expenses and methods of estimating their amounts for budgeting purposes. Developing and using the bases which provide the best predictions of estimated expenditures is an essential part of the budgeting process so that budgets for operating expenditures are accurate and useful.

Supplies versus Capital Expenditures

Both supplies and capital expenditures must be provided for in the operations of the not-for-profit organizations. Technically, supplies refers to those tangible assets, e.g., paper, pens, pencils, stamps, etc., which will be consumed within one year, while capital items are those tangible assets which will be used for periods longer than one year, e.g., land, buildings, office equipment, and typewriters. In practice, however, items which cost an arbitrary amount, i.e., $50, $100, or less, will be considered as part of supplies expense even though their use extends beyond one year. Wastebaskets, pencil sharpeners, and ashtrays are examples of such

items.   The cost of these are normally treated as
current expenditures since their cost doesn't warrant the necessary time and paperwork to keep track
of them along with the more expensive capital items.
In addition, these items are usually replaced on a
periodic basis so that the expenditures are spread
over a number of years.   Since these items are
included with supplies expense, however, when acquisition or replacement is planned it must be included
in the operating budget for that year.
    Other supplies which must be included in the
budget are determined by the needs of the organization.   Supplies for most governmental units consist
of forms and office supplies.   The list of supplies
for a hospital will include office supplies, nap-
kins, paper plates and cups for cafeteria and patient food service, and the dressings, medication,
and other disposable items used for patient care in
all areas of the hospital.   Many professional and
fraternal organizations may have few supplies other
than postage and stationery.   The estimated expenditures for supplies should be included in the budget,
even if small.   The estimates should also consider
planned levels of operation and any program increases or decreases.

ALTERNATIVE BUDGET PROCEDURES

    The operating budget may be prepared in several
ways.   One of the most common ways is to take the
prior year's budget and make appropriate adjustments, line by line for each item of revenue and
expenditure for each activity detailed in the budget.   These are then summed to develop budget totals.   One of the major difficulties with this
method is that it often leads to arbitrary adjustments of revenue and expenditure items and it does
not encourage alternative operating methods.   It
tends to perpetuate operations as they have always
been rather than requiring complete analysis of the
efficiency of current operations.
    Another method of developing a budget is to de-
termine overall revenues and/or allowable expenditures and then apportion certain percentages to
various activities.   It then becomes the responsibility of the activity managers to further apportion
the expenditures among the various items within
their activity basis.   This method, too, fails to
encourage alternative plans of operation.   It also

encourages spending of all allotted amounts for fear
that budgeted amounts would be cut the following
year. In order to combat these budget abuses, two
budget development procedures have received a certain amount of attention in recent years--the planning, programming, budgeting system and zero-base
budgeting. These budget theories are discussed in
the following sections.

Planning, Programming, and Budgeting System

The planning, programming, and budgeting system
(PPBS) of budget preparation first started to receive widespread attention in the early 1960s. Its
purpose was to provide a framework, or approach, to
decision making in the not-for-profit organization.
PPBS attempts to adapt successful decision
techniques used in the private sector to the public
sector and involves five distinct steps. First, the
overall goals and objectives of the not-for-profit
organization must be formulated. These goals should
be related to the various agencies or departments
within the organization and priorities assigned to
achieving these goals. Second, the organization
must search for and specify alternative programs for
meeting the desired objectives. These alternative
and current programs are then compared to determine
which is the most effective in achieving the goals.
Next, the total costs for each program are related to the benefits to be derived from them. It
is this particular step that can prove most trouble-
some. Collection of costs is often a time-consuming
and frustrating task, particularly since the total
costs should include not only the easily identifiable items such as wages and materials but the
less tangible social costs. For example, the rerouting of a highway will have readily identifiable
construction costs, but what will the social cost be
to the community that is now by-passed and will lose
business as a result? The measurement of benefits
is also very elusive. In private industry benefits
are derived from increased revenues and reduced
costs. Many public benefits simply cannot be measured. In the highway rerouting, what is the value
of the reduction in accidents that is expected?
Regardless of the problems involved, costs and benefits should be quantified in as accurate a manner as
possible for all the alternative programs specified
in step two.

The fourth step in PPBS is to select the most effective and efficient programs which meet the objectives and to integrate these into a comprehensive program of operation. The final step is the review and evaluation of each program adopted and implemented. This latter step provides control for current programs and develops information which becomes essential to the development of future budgets.

While a PPBS may require additional efforts to establish, its emphasis on goal specification and efficient programs was a much-needed step away from traditional budgeting, which tended to perpetuate the status quo. In order to establish PPBS, additional resources must generally be expended for personnel. The accounting system must also be upgraded to provide the necessary detailed cost information. PPBS must then achieve sufficient operating-cost savings to offset these required resources. If it does not, then it fails a cost-benefit analysis and should be abandoned. However, in adopting PPBS, it must be realized that initial costs will be much higher than they will be after several years of experience. As a result, costs and costs savings must be compared over a period of years and not just for the initial budget period or premature abandonment of the system will result.

Zero-Base Budgeting

The technique of zero-base budgeting was developed in the early 1970s by Peter Phyrr and applied first to private industry before it was adapted to not-for-profit organizations. The purpose of zero-base budgeting is to provide the mechanism for systematically reevaluating all programs and expenditures annually.

Zero-base budgeting requires an extensive budget preparation and review process. Traditionally, many budget reviews have been inadequate because they have focused on justification of increases in budgeted amounts rather than the total budget. There has been no in-depth analysis of overall cost-benefit relationships and evaluations of alternative methods of operation. Zero-base budgeting attempts to correct these shortcomings of the traditional budget process and also improve the channels of communication within the organization and foster better managerial decisions.

While the actual application of zero-base budgeting may vary somewhat from organization to organization, they all generally follow a basic four-
step procedure within the budget planning and review
process.

There are four major steps in the zero base
planning and budgeting process. First the
economic assumptions are developed for the
plan. Second, the "decision units" (the
budget units that will be evaluated) are
defined. Third, the decision unit managers
prepare analyses of their decision units.
Finally, middle and senior management make
budget funding decisions based on the
analyses prepared.[1]

The first step or economic forecast is generally
much more extensive than under traditional budget
procedures. Operating managers must analyze these
operations thoroughly and to do this they must develop rigorous economic assumptions. They must make
specific assumptions about the rates of inflation
affecting various aspects of their operations, and
they must determine how general economic conditions
will reflect on their operations. For example, a
city has imposed a general sales tax on goods sold
within the city as an additional source of revenue.
If the residents are free to make purchases in areas
outside the city which do not impose the sales tax,
then the revenue estimates must take into consideration that a certain amount of sales will be lost
because people will buy outside the city to avoid
the additional tax.

The decision unit of zero-base budgeting is somewhat similar to a responsibility center and is a
unit which performs certain identifiable activities
and incurs identifiable costs. The unit should be
defined in a way which facilitates in-depth analysis
of these activities and costs. Decision units in
the same organization should be similar in size and
should be under the control of a decision unit
manager who oversees the activities and budgets.

The third step, the analysis of the decision
unit, is the most critical to the zero-base budgeting process. The decision unit manager should specify the unit's goals, the resources consumed, and
the method of operation, preferably in written form.
It is also the decision unit manager's responsibil-

ity to analyze alternative methods of meeting the unit's goals through other modes of operation; e.g., subcontracting certain elements of the operations. At this point, the unit manager will generally require some assistance from the middle- and senior-level managers in developing alternative operating plans; however, the middle- and senior-level managers should be prepared to assist the unit manager at every step.

The final step in the zero-base budgeting process is the ranking of the decision units by priority. This function is performed by the upper-level managers and is the basis for funding decisions. When all decision units are ranked by priority, then funding is made available to those units with the higher priorities until all funding is exhausted.

One of the major benefits of zero-base budgeting is the involvement of all levels of management in a cost-benefit type of analysis for the entire budget. When budget preparations involve the entire management team, each member should be willing to work harder to meet budget objectives. It also encourages managers to constantly search for more efficient alternatives and abandon unnecessary costs.

While not all managers may support zero-base budgeting, it can be a powerful tool in achieving cost reductions. It may take time to achieve the changes in attitude and management style which will make zero-base budgeting most effective, but the investment in time very often has a substantial payoff in cost savings. It must, however, be noted that zero-base budgeting, too, can be defeated if managers do not view it with a positive attitude.

The Cash Budget

While the operating budget provides the revenue and expenditure data on which current operations are based, a cash budget provides another essential element in planning for operations. A not-for-profit firm must maintain revenues at a level to support current expenditures; in addition, however, the timing of the inflows and outflows of cash are important to ensure that cash is available to meet obligations and that excess cash does not remain idle.

It is important to understand that revenues and expenditures are not the same as cash inflows and outflows under the accrual and modified-accrual bases of accounting. While under the modified-accrual basis some revenues and expenditures may be recognized when cash is received or disbursed, accrual accounting principles require recognition of most revenues when there is an unrestricted right to receive them and expenditures when incurred. As a result, there may be substantial differences in the timing of revenues and expenditures and the inflows and outflows of cash. As a result, both an operating budget and a cash budget are necessary for effective management of the operations of the not-for-profit organization.

Cash management via the cash budget has two primary purposes. The first is to maintain the organization's solvency. The cash budget provides the details of expected cash inflows and outflows. Included in the cash budget are all items of cash inflows and outflows including capital expenditures, asset sales, and debt payments along with the inflows and outflows from daily operations. The budget ensures solvency by pinpointing those periods of cash shortages so that the organization can convert its temporary investments to cash or obtain loans to cover these shortages.

The second purpose of the cash budget is to determine those periods when excess cash is available and for how long it will be available. By doing so, the financial manager can invest these excess funds in revenue-producing assets to maximize the return for the available time period. The cash budget also forces management to analyze all elements of cash inflows and outflows specifically. Since many projections in the cash budget must be based on analysis of prior operations, it also helps management become aware of areas where cash management is weak. For example, a hospital receives the majority of its cash from billings to Medicaid and third-party health insurers. In an analysis of cash flows, it determines that there is an average four-month lag between patient services and the cash payment for these services. While a delay of one to three months in payment is often encountered with third-party payers, the four-month delay is excessive. An analysis of the billing process shows that the hospital does not submit a bill to the third-party payer for a patient until all charges are determined and totaled. Several departments in the hospital fail to submit their billings to the business office until two or more weeks after services are rendered. As a result, the business office holds all bills a minimum of three weeks and may hold them as long as six weeks prior to submission to the third-party payers. Further analysis shows that procedures could be streamlined so that departmental billings can be made within two days of service and final billings made to the third party within five business days of discharge--thus speeding collection by several weeks.

The basis for making a cash budget is the fundamental identity of:

Beginning Cash Balance + Cash Inflows - Cash Outflows = Ending Cash Balance

This identity can be used to establish a cash budget for any desired period of time. Cash budgets, however, are often determined for much shorter time intervals than operating budgets. It is common to find operating budgets prepared on a monthly basis with the monthly data aggregated for a period of a year or longer. Cash budgets, however, may be prepared for much shorter intervals, such as weekly or even daily. Since cash surpluses and shortages may exist for periods of less than a month, failure to invest or borrow for these short periods would be less than optimal. While these data may also be aggregated for monthly or annual periods, many savings can be effected or revenue increased by taking advantage of short-term investments, by delaying outflows or speeding up inflows by a few days, and by delaying borrowing until funds are actually required.

Example: The city of Westchester's new manager wants to establish a weekly cash budget for the month of February. Tax bills are sent out the latter part of December. If one-half of the bill is not paid by February 1, the entire balance becomes due on February 28. Tax bills were sent out totaling $2,500,000. Past experience indicates that 5 percent of tax bills become delinquent. Forty percent make the required one-half payment on February 1. The other 55 percent make their full payments by February 28 in the following pattern:

1st Week   5%
2nd week   10%

3rd week   15%
4th week   25%

The only other February revenue anticipated
is for dog licenses, which must be renewed
by February 28.   While some monies are collected earlier, the majority of the estimated $6,000 revenue from dog licenses is
assumed to be received during the fourth
week of February.

Expenses for the month are as follows:

Monthly salaried personnel
   (paid February 28) $ 40,000
Semimonthly payroll--including
   teachers' salaries (paid the
   end of the second and fourth
   weeks) $165,000
Operating expenses--paid during
   second week $ 65,000

The ending cash balance for the month of
January is $7,000.   The city always keeps a
minimum cash balance of $5,000.   From the
above data, the following weekly cash budget
can be constructed as shown on page 91.

This example illustrates the basics of a weekly
cash budget providing detailed data on anticipated
cash inflows and outflows.   The budget could then be
expanded to include the funds invested as disbursements of cash so that the ending cash balances would
always be $5,000.   Note that if this cash budget had
been for a period when revenues were less than
expenses the last line would have been an estimate
of additional cash requirements which could then be
met by selling investments or by borrowing funds as
an additional source of cash.

The Capital Budget

One of the most difficult budgets to prepare
accurately and the one most often neglected is the
capital budget.   The capital budget requires a relatively specific long-range plan of operation and
forecasts of future revenues and expenditures.   Capital budgets are generally developed for at least

February Cash Budget

	Week			
	1	2	3	4
Beginning cash balance	$ 7,000	$632,000	$ 652,000	$1,027,000
Cash receipts:				
Tax collections				
1/2 payments	500,000			
Full payments	125,000	250,000	375,000	625,000
Dog licenses				6,000
Cash available	632,000	882,000	1,027,000	1,658,000
Cash disbursements				
Monthly payroll	–			40,000
Semimonthly payroll	–	165,000	–	165,000
Operating expenses	–	65,000	–	
Ending cash balance	632,000	652,000	1,027,000	1,453,000
Minimum cash balance	5,000	5,000	5,000	5,000
Investable funds	627,000	647,000	1,022,000	1,448,000

five to ten years in the future. It is this long-range orientation that makes their preparation so difficult because it involves predicting the future. The capital budget, however, involves planning for major additions or replacements of existing plant and equipment which require substantial outlays of resources. Failure to adequately plan for these major expenditures may force cut-backs in services or delays in service expansion. Thus, it becomes a critical factor in ensuring that the required service levels are maintained at all times.

The capital budget constitutes a long-range planning tool which focuses on two areas--the replacement of major existing facilities and the expansion of current capacity. It is used to estimate the funds which will be required to carry out the planned replacement or expansion over a number of years. These funds may come from contributions, services, grants, revenue sharing, bond issues, or general revenues. The budget also details the amounts and timing of expenditures required for the new facilities. It must be emphasized, however, that the capital budget is totally dependent upon the long-range plans of the organization. Without a complete analysis of required future operations, a plan for the expansion and replacement of facilities cannot be formulated. For example, a suburban church has two Sunday services which have an attendance of approximately 90 percent capacity. The church is located in a growing suburb of a large metropolitan community. Two factors currently must be considered in expansion of the church. First, it will take almost one year for an addition to the church to be built. Second, in order to begin construction, the church must have a down payment of approximately 20 percent of the cost of the addition. The addition can then be financed over a ten-year period. Even though the church is not yet at capacity, it is estimated that capacity will be reached within the next two years. If the church does not prepare a capital budget now, it may not be able to have the expanded facilities ready when needed. The church must first determine as accurately as possible when the capacity of current facilities will be exceeded. It must also determine how long it feels it could operate at a level exceeding capacity before members become dissatisfied. Once this time table is determined, the church can work back to the date on which construction of the addition must begin and make plans to have the required down payment by that date.

In establishing even a simple capital budget for the church in the preceding example, it can be seen that the capital budget cannot be developed in isolation from the annual operating budgets. Unless the down payment and subsequent debt payments for the church addition can be obtained from extraordinary sources, provisions must be made within the operating budgets for these funds.

Due to the accounting procedures of certain forms of not-for-profit organizations, capital expenditures may also be accounted for as expenditures of the current operating fund. In addition, when funds for capital expenditures come from general revenues, they must be included in the operating budget for the current year. These funds may then be transferred temporarily to some form of restricted fund awaiting the actual capital investment. If funds are secured by debt, interest and principal payments may become the responsibility of the operating fund and must be included in the operating budget as

well. It must be understood then, that while the
capital investment budget is developed separately
from the operating budget, the operating budget may
include several items which are a direct result of
planned future or past acquisitions.

SUMMARY

The budgeting process for the not-for-profit
organization is an important tool which facilitates
planning for future operations and analyzing the
results of current operations. The budgeting process is a multistep process which should be under
the direction of a budget officer to facilitate
timely completion of the budget. The budget process
requires the specification of organization goals and
budgetary philosophy. These goals should be stated
in such a manner that they can be understood and
adhered to by all involved in the budget preparation. The actual budget preparation requires the
cooperation of many management personnel and should
be prepared by area of responsibility. The budget
should include estimates of all revenues and expenditures of the organization. As the budget moves
from lower-management levels to upper management,
similar expenditures are aggregated so that the
final budget contains totals for various categories
of revenues and expenditures by fund or by program.
Once prepared, the budget may go through several
revisions prior to formal approval. Once approved,
the budget may set a legal limit on the operating
expenditures for certain not-for-profit governmental
units; for others, the budget is merely a formality
required by the organization charter or bylaws. For
most not-for-profit organizations, however, the
budget provides one means of measuring their operations by using it to continually monitor planned
versus budgeted revenues and expenditures over the
budget categories.
Several illustrations of operating budgets follow
this summary. These illustrations are representative of only a small portion of not-for-profit
organizations. While many organizations of a particular type may have fairly standard budgeting
procedures, there are so many different types of
not-for-profit organizations, some with particular
accounting standards, others without, that truly
representative samples are impossible.

The latter part of this chapter briefly examined the planning, programming, budgeting system, and zero-base budgeting which are theories of budget preparation designed to encourage specification of goals and examination of alternative methods of operation to meet those goals. Finally, a discussion of cash budgets and capital budgets completed the chapter.

FIGURE 4.2
Budget Illustration I. The Central YMCA
Worksheet for Preparing 19X1 Expense Budget
(0000's omitted)

| | Actual Current Year | | | | |
	To date (8 mos.)	Estimate to end of year	Estimate total for year	Budget current year	Budget for new year
Building Expenses:					
Swimming pool					
Salaries & wages	10	5	15	14	20
Supplies	0.8	0.4	1.2	1.0	1.0
Maintenance	2	1	3	2.5	3.0
Tennis court					
Salaries & wages	4	2	6	8	6
Maintenance	6	1	7	6	
Racquetball courts					
Salaries & wages	6	3	9	10	8
Maintenance	8	2	10	10	5
Basketball courts					
Salaries & wages	2	1	3	4	4
Maintenance	4	8	12	12	6
Weight rooms & locker rooms					
Salaries & wages	4	4	8	5	8
Supplies	2	1	3	2	2
Maintenance	3	2	5	4	4
Totals excluding snack & sport shop	51.8	30.4	82.2	78.5	67
Snack bar*					
Salaries & wages	18	8	26	28	32
Food	35	18	53	50	60
Supplies	1	1	2	2	2
Maintenance	4	2	6	6	6
Sport shop*					
Salaries & wages	10	6	16	20	20
Sports equipment	20	10	30	25	30
Sports clothes	10	10	20	15	25
Maintenance	2	1	3	3	4
Total snack & sport shop	100	56	156	149	179
Total all areas	151.8	86.4	238.2	227.5	246.0

*These areas are self-supporting; thus they are presented after areas supported
by general membership fees.

FIGURE 4.3
Budget Illustration II. Badger City Chapter
Institute of Public Accountants
19X1 Oprating Budget

	19X0 Budget	19X0 Actual	19X0 Budget variance	19X1 Budget
Operating Fund Revenues				
Dues: Regular	2,000	1,950	<50>	2,300
Student	80	60	<20>	100
Retired	50	40	<10>	100
Meetings: Dinner	3,000	2,875	<125>	3,250
Luncheon	1,800	2,020	220	2,000
Breakfast	800	900	100	1,000
Other: Interest	200	185	<15>	200
Miscellaneous	100	250	150	200
Total revenues	8,030	8,290	260	9,150
Operating Fund Expenditures				
Dues to State Institute	500			
Meetings: Dinners	3,200	3,120	<80>	3,500
Luncheons	1,650	1,680	30	1,800
Breakfasts	600	675	75	800
Speakers	1,500	1,620	120	2,000
Other: Printing	350	295	<55>	350
Stationery	50	60	10	75
Postage	200	225	25	250
Public relations	300	280	<20>	300
Miscellaneous	100	140	40	150
Total expenses	7,950	8,095	145	8,975
Excess of revenues over expenditures	80	195	115	175

QUESTIONS

1. What role does the budget play in a not-for-profit organization?

2. What three types of budgets can an organization prepare? Explain briefly the purpose of each.

3. What is the budget cycle? Explain.

4. What is the purpose of the budget guidelines issued by the management or budget officer of a not-for-profit organization?

5. How does revenue in a not-for-profit firm differ from that of a profit-oriented firm for the budget process?

6. Distinguish primary and secondary revenue sources.

7. What problems may arise in forecasting revenues?

8. What types of expenditures must be estimated for budget preparation?

9. What is the difference between supplies expense and capital expenditure?

10. Describe several ways in which an operating budget can be prepared.

11. What is the PPBS system of budget preparation? Describe the basic steps in the PPBS budget's preparation.

12. What are the distinguishing characteristics of zero-base budgeting?

13. Why is a cash budget necessary?

14. Explain the fundamental identity used in cash-budget preparation.

15. What difficulties are encountered in the preparation of a capital budget?

PROBLEMS

1. Determine the cash inflows for the Germantown Community Hospital for the months of July and August using the following data.

Gross Billings	April	May	June	July	August
	$200,000	$240,000	$250,000	$250,000	$250,000
% Medicare	50	50	45	45	45
% Private Insurance Companies	40	40	45	45	45
% Individual Responsibility	10	10	10	10	10

Three-quarters of the Medicare claims are paid the 2nd month following service, the balance in the third month following. Forty percent of the claims to private insurance companies are paid within one month, 50 percent the following month, and the balance the third month. Of the charges which are paid by the individuals, 60 percent are paid in the month incurred; 20 percent the following month, 15 percent the next month, and the remainder is uncollectible.

2. Develop a cash budget detailing cash inflows and outflows for the Prince County Day Care Center for the months of January and February.

a. Revenues (paid in the month services are rendered) are expected to be $105,000 and $110,000 for January and February, respectively.
b. Salaries paid during the month are $42,000 (Jan.) and $34,000 (Feb.).
c. Rent is $6,000 per month.
d. Winter utility bills average $4,500.
e. Depreciation is $10,000 per month.
f. Food and other supplies paid currently are $10,000 per month.
g. Administrative expenses, insurance, and other miscellaneous expenses average $12,000 per month.
h. The center plans to add some equipment costing $20,000 in early January. A deposit of $5,000 has been made. One-half of the balance is due on delivery with the remainder payable within 30 days.

3. The finance committee of Redeemer Church must work out a quarterly cash budget for the construction of an education complex. Parishioners' pledges make up the major source of payment for the construction costs in the first year, with the balance financed through the local diocese. Using the following information, develop the quarterly cash budget and determine the amount and timing of any borrowing.

   a. Pledges of $200,000 have been obtained, which are to be paid in quarterly installments. Eighty percent of the pledges are expected to be paid when due. Ten percent are expected to be paid in the following quarter, 7 percent the next quarter, and 3 percent are expected to be uncollectible.

   b. Total first-year construction costs are estimated at $195,000. Payments must be made at the end of each quarter based on the percentage of the project completed less 10 percent, which is withheld pending project completion and acceptance. The project is expected to be 10, 35, 65, and 95 percent complete in the first through fourth quarters, respectively.

4. Andrews College has a separate store where a variety of clothing and incidental items are sold to students. In order to run the store efficiently a cash budget is desired. Using the following information, develop a cash budget for the months of January, February, and March.

   a. Sales are 60 percent cash; 40 percent on credit card collected the following month.

Actual and Forecasted Sales	
December	$44,000
January	36,000
February	35,000
March	32,000
April	34,000
May	38,000

   b. Inventories sufficient for two months' projected sales are maintained.
   c. Cost of goods sold is 45 percent of selling price.
   d. 50 percent of purchases for inventory are paid

for within 30 days and the balance within 60 days.

e. Rent is $2,500 per month.

f. Other operating expenses, paid in the month incurred, are projected at:

January	$15,500
February	12,000
March	11,500

5. Develop a cash budget for the months of September, October, and November for St. Mary's Hospital from the following information:

a.

Actual and Projected Revenues ($000)					
June	July	Aug.	Sept.	Oct.	Nov.
248	260	230	200	180	160

5 percent of revenue is collected in cash in the month of service, 10 percent of the balance on credit is collected in the month of service, 60 percent the following month, 28 percent the next, and the balance is uncollectible.

b. Variable costs of services are 40 percent of revenue.

c. Fixed overhead (excluding depreciation of $25,000 per month) is $100,000, paid as incurred.

d. The hospital maintains a $25,000 minimum cash balance and that is the beginning balance in September.

e. The hospital can borrow or invest in $1,000 units at the beginning of the month. It must pay 12 percent interest on funds borrowed and earns 7 percent on funds invested. Interest on short-term investments and borrowings is paid monthly at the beginning of the next month.

ENDNOTE

1. Stonick and Steenes, "Zero-Base Budgeting and Planning in Public Utilities," Public Utilities Fortnightly (Sept. 9, 1976), p. 26.

5

COST CONCEPTS AND ORGANIZATIONAL CONTROL

The previous chapter explored in broad terms the preparation of the operating budget and various theories on which its preparation can be based, as well as preparation of the cash and capital budgets. There are several other concepts directly or indirectly related to the actual preparation of the operating budget and its use as a control and evaluation device which must be considered. The first is the pattern of cost behavior. Costs may bear several types of relationship to output from direct (variable costs) to totally unrelated (fixed costs). It is essential to accurate budget preparation that the cost behavior patterns are understood.

There are also two types of operating budgets which can be prepared--flexible and static budgets. Static budgets are prepared for only one assumed level of activity, while flexible budgets are a series of static budgets, each prepared under differing assumptions about the level of activity. Flexible budgets provide a better basis for cost analysis when a substantial portion of the costs of operation vary with the level of output. Another important concept is that of standard costs and variance analysis. Standard costs may be developed for operations which are repetitive. When standard costs are feasible, variance analysis, the comparison of standard costs to actual costs, facilitates operating control.

Next, when revenues are related to costs, the concept of breakeven analysis may be useful to the not-for-profit firm. Then, since much of the control within the not-for-profit organization is based on comparisons of budgeted versus actual costs and revenues results, the role of the accounting system in budget evaluation is discussed. The accounting system is also explored as the primary source of information for management decisions. Finally, the functions of internal and external auditors are presented as the final step in the control process.

TYPES OF COSTS

In order to analyze costs of operations for preparing a budget, it is necessary to understand the behavior or patterns of various types of costs. The two most common types of costs to be considered are variable costs and fixed costs. While these costs are generally defined and explained with reference to a manufacturing firm, their definitions are adaptable to the not-for-profit enterprise. Variable costs are those costs which fluctuate in direct proportion to some measure of output. In the manufacturing firm, direct materials costs are used as an example of a strictly variable cost since, as output increases, the amount of input material also increases. Fixed costs are those costs which remain constant regardless of the level of output or activity. Property taxes on a manufacturing plant remain the same whether the plant produces one or one million units in a given period.

In the analysis of these costs in relation to the not-for-profit organization, it is necessary to define several additional cost behavior patterns. Semivariable costs are those costs which possess a fixed as well as a variable portion; i.e., they will vary within a certain range of activity but will not be zero at zero activity. Certain types of telephone service fit this category. If telephone service is provided for a flat fee with an additional charge per phone call, a semivariable cost results. Another type of cost is the step cost. Step costs are fixed over a certain range of activity and increase in steps as activity increases. Costs of supervisory personnel usually follow a stepped pattern. Figure 5.1 is a graphical representation of

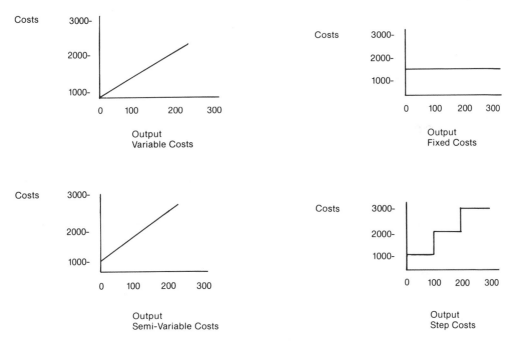

Figure 5.1   Types of organization cost patterns.

fixed, variable, semivariable, and step costs.

Few not-for-profit organizations will have truly variable costs unless they happen to be engaged in some activity which requires the use of raw materials and/or labor based on output. A sheltered workshop for the mentally retarded may base employee compensation on piecework. Most costs, however, will fall into one of the other categories. The salaries of hospital administrators or governmental officials are fixed. Most utility costs are determined by a fixed fee plus a variable portion depending upon use. The welfare department may employ one social worker for every 100 cases; as the number of cases exceeds a multiple of 100 an additional caseworker must be hired, resulting in a stepped cost pattern. The objective of understanding these cost behavior patterns is to be able to identify them and then try to operate in a manner which reduces overall costs to an optimum level. It is also important to budget preparation that the type of cost behavior is accurately recognized so that the budgeted costs truly reflect costs at the anticipated activity level.

TYPES OF BUDGETS

The Static versus The Flexible Budget

The nonprofit organization may prepare its budget in one of two forms, as a static budget or a flexible budget. When a static budget is prepared, a singular set of assumptions is made regarding the level of activity of the organization and the budget figures are based solely on that activity level. The flexible budget is in reality a series of static budgets since budget figures will be presented for several levels of activity. Whether preparing a static or flexible budget, it is important to understand the behavior of various costs, whether they are fixed, variable, semivariable, or stepped, as explained in a preceding section.

In preparing the static budget, only one level of activity is considered. The fixed costs such as rent or depreciation are independent of the level of activity chosen. The other costs, however, are determined in whole or in part by this activity level. Once an estimate of the activity level is made, the variable, semivariable, and stepped costs are determined for this level and along with the fixed costs constitute the budgeted costs for that activity.

For example, the Department of Social Services estimates the average caseload over the year will be 20,000 clients. Each social worker is expected to handle an average of 400 clients at any one time at an average salary of $18,000 per year. There is one supervisor for each 10 caseworkers at a salary of $25,000 per year. Fringe benefits are $5,000 per employee. Fixed costs of $800,000 per year are incurred for rent and utilities. Supplies cost an average of $1 per month per client. The static budget for the social services department can be developed in the following manner:

Caseworkers:	200,000/400 = 50@ 18,000	900,000
Supervisors:	50/10 = 5 @ 25,000	125,000
Fringe benefits:	55 @ 5,000	275,000
Supplies:	20,000 x $1 x 12	240,000
Fixed expenses:		800,000
		$2,340,000

The static budget works well in situations where most costs tend to be relatively fixed. A library may employ a certain number of employees to provide the services regardless of how many persons take advantage of these services or the number of books borrowed. In other words, the library staff must be available to provide the services whether anyone uses them or not. The budget will be the same for these basic services up to a level of activity which requires multiple persons to service certain activities. A static budget may be adequate since there may be little opportunity to vary the costs as the activity level fluctuates. When it is possible to vary certain costs as activity varies, the flexible budget may provide a better mechanism for assessing efficiency of operations.

The flexible budget is a series of static budgets developed for various levels of activity.

For example, the social services department in the previous example decides to develop a flexible budget on a monthly basis. The expected level of activity is still 20,000 clients on an average. Due to an uncertain economic climate, the number of clients could be as low as 18,000 or as high as 24,000 in a month. It is possible to lay off caseworkers; however, certain fringe benefits with an annual cost of $3,000 must be continued. Additional temporary caseworkers may be hired at $20,000 per year with no added costs for fringe benefits. A flexible budget for 18,000, 20,000, 22,000, and 24,000 clients is prepared as follows: [All other information from the previous example is the same].

Flexible Budget

Monthly costs	Activity level - No. of clients			
	18,000	20,000	22,000	24,000
Labor	67,500	75,000	83,333	91,667
Supervisors	10,417	10,417	10,417	12,500
Fringe benefits	22,083	22,917	22,917	22,917
Supplies	18,000	20,000	22,000	24,000
Fixed expenses	66,667	66,667	66,667	66,667

There are several things that should be noted about this flexible budget. First, there are several cost patterns represented in this budget. Supplies are a variable expense and labor can be considered variable although it increases in small steps at each 400-client interval. The supervisor and fringe benefit costs are both stepped costs. Second, this budget highlights the fact that adherence to a budget must be tempered by consideration of the activity level. Since activity levels are an integral part of the budget, any comparison of actual costs to budgeted costs should be made to those of the activity level closest to actual. The flexible budget, which incorporates the various activity levels, facilitates this comparison. On the other hand, the static budget often leads to absolute dollar comparisons without consideration for activity level. The danger exists, then, that an operation will be judged efficient when actual expenses are less than budgeted simply because the activity level is below the budgeted level; similarly, an operation with expenses in excess of budgeted amounts as a result of increased activity will be considered inefficient. The flexible budget aids in overcoming this deficiency. Another concept which will also aid in this type of comparison is that of standard costs and variance analysis discussed in the following section.

STANDARD COSTS AND VARIANCE ANALYSIS

A concept often used in budget preparation is that of standard costs. The budget contains costs for total activities, whereas standard costs are developed for a single activity unit. Thus, when standard costs are multiplied by the expected activity level, the total budgeted costs for that activity result.

Standard costs have their most widespread application in manufacturing firms where standards are developed for materials, labor, and fixed and variable overhead. As the firm operates, the actual results of operations are compared to the standards set for operations. The differences, called variances, are then analyzed as to cause as a means of improving future operations.

In order to develop standards, costs must be estimated for material, labor, and overhead for each type of unit output. Standards may be developed

based on one of several assumptions regarding operations, and the type of standard developed affects
the analysis of variances. If the standards which
are initially developed remain unchanged over the
years of operations, then the standards are called
basic cost standards. This type of standard generally leads to greater and greater unfavorable variances the further the operations are from the time
the standards were set. Their primary usefulness is
in trend analysis, but as procedures and products
change these trends may be obscured. As a result,
base standards are seldom used in favor of setting
new standards at periodic intervals.

Standards may also be set based on a theoretically ideal set of operating conditions. These standards are often termed perfection standards and are
based on achieving maximum efficiency. This type of
standard, too, may lead to significant unfavorable
variances; variance analysis must then be based on
some expected level of unfavorable variances. This
type of standard often has some unfavorable behav-
ioral aspects; i.e., workers may feel defeated by
this type of standard. There are, however, situations where it may motivate workers to improve
their operations. The use, then, of perfection
standards often hinges on the effect on workers.

The most common type of standard that is set is
the currently attainable standard. This is a standard that requires reasonable efficiency to achieve
but allows for some downtime or operation at less
than 100 percent of capacity. Currently attainable
standards are usually set tight enough to instill a
real sense of accomplishment when attained but not
so tight that large unfavorable variances always
result.

As previously mentioned, standards are usually
developed for materials, labor, and fixed and variable overhead. The not-for-profit firms will find
the most use for labor standards since they are
generally service-oriented. It should be emphasized, however, that it is difficult to develop
standards for operations that are unique or nonre-
petitive. Labor standards in manufacturing firms
are usually developed by engineers who study the
operations and break them down into a succession of
repetitive steps. In service organizations, it may
be difficult to develop meaningful standards because
the services must be provided to meet individual
problems rather than meet repetitive situations.
However, where this repetition exists, standards can

be very useful. The balance of this discussion on standards and variance analysis will center on labor standards only. Any one of the many current cost accounting texts available will provide a complete discussion of standards and variance analysis for materials and overhead.

Labor standards are developed for particular tasks by estimating both the time and cost of labor to perform a particular task. The estimation of time is often made by a trained observer focusing over a period of time on one or more persons performing the task in question. (In manufacturing firms, this conjures up the image of the engineer walking around with a stopwatch and clipboard.) In the not-for-profit organization, the standards should be set by management, including the supervisor directly responsible for the department for which the standards are being set. If the standards are simply imposed by upper management, the supervisors who must maintain the standards may fail to accept them as reasonable and fail to provide the necessary leadership.

It is important to consider both the time and cost of labor in setting standards. They should be based on the wages or salary of someone qualified, but not overly qualified, to perform the task. In many manufacturing firms, union negotiations set the salaries for particular types of labor. In governmental and not-for-profit organizations (such as schools and hospitals) a similar situation exists either through union negotiations or through a well-specified pay-rate structure. If the pay rates are in question, there are generally several sources of information available for setting rates, such as other not-for-profit organizations or private industries with people performing similar functions. In addition, state or private employment agencies or state or federal agencies which maintain statistical employment data may be consulted; i.e., the Bureau of Labor Statistics prepares extensive wage data which may provide a foundation for setting standards.

Once standards are set, the actual labor costs of performing the task are compared to these standards, with the differences called variances.

For example, the local government has purchased a computer facility which will be used to store all property tax information. Punch cards will be used to input data to the system. The government plans to hire two keypunch operators. Using an average property tax record, the supervisor determines that each keypunch operator should be able to keypunch 80 records per hour. The local office of the state employment agency reports that the starting salary for key punch operators is $5.60 per hour. Thus, a standard of $0.07 per record is set. The city has 96,000 property tax records to enter on punch cards. Thus the total budgeted costs are $6,720.

The city hires only one starting keypunch operator (A) at $5.60 per hour; the second keypunch operator (B) has two years experience and is paid $6.20 per hour. After an initial two-week training period, information is gathered on actual versus standard costs for the third week. Keypunch operator A completes 2900 records while keypunch operator B completes 4050 records during the 40-hour work week, resulting in the following standard and actual costs:

	Standard Costs	Actual Costs
Keypunch Operator A	2900 x 0.07 = $203.00	40 hr @ 5.60 = $224
Keypunch Operator B	4050 x 0.07 = 283.50	40 hr @ 6.20 = $248

Keypunch operator A has an unfavorable variance of $21 while keypunch operator B has a favorable variance of $35.50. Favorable variances result when actual costs are below standard costs but unfavorable variances result from actual costs exceeding standard.

Labor variances may be subdivided into two parts: efficiency and rate variances. The $21 and $35.50 variances are total variances caused by differences in both the output (efficiency) and wage (rate). These may be separated in the following manner:

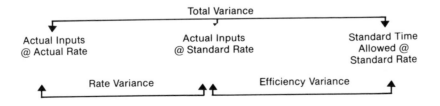

For keypunch operator A this is:

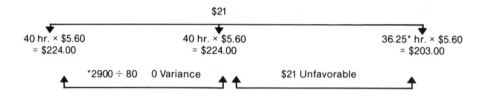

The entire $21 unfavorable variance for keypunch operator A is an efficiency variance.

Keypunch operator B has the following variances:

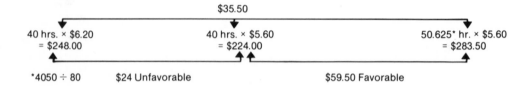

Keypunch operator B's $35.50 favorable variance is made up of a $24 unfavorable wage rate variance (since the operator is paid $6.20 per hour rather than the standard $5.60) and a $59.50 favorable efficiency variance.

The primary importance of this information is in the manner it is used beyond this point to improve operations. The supervisor should carefully examine the work of keypunch operator A, asking such questions as:

"Is this operator failing to work to capacity?"

"Is this operator's inexperience the reason for the inefficient operation? If so, is there a definite improvement as time progresses?"

"Since operator B meets the efficiency standard easily, would it be better to replace A with another operator whose experience is similar to B's?"

It is even proper to question the standards. Since B meets the standard so readily, should they be tightened? Would this greater challenge affect A in the desired manner? Would this have either a

positive or negative effect on B? The variances
themselves offer no solutions to problems; they do,
however, highlight the areas which need examination.
Often no clear-cut answers to the problems are evident, and supervisors must go beyond obvious
answers. Unfavorable variances do not always mean
poor quality labor but may result from unrealistic
standards. Similarly, favorable variances may only
indicate that standards are set too loosely. As in
many other areas of management, experience in supervising within a standard cost-variance analysis
framework will be the greatest asset in using these
data to analyze and improve performance.

Breakeven Analysis

Breakeven analysis is a tool used most
effectively in the private sector. Unfortunately,
its applicability to the not-for-profit sector is
limited. There are, however, instances where it may
be used directly or adapted to the not-for-profit
firm (particularly a client-oriented organization)
and should not be ignored.
The breakeven point is defined as that level of
activity where total revenues equal total expenses;
i.e., profit is zero. Theoretically, the not-for-
profit organization should always operate at a
breakeven point, by definition. The difficulty in
applying this tool to many not-for-profit organizations is that breakeven analysis presupposes a direct relationship between revenues and outputs.
Again, this relationship simply does not exist in
many areas of the public sector.
It is also understood in breakeven analysis that
costs can be broken down into variable and fixed.
The purpose of breakeven analysis is to determine
the level of output where revenue covers not only
the variable costs but the fixed costs as well.
In order to understand traditional breakeven
analysis, two additional terms need defining:

Sales revenue = No. of units x unit price
Unit contribution margin =
          Unit price - Unit variable costs

The traditional breakeven equation may take either
of two forms, one based on total revenues and costs
and one based on the unit contribution margin. The
first form is referred to as the equation technique

and is:

Sales revenue = Variable costs + Fixed costs

If X equals the number of breakeven units, $1.00 is the selling price per unit, variable costs = $0.50 per unit, and fixed costs are $1,000, the equation may be restated as:

$$1.00 \ X = 0.50X + 1000$$
$$0.50 \ X = \$1000$$
$$X = 2000 \ units$$

The unit contribution approach basically states that the unit contribution margin is available to cover fixed costs. The contribution technique then finds the number of units which need to be sold to cover fixed expenses or:

$$\text{Breakeven units} = \frac{\text{Fixed expense}}{\text{Unit Contribution Margin}}$$

In the example above this is:

$$X = \frac{1000}{0.50}*$$

*This 0.50 represents the unit contribution margin which is selling price less variable costs per unit of $1.00 - 0.50.

Figure 5.2 is a graphic representation of breakeven analysis.

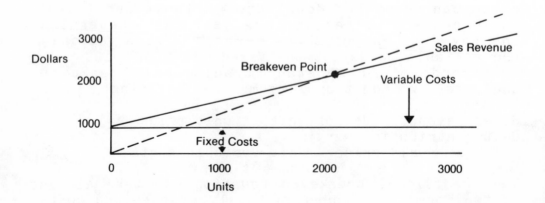

FIGURE 5.2 Breakeven chart.

In traditional breakeven analysis, given that the assumptions regarding cost behavior and revenue are reasonable, the number obtained is exactly how many units must be produced and sold before any profit is realized.

Can this technique be used in the public sector? The answer is definitely yes, though some creativity in application may be required. First, in not-for-profit organizations where services are charged for on a unit basis, it may be used to establish the unit charges.

> **Example:** A university athletic department wishes to provide student tickets to basketball games at home at a reasonable cost, but at a cost which covers only its proportionate share of fixed and variable expenses. Total fixed costs of the basketball team are $300,000 annually. However, the team plays only 50 percent of its games at home; there are 12 home games and variable costs per home game are $0.30 per ticket. The athletic department allocates 25 percent of the 10,000 tickets for at-home games to students. How much must student tickets sell for to break even on them if 100 percent of the tickets are sold?
>
> The selling price of the 2500 student tickets must cover 25 percent of the home game fixed and variable costs.
>
> ```
> Fixed costs/home game = 150,000 ÷ 12   =   $12,500.00
> Variable costs/home game (10,000 x $0.30)    3,000.00
> Total costs/home game                       15,500.00
> Allocated to student tickets @ 25%           3,875.00
> Cost/ticket = 3875/2500              =           1.55
> ```
>
> What would the answer be if only 75 percent of the tickets are sold?
>
> ```
> Fixed costs/game                      =  $12,500.00
> Variable costs (10,000 x 0.75 x 0.3)       2,250.00
> Total costs/home game                     14,750.00
> Allocated to student tickets @ 25%         3,687.50
> Cost/ticket = 3687.50 ÷ (2500 x 0.75)          1.97
> ```

This example shows that the fewer the units sold, the higher the price per unit must be to break even.

This aspect of breakeven analysis leads to additional applications.

>**Example:** A municipality is deciding whether to establish its own sanitation department or allow residents to contract with private firms for garbage collection. The city has 10,000 households, all of which would be assessed for garbage collection on their property tax bills if the city establishes a sanitation department. The taxes would have to cover the full costs of operating the sanitation department. Estimated annual costs are:

Labor:	8 - 2 man crews @ 20,000/yr./man	$320,000
	1 Supervisor	30,000
	Fringe benefits	50,000
Trucks:	Gasoline & maintenance	75,000
	Depreciation/year	200,000
Overhead:	Added clerical and administrative costs	30,000
	Total annual costs	705,000
	Cost per household	$70.50

The city would have to add a minimum of $70.50 per household to the tax bill to break even on a garbage collection service. If the residents can contract for private garbage service at a cost of less than $70.50 annually, or, alternatively, if the city can contract with a private firm to provide the service to all residences for less than $70.50 per household per year, the city should not establish its own sanitation department.

The Accounting System and Budget Evaluation

The accounting department in a not-for-profit organization may have many diverse responsibilities. It's primary responsibility is the recording of all the monetary transactions in the accounting records and the preparation of periodic financial statements. As explained in Chapter 2, however, the system of fund accounting may require maintenance of accounting records for many types of funds and numerous funds of each particular type. In addition, individual statements are prepared for each fund and combined statements may be prepared for all funds and/or for all funds of a particular type.

The accounting department may also have a major role in the billing and collection of revenues, payment of bills, and preparation of payroll. Since the accounting department should also be able to provide the information necessary for management decisions and day-to-day control of operations, the design of the accounting system is a critical factor in its ability to meet the various masters it must serve.

In the majority of not-for-profit organizations, the budget is the foundation for control of operations. Expenditures often must be curtailed when budgeted amounts are exceeded or additional funds appropriated to cover them. Operating managers cannot, however, maintain day-to-day control over expenditures if the accounting system is not designed to prepare the necessary data to do so. In a very small organization it may be possible to collect data manually from the accounting records to meet control requirements. In larger organizations, accounting records are often processed and maintained with the aid of computers. Whether the organization maintains its own computer facility, uses time-sharing, or uses a service bureau, the accounting records must be maintained in a manner which ties into budgeted amounts. This can be done by a coding system in which budget codes are paired to codes for actual transactions. For instance, revenues could carry a general code of 900; patient service revenues could be 70; and revenues from laboratory facilities could be a 4. Thus, when recording transactions for lab services, the accounting record would be coded as 974. Budgeted revenues for lab services could be some variation of 974 such as 974 B. The system could then provide both the actual and budgeted revenues for lab services with a minimum of difficulty. While this is an overly simplified example of system design, it illustrates the feasibility of tieing budgeted and actual data together through computer facilities.

A second consideration in system design is that the accounting reports provided to operating managers must have sufficient detail so that problem areas can be identified and appropriate corrective actions taken.

For example, the central offices service of a municipality provides typing and duplicating services for all administrative areas. The typing pool consists of four clerk-typists and one statistical typist, while two persons normally run the duplicating equipment and do all necessary filing; for the last month, however, the department has operated with only one person in duplicating services.

Budgeted salaries for the current month are:

4	Clerk-typists	@	800/mo.	$3,200
1	Statistical typist	@	1,000/mo.	1,000
2	Clerks	@	650/mo.	1,300
				$5,500

The manager receives actual data for the month indicating actual salaries paid of only $5,200, or $300 under budget. The manager, however, recognizing the limitation of this summary figure, requests a breakdown of salaries by position and by regular and overtime pay. He receives the following:

	Regular	Overtime
4 Clerk-typists	$3,120	$270
1 Statistical typist	1,000	200
1 Clerk	660	50
	$4,780	$420

The manager can now see that while he is substantially under budget for clerks, he is well over budget for the other areas. He must now determine the answers to a series of questions concerning these operations to assess the situation and take any necessary corrective actions. Some of these questions might be: (1) Are the clerk-typist and the statistical typist receiving overtime for their own work or for picking up some of the duplicating services? (2) If they are doing their own work, is this a temporary phenomenon or has the workload increased to the point that an additional part-time person would be more economical? (3) If they are providing duplicating services at overtime rates, why is the statistical typist doing a larger proportion of it at the higher rate? (4) Since overtime hours do not equal full-time hours, is a backlog developing? (5) If there is a backlog, should an additional part-time person be hired as soon as possible rather than paying overtime rates? While these questions do not cover the complete range of possibilities, it should be clear that a manager should have detailed budgeted and actual information in order to accurately assess possible problem areas. Again, the accounting system must be designed so that it is able to provide this kind of detailed information, and the accounting entries must conform to budgetary entries.

A Management Information System

The accounting system may form a part of an overall organization information system. Control in a not-for-profit organization may take forms other than a comparison of actual to budgeted data stated in a dollar format. As discussed in Chapter 3, the lack of relationship between revenues and expenditures in many not-for-profit organizations complicates the control of operations. It may be necessary to develop measures of efficiency on some basis other than costs relationship to revenue or budgeted versus actual costs; e.g., cost per client served. If the organization has an information system that provides not only financial data but nonfinancial data, a variety of reports may be generated which can help the manager in assessing the efficiency of operations.

The persons managing not-for-profit organizations may not have the necessary expertise to analyze all their data-processing needs. Outside consultants may be required to assist in the design of reports to facilitate the accurate analysis of operations, to help select the computer hardware which is the most efficient for its particular needs, and to help select the software packages or write specialized programs to meet data requirements.

The decision to establish either a computerized accounting system or a management information system can be viewed in the context of the capital budgeting decision, as discussed in Chapter 11. Many public accounting firms have management advisory services sections which will analyze an organization's needs and make recommendations, as will a number of outside consulting firms. If the cost of the system can be justified on the basis of improved operations, then it should be considered.

Auditing for Control

The not-for-profit organization may benefit in several respects from auditing procedures. As discussed briefly in Chapter 2, external auditors may be employed to verify the fairness of the financial statements of the organization. This attest function takes on special significance in the not-for-profit organization because of its position of public trust. The independent audit provides assurance to the public that the results of operations presented in the financial statements are fair and in conformity to generally accepted accounting principles established for that type of organization. This function itself serves as a control device on the maintenance of adequate, accurate accounting records.

There are other functions that auditors can perform, but first internal and external auditors must be distinguished. Internal auditors are skilled accountants who work for the organization itself but are independent of the actual accounting department, reporting directly to the director or board of trustees of the organization, for example. External auditors work for public accounting firms and are hired to perform certain specific tasks by the organization. While internal and external auditors may be able to provide many of the same services, only outside auditors may express an opinion on the financial statements of the organization. Many not-for-profit organizations are not large enough to employ one or more full-time internal auditors and may have to rely totally on external auditors; if, however, the organization is sufficiently large, the services of a full-time internal auditor may be extremely valuable in controlling operations of the organization. First, in not-for-profit organizations which have legally binding restrictions on expenditures exceeding appropriations, auditors can watch to see that expenditures and encumbered amounts do not exceed appropriations. They can also verify that expenditures are actually made for the appropriated items. These "watchdog" functions can usually be provided by internal auditors on an ongoing basis. If not, this task must fall on management.

Internal and external auditors can also provide "management" audits. These audits are designed to evaluate the effectiveness of various management functions. They can be rather routine; e.g., making sure the controls over cash, accounts receivable, and the bank accounts are maintained; or they can be quite complex; e.g., assessing the effectiveness of the system on snow removal during major snow storms. This latter example falls into a distinct class of management audits called program audits.

Program audits are specially suited to many types of not-for-profit organizations. Many not-for-profit organizations have specific functions to perform which are met by a planned operation or program. The program audit is designed to evaluate both the effectiveness and efficiency of the program in meeting its specific objective. If there are areas in which improvements can be made, the auditor should not only point these out but make suggestions for changes in operations to correct the inefficiencies. For example, the duplicating department of a local government was running substantially over its budget for several months because of overtime hours. The internal auditor, in looking at this situation, found the property tax division had changed their own procedures in a way which doubled the amount of work they sent to the duplicating department. Prior to this change, the duplicating department had determined that the type of duplicating equipment was adequate for their workload and no equipment changes were necessary. With this change, however, the machines could not produce the volume required in an eight-hour day. The internal auditor recommended and studied alternative duplicating machines. A slower machine was replaced with a high-speed duplicating machine, eliminating the overtime at only a slight increase in machine costs.

Management and/or program audits can be effective in assessing the efficiency of equipment as illustrated in this example. They can also be effective in assessing the managerial capabilities of various persons within the organization as well as evaluating overall programs. The concern of any control system, however, whether it is a budget system or periodic operational audit, is to permit management to evaluate the operation of the organization so that future operations can be improved. A great deal is written about the preparation of the budgets, but careful analysis of the results of operations provides another necessary step in maintaining operating efficiency. To prepare budgets, statistical data, and accounting data without using the information to improve future operations, is an enormous waste of resources. No control system will work unless it first is used.

SUMMARY

Preparation of the operating budget is extremely important to a not-for-profit organization since it may be the basic management control device. Several concepts are useful to budget preparation and its control features such as flexible budgets, standard costs, and variance analysis. In addition there may be times when the concept of breakeven analysis may be useful for decision making by the not-for-profit firm. These concepts were covered briefly in this chapter; for a more complete discussion a cost accounting text should be consulted.

This chapter also reviewed the accounting system's role in providing the necessary data for improving operations. If budgeted data are used as a major control tool, then the results of operations should be correlated to budgeted amounts. The accounting system may also form only one part of a management information system which could provide data in other than monetary terms. Finally, the role of external and internal auditors was discussed. While they often perform similar functions, only external auditors can express an opinion on financial statements. Internal auditors, however, work for the organization and are available on a continuing basis.

QUESTIONS

1. Distinguish between static and flexible budgets.

2. Describe several cost behavior patterns and give examples of each.

3. Explain standard costs. How are they related to variance analysis?

4. How are standard costs developed and on what basis?

5. What are rate and efficiency variances related to labor costs?

6. What purpose does variance analysis serve?

7. What is breakeven analysis and when is it applicable to not-for-profit organizations?

8. How can the accounting system facilitate budget evaluation?

9. What role can a management information system play in a not-for-profit organization?

10. What functions can auditors perform in a not-for-profit organization?

11. What is the difference between internal and external auditors?

PROBLEMS

1. Prepare a static expense budget for the year 198X for Home Hospital using the following information.

Avg. no. of nurses per day	200
Avg. salary per day per nurse	$64
Avg. fringe benefits per day per nurse	$10
Avg. no. of nursing supervisors per day	25
Avg. salary per day per supervisor	$80
Avg. fringe benefits per day per supervisor	$15
Avg. no. of head nurses	10
Avg. salary per day per head nurse	$100
Avg. fringe benefits per day per head nurse	$20
Avg. no. of patients per day	250
Avg. cost of drugs per patient per day	$10
Avg. cost of supplies per patient per day	$25

Fixed Expenses - Monthly

Utilities	$14,000
Depreciation	40,000
Maintenance & housekeeping	18,000

2. Develop an annual static expense budget for a parochial school from the following information.

8 full-time teachers @ $12,000/year
4 part-time special resource teachers @ $4,000/year

Fringe benefits per full-time teachers =
$3,000/year

Monthly Utilities $2,000
        Depreciation   4,000
        Maintenance   1,500
        Supplies   500

3. Develop a flexible expense budget for the month of May for the maternity floor of the Whitehall Hospital from the following information. Total number of patient days expected ranges from 200 to 250 in 10-patient increments. One and one-half nurses are required per patient-day at a cost of $1,200 per nurse per month. One supervisor is required for every multiple of 20 nurses at a cost of $1,500 per month.

4. Develop a flexible expense budget for June for a local mental health clinic run by Banning County from the information provided. The number of clients per month averages 1,000 but could be as low as 700 and as high as 1,200 budgeted in 100-patient increments. Each therapist sees an average of 120 patients per month. Each of the therapists employed receives a guaranteed $800 per month regardless of the patients seen. They also receive an additional $20 per patient for each patient they see over 40 per month. Fringe benefits are $200 per month plus 8 percent of salary over $800 per therapist. One supervising psychiatrist is employed at a cost of $4,000 per month. Secretarial expenses are $1,200 per month. When the patient load exceeds 1,000 per month, an additional part-time person is hired at $400 per month. Insurance processing and billing costs are $1 per patient per month in addition to the secretarial expense.

5. Determine the total, rate, and efficiency variances for nursing services at Memorial Hospital for the month of April.

Budget: 8,000 hr nursing services @ $16.00/hr

Actual: 4,000 hr nursing services @   15.50/hr
          2,500 hr nursing services @   16.25/hr
          2,000 hr nursing services @   16.50/hr

6. Social work supervisors at the local United Services Agency are trying to improve performance by the development of accurate budgets and variance analysis. In an initial month-long trial period, the following results were obtained. Prepare total, rate, and efficiency variances for each category of social worker and for the department as a whole.

Budgeted amounts:
Class I: 154 man-days @ $70/day
Class II: 110 man-days @ $85/day
Class III: 44 man-days @ $95/day

Actual results:
Class I: 66 man-days @ $68/day
               77 man-days @ $75/day
Class II: 66 man-days @ $85/day
               55 man-days @ $87/day
Class III: 40 man-days @ $93.50/day

7. How many units of an item must a rehabilitative workshop sell in order to break even under the following conditions: fixed expenses are $15,000, selling price is $2.00 per unit, and variable costs are $0.65 per unit.

8. What is the contribution margin and annual breakeven volume for license plates manufactured at the state prison? The license plates are sold to the state for $6.00 a pair; labor costs $1.25 per plate and materials $0.65 per plate. Fixed costs for the manufacturing facilities are $620,00 annually.

9. Lakewood City has a crew of mechanics to maintain its fleet of garbage trucks and snow removal equipment.

Annual costs are:

Labor: 20 men   @ $18,000/year/man
         2 supervisors   @ $24,000/year/man
Fringe benefits: Men $120,000/year
                  Supervisors   16,000/year
Facilities rent   48,000/year
Material & supplies   8,000/year
Repair parts   65,000/year
Utilities   9,000/year

The city can obtain a maintenance contract on its 350 pieces of equipment at the following rates:

        100 pieces @ $1,200 annually
        100 pieces @ 1,500 annually
         50 pieces @ 2,000 annually
        100 pieces @ 3,000 annually

Assuming either method provides an adequate level of service, should Lakewood continue to operate its own service department?

6

OVERVIEW OF WORKING CAPITAL MANAGEMENT

Working capital management refers to the management of an organization's current assets and current liabilities to maintain them at appropriate levels. Current assets are cash and other liquid assets; e.g., short-term investments, accounts receivable, and inventories, which would normally be converted into cash within one year's time. Current liabilities are obligations which will be discharged through the use of current assets and consist primarily of accounts payable, notes payable, wages, and other payables.

Working capital management should be of primary importance to the not-for-profit organization. If the not-for-profit organization's level of working capital is too low, it will not be able to pay its bills when they become due. On the other hand, if the level of working capital is too high, the organization is not employing its resources in an efficient and effective manner.

One of the characteristics of not-for-profit organizations is their stewardship responsibility for the funds they receive. This fiduciary responsibility results in the use of the "fund accounting" technique discussed in Chapter 2. A characteristic of this technique is that accounting for long-term assets and long-term debt is most often accomplished

through the use of nonoperating funds or group accounts. Consequently, the current operating funds
for most not-for-profit organizations are made up
exclusively of working capital items. In general,
then, the current fund balance indicates the resources available for current operations.

This chapter addresses the three fundamental
questions associated with working capital management[1]:

1. Why should the organization invest in current
   assets (or working capital)?
2. What level of current assets should the organization carry?
3. How should the current assets be financed?

The subsequent three chapters will devote attention
to the determination of the levels of individual
current assets and current liabilities.

NATURE AND IMPORTANCE OF WORKING
CAPITAL MANAGEMENT

A not-for-profit organization has to have an
asset base, containing both current and fixed assets, in order to provide services on a continuing
basis. Fixed assets, those items expected to be
held and used for more than one year, are obviously
mandatory for the provision of services. Land,
buildings, and equipment are necessary for almost
every not-for-profit organization. It is not possible, however, to provide productive services with
fixed assets alone. Fixed assets have to be combined with current assets to achieve their productive potential. For example, a hospital has to
invest in inventories of food, drugs, linens, and
other supplies in order to provide patient care. In
addition, it must also invest in accounts receivable
since the majority of patients' bills are paid by
third parties. Working capital serves as the catalyst which changes the productive potential of fixed
assets into productive services.[2]

The mechanism by which working capital serves as
a catalyst for converting fixed assets into productive services can be illustrated by means of the
following example.

Table 6.1 shows the combined balance sheet
for the various funds of the Johnson Dia-

betes Research Center as of June 30, 19X0.
Johnson Diabetes Research Center is a nonprofit organization which provides treatment
for diabetes and conducts research into the
causes of the disease.   The research center

TABLE 6.1

Johnson Diabetes Research Institute
Balance Sheet
June 30, 19X0

Assets

| | Unrestricted | | Funds for | | |
	General fund	Investment fund	specified purposes	Endowment funds	Total funds
Current assets					
Cash	$30,000	1,400	$12,300	$9,400	$53,100
Marketable securities at cost		154,000	153,000	1,340,000	1,647,000
Contract receivables	4,500				4,500
Other receivables	76,400				76,400
Inventories of books and supplies	8,500				8,500
Total current assets	$119,400	$155,400	$165,300	$1,349,400	$1,789,500
Fixed assets at cost					
Land	60,000				60,000
Buildings	1,050,000				1,050,000
Vehicles	15,300				15,300
Total	$1,125,300				$1,125,300
Less: accumulated depreciation	(634,000)				(634,000)
Net fixed assets	491,300				491,300
Total assets	$610,700	$155,400	$165,300	$1,349,400	$2,280,800

Liabilities and net worth

| | Unrestricted | | Funds for | | |
	General fund	Investment fund	specified purposes	Endowment funds	Total funds
Accounts payable	$58,700				$58,700
Witholding taxes	4,000				4,000
Grants paid in advance	25,200				25,200
Interfund payable (receivable)	21,000	$(22,000)	$(6,250)	7,250	-
Total liabilities	$108,900	$(22,000)	$(6,250)	$7,250	$87,900
Fund balances	501,800	177,400	171,550	1,342,150	2,192,900
Total liabilities and fund balances	$610,700	$155,400	$165,300	$1,349,400	$2,280,800

Adopted from a similar example in Malvern J. Gross, Jr. and Stephen F.
Jablonsky, Principles of Accounting and Financial Reporting for Nonprofit
Organizations (New York: John Wiley & Sons, Inc.), p. 101.

receives its revenues from grants and contracts, contributions and legacies, investment income, and gains on the sales of
investments. The annual drive for contribu-

tions is over, so no additional cash contributions or pledges are expected. All $58,700 of accounts payable and the $4,000 in withholding taxes shown in Table 6.1 are due July 31, 19X0. How can the Johnson Diabetes Research Center pay these bills when they become due?

Johnson's working capital position in terms of restricted and unrestricted funds is presented separately in Table 6.2 to aid in examining their ability to pay their bills. The restricted column in Table 6.2 shows that $12,300 in cash and $153,000 in market

Table 6.2

Working Capital of Johnson Diabetes Research Center December 31, 19X0

	Current assets		
	Unrestricted	Restricted	Total
Cash	$40,800	$12,300	$53,100
Marketable securities	1,494,000	153,000	1,647,000
Contract receivables	4,500	-	4,500
Other receivables	76,400	-	76,400
Inventories of books and supplies	8,500	-	8,500
Total current assets	$1,624,200	$165,300	$1,789,500

	Current liabilities		
	Unrestricted	Restricted	Total
Accounts payable	$58,700	-	$58,700
Witholding taxes	4,000		4,000
Grants paid in advance	25,200		25,200
Total current liabilities	$87,900		$87,900

able securities are earmarked for specific purposes and would not be used for current operations not meeting the specified purpose. In the unrestricted fund, however, the Johnson Diabetes Research Center has $62,700 in bills coming due on July 31, 19X0 and has only $40,800 in unrestricted cash on hand. The difference of $21,900 has to come from the conversion of other current assets in the unrestricted fund into cash.

The $1,536,300 difference between unre-
stricted current assets and current liabilities is available for meeting the cash deficit of $21,900. The most likely source for
meeting this deficit is the $1,494,000 in
unrestricted marketable securities. Marketable securities are readily converted into
cash with little risk of loss of the initial
invested capital. This deficit could also
be covered by conversion of accounts receivable into cash, either by the collection of
pledges or receivables for services rendered. In some instances this deficit could
be made up by converting inventory into
cash. This is highly unlikely, however, for
the research center since their inventory
consists of books and supplies which are not
readily converted to cash, unlike inventories of finished goods.

This example illustrates the role of working
capital in the operation of a not-for-profit
organization. Cash and other assets which
can be transformed into cash are used to pay
employee salaries and to obtain raw materials, supplies, and other factors of production necessary for the provision of
services. The Johnson Diabetes Research
Institute could not supply treatment for
diabetes nor conduct research into the
causes of the disease with fixed assets
alone. With fixed assets alone, the Johnson
Institute would be just a collection of
land, buildings, and equipment. Working
capital allows the organization to become a
productive entity. Cash and assets easily
converted into cash are the conversion me-
dium for all transactions of the organization. Consequently, working capital must be
managed properly for the efficient and effective operation of the not-for-profit
organization.

Figure 6.1 illustrates the cash flow cycle
of the Johnson Diabetes Research Institute.
The level of cash is increased by cash contributions, cash payments for treatment,
grants, cash from the yield on or from the
sale of marketable securities, or by collection of accounts receivable. The cash level

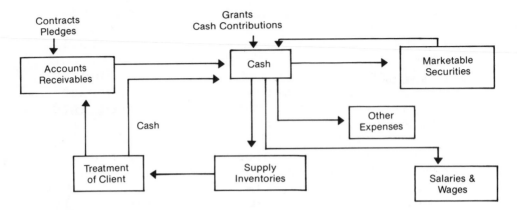

FIGURE 6.1 Cash flow cycle--Johnson Diabetes Research Center.

is reduced by cash outlays for salaries and wages, for other expenses such as telephone and travel expenses, and for supply inventories. The treatment of a client increases either the level of accounts receivable or cash, depending on whether it is a credit or cash transaction, while the collection of a pledge or a receivable for treatment on credit reduces the level of accounts receivable and increases the level of cash.

If the cash flow cycle occurred instantaneously, there would be no need for an investment in working capital. Figure 6.2 pictures the timing of two cash flow streams--a cash inflow stream and a cash outflow steam. The two cash flows are perfectly synchronous in the top panel. A cash inflow of $100 occurs every two weeks coincidentally with a cash outflow of $100. There is no need to maintain a cash balance or to hold current assets which can be quickly converted to cash, since the $100 payment every two weeks can be made from the $100 cash inflow which occurs at the same time. Now examine the bottom panel of Figure 6.2. The cash inflows of $100 occur every two weeks while the cash outflows occur at a rate of $50 every week. In order to pay its bills on time, the organization will have to maintain a level of working capital of $50 either in cash or an asset converted into cash, to make the $50 payment which comes due every odd week. Otherwise, every other payment will be a week late. Delays in cash inflows or unforeseen changes in the magnitude of cash flows will only compound the problem.

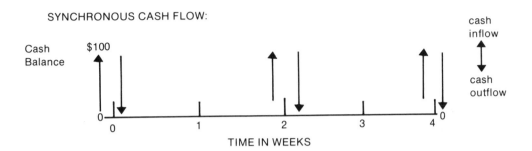

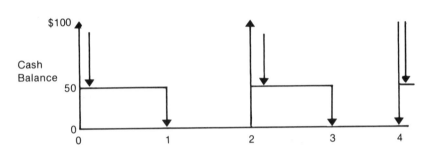

FIGURE 6.2   Timing of cash flows.

Unfortunately, cash inflows do not necessarily match cash outflows. Some level of cash is needed in order to pay bills not perfectly matched with cash inflows. Marketable securities, which are quickly and easily converted into cash, provide funds for emergencies and take up the slack when cash inflows do not coincide with cash outflows. Inventories are necessary for converting fixed assets into products and productive services. Accounts receivables are usually necessary to provide flexibility in the provision of service. An adequate level of investment in current assets contributes toward a smooth, efficient, and uninterrupted operation, thus enhancing the quantity and quality of services provided.

TRADE-OFFS IN DIFFERENT
LEVELS OF WORKING CAPITAL

The nature of the trade-offs involved in different levels of working capital can be envisioned by thinking of working capital as a pool of funds available for making cash outlays. Figure 6.3 shows

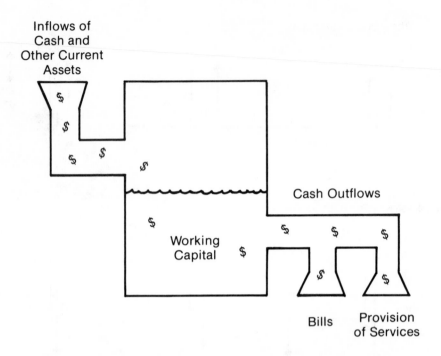

FIGURE 6.3 Adequate working capital pool.

this concept of working capital. When the cash
inflows are combined with a pool of working capital,
the not-for-profit organization is able to pay its
bills on time and to provide a certain level of
services. If cash inflows increase, more cash can
be drawn from the working capital pool without reducing its level, e.g., to increase the level of
services provided. A decrease in cash inflows will
cause a decrease in the level of the working capital
pool available for the payment of bills and for the
provision of services if these payments do not also
decrease. An increase in cash outflows for unexpected bills or services can also be accommodated by
reducing the level of the working capital pool.

A trade-off exists between the not-for-profit
organization's ability to provide services and its
ability to pay its bills on a timely basis. The
not-for-profit organization exists in order to provide service, not to invest in assets which generate
a profit. The level of services can be increased by
reducing the level of investment in working capital.
The ability of the organization to pay its bills on
time, however, is decreased. Since the pool of
funds to provide for unexpected decreases or delays
in cash inflows is smaller, the ability to accommo-
date any increase in cash outflows is reduced. Con-

sequently, the chances of not being able to pay
bills when they become due and of having to reduce
the level of services is increased. The risk exposure of not paying the bills on time can be reduced
by increasing the size of the working capital pool.
This results, however, in a reduction of the ability
to provide services. Therefore, the management of
working capital must consider this trade-off between
services provided and payment of bills.

AN OVERVIEW OF THE FINANCING
OF CURRENT ASSETS

The financial manager of the not-for-profit organization can select either short- or long-term
sources for the financing of current assets. The
major short-term sources of financing are accounts
payable (or trade credit), other liabilities, and
short-term loans. The primary long-term sources of
financing are long-term loans and funds from contributors. The relative composition of the total
financing (right-hand side of balance sheet) of ten
representative not-for-profit organizations from
Table 1.2 is repeated in Table 6.3. Accounts pay-

TABLE 6.3

Relative Composition of Financing of Ten
Representative Not-for-Profit Organizations

Type of organization	Source of financing (%)				
	Accounts payable	Borrowing	Other liabilities	Funds	Total financing
1. Charity	2.1	4.1	4.5	89.4	100.1
2. Hospital	5.3	51.9	13.8	29.1	100.1
3. Voluntary health	2.4	0	37.9	59.7	100.0
4. Museum	1.6	0.6	3.5	94.3	100.0
5. Research	7.4	13.5	26.3	52.8	100.0
6. Municipality	2.1	46.6	7.6	43.7	100.0
7. Conservation	31.9	33.5	23.3	11.3	100.0
8. Symphony	5.7	0	26.4	67.9	100.0
9. Church	0.8	39.9	5.9	53.4	100.0
10. Youth	7.6	6.6	3.6	82.1	99.9

able varies from less than 1 percent of total financing for the church to almost 32 percent for the
conservation organization. Two of the organizations
do not utilize loans, while the hospital receives
over one-half of its funds from loans. Funds, a

source provided by contributors, represents from 11 percent to over 94 percent of total financing.

To enhance its ability to provide service, the not-for-profit organization should attempt to operate at minimum cost. Accounts payable (if cash discounts are not lost) and other liabilities are virtually costless. Generally, the cost of short-term borrowing is less than the cost of long-term borrowing, as evidenced by an examination of the term structure of interest rates.

The term structure of interest rates refers to the relationship between the maturity of debt and its cost. The pattern of interest rates (or yields) as a function of the length of time money will be borrowed (or maturity) is known as the yield curve. The yield curve is typically used to illustrate the term structure of interest rates. Yield curves which indicate higher interest rates the longer the time to maturity are known as upward-sloping yield curves. Conversely, yield curves depicting lower interest rates in the longer term are known as down-sloping yield curves. In practice, the yield curve has taken on many different shapes, but the most common is the upward-sloping yield curve. For example, interest rates (yields) as of April 4, 1978 were considerably higher for long-term U.S. Treasury obligations than for short-term maturities. This relationship is shown in Table 6.4 and is graphed in Figure 6.4 which illustrates that there was a cost differential of borrowing for the U.S. Government between shorter-term and longer-term maturities. This differential was probably greater for not-for-profit organizations since they could not borrow at the same rate as the U.S. Treasury, which issues securities with no risk of default.

Although short-term financing is usually less costly than long-term financing, it involves a greater risk of not being able to pay bills on time. The not-for-profit organization must arrange for new financing as the short-term financing becomes due. With more frequent refinancing, the probability of encountering difficulty in borrowing new money increases. Banks can experience a shortage of loanable funds or the not-for-profit organization may have temporary financial difficulties. Long-term financing involves less periodic financing; consequently, the chances of disruption in service because of not being able to finance current assets is reduced.

As an example of short-term versus long-term financing, consider the following.

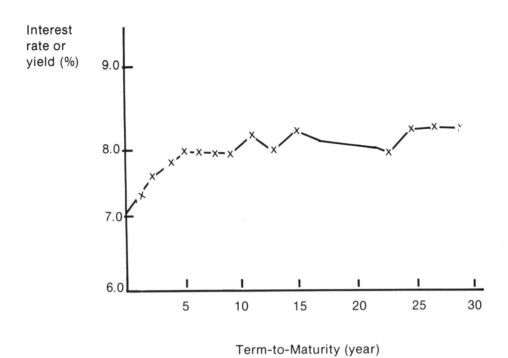

FIGURE 6.4 The yield curve for treasury bonds as of April 4, 1978.

Organization A borrows $10,000 for one year at a 10 percent interest rate to finance its current assets. Organization B uses a five-year note, payable in equal annual installments at a 10 percent interest rate to finance its current assets.

At the end of year one, Organization A must pay $1,000 in interest and refinance the $10,000. If short-term rates have increased to 12 percent, the organization has to pay $1,200 in interest during year two. Even worse, Organization A may not be able to refinance the loan due to a shortage of loanable funds or some other unforeseen event; as a result it would be unable to pay its bills when they become due. On the other hand, Organization B, with its longer-term loan, would pay $2,637.97 in principal and interest at the end of years one through five.[3] The 10 percent interest rate would be locked in for each of the five years. More importantly, Organization B would not have to worry about refinancing the $10,000

TABLE 6.4

The Term Structure of Treasury Obligations
(as of April 4, 1978)

Coupon rate	Maturity date	Bid price	Ask price	Yield
6 1/2s	1978 April	99.29	99.31	6.78
5 7/8s	1979 April	98.14	98.18	7.30
6 7/8s	1980 May	98.15	98.19	7.61
7 3/8s	1981 May	98.28	99	7.75
7s	1982 May	100.14	100.22	7.80
7 7/8s	1982 May	99.21	99.23	7.94
7 1/4s	1984 Feb	96.18	96.22	7.97
7 7/8s	1986 May	98.27	99.30	8.02
7 5/8s	1987 Nov	96.27	93.31	8.09
8 1/4s	1990 May	100.22	101.60	8.00
7 1/4s	1992 Aug	92.20	92.10	8.17
7 1/2s	1988–93 Aug	94.40	95.40	8.06
7s	1993–98 May	89.14	90.14	7.96
8 1/2s	1994–99 May	101.18	102.20	8.27
7 7/8s	1995–00 Feb	95.20	95.28	8.28
8s	1996–01 Aug	96.22	96.30	8.30
8 1/4s	2000–05 May	99.40	99.12	8.31
7 5/8s	2002–07 Feb	92.20	92.28	8.27

NOTE: Bid and ask prices are quoted in 32nds. For example, 99.29 means 99 29/32.

Source: Wall Street Journal, April 5, 1978, p.38.

for five years and would not be affected by a shortage of loanable funds.

One way of minimizing the risk of being unable to pay off maturing obligations is to match asset and liability maturities. For example, accounts receivable would be financed with a loan with a maturity equal to the average time it takes to convert accounts receivable into cash. By using this strategy the asset is converted into cash at the exact time it is needed to meet a maturing obligation. This type of strategy is shown in Figure 6.5 where the organization's asset base is increasing over time. The fixed assets are financed with long-term funds; that is, with long-term loans, or funds from contributors. A portion of current assets, the minimum

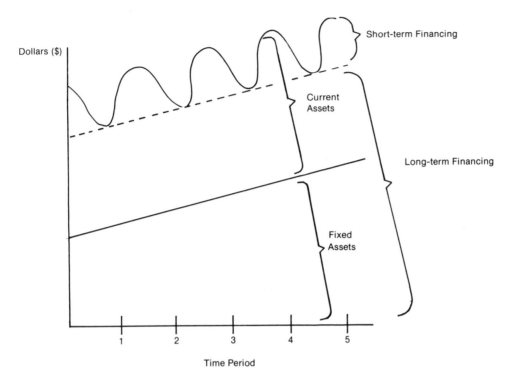

FIGURE 6.5   Matching asset and liability maturities.

level needed for effective operations, is also financed with long-term funds. A portion of current
assets will vary with the operating cycle of the
organization. A municipality's level of cash, for
example, will be highest at the time ad valorem
taxes are collected. This level will decrease during the year as the city provides services. This
temporary investment in current assets will be liquidated and not replaced within the current year.
The temporary investment in current assets is financed with short-term funds.

   This strategy of matching asset and liability
maturities is known as the hedging principle. The
hedging principle can be stated very simply: Permanent investments in assets should be financed with
long-term sources of financing and temporary investments should be financed with short-term sources of
financing.[4] The rationale underlying the hedging
principle is straightforward. For example, a university experiencing a seasonal expansion in accounts receivable at registration should finance the
increase with current liabilities since financing is
needed for a limited period of time. The current
liabilities will be paid from the cash generated by

collection of tuition payments. Financing with a
long-term source would mean the university would
still have the funds from the long-term source after
the accounts receivable have been collected. This
would result in "excess" liquidity which could be
used to provide additional service. Also, the university may be paying interest charges on funds no
longer needed for operations.

Other maturity-matching strategies are possible.
A more conservative approach is shown in Figure 6.6.

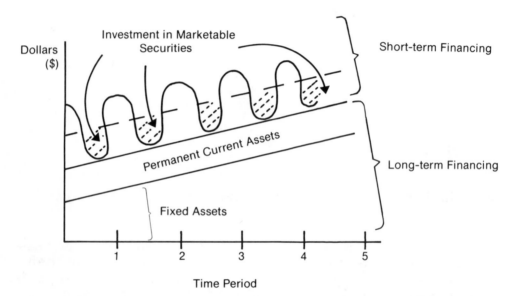

FIGURE 6.6 Conservative strategy.

Long-term financing exceeds the level of fixed assets and permanent current assets. Short-term financing is used to meet peak seasonal demands for
funds, while the remainder of seasonal needs are met
by storing up liquidity. This is accomplished by
investing long-term funds not needed for seasonal
needs in marketable securities. The risk of not
being able to pay bills on time is reduced by this
strategy. The not-for-profit organization, however,
has to pay interest on the long-term funds during
the entire period so this strategy is more costly
than the matching strategy.

A third strategy is shown in Figure 6.7. In this
case, the organization finances part or all of its
permanent current assets with short-term funds.
Failure to renew the short-term commitment is most
serious since the organization is faced with loss of

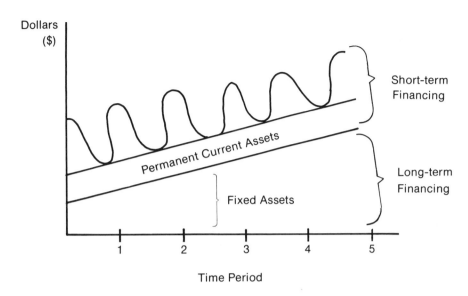

FIGURE 6.7 Aggressive strategy.

use of part of its minimum level of current assets.
The interest cost of this strategy should be less
than the previous two strategies discussed since a
higher proportion of cheaper short-term debt is
used.

SUMMARY

Working capital management refers to the management of current assets and current liabilities.
Current assets consist of cash and assets which will
be converted into cash in a year's time. Current
liabilities are obligations which have to be discharged within a year. The not-for-profit organization must invest in current assets because cash
inflows and cash outflows are not synchronous and
instantaneous. Current assets are required in order
to convert fixed assets into units of service. The
need for current assets is a function of the cash
cycle. The cash cycle refers to the activities of
converting cash into productive services.
The determination of the proper aggregate level
of current assets involves a trade-off between the
ability to provide service and the ability to pay
bills on time. The higher the level of current
assets, the greater the chances of paying bills on
time. A higher investment in current assets, however, reduces the organization's ability to provide

services since more funds are tied up in idle assets.

The current assets financing decision involves a trade-off between the cost of financing and the risk of not being able to pay bills on time. Three different strategies for determining the mix between short- and long-term financing were presented. A hedging strategy of matching asset and liability lives reduces the risk of not being able to pay bills on time. A more conservative strategy of financing part of current assets with long-term funds reduces the risk of not being able to pay bills on time but increases cost. The most aggressive strategy is to finance part of the fixed assets with short-term financing.

The management of working capital is covered in more detail in the next three chapters. The management of cash and short-term securities is covered in Chapter 7, while accounts receivable and inventory management are discussed in Chapter 8. The financing of current assets is covered in additional detail in Chapter 9.

QUESTIONS

1. Define working capital. Give several examples of accounts which are included in working capital.

2. What is the primary purpose for working capital within the not-for-profit organization?

3. Develop a probable cash flow cycle, similar to Figure 6.1, for a community hospital.

4. Why does a firm need to maintain a positive balance in working capital?

5. What trade-offs exist with various levels of working capital?

6. Why should any effort be expended in managing the working capital of a not-for-profit organization, when it is not interested in "making a profit"?

7. What trade-offs exist in the determination of the maturity of the source used to finance the acquisition of a current asset?

ENDNOTES

1. O. Maurice Joy, Introduction to Financial Management (Homewood, Ill.: Richard D. Irwin, Inc., 1977), p. 405.
2. Howard J. Berman and Lewis E. Weeks, The Financial Management of Hospitals, 2d ed. (Ann Arbor, Mich: Health Administration Press, 1974), p. 212.
3. See Chapter 10 for a discussion of how to calculate the size of the principal and interest payments.
4. John D. Martin, J. William Petty, Arthur J. Keown, and David E. Scott, Jr., Basic Financial Management (Englewood Cliffs, New Jersey: Prentice-Hall, Inc., 1979), p. 155.

7

CASH MANAGEMENT AND SHORT-TERM INVESTMENTS

In recent years, not-for-profit organizations have faced the twin onslaught of inflation and recession. Expenditures have increased as a result of the increased demand for services and of inflationary increases. At the same time, it has been difficult to increase revenues because of the heavy burden placed on donors and taxpayers from increases in the cost of living. The squeeze between increasing expenditures and inadequate revenues has emphasized the need for not-for-profit organizations to optimize their use of available resources. It is imperative that not-for-profit organizations manage their cash balances and cash flows in an effective and efficient manner to meet the challenge of these external pressures.

Cash management, an important component of financial management, is a complex activity involving a large number of variables, constraints, and alternatives which have to be considered. This chapter presents a broad, comprehensive approach to cash management which provides practical guidelines for the administration of cash balances and cash flows. There are four major parts to the chapter. The first part presents the cash management system, the motives for holding cash and short-term securities, along with the objectives and nature of cash manage-

ment.   Methods of speeding up cash collections,
basic elements of cash control, and the slowing down
of cash disbursements are discussed in the second
part.   Strategies and techniques for determining the
appropriate level of cash balances are introduced
briefly in the third part, while the management of
short-term investments is presented in part four.
This chapter also contains two appendices: Appendix
A which presents in more detail a cash control
system and Appendix B, which includes mathematical
models for determination of adequate cash balances.

THE CASH MANAGEMENT SYSTEM

Before discussing the cash management decision,
we need to define what is meant by the terms "cash"
and "short-term" investments. Cash is currency on
hand or in checking accounts with banks.[1] Cash is
the most liquid of assets because of its immediate
availability for use in the payment of bills. Cash
is characterized by a lack of earning power since
interest is not always paid on checking accounts.[2]
Short-term investments, also known as marketable
securities, are assets which can readily be converted into cash with little or no loss of capital.
Short-term investments provide a return and, at the
same time, provide a cushion or buffer for unantici-
pated cash needs. Common types of short-term investments are certificates of deposit, U. S. Treasury bills, repurchase agreements, commercial paper,
and money market funds.
A potential source of additional revenue exists
for not-for-profit organizations. This source is
the interest which can be earned on the investment
of operating funds that would otherwise remain temporarily idle. Cash balances are generated because
cash receipts do not necessarily occur simultaneously with the needs of an organization to meet its
cash commitments or disbursements. The management
of cash balances presents a dilemma. If cash is
held in excess of that required to bridge the gap
between cash receipts and cash disbursements, then
returns from suitable alternative uses are foregone.
On the other hand, if inadequate cash is held, the
organization may not be able to pay its bills when
they become due.
Organizations may choose to treat the management
of cash balances as a residual decision with their
level increasing or decreasing with increases or

decreases in the gap between cash receipts and cash disbursements. Or, preferably, organizations may attempt to manage the level of cash balances in an optimum manner, so that maximum returns are received from the investment of funds that would otherwise remain temporarily idle. Improved cash management can result in additional revenue for the not-for-profit organization with little or no increase in risk or expense. Consequently, the financial goals of cash management for a not-for-profit organization should be:

Availability--to optimize the amount of cash available, both to meet daily cash needs and to increase the funds available for investment.

Yield--to earn the maximum return on the temporarily idle funds available for investment.

The achievement of the goals of cash management requires a consideration of several related elements. The elements of cash management which should be considered by the financial manager are shown schematically in Figure 7.1. Each of the elements, which are discussed below, have to mesh together and relate to the two-fold goals of cash management.

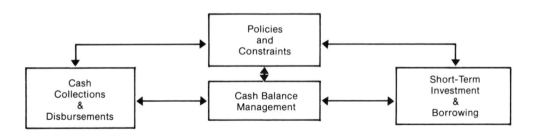

FIGURE 7.1 Elements of a cash management system.

A number of policies and constraints limit the ability of a not-for-profit organization to achieve optimum cash management. For example, various state, local, and federal laws restrict the cash management practices of local governments by "determining when monies can be collected, when obligations must be paid, where deposits can be placed and what securities can and cannot be purchased."[3] Charities may be limited in their cash collection practices by restrictions placed on them by fund-raising organizations. A professional organization may have a policy that all accounts payable have to be paid by the due date.

Risk is a constraint that has to be considered in achieving cash management goals. In this case, risk is the possibility of losing a portion of the investment. A higher yield on investments can usually be earned by assuming a higher level of risk. Risk has to be limited, however, since loss of principal will diminish the organization's ability to pay its bills. The financial manager must consider both the various policies and constraints in carrying out a cash management program.

Effective cash collection and disbursement procedures are an important part of a cash management program. The speed and timing of cash collections and disbursements affect the size of the cash balance. If cash cn be collected as fast as possible and kept as long as possible then cash availability is maximized.

The financial manager has to develop appropriate policies and procedures to effectively manage cash balances. The financial manager needs to minimize cash balances if yield is to be maximized since cash is a nonincome-producing asset. On the other hand, a large cash balance enhances the organization's ability to pay its bills on time. One of the financial manager's major decisions then is to decide on the level of cash balances considering this trade-off. A critical minimum balance has to be maintained in order to pay bills promptly and to provide a buffer against unforeseen events. Any balance held above the critical minimum cash balance, however, involves an opportunity cost since the cash could earn a return if invested.

Short-term investments represent a vehicle for earning a return on idle cash, for financing cash requirements at short notice, and for investing excess cash for short periods of time. There are numerous alternatives for short-term investments; consequently, there are numerous alternatives of yields, risk, maturities, and transaction costs to be considered in meeting the particular needs of an organization. The financial manager needs to employ appropriate decision rules to help determine which securities to purchase, when to purchase them, the amounts to be purchased, and their respective maturities. In some instances, the liquidation of short-term investments will not provide enough cash to meet required cash outlays. Short-term borrowing may represent a means of meeting interim cash requirements prior to the receipt of revenues from donations, sales, or the collection of taxes.

CASH COLLECTIONS AND DISBURSEMENTS

The relationship between cash collections, cash disbursements, and the cash balance is shown in Figure 7.2. The figure is helpful in illustrating that the level of the cash balance is influenced by both the speed and the timing of the cash collections and disbursements.

Cash Collections

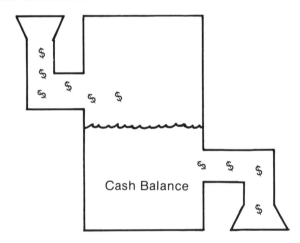

Cash Balance

Cash Disbursements

FIGURE 7.2   Relationship between cash collections, disbursements, and cash balance.

If $500 in cash is received and deposited every day and a $500 check is drawn daily, then, theoretically, the average balance would be zero. Usually, cash inflows and cash outflows are not perfectly synchronized, so a cash balance is required. For example, if on a particular day cash inflows are only $300 but cash outflows are $500 then the organization would need a $200 cash balance to pay its bills when due. The faster cash is collected, the smaller the cash balance required. Accelerated cash inflows increase the probability of being able to synchronize cash inflows and cash outflows, allowing cash to be invested for a longer time. As a result, the opportunity cost of holding idle cash is reduced. Slowing cash outflows also has the same effect as speeding up cash inflows. An appropriate strategy for the financial manager of a not-for-

profit organization would be speed-up cash collections and slow-down cash disbursements as much as
possible within the limits of the organization's
policies and constraints. Either strategy, accelerating cash inflows or slowing cash outflows, will
reduce the size of the required cash balance,
freeing additional funds for investment and providing an increased return.

Speeding-Up Cash Collections

The control that a not-for-profit corporation has
over its cash collections is often subject to many
restrictions. Property tax bills for a local government may not be mailed out before a certain date.
Hospitals cannot usually bring enough pressure to
bear on third-party payers to force them to speed up[4]
or change the timing of their payment schedule.
University cash flows are closely tied to registration dates. Although restricted, the not-for-profit
organization can still have substantial impact on
the timing of cash inflows. For example, a not-for-
profit foundation may elect to have six fund drives
during the year, geared toward different potential
donors rather than two. There are several methods
available for speeding-up cash inflows by reducing
the time between payment of a check by a customer or
donor and the time the organization has use of the
funds. In addition, the section on managing accounts receivable in Chapter 8 discusses methods of
accelerating the conversion of accounts receivable
into cash.
A not-for-profit organization does not have immediate use of a customer's or donor's money. There
is a waiting period from the time the check is
mailed until the funds are credited to the not-for-
profit organization's checking account. This period
results in what is known as deposit float--mail
time, internal recording and processing time, and
check-clearing time. The longer the delays the
greater the magnitude of the deposit float. As
shown in the bottom panel of Figure 7.3, delay
caused by deposit float can be significant. If, on
the average, it takes two days mail time, three days

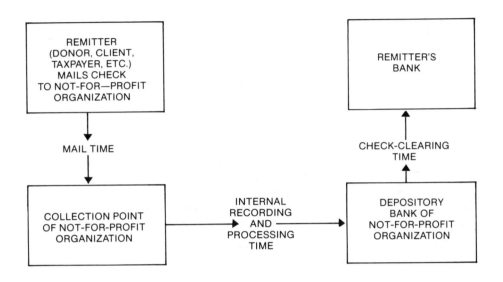

COMPONENTS OF DEPOSIT FLOAT

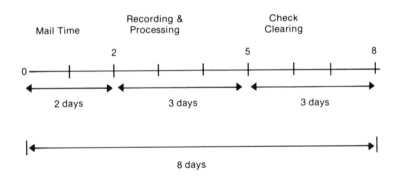

TIME DIAGRAM OF DEPOSIT FLOAT

FIGURE 7.3 Deposit float.

for internal processing, and three days for a check
to clear the banking system, the organization must
wait eight days before it has use of the funds.
There are, however, several methods available for
reducing this deposit float.

One method of reducing the interval between the mailing of a check and the time the not-for-profit organization has use of the funds is by use of a lock-box system. Under a lock-box system, customers and/or donors in an area with many customers and/or donors are directed to mail their checks to a post office box. A representative of the bank then picks up the checks daily and deposits them in the organization's account in the bank. The organization is notified of the aggregate amounts collected daily and the paper work is forwarded for processing. The lock-box system removes one step in the deposit process and makes funds available more quickly. As a result, a lock-box system can reduce transit and processing time by two or three days.

Lock-box systems can also be employed by large governmental units or charitable organizations to speed-up their cash inflows. Local governments can make arrangements for one or several banks to receive tax and utility payments directly using preaddressed return receipt envelopes. The banks would then deposit all receipts on a daily basis and inform the municipal financial manager of the aggregate amounts.

Before adopting a lock-box system, it is generally necessary to make a cost/benefit analysis.[5] The benefits of the lock-box system are the return on the added funds from speeding-up the cash inflows and/or a reduction in internal processing costs. The cost of the system is the fixed monthly fee usually charged by the bank plus a per-item processing charge.

The increase in usable balances (BAL) generated by implementation of a lock-box system is calculated by multiplying the number of checks processed per day (NUM) times the average value per check (AVG) times the number of days of reduced transit time (TIM), or:

$$BAL = (NUM) \times (AVG) \times (TIM) \qquad \text{(Equation 7-1)}$$

The annual dollar returns on the added funds (ADR) from a lock-box system depend on the increase in usable balances (BAL) and the annual interest rate (INT) earned by investing the increase in usable balances, or:

$$ADR = (BAL) \times (INT) \qquad \text{(Equation 7-2)}$$

The total annual cost (ATC) of operating the lock-box system is based on the processing cost per check charged by the bank (UC) times the number of checks processed per year (ANU), resulting in:

$$\underline{ATC} = \underline{UC} \times \underline{ANU} \qquad \text{(Equation 7-3)}$$

The breakeven point occurs where benefits of the system equal the cost of the system, or:

$$\underline{ADR} = \underline{ATC} \qquad \text{(Equation 7-4)}$$

The lock-box system should be implemented if the benefits are greater than the costs; i.e., $\underline{ADR} >$ $\underline{ATC}$. Otherwise, the lock-box system should be rejected. The following example illustrates the trade-offs involved in the lock-box system decision.

> The city of Alexander is considering implementation of a lock-box system for the commercial customers of its electrical utility system. It is estimated that implementation of the lock-box system will reduce mail time and internal processing time by three days. The 5,000 commercial customers have an average $300 monthly electrical bill. The city of Alexander presently earns 9 percent on its short-term investments. If the bank charges $0.25 to process each check, should the lock-box system be implemented?
>
> First, the number of checks processed per day (NUM) is determined assuming 21 working days in a month and that checks are received at a constant daily rate:
>
> $$\underline{NUM} = \frac{5,000}{21} = 238.1 \text{ checks per day}$$
>
> The increase in usable balances is calculated by using Equation 7-1:
>
> $$\underline{BAL} = (\underline{NUM}) \times (\underline{AVG}) \times (\underline{TIM})$$
>
> $$= 238.1 \times \$300 \times 3$$
>
> $$= \$214,290$$
>
> Implementation of the system will free an additional $214,290 for investment. Note that Equation 7-1 was solved on a daily

basis; it could have been solved on a monthly, or some other basis, as well. The
$214,290 can be invested for the entire year
at 9 percent so the annual dollar return
(ADR) is equal to:

$$ADR = (BAL) \times (INT) \qquad \text{(Equation 7-2)}$$

$$= (\$214,290) \times 0.09$$

$$= \$19,286.$$

Consequently, implementation of the system
will result in an annual benefit of $19,286.

The annual checks processed per year (ANU)
is equal to:

$$ANU = 5,000 \times 12 = 60,000$$

since each of the 5,000 customers is billed
on a monthly basis, or twelve times a year.
The total cost of implementing the lock-box
system is calculated by Equation 7-3:

$$ATC = (UC) \times (ANU)$$

$$= \$0.25 \times 60,000$$

$$= \$15,000$$

In this case, ADR ($19,286) is greater than
ATC ($15,000). Since the benefits are
greater than the cost, the lock-box system
should be implemented. Implementation of
the system results in an annual incremental
earnings of $19,286 minus 15,000 or $4,286.

Wire transfers and branch deposits may also be
used to speed up cash collections. A wire transfer
involves the use of the Federal Reserve wire system
to electronically move balances from one bank to
another. It is a method of minimizing transit time
in check collection. The cost of a wire transfer
ranges between $1 and $5, so it is economical only
for larger transfers, such as the transfer of bond
proceeds. In states which allow branch banking, use
of branch deposits can also speed up cash collections. Arrangements can be made to accept deposits
in outlying branches and have them immediately cred-

ited to a central account at the main bank.

Cash Collection Procedures

Probably the easiest and simplest method to speed up cash inflows is to establish procedures for depositing currency and checks into bank accounts as quickly as possible. For a small organization with only one cash collection point and one bank account this can be accomplished with a minimum amount of effort. A large not-for-profit organization with several collection points and several different bank accounts may require considerably more effort. To improve internal processing of cash collections each department that receives cash payments should have:

1. Revenue collection policies and procedures for each major source of revenue.
2. Special deposit procedures to handle major revenue processing problems. Examples of special revenue problems would be the quarterly collection of registration fees by universities or the annual collection of property taxes by local governments.
3. Established deposit procedures for each type of revenue and collection location.[6]

A checklist of detailed procedures for collecting every revenue source should be prepared. An example for a municipality is presented in Table 7.1. Such detailed processing procedures reduce the probability of loss or theft of cash along with facilitating the efficient use of the organization's cash balance. Basic differences between profit-oriented and not-for-profit organizations[7] often lead to wide variations in management practices, accounting, and operational procedures. One primary area where these variations occur is in control procedures for the collection of contributions--a problem seldom faced by profit-oriented firms. Voluntary health and welfare organizations, which derive their revenues primarily from voluntary contributions, serve as a useful model to describe some basic guidelines to ensure adequate internal control and accurate accounting.

The voluntary nature of the revenue received by health and welfare organizations, such as United Way, causes internal accounting procedures to take on added significance. In profit-oriented organiza-

TABLE 7.1

Checklist of Detailed Procedures in Collection of Revenue Sources for a Municipality

---

Licenses and permits
* Deposit all monies intact.
* Maintain a list of all delinquent licenses or permits and strictly enforce collection of delinquencies uniformly.
* Require all licensees or permit holders to display their licenses and/or permits. Instruct government offices to look for such licenses and/or permits and notify the collection agency when violators are suspected.
* If fees are based on gross receipts, utilize reports submitted to other government agencies, such as taxes paid the state treasury, to verify such gross receipts.

Parking lots, golf courses, swimming pools
* Indicate in plain sight at all locations, a schedule showing the full range of fees.
* If tickets are used, design a standard format for use at all locations.
* Check all cash register receipts to ensure that cash and ticket counts reflect recorded frequency and monetary totals.
* Rotate attendants through different facilities and work schedules at frequent intervals.
* Practice close supervision and surveillance.
* Have all keys to lock boxes, cash registers, etc., under control of authorized supervision and not available to attendants.
* Schedule frequent unannounced visits by internal auditors who will review inventory of tickets, count cash, require authorization for all exemptions, etc.

Parking meter collections
* Establish, number, and describe meter routes.
* Select coin collection equipment that will be secure against theft.
* Consider maintaining weight records by route.
* Rotate the schedule of route collection periodically.
* Collect coins at hours which coincide with heavy traffic.
* Safeguard keys to coin meter receptacles; issue daily to coin collectors.
* Mutilate and destroy worn keys.
* Order new keys only on authorization of responsible persons.
* Require meter collectors to wear distinctive uniforms.
* Supervise the coin counting process.
* Ensure the security of the coin counting area.
* Have meter collectors report the location of all broken,

TABLE 7.1 Cont.

stuck, or pilfered meters as they are discovered.
* Maintain dollar and/or weight records to provide for periodic comparisons of collections for each weight.
* Issue receipts daily to collectors.
* Establish procedures to make reconciliations of cash deposits. If coin counting machines which register total values are used, such values can be reconciled to deposits.
* Schedule periodic unannounced reviews of all phases of operation. Spot-check collection and counting procedures, personnel rotation, revenue comparisons, etc.

Property taxes, parking and vehicle code fines, sales taxes, gasoline taxes, cigarette taxes, liquor license fees, and motor vehicle fees
* Establish written contracts with other agencies as provided by law.
* Periodically test receipts to treasury record to verify that all receipts are properly and timely deposited.
* Request confirmation from agencies doing the collecting and distributing, and compare information received from them with the municipal records.

Federal and state grants
* Prepare status reports for each grant. These reports show such data as:
  * grant description;
  * granting agency;
  * total amount of grant;
  * terms and restrictions concerning the use of the grant; and,
  * anticipated payment terms of the grant.
* Bill granting agency as soon as permitted by grant guidelines.

Source: Phillip Rosenberg, C. Wayne Stalling, and Charles K. Coe, A Treasury Management Handbook for Small Cities and Other Governmental Units (Chicago: Municipal Finance Officers Association, 1978), pp. 53-54.

tions, sales and gross profit figures provide useful check points which are not present in a not-for-profit enterprise. In a business organization, cash or checks received through the mail are usually in payment of some account or accompany an order for goods. Consequently, the initial record is usually subject to subsequent verification through statements mailed to customers or merchandise shipped. A system which requires mailing of receipts for all voluntary contributions, however, is expensive and usually does not provide full control.

Since voluntary health and welfare organizations do not ordinarily exchange assets for contributions received, most revenue must be controlled by internal means. The voluntary nature of donations and the use of volunteer personnel in the fund-raising efforts often inhibit the development of good control procedures.

Adequate control over the collection of donations requires that the system design assure:

1. An official record is made of all donations received.
2. Control of the official record and physical control over the donations are immediately separated.
3. The record is subsequently checked against bank deposits.[8]

More specific guidelines for the control of donations to voluntary health and welfare organizations are outlined in Appendix A of this chapter. These procedures are, of course, applicable to other types of not-for-profit organizations, such as churches and scholarship funds which are dependent on donations as a major source of revenue.

Slowing-Down Cash Disbursements

To maximize cash availability, the not-for-profit organization needs to delay cash disbursements to the last possible moment. This practice, however, has to be tempered by the fact that consistently late payments may result in increased prices, unhappy vendors, and poor community relations. Obviously, the not-for-profit organization does not want to delay cash disbursements to its clients, since this will reduce services and possibly place undue hardships on them.

The not-for-profit organization has a critical need for a system to manage cash disbursements. Invoices should be analyzed as they are received to determine payment dates. The invoices can then be filed and disbursements made on the payment dates. The following factors need to be considered in the determination of payment dates: "...the discounts available, the standard policies for handling different types of invoices, the past history of the

vendor for requiring rapid payment, and the method
by which the payment will be made (e.g., mail or
pick-up)."[9]   The use of discounts can result in very
significant savings.   The cost of foregoing the
discount on accounts receivable is discussed in
Chapter 8.

Consolidation of Accounts

The use of fund accounting by most not-for-profit
organizations may lead to ineffective cash management.   With fund accounting, funds restricted for
specific purposes are segregated and their receipt
and disposition are reported separately.   Often,
not-for-profit organizations will have separate bank
accounts for each of the funds and sometimes separate accounts are maintained for the different functions within each major fund.   While separate bank
accounts may be helpful for control of the various
funds, effective cash management is impeded by the
proliferation of bank accounts which have their own
separate cash flow patterns and their own balances.
Numerous bank accounts lead to higher clerical
and administrative costs as well as higher banking
costs.   It is also more difficult to obtain timely
and accurate information regarding the overall cash
position of the organization.   Investable funds are
fragmented into several small investments.   Consolidation of the various bank accounts may reduce costs
and provide a larger pool of cash available for
investment.
Several methods are available for achieving the
advantages of a large pool of cash without sacrific-
ing the control afforded by separate bank accounts.
One technique, advocated for municipalities, is
based on using a single concentration account for
all cash receipts along with separate zero-balance
accounts for all cash disbursements.[10]   This technique for the consolidation of accounts is outlined
in Figure 7-4.   Using this method, all cash receipts
are placed in a concentration account, usually a
demand deposit.   Separate checking accounts are used
for all disbursements, except that they are maintained at a zero balance.   Funds are transferred
automatically from the concentration account to the
various disbursement accounts to cover overdrafts
created as a result of the checks drawn on the zero-
balance accounts.   Excess cash in the concentration
account is invested in short-term securities.

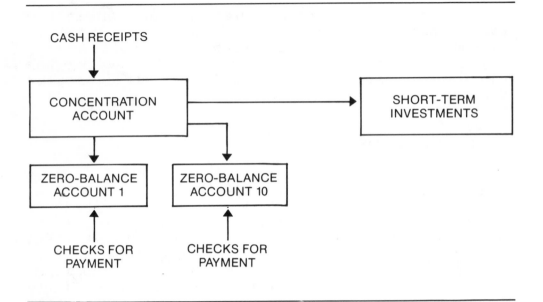

FIGURE 7.4 Technique for the consolidation of accounts.

This consolidation technique has three principal advantages. The zero-balance accounts eliminate the cash balances which would remain in separate accounts. Disbursement float time, the time from when the check is written to the time it is charged against the bank account, becomes irrelevant and the pooling of funds increases the cash available for investment purposes.

DETERMINIZATION OF THE MINIMUM CASH BALANCE

If a not-for-profit organization is collecting, processing, and disbursing cash as efficiently as possible, its next problem is to determine the minimum cash balance to be kept in its checking account. This is a complex problem due to the uncertainty associated with the cash flows and the difficulty of accurately measuring the costs of having too much or too little cash. There may also be numerous other factors which impinge upon this problem; nevertheless, it is a problem that has to be addressed if the not-for-profit organization is to effectively and efficiently manage its cash.

Internally or externally imposed constraints may dictate the size of the minimum cash balance for the not-for-profit organization. The use of bank credit as a source of financing may be tied to a compensating balance requirement. That is, the bank may require maintenance of a certain minimum cash balance as a condition for various services and for commitments to lend. On the other hand, the not-for-profit organization may decide to hold a cash balance in a bank in order to establish a relationship for future borrowing. If this imposed cash balance is greater than the minimum balance required by operating conditions, then the imposed balance becomes the minimum checking account balance. In other cases, however, the minimum cash balance needs to be determined by carefully considering the trade-off between the opportunity cost of holding too much cash and the cost of being short of cash. Several mathematical models have been proposed which provide insights into the cash balance decision. These models aid in making the trade-offs explicit and in identifying important factors in the decision process. Appendix B discuss two such mathematical models for determining minimum cash balances, depending on the nature of the cash flows.

MANAGEMENT OF SHORT-TERM INVESTMENTS

If cash receipts and disbursements could be forecasted with certainty, the organization would maintain a cash balance sufficient to meet disbursements, and no more. This is not a world of certainty, however, so short-term securities are held as a buffer for uncertainty and as a means of earning a return on temporarily idle cash. The types of securities and the strategies appropriate for short-term investments need to be examined.

Types of Securities[11]

The types of securities appropriate for the investment of temporarily idle cash balances are known as marketable securities. Marketable securities are highly liquid, interest-earning, relatively risk-free paper assets. Common stock, preferred stock, and corporate bonds provide earnings in the form of dividends or interest but they are not highly liquid without risk of significant price changes. Market-

able securities are money or short-term market instruments that are highly salable and are relatively
risk-free of default on principal and interest payments and on major changes in their value. Included
in this definition of marketable securities are
several instruments.

Treasury Bills

Treasury bills and Treasury certificates are
short-term debt instruments of the U. S. Government.
T-bills, as Treasury bills are often called, are
initially offered in $10,000 denominations with 91-
and 182-day maturities and, infrequently, certificates are issued with 9- and 12-month maturities.
T-bills are noninterest-bearing notes; however, they
are sold at a discount, i.e., at a price less than
their face value of $10,000. Their yield or inter-
est return is computed on the difference between the
purchasing and selling (or maturity) price.
The "yield rate" or annual rate of return on this
type of investment can be calculated using the following formula:

$$\underline{Y} = \frac{SP - PP}{PP} \times \frac{360}{H} \qquad \text{(Equation 7-5)}$$

$\underline{Y}$ is the annualized holding-period yield, $\underline{SP}$ the
selling price, $\underline{PP}$ the purchase price, and $\underline{H}$ the
number of days in the holding period. For example,
consider a 91-day T-bill purchased for $9,800. Ap-
plication of Equation 7-5 yields the following results:

$$\underline{Y} = \frac{(\$10,000 - 9,800)}{\$9,800} \times \frac{360}{91}$$

$$\underline{Y} = (0.0204) \times (3.9560) = 0.0807$$

$$\underline{Y} = 8.07\%$$

Consequently, this T-bill earns 8.07 percent on an
annualized basis.
A very large secondary market exists for Treasury
securities, allowing buying and selling to take
place any time between issuance and maturity dates.
Since this makes the Treasury bill highly liquid and
the government cannot default on principal repayment, they are a very attractive investment for idle

cash. These factors, however, also result in the yield on these securities being, in general, the lowest of all money market instruments.

Government Agency Securities

Several agencies of the U. S. Government, e.g., the Federal Intermediate Credit Banks, Banks for Cooperatives, Federal Land Banks, Federal Home Loan Banks, and the Federal National Mortgage Association, offer instruments with normally higher yields than Treasury bills. The secondary market for these securities is large but their liquidity is not quite as good as that of Treasury bills, which accounts for the yield spread between T-bills and these securities.

Certificates of Deposit

Certificates of deposit (CDs) are time deposits of commercial banks. The largest commercial banks provide the most liquid CDs, which are actively traded on the secondary market. The bulk of the transactions in the secondary market are in round lots of $1 million or multiples thereof; odd lots are transactions in multiples of $100,000 and $250,000. Again, the secondary market for CDs is not as large as that for Treasury bills but it is sufficient in size to make CDs bear an interest rate just slightly higher than the yield on Treasury bills.

Commercial Paper

Commercial paper is perhaps the oldest of all money market instruments. Commercial paper is a negotiable, short-term promissory note issued by well-known corporations in such fields as manufacturing, retailing, finance, transportation, and mining, usually for a period of 270 days or less. These notes are available in face amounts of $100,000, $250,000, $500,000 and $1,000,000 and in combinations of these amounts. The National Credit Office (a subsidiary of Dun and Bradstreet) rates commercial paper as prime, desirable, and satisfactory. Most commercial paper is rated as prime. The secondary market is not as large as the market for

T-bills, CDs, and government securities but it is
adequate for providing a fair amount of liquidity.
Yields are generally higher than the interest rate
on T-bills and are comparable with other money market instruments.

Repurchase Agreement

A repurchase agreement is not a specific security; rather, it is a contract whereby a bank or
government security dealer sells a marketable security, such as a T-bill, to the organization and
agrees to repurchase the security at a specified
higher price at a specified point in time. This
type of arrangement offers a tailor-made maturity
date, guaranteeing the organization a certain level
of cash at a specific date. The investment is safe
since the security serves as collateral for the
transaction.

Money Market Funds

A money market fund is a mutual fund which invests in marketable securities. The money market
fund pools cash from many investors and purchases
commercial paper, CDs, and Treasury securities. In
return, the investor receives a pro rata share of
the income of the fund. A sales commission is not
usually charged, but there is usually a small management fee (on the order of 0.75 percent). The
amount of cash invested in money market funds has
grown rapidly--from $16 billion in the Spring of
1979 to $117 billion in April, 1981. At that time,
the funds were yielding an annual return of more
than 14 percent compared to the 5.5 percent available on passbook savings accounts.

Money market funds offer several benefits to the
not-for-profit organization, especially smaller
ones. The investment portfolio is managed by the
fund so the not-for-profit organization does not
have to develop expertise, nor expend effort in that
area. The yields can be much higher than those
available on savings accounts, with only a minimal
increase in risk of loss of principal. Most savings
accounts are insured up to a maximum of $100,000 by
the federal government. The money market funds
invest in Treasury securities, which have no risk of
default of principal, and other instruments such as

CDs and commercial paper which have only a small risk of default. These funds usually compound interest daily and there is no minimum holding period required. Most funds allow investors to write checks against their accounts, in minimum amounts of $250 or $500, so the shares can be converted into cash very quickly.

Objectives of Short-Term Investment

Maximization of interest income from investments in marketable securities should not be the primary consideration of the financial manager of a not-for-profit organization. Recall from the discussion of the cash management system that the objective should first be to have sufficient cash on hand to pay bills and, second, to maximize the return on temporarily idle funds. The various types of marketable securities and their variations in yields and maturities allow a great deal of investment discretion and flexibility. Cash budgets and the determination of the desired cash balance are required prior to any decision regarding investment in short-term securities.

As developed in Chapter 5, the cash budget is a plan which attempts to determine the amounts and timing of cash inflows and outflows along with cash surpluses and shortages. In the event of a shortage, the organization must plan to borrow funds; if there is a surplus, the firm should invest these temporarily idle funds. A shortage or surplus cannot, however, be determined until the desired cash balance is computed. Appendix B to this chapter suggests two methods of calculating the desired cash balance.

The organization's cash budget will provide the estimated ending cash balance for the various subperiods of the year. An abbreviated cash budget is presented in Table 7.2. This ending cash balance is compared with the desired cash balance to determine the amount of investable funds available per subperiod (or the amount of short-term financing required). Smith Memorial Hospital, in Table 7.2, has $133,333 in investable funds for the month of January, 19X0. This amount is uncertain, because the estimation of future cash receipts and disbursements is, at best, subject to considerable error.

In selecting the investment instrument for idle cash, the primary consideration is liquidity and

TABLE 7.2

Smith Memorial Hospital
January, 19X0

Beginning cash balance	$ 28,726
ADD: Cash receipts	318,078
EQUALS: Total cash available	$346,804
LESS: Cash disbursements	184,745
EQUALS: Cash available	$162,059
LESS: Required ending cash balance	28,726
EQUALS: Investable funds	$133,333

only secondarily should the financial manager seek
the highest return. An appropriate amount of cash
should first be invested in the most liquid of money
market instruments--Treasury bills. The appropriate
amount can be determined only by considering the
unique features of the organization. An appropriate
amount might be that portion of the available
$133,333 not specifically earmarked for future use.
If, for example, $33,333 and $20,000 will be required in 30 days for bond interest and equipment
purchases, respectively, the $53,333 committed to
these uses could be invested for 30 days in CDs at a
higher interest return but with less liquidity than
Treasury bills. The remaining $80,000 could then be
invested until needed in more liquid Treasury bills
at a lower return, as a ready reserve.
    If the organization follows the above strategy
and invests $53,333 in 30-day CDs and $80,000 in T-
bills, the financial manager must still decide which
maturity of T-bills to purchase. He may match maturity and holding period; that is, since the cash is
expected to be idle for at least 30 days, he may
purchase a bill with a 30-day maturity. He could,
however, purchase a 60-, 90-, or 180-day maturity
bill and sell it at the end of his 30-day holding
period or whenever the cash was needed. Since the
bill market allows the financial manager to sell the
bill at any time, any of the above strategies assures liquidity.

It should again be noted that the highest interest rate is not always the best rate. Safety and liquidity are vital considerations for not-for-profit organizations. Excess cash should be invested only in securities that will mature or can be liquidated prior to the time the funds are required for operating purposes. In addition, projected future interest rates must be considered. Even if the cash will not be needed for operating purposes, the rates projected to be available when the investments mature are a factor in the investment decision. If very low rates are predicted for that time, it might be better to purchase securities that mature prior to the drop in interest so that the money may be reinvested while the rates are still high. Even though the yield on the shorter-term securities may be lower initially, the combined return of the investment sequence will be greater.

General economic conditions affect interest rates, which in turn determine the behavior of securities in both primary and secondary markets. Confidence in a particular security can also affect its behavior. Confidence is determined by an investor's perceptions of the financial condition of the institution or collateral behind the security. It tends to be most important in determining the strength and activity of a security in the secondary market. For instance, Treasury bills are always very active in both primary and secondary markets because they are backed by the U.S. government. The commercial paper of corporations may not enjoy the same degree of confidence. Understanding how markets behave under a variety of conditions and gaining a feel for how various securities are affected is a skill acquired through day-to-day experience and the study of the characteristics of securities.

SUMMARY

This chapter has discussed various aspects of a cash management program for not-for-profit organizations. Effective cash management will allow a return to be earned on otherwise idle cash and, at the same time, provide an adequate level of liquidity. The overall cash management problem requires a consideration of: (1) cash collections and disbursements, (2) cash balance management, and (3) short-term investment and borrowing. Each of these elements has to fit within the policies and constraints of the organization.

The proper management of cash flows dictates that the financial manager attempt to speed-up cash collections and slow-down cash disbursements as much as possible. This must be accomplished, however, within the limits of the organization's policies, taking into consideration the costs involved. An improved operating procedure for depositing currency and checks is one of the easiest ways of speeding-up cash collections. Lock-box systems can be used to accelerate cash availability.

Short-term assets are held in order to provide a buffer for the uncertainty associated with cash receipts disbursements and to earn a return. Liquidity is the primary consideration, with return being secondary. Several alternatives are available for investment of such reserves. These include U.S. Treasury bills, certificates of deposit, Federal agency issues, commercial paper, repurchase agreements, and money market funds.

QUESTIONS

1. Define the following terms:
   Cash
   Concentration account
   T-bills
   Short-term investments
   Lock-box system

   Zero-balance account
   Money market fund
   Deposit float
   Wire transfer
   Discount

2. What is the major disadvantage of holding cash?

3. Why would a not-for-profit firm invest in short-term marketable securities?

4. What alternatives are available when available cash fails to meet cash requirements?

5. How may the cash manager reduce the size of the required cash balance?

6. What alternatives are available for speeding-up cash flows?

7. What factors must be considered when payments for bills are slowed?

8. What accounting procedure for not-for-profit organizations may lead to ineffective cash man-

agement?

9. What types of marketable securities may a not-for-profit organization invest in?

10. What are the objectives of investing in marketable securities?

PROBLEMS

1. What is the opportunity cost of holding $400,000 in cash which was not needed for three months and which could have been invested at 8 percent interest?

2. The city of Midvale collects annual property taxes on June 1. These funds have remained in a checking account for the entire year for payment of bills on the last day of each month. If total property taxes are $3,000,000 and average monthly bills paid total $250,000, how much interest is the city losing at the current 6 percent interest rate by failing to invest idle funds?

3. The Central City United Fund bills pledges on a monthly basis. It is considering the use of a lock-box system for cash collections since office personnel is limited and it takes an average of 7 days to process pledge payments for deposit in the bank. They receive an average of 100 pledge payments on each of the 22 working days per month. The average pledge payment is $25. If the current interest rate on short-term investments is 6 percent, how much money could the city save by using a lock box which would allow deposit of pledges the day received?

4. If the Central City Bank charges Central City $0.05 to process each pledge payment received, in addition to a flat fee of $500, should Central City adopt the lock-box arrangement? (Use the data provided in problem 3 to complete this problem.)

5. The Crippled Children's Hospital receives funds twice a month from its national supporting foundation for the payment of operating expenses. The national foundation mails cashier's checks,

which average $200,000 each, five days prior to the 1st and 16th of the month. Should the national foundation switch to wire transfers if the average transfer costs $5 and current interest rates are 6 percent?

6. (a) What is the asking price for a $10,000 security which has a 60-day maturity and an ask yield of 9.6087 percent? (b) What is the ask yield of a 10,000 face value Treasury bill if the asking price is $9,925 and it has a 30-day maturity?

7. The comptroller of the State of Utah has several investment alternatives based on "riding the yield curve." Compare the yield earned on the security if held to maturity for the following cases:
   (a) Purchase a 30-day T-bill at $99.65; sell 15 days later at $99.90.
   (b) Purchase a 90-day T-bill at $98.55; sell 60 days later at $99.40.
   (c) Purchase a 180-day T-bill at $98.05; sell 30 days later at $98.45.

ENDNOTES

1. Checking accounts with banks are also known as demand deposits because the funds may be transferred or withdrawn "on demand" by presentation of a check.
2. It is possible to earn interest on accounts, like "NOW" accounts and share-draft accounts, which are similar to checking accounts. After the service charges are deducted, however, the returns on these accounts are usually very low.
3. Frank M. Patitucci and Michael H. Lichtenstein, Improving Cash Management in Local Governments (Chicago: Municipal Finance Officers Association, 1977), p. 4.
4. Howard J. Berman and Lewis E. Weeks, The Financial Management of Hospitals. 2d ed. (Ann Arbor, Mich.: Health Administration Press, 1974), p. 302.
5. This analysis is based on Phillip Rosenberg, C. Wayne Stallings, and Charles K. Coe, A Treasury Management Handbook for Small Cities and Other Governmental Units (Chicago: Municipal Finance Officers Association, 1978), pp. 58-59.

6. Patitucci and Lichtenstein, p. 27.
7. These differences are discussed in Chapter 1.
8. Accounting and Financial Reporting, A Guide For United Ways and Not For Profit Human Service Organizations, United Ways of America, Alexandria, Va., 1974, page 29.
9. Rosenberg, Stallings, and Coe, p. 61.
10. Ibid, p. 63.
11. This section is primarily from: Jerome Osteryoung and Daniel McCarty, Financial Management: Analytical Technique, (Columbus, Ohio: Grid Publishing, Inc., 1980, pp. 104-106.

APPENDIX A

This appendix outlines simple guidelines for the control of collection of donations to a voluntary health and welfare organization.

Control over donations may be divided into two general areas—office control and field control. Office control involves control over donations initially received through the mail or in person at the office of the agency. Field control involves control over donations which are received by volunteers in the field.

CONTROL OF OFFICE COLLECTIONS

Ideally, two employees should jointly control incoming mail and prepare a record of amounts received. The record should take the form of a multicopy prenumbered receipt book listing amounts received, which are then totaled and initialled by these employees. This record should be routinely compared with bank deposits, preferably by a person not having access to the donations.

It should be recognized that possible alternatives exist if dual control of incoming mail cannot be established. In some localities, banks will provide a service whereby all mail directed to a participating agency is controlled by the bank. Authenticated deposit slips and a list of deposits are then provided by the bank. Test mailing of contributions can be made by some form of auditing or as an protective agency aid to the detection of possible fraud.[1]

CONTROL OF FIELD COLLECTIONS

In most voluntary health and welfare organizations, the fundraising effort is divided into at least three fairly distinct activities. These activities include door-to-door solicitation, special events, and business solicitation. While there is no standard organizational structure, it is helpful to break a geographical area down into small sections so that a separate volunteer group carries out the fund-raising activity in each area. The responsible persons in each area are a chairman and a treasurer, with a separate chairman for each major fund-raising activity reporting to an area chairman. The activity chairmen, in turn, should appoint subchairmen for subdivisions of their area.[2]

Typically, a door-to-door solicitor should have ten to twenty family units to contact. A neighborhood captain should be responsible for about ten door-to-door solicitors and a division captain should be responsible for about ten neighborhood captains. Each solicitor should be provided a kit which includes identification authorizing solicitation of contributions in the name of the organization, envelopes and receipt forms for contributions, printed materials to aid in soliciting donations, and a report form for reporting the amounts collected. These workers' kits should be distributed through the chain of command on the basis of organizational reports showing the numbers of workers enlisted. The organizational reports may be checked against a detailed street map and city directory by the area chairman.

Control over the flow of promotional and other material through this chain of command and over the flow of reports and donations back to the top is the key to good control over this phase of the fund-raising operation. Separation of control over the donations themselves from control over the reports of donations received should be made as low in the chain of command as practicable.

Complete control over the door-to-door solicitor is usually not possible. Effective control could be attained only if door-to-door solicitation is done by a team of workers who maintain dual control over contributions until a permanent record is established. The use of prenumbered duplicate receipts or a follow-up solicitation of those not reported as contributors will provide additional control.

The cash donations available to any one door-to-door solicitor will usually be very small. Larger donations are usually made by check, payable to the organization. The small amount available to each solicitor, and the requirement that each

worker make a report, usually provides reasonable assurance
that there has been no material diversion of donations at this
level.[3]

More control can usually be exercised over the neighborhood
captain than over the door-to-door solicitor. The captain
generally has the responsibility of getting a signed report
from each worker summarizing these reports, and then turning
over the money, individual reports, and summary reports to the
division captain. The division captain checks the neighborhood
captain's report with individual worker's reports, proving the
amount of money turned in. The division captain should also
check to see that all workers in the division have reported and
prepare a summary report of all donations collected in this
area.

At no later than this point in the procedure, the donations
themselves and the record of the donations should be separated.
Donations should be turned over to the treasurer along with
copies of the summary reports of the neighborhood captains.
The original reports and the supporting detailed reports of
individual solicitors should be turned over to the area chairman. The area chairman should check that a report is received
from each person to whom material was supplied. These reports
should then be recapped and checked against the amounts deposited by the treasurer.[4]

The basic elements of good control are present if the cash
received and related reports are separated in the structure
before the reports are received by the chairman responsible for
checking the flow of materials to workers. If the chairman
actually performs his function of checking and follow-up, there
is reasonable assurance that the reports show substantially all
of the amounts actually received from contributors. Subsequent
tie-in of these reports to the amounts deposited completes the
chain of control.

SPECIAL EVENTS

As the name implies, special events can encompass a variety
of activities to raise revenue; e.g., fund-raising dinners,
dances, and street sales of various items. The methods of
ensuring adequate control will depend on the nature of the
event.[5]

For a fund-raising dinner and/or dance, good control can be
established over tickets. The person handling the collections
can be required to account for the tickets and collections,
with a subsequent check against meals served.[6]

For street sales or collections, each person authorized to
solicit funds will normally have access to limited amounts of
money. If the procedures are designed to ensure that each
solicitor reports in, and controls are established at the

reporting point, good control can be developed up the chain of command.

In all cases it is essential that the initial record be established at the earliest practicable moment and separated from the custodianship of the amounts collected. It is also essential that the initial record is subsequently verified against the amounts deposited in the depository of the agency.[7]

Business Solicitation

The campaign for donations from a business community of large individual donors is usually organized and controlled along the same lines as the door-to-door campaign. The major difference is each worker is often furnished the names of each prospective donor to be contacted, along with a card for each pledge or contribution expected. The personal solicitor will collect very little cash, as donations will most likely be made in the form of checks payable to the organization. In those cases where pledges are significant, the organization must control subsequent collections and the proper recording of the pledges receivable.[8]

Administrative

In practically all fund-raising campaigns there are administrative controls which supplement the detailed control procedures for donations. Three of these administrative controls are:

1. comparison of results with prior campaigns or knowledge of expected contributions
2. staff knowledge of type and intensity of fund-raising activities in each area
3. feed-back reports to key personnel in each area

Fund-raising statistics for past campaigns in each area are usually compared with current fund-raising results. In many cases this is formally developed into a fund-raising budget for the current year. Average per capita giving data for other areas and other types of campaigns in the same areas are often used extensively by agency personnel in checking donations received.[9]

Personnel on the field staff of the agency are usually assigned direct responsibility for certain areas within the overall territory covered by the agency. Their responsibility includes the organization and execution of a fund drive on an efficient basis. The staff maintains close contact with the chairmen in the organization structure and monitors fund-raising activities and reported results in their areas. If reported donations are less than what they think should have been in an area, the system of control may have broken down. Such a situation would probably trigger an investigation to determine the cause or causes of this problem.

Finally, a mailing list of all key volunteer personnel in each area should be maintained. As the campaign progresses, periodic reports are usually mailed to these persons showing the receipts by area. Any significant difference between the donations reported and the amount expected by these key persons would probably be questioned.[10]

While many individual organizations have policies and procedures which are effective for a given organization, little standardization exists in the area of contribution collection control. Consequently, the simple procedures outlined in this appendix are not always judiciously followed.[11] However, it would be beneficial for any not-for-profit organization which solicits contributions to employ a uniform, well-defined, and structured system of controls over the collection of contributions.

QUESTIONS

1. Describe the organizational structure of a door-to-door solicitation.

2. What types of control procedures can be exercised in a door-to-door solicitation?

3. What administrative controls may be exercised for a fund-raising campaign?

ENDNOTES

1. Audits of Voluntary Health and Welfare Organizations, An AICPA Industry Audit Guide, AICPA, New York:1964, pp. 32-34.
2. Ibid, page 35.
3. Ibid, page 37.
4. Ibid, page 38.
5. The Charitable Organization, Its Function and Purpose, Nelson O. Wax, Englewood Cliffs, N.J.: Prentice Hall, 1975, pp. 157-160.
6. Ibid, page 165.
7. Ibid, page 169.
8. Accounting for the Non-Profit Organization, Harvey A. Mossman, New York: McGraw-Hill, 1975, p. 235.
9. Ibid, page 240.

10. <u>Ibid</u>, page 241.

11. <u>Accounting in the Non-Profit Sector</u>, Andrew Mandel, Hinsdale, IL, The Dryden Press, 1973, pp. 214-220.

APPENDIX B

Various mathematical models have been developed for determining the optimal balance between cash and marketable securities. Two of these models, the Baumol Model for certain cash flows and the Miller-Orr Model for uncertain cash flows are discussed in this appendix.

The not-for-profit organization's beginning and ending cash balances for any time period are related by the following equation:

$$\underline{ECB} = \underline{CI} - \underline{CO} + \underline{BCB} \qquad \text{(Equation 7B-1)}$$

where $\underline{ECB}$ is the ending cash balance, $\underline{CI}$ the cash collections, $\underline{CO}$ the cash disbursements, and $\underline{BCB}$ the beginning cash balance. With constant collections and disbursements, the determination of the minimum cash balance is a simple matter. Collections and disbursements are known with certainty, and there is always a constant difference between them. In practice, however, collections and disbursements are likely to vary over the month and over the year. Some of the variations may be accurately predicted, while others may not be predicted at all.

Suppose cash flows which are reasonably foreseeable are separated from the organization's total cash flows. The cash

176

flows which are separated are the receipts and disbursements which vary, but whose size and timing are known with a high degree of certainty. Examples of such cash flows are: proceeds from the sale of bonds, payroll payments, property tax receipts, pledge receipts, capital expenditures, principal and interest payments, and interest income. Determination of the minimum cash balance with certain cash flows is actually an inventory problem in which the cost of having too little cash is balanced against the opportunity cost of having too much cash.

BAUMOL MODEL

William J. Baumol first applied inventory theory to the determination of the optimal cash balance in the early 1950s and the model has been improved by other writers since that time.[1]   Cash is treated as an inventory item with two types of relevant costs: (1) the opportunity cost of keeping funds in cash and (2) the fixed transaction cost of shifting from marketable securities to cash and vice versa. It is assumed the cash flows are known with certainty and occur at a constant rate. A single sum of cash is received at the beginning of the period and disbursements occur at a constant rate. Alternately, one could assume a series of uniform receipts and a single disbursement.

The organization keeps $\underline{C}$ dollars of the initial cash receipts in the form of cash and invests the remainder in short-term securities. These cash flows are depicted in Figure 7B.1. Since disbursements occur at a constant rate, the cash balance

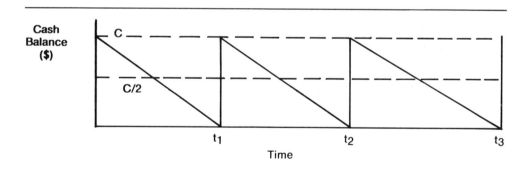

FIGURE 7B.1   Baumol model cash flows.

declines uniformly from its initial balance of $\underline{C}$ to zero at time $\underline{t}_1$. $\underline{C}$ dollars of securities are sold instantaneously at $\underline{t}_1$ to replenish the cash balance and the process repeats itself until the end of the planning period. A change in the value of $\underline{C}$ produces two opposite effects. A reduction in $\underline{C}$ reduces the average cash balance, which is simply C/2, thereby lowering the opportunity cost since more funds may be invested in short-term securities. At the same time, a lowering of C results in a greater number of security transactions during the planning period, resulting in increased transaction costs. The trade-off between these two types of costs is shown in Figure 7B.2. The objective is to select the value of C, the size of the

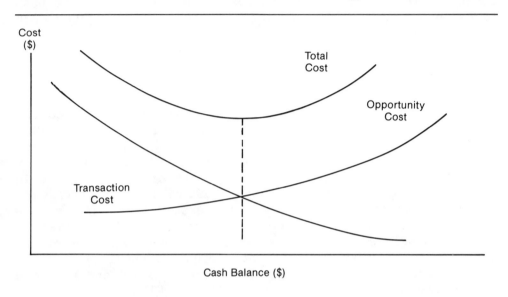

FIGURE 7B.2 Trade-off involved with Baumol Model.

security transaction, so as to minimize total costs.

Based on these assumptions, which are the same as those underlying the standard inventory EOQ model discussed in the following chapter, Baumol obtained the following formula for the optimal value of C which minimizes total costs:

$$\underline{C} = \sqrt{\frac{2\underline{b}\underline{T}}{\underline{i}}} \qquad \text{(Equation 7B-2)}$$

where C is the size of the initial cash balance and the value of marketable securities transactions, $\underline{b}$ the fixed cost per transaction, $\underline{T}$ the total cash outlay per period, and $\underline{i}$ the interest rate per period on marketable securities (the opportunity rate).

Using the Baumol model the average cash balance ($\underline{ACB}$) is:

$$\underline{ACB} = \underline{C}/2 \qquad \text{(Equation 7B-3)}$$

The total cost of operating the system ($\underline{TC}$) is:

$$\underline{TC} = \underline{b}\ (\underline{T}/\underline{C}) + [(\underline{C}/2)\underline{i}] \qquad \text{(Equation 7B-4)}$$

The total cost is the sum of the transaction cost $[b(T/C)]$ and the opportunity cost $[(C/2)i]$.

Examination of the model reveals some important relationships between the variables. An increase in transaction costs or a decrease in interest rates results in a higher cash balance. Economies of scale, however, are present. A four-fold increase in transaction costs results in a doubling of the cash balance. The following example illustrates the application of the Baumol Model to the cash balance problem.

Baumol Model Illustration

The Finance Officers Association has annual cash outlays of $850,000. These cash outlays occur at a constant rate and are highly predictable. Currently, the Finance Officers Association earns 9 percent on its investment in short-term securities. The association has estimated that each security transaction costs $30. The association is concerned with determining the optimal size of each security transaction. The association would also like to determine its average cash balance, the number of transactions conducted during the year, and the total cost of managing its transaction's cash balance.

Application of the Baumol Equation 7B-2 results in the following:

$$C = \sqrt{\frac{2bT}{i}} = \sqrt{\frac{2(30)850,000}{0.09}} = \sqrt{566,666,667} = \underline{\$23,805}$$

Consequently, the optimal transaction size is $23,805. Every time the association runs out of cash, $23,805 of securities are sold to replenish the cash balance. The average cash balance is equal to

$$\frac{C}{2} = \frac{\$23,805}{2} = \underline{\$11,903} \qquad \text{(Equation 7B-3)}$$

Assuming a 360-day year, the number of transactions per year is,

$$\frac{T}{C} = \frac{\$850,000}{23,805}, \text{ or 36 transactions per year.}$$

The total cost is equal to the sum of the transaction cost and the carrying cost.

Total cost = Transaction cost + Carrying cost

$$\text{Total cost} = b\,\underline{\frac{T}{C}} \;+\; \underline{\frac{C}{2}\,i}$$

$$= 30\frac{(850,000)}{23,805} + \frac{(23,805)}{2}\,0.09$$

(Equation 7B-4)

$$= \$1,071.20 + 1,071.23 = \underline{\$2,142.43}$$

MILLER-ORR MODEL

The Baumol model illustrates cash balance management when cash flows are known with certainty. Often, certain types of cash flows cannot be estimated with any degree of precision. Examples of such types of cash flows are cash payments and federal government grants. The Miller-Orr model has been developed and tested for the daily management of uncertain cash flows.[2]

Miller-Orr is a control-limit model. As long as the daily cash balance remains within a lower and upper limit, no action is taken. A violation of either limit is a signal that corrective action is needed. The general nature of the Miller-Orr model is illustrated in Figure 7B.3. The daily cash balances

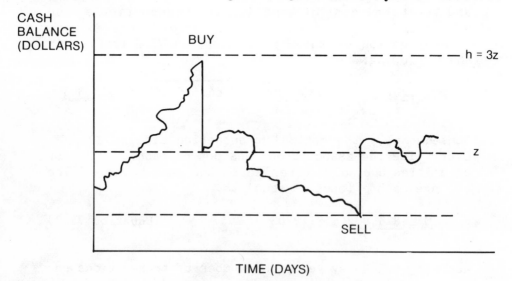

FIGURE 7B.3 Diagram of the Miller-Orr model.

are allowed to wander between the upper control limit, $\underline{h}$, and the lower control limit, $\underline{1}$. The lower control limit, $\underline{1}$, is usually determined by the compensating balance requirement of the organization's bank. The lower limit could be zero if there were no compensating balance requirement. In addition to these two limits, a return point, $\underline{z}$, is specified. Operation of the model is as follows: When the upper control limit, h, is reached, h-z dollars of marketable securities are purchased, which returns the cash balance to z. If the lower limit, l, is reached, z-l dollars of marketable securities are sold, restoring the cash balance to z. The average cash balance using this system is approximately equal to (z+h)/3.

Use of the Miller-Orr model requires determination of the h and z values. The value of z is found by using Equation 7B-5:

$$z = \sqrt[3]{\frac{3b\sigma^2}{4i}} \qquad \text{(Equation 7B-5)}$$

The cost per security transaction, or brokerage fee, is represented by b. The variance of the daily cash balances, a measure of uncertainty, is denoted by σ^2. The opportunity cost of cash balances is represented by i, the daily interest rate earned on marketable securities. The interest rate, i, and the brokerage fee, b, can be readily obtained. The value of σ^2, the variance of the daily cash balance, is more difficult to obtain.

One approach to the determination of variance is to use historical daily cash balances for the previous year.

This approach is illustrated by Professors Jerome Osteryoung and Daniel McCarty using the following example[3]: The use of historical data requires assuming that (1) the past daily cash balances were random events and (2) the future cash balances will move in a random fashion. The data in Table 7B.1 illustrates

TABLE 7B.1

Range, Frequency, and Probability of Cash Balances Last Year

(1) Cash balance range	(2) Number of days	(3) Middle value	(4) Probability
$ - 0 - to $ 9,999	30	$ 5,000	30/360
10,000 to 19,999	60	15,000	60/360
20,000 to 29,999	180	25,000	180/360
30,000 to 39,999	60	35,000	60/360
40,000 to 49,999	30	45,000	30/360

Source: Jerome S. Osteryoung and Daniel E. McCarty, Analytical Techniques For Financial Management (Columbus, Ohio: Grid Publishing, Inc., 1980), p. 104.

actual ranges of daily cash balances over the past year (Column 1) and the number of days cash balances fell within a given range (Column 2). Column 3 indicates the middle value of each range and Column 4 is found by dividing Column 2 by 360, the number of days in a finance year, and provides the probabilities necessary to calculate the variance.

Columns 3 and 4 can be used to compute the variance by employing Equation 7B-6.

$$\sigma^2 = \sum_{j=1}^{m} \left[(\underline{X}_{\underline{j}}) - \underline{E}(\underline{X}_{\underline{j}}) \right]^2 (\underline{P}_{\underline{j}}) \qquad \text{(Equation 7B-6)}$$

The Greek symbol sigma, σ, in Equation 7B-6 denotes that the various values, from $\underline{j}=1$ to $\underline{j}=\underline{m}$ are summed. X_j represents the middle value of each of the $\underline{m}$ ranges. $E(X_j)$ is a symbol which represents the expected value, or average value, of the mid-points of all of the ranges. P_j is the probability of the cash balance being within the $\underline{j}$ range. The computations of the variance are carried out in Table 7B.2. The values in Column 6 of Table 7B.2 are summed to obtain the variance, which is equal to $100,000,000.

TABLE 7B.2

Variance Computations for Daily Cash Balances

(1) Prob. $(\underline{P}_{\underline{j}})$	(2) Cash balance $(\underline{X}_{\underline{j}})$	(3) Product $(\underline{X}_{\underline{j}}) \times (\underline{P}_{\underline{j}})$	(4) Deviation $[(\underline{X}_{\underline{j}})-\underline{E}(\underline{X}_{\underline{j}})]$	(5) Squared deviation $[(\underline{X}_{\underline{j}})-\underline{E}(\underline{X}_{\underline{j}})]^2$	(6) Product of probability and squared deviation $[(\underline{X}_{\underline{j}})-\underline{E}(\underline{X}_{\underline{j}})]^2(\underline{P}_{\underline{j}})$
30/60	$ 5,000	$ 417	$(20,000)	$4 x 10^8	$ 33,333,333
60/360	15,000	2,500	(10,000)	1 x 10^8	16,666,667
180/360	25,000	12,500	– 0 –	– 0 –	– 0 –
60/360	35,000	5,833	10,000	1 x 10^8	16,666,667
30/360	45,000	3,750	20,000	4 x 10^8	33,333,333

$\underline{E}(\underline{X}_{\underline{j}}) = \sum_{j=1}^{m} (\underline{X}_{\underline{j}}) \, (\underline{P}_{\underline{j}}) = 25,000$ Variance = $100,000,000

Source: Jerome S. Osteryoung and Daniel E. McCarty, Analytical Techniques for Financial Management (Columbus, Ohio: Grid Publishing, Inc., 1980), p. 105.

The return point, $\underline{z}$, for the model can be obtained using this variance, and assuming a brokerage fee of $90, a compensating balance of $15,000, and an annual interest rate of 7.2 percent. The daily interest rate is 0.072/360 or 0.02 percent. The return point is:

$$\underline{z} = \sqrt[3]{\frac{(3)(\$90)(\$100,000,000)}{4(0.0002)}} = \underline{\$32,317}$$

The model specifies the upper control limit as three times the return point or $96,951. That is, when the cash balance reaches $96,951, $\underline{h}-\underline{z}$, or $64,634, should be invested in marketable securities. When the cash balance reaches $15,000, then $17,317 of marketable securities should be sold to return the cash balance to $32,317. An average cash balance approximately equal to (32,317 + 96,951)/3 or $43,089 can also be determined from the model. This example uses daily cash balances and the daily interest rate. The model can be applied using other time periods as well. For example, if done on a monthly basis: the monthly variance of the cash flows and the monthly interest rate would be used in Equation 7B-5.

Both the Baumol and Miller-Orr models specify that any excess cash is invested in short-term securities. Short-term securities are a vehicle for earning a return on temporarily idle cash. The numerous alternatives for investment in such securities were discussed in the main text of Chapter 7.

PROBLEM

1. The New York Port Authority experiences a variance in its daily cash balance of $2,777,700,000. Determine the average cash balance by the Miller-Orr model if brokerage fees are $250 per transaction and the current interest rate on marketable securities is 12 percent. Using this average cash balance as the required beginning and ending balance, determine the amount of investible funds on April 10th if cash receipts are $724,000 and disbursements are 478,000.

2. The city of La Mesa expects $100,000 in cash transactions during the current month. If idle funds can be invested in marketable securities at 8 percent interest and brokerage fees are $25 per transaction, determine (a) the cash balance La Mesa should have at the start of the period; (b) the average cash balance for the month; (c) the number of cash conversions; (d) the total cost of holding cash. (Use the EOQ model.)

184

3. Dupage County Hospital estimates its monthly cash transactions at $1 million. What is the optimal cash conversion if the cost of each conversion is $100 and marketable securities are currently earning 11 percent interest per year?

4. A local social service agency expects cash transactions of $400,000 next month. If brokerage fees and interest on marketable securities are $25 and 10 percent, respectively, what should the average cash balance be next month? If the interest rate on marketable securities increases to 14 percent, what happens to the average cash balance? Explain.

5. Using the Miller-Orr model, determine the upper limit, return point, and the average cash balance for Elmhurst Community College under the following conditions:

Range and frequencies of cash balances:

Cash balance range, $	Number of day
0- 29,999	40
30,000- 59,999	120
60,000- 79,999	160
80,000-100,000	40

Interest rate on marketable securities = 10 percent

Brokerage fees=$25/transaction

ENDNOTES

1. William J. Baumol, "The Transactions Demand for Cash: An Inventory Theoretic Approach, "Quarterly Journal of Economics, Vol. 66 (November 1952), pp. 545-556.
2. Merton H. Miller and Daniel Orr, "A Model of the Demand for Money by Firms," Quarterly Journal of Economics, Vol. 80 (August 1966), pp. 413-435.
3. Jerome Osteryoung and Daniel McCarty, Financial Management: Analytical Techniques (Columbus, Ohio: Grid Publishing, Inc., 1980), pp. 102-103.

ACCOUNTS RECEIVABLE AND INVENTORY MANAGEMENT

Two types of current assets most not-for-profit organizations have other than cash and marketable securities are accounts receivable and inventory. The effective management of these assets is critical to the not-for-profit organization since they frequently must commit large amounts of funds to them.

Many not-for-profit organizations provide services for which customers are billed on a periodic basis subsequent to the providing of services. For example, a municipality may provide refuse collection services billed on a monthly, bimonthly, or quarterly basis. The not-for-profit hospital bills a patient upon dismissal from the hospital, rather than when the charges are incurred. Debts owed an organization by recipients of their services, or their agents, are known as accounts receivable. Although necessary for smooth operations, accounts receivable have to be managed efficiently and effectively to ensure accomplishing the objectives of the not-for-profit organization.

Many not-for-profit organizations must invest in inventories such as supplies, food, linens, and other items in order to convert fixed assets into services. The effective and efficient management of inventories enhances the not-for-profit organization's ability to provide services. This chapter develops techniques for managing the investment in these two current assets.

ACCOUNTS RECEIVABLE MANAGEMENT

Accounts receivable may be viewed as a loan extended to the recipient of services by the not-for-profit organization. Some of this debt is generated as a normal by-product of the manner in which services are provided. For example, it is too costly and inconvenient for cities and counties to collect for services such as sewers and electricity as the services are provided. Instead, a loan is extended and the customer is billed on a periodic basis.

The type of not-for-profit organization is a major factor influencing the level of accounts receivable. For instance, the not-for-profit hospital is in the credit business to a substantial degree, but not by choice. The not-for-profit hospital usually does not have the option of accepting only the most credit-worthy customer. Likewise, universities accept students, clubs accept members, and cities provide services based on criteria other than credit worthiness.

Both the profit-oriented firm and the not-for-profit organization must take measures to keep the amount and quality of accounts receivable in check. The not-for-profit organization, however, has less flexibility than the profit-oriented firm. Many not-for-profit organizations do not enjoy the luxury of determining to whom they will or will not extend credit. The not-for-profit organization must seek to effectively manage, and, if possible, to minimize its investment in accounts receivable.

Costs of Accounts Receivable

There are costs associated with carrying accounts receivable which must be considered in determining the level of investment in this current asset. The relevant costs attached to the management of accounts receivable for not-for-profit organizations can be separated into three general categories: (1) financial carrying costs, (2) routine collection and credit costs, and (3) bad-debt expenses.

Financial carrying costs are the opportunity costs associated with accounts receivable. Funds are tied up in accounts receivable when loans are made to the recipients of services. If these funds were not invested in accounts receivable, they could be invested elsewhere. The lending organization incurs an opportunity cost equal to the rate of return which could be earned from an alternative investment times the size of the investment. If funds have to be borrowed to finance all or part of the investment in accounts receivable, then the cost is equal to the interest rate times the size of the loan plus any opportunity cost on unborrowed funds. In either case, the financial carrying cost is directly related to the size of the investment in accounts receivable and they exist for the entire period in which funds are committed to accounts receivable.

The second category of costs, routine collection and credit costs, results from the operating expenses associated with the organization's extending credit. Costs for personnel, postage, stationery, computer time, and other resources have to be incurred in order to bill the organization's customers and process their payments. Not all bills will be paid in a timely fashion, even with careful screening by the credit department. Costly steps have to be taken if the collection efforts of the credit department are unsuccessful. A lawyer may have to be hired or a collection agency utilized. Either of these actions could result in a collection expense from 10 percent to as much as 50 percent of the outstanding balance. As a last resort, the entire amount of the overdue balance may have to be written off as a bad debt. This third category, delinquency costs, can be quite expensive.

Investment in Accounts Receivable

The general credit policy of an organization is established by its credit standards, credit terms, and collection policy. All of these variables are controllable by a profit-oriented firm. Many not-for-profit organizations, however, have control only over their collection policy.

Credit standards are the guidelines used to determine which customers will receive credit and the amount of credit extended. Credit standards establish the level of risk the organization is willing to accept as a result of extending credit. The not-for-profit organization is usually not in a position to determine which clients will or will not receive

service based on their credit worthiness. Credit
terms define the time for which credit is extended
and the discount given for the early payment. In
many instances, credit terms for not-for-profit
organizations are dictated by third parties, e.g.
the Medicare program pays a substantial portion of
hospital charges as directed by federal policy.

Collection policy refers to the procedures and
guidelines used by an organization to collect accounts receivable. It includes the routine billing
and collection of accounts receivable as well as
their collection when they are past due. Not-for-
profit organizations generally have more control
over credit policy than they do over credit standards and credit terms. Cities can force the sale
of property if taxes are not paid by certain dates.
Clubs can cancel memberships if dues are not paid on
time. Universities can cancel the registration of
students if tuition payments are delinquent.

Billing System

Many not-for-profit organizations provide services for which a fee is charged. The client serviced should be presented with a bill at the time
services are provided, or shortly thereafter. A
system should be established to monitor the progress
of payments on accounts. With the availability of
computer time or packages at reasonable prices,
computerized billing has become more widespread.

A computer can be used to generate bills at the
appropriate time following delivery of service. The
computer can also be programmed to monitor accounts
receivable automatically to determine whether bills
have been paid or not. If payment is not received
after a certain period of time has elapsed, the
computer can generate a letter or a notice to send a
letter. If payment is not received after several
letters have been sent, more drastic action is
needed. Some of the possible actions are discussed
in the next section on collection procedures.

Collection Policy Decision

The collection policy decision depends on a
trade-off between direct billing cost, financial
carrying costs, and bad debt expense. To illustrate
one such trade-off, consider the problem of deter-

mining the frequency of billing for a municipal utility which results in the lowest annual cost for managing accounts receivable.[1] Local governments provide many services for which they bill their customers on a periodic basis. A substantial portion of these accounts receivable are a result of providing utility services such as water, sewer, garbage pickup, gas, and electricity. An important decision in the management of these accounts receivable is how frequently customers should be billed.

To illustrate, assume that a typical customer of Alexander City Utilities pays $90 per month for city utilities, and thus has an annual bill of $1,080. Assume also that it costs $1.25 for each bill to be processed; that bad debt losses average 1 percent of the average level of accounts receivable if billed monthly, 2 percent if billed bimonthly, and 2.5 percent if billed quarterly; and that the financial carrying costs are 10 percent of the average level of accounts receivable. Alexander City is trying to decide whether to continue to bill on a monthly basis or to change to a bimonthly or quarterly basis.

The information necessary for this type of decision on an individual customer basis is given in Table 8.1. It is also assumed that the typical customer's obligation increases

TABLE 8.1

Data for Billing Frequency Decision

Billing frequency	Quarterly	Bimonthly	Monthly
Bill size	$270.00	$180.00	$90.00
Average receivables	135.00	90.00	45.00
Financial carrying costs	13.50	9.00	4.50
Bad-debt costs	3.38	1.80	0.45
Direct billing costs	5.00	7.50	15.00
Total annual costs	$ 21.88	$ 18.30	$19.95

at a constant rate during the billing cycle and is reduced to zero every time a payment is made. With a quarterly billing cycle for a $1,080 annual bill, four $270 payments will be made. The average level of accounts receivable is one-half of $270 or $135. The financial carrying cost is equal to 10 percent times the average receivable level or $13.50 per year. Bad-debt loss averages 2.5 percent of the average level of receivables or $3.38 per year. The direct billing costs are simply $1.25 per bill times 4 bills per year or $5.00 per year. The total annual cost per customer of billing customers on a quarterly basis is the sum of the three types of costs, or $21.88 per year.

Calculations for billing on a bimonthly and monthly basis are performed in a similar manner. If bimonthly billing is used, the financial carrying costs, bad-debt costs, and direct billing costs are $9.00, $1.80, and $7.50, respectively, resulting in an annual cost per customer of $18.30. Similarly, with monthly billing, the financial carrying cost is $4.50, the bad-debt cost is $0.45, and the direct billing cost is $15.00, in which case the total annual cost would be $19.95. This analysis shows that bimonthly billing should be used since this the least expensive of the three alternatives considered.

Collection Techniques

Collection policy also includes decisions regarding the collection of past-due accounts. A number of different collection techniques can be employed as an account becomes increasingly overdue. Basic collection techniques are discussed below in the order typically found in the collection process.[2]
The first step normally, after an account receivable becomes overdue, is to send a polite letter reminding the customer of the overdue obligation. If payment is not forthcoming, a second more-demanding letter is sent, followed by a third letter if necessary. If the letters prove unsuccessful, a telephone call personally requesting immediate pay-

ment may elicit results. Sending someone personally to the customer to attempt to work out a payment schedule can also be an effective collection procedure. Finally, an uncollectible account can be turned over to a collection agency or an attorney for collection. The fees, however, for this type of procedure are typically quite high. The most stringent step in the collection process is direct legal action. The action is quite expensive and may force the customer into bankruptcy. It must be noted, however, that several of these techniques are not viable for certain types of not-for-profit organization. For instance, it is doubtful that churches would proceed beyond the telephone call stage.

The decision to use a collection agency involves the trade-off between a higher expected amount of funds to be collected using this procedure and the higher costs of collection. This decision is illustrated for Smith University. Smith University has recently experienced difficulty in collecting tuition from previous quarters for three students. The university has cancelled enrollment for the present quarter and is considering the use of a collection agency to collect the overdue obligations.

The amounts owed and the estimated probabilities of collecting at least one-half of the amounts owed by the three students are:

Student	Amount Owed	Probability
A	$2,500	0.10
B	1,780	0.20
C	3,600	0.07

Collection expenses will amount to $150 if Smith pursues collection on its own. If a collection agency is used, the fee is 60 percent of the amount collected. In return for this substantial fee, the agency is able to double the probability of collecting at least one-half of the amounts owed by employing "special methods." Smith University must decide whether to continue to pursue the bad accounts on their own, or turn them over to the collection agency.

The criterion to use in this type of decision is to select the alternative which has the highest net expected value. The expected value is the probability of an event times the potential outcome. Table 8.2 shows the net expected value of collection if Smith University attempts to collect the funds owed on their own--or a net expected amount of $279.

TABLE 8.2

Calculation of Net Expected Amount if Collected by University

Student	Amount owed	One-half of amount owed	Probability	Outcome
A	$2,500	$1,250	0.10	$125
B	1,780	890	0.20	178
C	3,600	1,80	0.70	126
		Total outcome		$429
		Collection expense		150
		Net expected amount		279

If the university turns its collections over to an agency, the net expected amount of collection is calculated as shown in Table 8.3. While the probability of collection doubles, the cost of collection goes from $150.00 to $514.80. In spite of the increased collection cost, Smith University is ahead by using the collection agency, since this alternative has the highest net expected value.

TABLE 8.3

Calculation of Net Expected Amount if Collected by Collection Agency

Student	Amount owed	One-half of amount owed	Probability	Outcome
A	$2,500	$1,250	0.20	$250.00
B	1,780	890	0.40	356.00
C	3,600	1,800	0.14	252.00
		Total outcome		$858.00
		60% collection expense		514.80
		Net expected amount		$343.20

In addition to the previously discussed
techniques for collecting overdue accounts,
discounts may be used to encourage prompt
payment. A 1 percent reduction in tuition
if paid early will speed up the collection
of accounts receivable, but at a cost of the
reduced revenues due to the discount.

The use of bank credit cards such as Visa and
Master Card can also speed up collections. The
credit cards are held by several million people and
are accepted by most businesses. Many not-for-
profit organizations, such as hospitals and universities, now accept credit cards. The key characteristics of a credit card agreement usually require
that:

1. the organization agrees to accept the client's
    credit card for payment of amounts owed

2. the organization pays a service charge of 3 to 5
    percent of the amount of each charge submitted

3. the organization must maintain an account at the
    bank issuing the credit card

4. the issuing bank agrees to pay all accounts
    quickly by depositing funds in the organiza-
    tion's account at the issuing bank

5. the bank determines the client's credit worthi-
    ness and has no recourse for uncollectible
    accounts[3]

The use of credit cards accelerates cash collections
and reduces collection efforts at the expense of a
service charge to the issuing bank for each charge
submitted.
    The decision rule whether to accept bank cards or
not is straightforward. If the benefits of reducing
the investment in accounts receivable and collection
costs and eliminating bad-debt expense exceed the
cost of the bank fee, then the credit cards should
be used. This decision is illustrated for Williams
Memorial Hospital in Table 8.4.

Williams Memorial Hospital's credit charges
average $5 million per year. The typical
patient pays his bill in 36 days. The hospital estimates it will take 5 days to pro-

cess credit card charges and have the funds deposited in its account at the bank. The opportunity cost of funds tied up in accounts receivable is 6 percent. The hospital currently has to write off 3 percent of its credit charges as bad debts, or $150,000 per year. In addition, implementation of the bank credit card system would eliminate the need for three positions in the credit and collection department at an annual savings of $50,000.

Daily credit charges, assuming a 360-day year, are $13,888.89. Multiplying the credit charges per day times the average age of accounts receivable results in the average level of accounts receivable of $500,000 under the present system and $69,444 with the bank credit card system. Implementation of the credit card system allows a reduction of $430,556 in the average level of accounts receivable. Since accounts receivable carry an opportunity cost of 6 percent, the reduction in accounts receivable saves the hospital $25,833 per year. The cost of the bank credit card system is 4 percent of the credit charges, or $200,000 for the $5,000,000 in annual credit charges.

TABLE 8.4

Bank Credit Card Decision for Williams Memorial Hospital

Assumptions

Average annual credit charges	$5,000,000
Average age of accounts receivable (present)	36 days
Average age of accounts receivable (credit card)	5 days
Carrying cost per year	6%
Bad-debt expense (3% of credit charges)	$150,000
Bank credit card fee per credit charge	4%
Present cost of credit and collections dept.	$160,000
Savings in credit and collections department with credit card system	$50,000

Table 8.4 Cont.

Calculations

Credit sales per day $= \dfrac{\$5,000,000}{360} = \$13,888.89$

Average accounts receivable--present system:
= $13,888.89 x 36 days = $500,000

Average accounts receivable--credit cards:
= $13,888.89 x 5 days = $69,444

Reduction in accounts receivable:
$500,000 - $69,444 = $430,556

Saving from reduction in accounts receivable:
$430,556 x 0.06 = $25,833

Cost of bank credit card system:
$5,000,000 x 0.04 = $200,000

Comparison of Benefits and Costs

Benefits
Savings from reduction in accounts
  receivable $ 25,833
Reduction in collection costs   50,000
Elimination of bad-debt expense   150,000
                         Total benefits $225,833

Cost
Total bank credit card fees   200,000
                         Benefit--cost $ 25,833

Application of the decision rule calls for a
comparison of benefits and costs. The total
benefits from the reduction in accounts
receivable, reduction in collection costs,
and elimination of bad-debt expense are
$225,833. The cost of the bank credit card
system is $200,000. Acceptance of the cre-
dit card system would result in a net savings of $25,833 per year so it should be
adopted.

INVENTORY MANAGEMENT

The investment of funds in inventory is critical
for not-for-profit organizations in two ways.
First, the majority of not-for-profit organizations
have some funds invested in inventories and, second,
having insufficient inventory on hand frequently
means inability to provide services. These two

elements demand that careful attention be given the level of inventory maintained by the not-for-profit organization.

Many profit-oriented firms have three distinct types of inventory--raw materials and supplies, work-in-progress, and finished goods. In this discussion, emphasis will be placed on supplies inventory since the vast majority of not-for-profit organizations are service-oriented and supplies constitute their only type of inventory. Some types of not-for-profit organizations, however, may be involved with all three types of inventory. For example, the Industries Division of the Pennsylvania Bureau of Correction operates eighteen production plants in eight state correctional institutions.[4] These plants produce furniture, upholstery, mattresses, garments, cardboard, shoes, underwear, hosiery, soap, detergent, lumber, metal shelves, bookcases, and a host of other products. The techniques discussed for supplies inventory are also applicable for work-in-progress and finished goods inventories.

An Overview of Inventory Management

The amount of inventory held by a not-for-profit organization will depend on several factors such as type of organization, level of activity, size, length of service cycle, and durability of the inventory. Supplies expense is typically the largest nonwage cost element for a hospital. A certain amount of material and supplies must be on hand to meet the inflow and outflow demands of the service cycle of the organization. In addition, a safety stock is desirable in order to provide a cushion for unusual demand for the product or service or for delays in receiving materials and supplies. However, management cannot keep unlimited amounts of inventory on hand because of the costs associated with holding inventory. Inventory demand must be weighed against the carrying costs in order to determine an optimal level of inventory.

There are three basic costs involved with inventory: (1) the cost of carrying the inventory once it is acquired, (2) the cost of ordering the inventory, and (3) the costs of running out of the inventory. The carrying costs include: the opportunity cost of funds tied up in inventory, storage of the inventory, depreciation or obsolescence, and insurance. Ordering costs include all expenses related to acquisition of the inventory such as the cost of placing the order, shipping and handling expense, inspection costs, and the opportunity cost of lost quantity discounts.

The significance of the third type of cost, the cost of running out of inventory or stockout cost, will depend on the type of organization and inventory item. For a hospital, the stockout cost is probably the most critical and most difficult cost component to measure.[6] The stockout cost for a hospital has to be measured in terms of the tangible cash costs of not being able to provide patient care and in terms of the intangible, and difficult to measure, costs of illness, pain, and death. On the other hand, if a school district runs out of supplies, the teachers may simply do without or buy their own supplies.

There are several decisions involved in inventory management, but the three basic ones are: (1) the amount to order at any one time, (2) when to place the order, and (3) how much extra inventory to carry as protection against stockouts.[7] These decisions involve a consideration of trade-offs between the various inventory costs. The costs of carrying inventory, such as the opportunity cost of funds committed to inventory, increase as the size of inventory increases. On the other hand, the chances of a stockout decrease as inventory increases, so stockout costs decrease with larger inventory. The frequency of orders decreases as the size of the inventory order increases, thereby reducing ordering costs. Figure 8.1 depicts the trade-offs involved, and indicates that there is a level of inventory which minimizes total inventory costs.

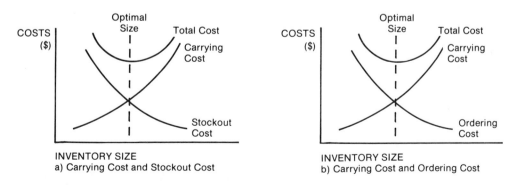

a) Carrying Cost and Stockout Cost

b) Carrying Cost and Ordering Cost

FIGURE 8.1 Trade-offs involved in inventory management.

Economic Order Quantity

The Economic Order Quantity (EOQ) model is a widely used method to address the first of the three basic inventory management decisions, the quantity to order at any one time. As shown in Figure 8.1 (b), management must consider the trade-off between inventory carrying costs and order costs. The EOQ method allows us to determine the order size which results in the lowest total cost.

The EOQ model is summarized in Figure 8.2. To determine the EOQ (Q in Equation 8-2), we must know the inventory usage per period, S; the per unit carrying costs, C; and the ordering costs, O. The model assumes usage is known with certainty and occurs at a constant rate.

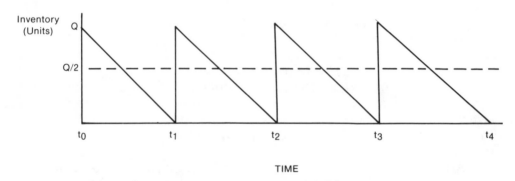

FIGURE 8.2   EOQ model.

The organization orders the EOQ Q, initially. The inventory is used at a constant rate until it is reduced to zero at t_1, at which time it is instantaneously replenished to level Q. Consequently, it is assumed there is no lead time involved in acquiring inventory. This pattern of usage, ordering, and delivery is repeated during the planning period. With no safety stock, the average inventory level will be Q/2.

The objective of the EOQ model is to minimize the total cost of inventory. The model does not consider stockout costs, so the total inventory costs are only carrying costs plus the ordering costs. The carrying cost of inventory for the year is equal to the average inventory (Q/2) times the per unit carrying costs, or CQ/2. The number of orders per year is equal to the usage, S, divided by the order quantity, Q. The total ordering cost per year is equal to the number of orders per year times the cost per order, or SO/Q. Thus, the equation for the total cost of inventory, T is:

$$T = \frac{CQ}{2} + \frac{SO}{Q}$$ (Equation 8-1)

From Figure 8.1(b) it can be observed that minimum total cost occurs when ordering and carrying costs are equal. Equating these two costs results in[8]:

$$\frac{CQ}{2} = \frac{SO}{Q}$$

$$CQ^2 = 2SO$$ (Equation 8-2)

$$Q^2 = \frac{2SO}{C}$$

$$Q = \sqrt{\frac{2SO}{C}}$$

Equation 8-2 is the EOQ equation for determining the order quantity which results in the best trade-off between ordering and carrying costs.

Basic EOQ Example.   The pharmacy of Williams Memorial Hospital uses 720,000 units of Drug A per year. The ordering cost of the drug is $20 per order and the carrying cost is $2.50 per unit per year. The economic order quantity, using Equation 8-2, would be:

$$Q = \sqrt{\frac{2SO}{C}}$$

$$= \sqrt{\frac{2(600,000)20}{2.50}} = \sqrt{\frac{24,000,000}{2.50}}$$

$$= \sqrt{9,600,000} = 3098.39$$

or $\underline{3098\ units}$ per order

The total costs per month, using Equation 8-1, would be:

$$T = \frac{CQ}{2} + \frac{SO}{Q}$$

$$= \frac{(\$2.50) \; 3{,}098}{2} \; + \; \left(\frac{600{,}000}{3098}\right) \; \$20$$

$\underline{T} = \$3972.50 + \$3873.47$

$\underline{T} = \underline{\$7745.97}$ per year or $\underline{\$645.50}$ per month[9]

Ordering Policy

The ordering frequency can be derived from the $\underline{EOQ}$ approach. The frequency of orders is equal to $\underline{S/Q}$. Dividing the length of the planning period, $\underline{N}$, by the frequency of orders results in the time between orders, $\underline{t}$. This relationship is expressed below:

$$\underline{t} = \frac{N}{\underline{S/Q}} = \frac{N\underline{Q}}{\underline{S}} \qquad \text{(Equation 8-3)}$$

Continuing with the previous example of Williams Memorial Hospital:

$$\underline{t} = \frac{N\underline{Q}}{\underline{S}} = \frac{(365 \text{ days}) \; (3098)}{600{,}000} = 1.88 \text{ days}$$

An order of 3098 units of Drug A would be placed approximately every 1.88 days.

Instantaneous reordering and restocking of inventory is an unrealistic assumption. There is usually a lead time or delay between the time an order is placed and when it is received. This situation is shown graphically in Figure 8.3, where lead time is identified as $\underline{L}$ and the reorder point as $\underline{R}$. R, the reorder point or level of inventory at the time of reorder, is calculated as follows:

$$\underline{R} = \frac{S}{N} \text{ x } \underline{L} \qquad \text{(Equation 8-4)}$$

S/N is the daily usage rate and $\underline{L}$ is the lead time in days. An order of $\underline{Q}$ amount would be placed when the inventory level reaches $\underline{R}$. With constant usage, the order would be received at the time the inventory level is depleted.

Continuing with the same example of Williams Memorial Hospital and assuming a one-day lead time, the reorder point is:

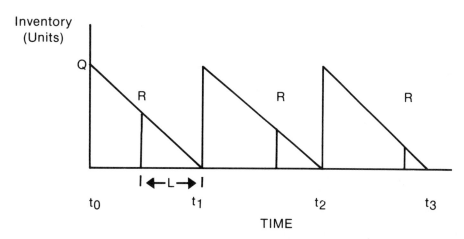

FIGURE 8.3   EOQ model with lead time.

$$\underline{R} = \frac{\underline{S}}{\underline{N}} \times \underline{L}$$

$$= \frac{600,000}{365} \times 1$$

$$= 1643.84 \text{ or } 1,644 \text{ units}$$

So an order would be placed when the inventory level reached 1644 units of Drug A. At the daily rate of usage of 1644 units the new order would arrive at the same time the inventory level was depleted.

Safety Stock

Having examined two of the basic inventory management decisions, the third: "How much protection do we provide against stockouts?" must be considered. This decision is approached through consideration of safety stocks, or buffer stocks as they are sometimes known. Safety stocks are maintained in order to provide protection against unexpected variations in lead time and in usage. The safety stock is a level of inventory maintained at all times, except for unplanned usage. Figure 8.4 graphically shows inventory levels with a safety stock, $\underline{B}$, maintained. An increase in usage occurs in period 2, depleting the safety stock to level $\underline{B}_2$. A longer lead time than expected, such as at $\underline{t}_3$, causes depletion of the safety stock to level $\underline{B}_3$.

With a safety stock, the maximum inventory is $\underline{B}$ + $\underline{Q}$. The average inventory shifts upward by the level of safety stock becoming $\underline{Q}/2 + \underline{B}$. The $\underline{EOQ}$ equation

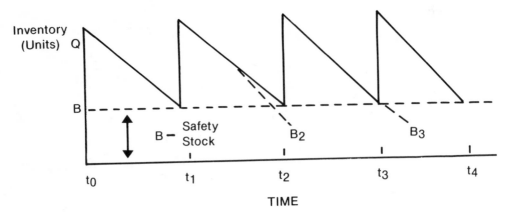

FIGURE 8.4 **Inventory levels with safety stock.**

remains the same, since the cost of carrying the safety stock is a constant that does not vary with the order size.

The level of safety stock to be carried depends upon the risk of stockout the not-for-profit organization is willing to assume. The higher the level of safety stock the lower the risk of a stockout but the greater the carrying cost. As mentioned previously, the cost of a stockout can vary tremendously, depending on the type of organization and the type of supply item. Certain types of supplies have to be maintained in a hospital at all times because a stockout could mean pain, suffering, or even death. A shortage of stationery, however, is not as critical.

To illustrate the determination of the level of safety stock in cases where a stockout can be tolerated, assume that Williams Memorial Hospital presently has no safety stock and orders 15,000 paper plates per month.

Due to variations in usage, the hospital finds it necessary to establish an optimal safety stock. The estimated probability for usage of the paper plates is shown below:

Usage (units)	Probability
13,500	0.04
14,000	0.07
14,500	0.17
15,000	0.32
15,500	0.20
16,000	0.10
16,500	0.06
17,000	0.04

It takes two days to place an order and receive delivery. The average monthly carrying cost is $0.15 per unit and stockouts are estimated to cost $3.00 per unit. The hospital desires to determine the optimal level of safety stock if it continues to order 15,000 paper plates per month.

The optimal safety stock is that level which has the lowest total inventory cost for the level of stockout risk the organization is willing to assume. The total inventory cost is a function of the expected stockout cost and the safety stock carrying cost. Equation 8-5 expresses this relationship mathematically:

$$\underline{KS} = \left[\sum_{\underline{j}=1}^{n} (\underline{D}) \ (\underline{P}_{\underline{j}}) \ (\underline{N}_{\underline{j}}) \right] + (\underline{C}) \ (\underline{B})$$

(Equation 8-5)

where $\underline{KS}$ is the total cost of safety stock, $\underline{D}$ the per unit stockout cost,[10] $\underline{P}_{\underline{j}}$ the probability of a shortage $\underline{j}$, $\underline{N}_{\underline{j}}$ the size of shortage $\underline{j}$, C the per unit carrying cost of inventory, and $\underline{B}$ the number of units in the safety stock.

The data for a safety stock analysis are shown in Table 8.5. Column 1 shows different safety stock levels, $\underline{B}$, for a monthly order quantity of 15,000. The size of the stockouts associated with different levels of safety stock are shown in Column 2. Stockout costs, (D x $\underline{N}_{\underline{j}}$), for different combinations of safety stock and stockouts are shown in Column 3. For example, if the hospital orders 15,000 units and maintains a safety stock of 1,000 units, two possible shortages may occur. The number of units available during the month is 16,000, the 15,000 ordered plus the safety stock. If usage is 16,500 units, a shortage of 500 units is experienced. The probabilities of these two stockouts occurring are shown in Column 4.

TABLE 8.5

Safety Stock Analysis—
Williams Memorial Hospital
15,000 units ordered per month

(1) Safety stock ($\underline{B}$)	(2) Stockout ($\underline{N}_j$)	(3) Stockout cost @ 3.00 unit ($\underline{D}$ x $\underline{N}_j$)	(4) Prob. ($\underline{P}_j$)	(5) Expected stockout cost ($\underline{D}$ x $\underline{N}_j$ x $\underline{P}_j$)	(6) Carrying cost @ $0.15 unit ($\underline{C}$ x $\underline{B}$)	(7) Total cost ($\underline{K}_5$)
2,000	0	$0	0	$0	$300	$ 300
1,500	500	1,500	0.04	60	$225	$ 285
1,000	1,000	3,000	0.04	120	-	-
	500	1,500	0.06	90	-	-
				$ 210	$150	$ 360
500	1,500	$4,500	0.04	$ 180	$ -	$ -
	1,000	3,000	0.06	180	-	-
	500	1,500	0.10	150	-	-
				$ 510	$ 75	$ 585
0	2,000	$6,000	0.04	$ 240	$ -	$ -
	1,500	4,500	0.06	270	-	-
	1,000	3,000	0.10	300	-	-
	500	1,500	0.20	300	-	-
				$1,110	$ 0	$1,110

The expected stockout cost for each shortage is shown in Column 5 and is obtained by multiplying Column 3 by Column 4. The carrying cost of the safety stock, obtained by multiplying the per unit carrying cost by the safety stock Level $\underline{B}$, is shown in Column 6. The total cost for a certain level of safety stock is the sum of Columns 5 and 6 or $360 for the 1,000 unit safety stock.

With a safety stock of 1500 units, there could be inventory shortages of 500 units. Although the cost of a possible stockout is relatively low, the carrying cost of the safety stock is relatively high. Together, however, their combined costs are lowest for a safety stock of 1,500 units. Consequently, this is the optimal level of safety stock. However, the hospital has to be willing to accept a 4 percent chance of a stockout occurring.

The not-for-profit organization can also maintain a safety stock as protection against variations in lead time. This type of decision is analyzed in a manner similar to the previous example, except the organization has to estimate the probabilities associated with different lead times instead of usages.

SUMMARY

This chapter focused on the management of two current assets--accounts receivable and inventory. The objective of accounts receivable management for the not-for-profit organization is to select the set of collection policies to minimize the overall costs of accounts receivable. Collection policies are the guidelines used to collect accounts receivable when they are due or past due. This type of decision involves a consideration of the financial carrying costs, routine collection and credit costs, and bad-debt expenses.

The amount of funds invested in inventory involves a trade-off between three types of costs. The basic EOQ model, which involves a trade-off between ordering costs and carrying costs, was developed to determine the optimal order size under conditions of certainty. This model was later extended to incorporate lead time. Finally, a safety stock analysis was presented for instances in which there are variations in usage and/or lead time.

QUESTIONS

1. What are accounts receivable and how are they generated?

2. What costs are associated with the carrying of accounts receivable?

3. What difficulty does a not-for-profit organization have in setting credit standards?

4. What does the term collection policy mean and what trade-offs exist in its establishment?

5. Briefly describe the basic collection techniques a not-for-profit organization can use.

206

6. How does the use of credit cards aid in the collection of cash?

7. What factors must be considered in the use of credit cards for payment of goods or services?

8. What is the most common type of inventory carried by a not-for-profit organization and why is its management important?

9. What costs are associated with the carrying of inventory?

10. What is meant by a stockout and why is its cost important to inventory management?

11. What is the economic order quantity and how is it determined?

12. What is safety stock and how does it relate to inventory management?

PROBLEMS

1. The Canton Power and Light Company has been billing on a bimonthly basis for many years. Due to the recent increases in the average size bill and high interest rates, it is considering switching to monthly billing. Using the following data, determine whether the utility should switch to monthly billing. The average receivables outstanding is one-half the average bill.

Billing frequency	Monthly	Bimonthly
Avg. bill	$75	$150
Processing cost/bill	$ 3	$ 3
Financial carrying cost	18%	18%
Bad-debt expense (As % of average accounts receivable)	0.5%	0.75%

2. The United Charities has been billing pledges on a quarterly basis for many years. In the recent recession, however, a discussion took place on the feasibility of increasing the billing frequency to speed collection and reduce unfulfilled pledges. Using the following data, determine whether United Charities should alter

its billing frequency. Pledges are collected evenly over the billing period.

Bill frequency	Monthly	Bimonthly	Quarterly
Average pledge	$ 50	$100	$150
Processing cost/bill	1.50	1.50	1.50
Financial carrying cost	12%	12%	12%
Dishonored pledges (as a % of average pledges)	3%	5%	7%

3. The financial manager of a privately owned emergency clinic must decide whether to pursue collection procedures against certain accounts or sell them to a collection firm, receiving a percentage of their face value. Using the following information, should the financial manager try to collect all accounts, sell them, or collect some and sell others?

Age of Account	Amount	No. of Customers	Cost of Collection/ Account	Probability of Collection	Selling Price, % of Face Value
60-90	$50,000	200	$15	0.6	50%
90-120	30,000	90	20	0.4	20%
120 +	15,000	65	25	0.2	10%

4. The local technical school has failed to collect student tuition and fees in certain cases and is considering a collection agency. The number of students, amounts owed, and probability of collecting amounts owed are as follows:

No. of students	Amount owed/student	Probability of collection
24	400	0.30
17	250	0.20
23	150	0.40

Collection expenses are $30 per student if pursued through the college business office. If a collection agency is hired, their fee is 40 percent of the amount collected, but the probability of collection is increased by 50 percent. Should the school pursue collection on its own or use the agency?

5. Monarch County Hospital receives most of its revenue from Medicare and insurance payments for services. As a county hospital, however, it

cares for all persons regardless of their ability to pay. They must decide whether to pursue collection procedures against their private paying patients themselves or turn them over to a collection agency. Several categories of patients, amounts owed, and probability of collection are itemized below:

No. of patients	Avg. size of bill due	Probability of collection
110	$125	0.4
70	500	0.3
20	1,500	0.25
5	5,000	0.15

Collection expenses are $60 per patient if pursued by the hospital collection department. If a collection agency is used, they keep 50 percent of all monies collected but the probability of collection is doubled. Should the hospital pursue collection procedures itself or use the collection agency?

6. A parochial school is considering offering a 5 percent discount if payment of the entire year's tuition is made on September 1. It normally bills on September 1 and February 1. Seventy-five percent of the tuition is paid within 30 days, 15 percent within 60 days, 5 percent within 90 days, and 5 percent within 120 days. If the school can invest the funds received at 10 percent and it has 500 students who pay $1000 each tuition, should the school offer the discount? The percentage of each payment group expected to take advantage of the discount is as follows:

No. of days prior to payment	
30 days	50%
60	25
90	10
120	5

7. The local scouting organization is considering using credit cards for the payment of donations to its annual fund-raising campaign. The total amount pledged, rather than paid immediately by cash, is $210,000. The average time it takes for a pledge to be collected is 90 days. Credit

card processing requires an average of 10 days before the money is deposited in the organization's bank account. Funds received through this process could be invested at 10 percent interest immediately. The organization writes off approximately 5 percent of its pledges as uncollectible. Using credit cards would eliminate one-half a clerical person and save $7,200 annually. The credit card company charges a fee of 5 percent for its services. Should the organization use credit cards for collection of pledges if one-half of the total amount pledged is expected to be paid by credit card?

8. What is the economic order quantity for an item which has usage, carrying, and ordering costs of (a) 750,000, $0.50, and $30, respectively; (b) 2,000,000, $0.15, and $40?

9. What is the economic order quantity for an item with an annual usage of 5,000,000, order costs of $25 per order, and carrying costs of $0.001 per item?

10. Determine the frequency of orders for items (a) and (b) in problem 8.

11. Determine the frequency of orders for the item in problem 9.

12. The local cancer society provides bandages for cancer patients but needs to minimize its inventory carrying costs and is not sure how much safety stock to maintain. The organization places orders in 5,000-unit lots. Inventory carrying costs are $0.05 per unit; if they run out, however, it costs them $2.50 per unit to obtain bandages from the local hospital. Probable distribution of bandages in a period is as follows:

Probability	Units distributed/period
0.1	3,800
0.1	4,200
0.15	4,600
0.3	5,000
0.15	5,400
0.1	5,800
0.1	6,200

What level of safety stock should be maintained if the analysis considers safety stock in 400-unit increments?

13. Community Hospital is unsure of the level of inventory of disposable sheets to maintain. Annual demand for sheets is 50,000 units. It costs $8 to place an order, and the carrying cost is $50 per 1,000 units. Demand per period is expected to deviate from the economic order quantity by the probabilities and percentages below. The cost of running out of disposable sheets is $0.25 per unit. What economic order quantity and safety stock should Community Hospital maintain? (Safety stock is maintained in 100-unit increments.)

Percent deviation from EOQ	Demand probability
-10	0.1
-5	0.2
0	0.4
+5	0.2
+10	0.1

ENDNOTES

1. Adapted from: John D. Stowe and John Leslie King, "Billing Cycles for Municipal Utilities," Special Bulletin 1977A, April 16, 1977) (Chicago: Municipal Finance Officers Association, 1977).
2. Lawrence J. Gitman, Principles of Managerial Finance, 2d ed. (New York: Harper and Row, Publishers, 1979), p. 203.
3. Horward J. Berman and Lewis E. Weeks, The Financial Management of Hospitals, 2d ed. (Ann Arbor, Mich,: Health Administration Press, 1974), p. 288.
4. Sistansu S. Mitha, Akron Business and Economic Review, Vol. 9, No. 1, (Spring, 1978), p. 46.
5. Berman and Weeks, p. 251.
6. Ibid., p. 266.
7. Ross H. Johnson and Paul R. Winn, Quantitative Methods for Management (Boston: Houghton Mifflin Co., 1976), p. 182.
8. Equation (8-2) may also be derived by calculus, differentiating Equation (8-1) with respect to Q

and setting the derivative equal to zero. The steps are:

$$\frac{dT}{dQ} = \frac{C}{2} - \frac{SO}{Q^2} = 0$$

$$= CQ^2 - 2SO = 0$$

$$Q^2 = \frac{2SO}{C}$$

$$Q = \sqrt{\frac{2SO}{C}}$$

9. The ordering and carrying costs are not equal because of rounding error.

10. Due to the complex nature of this type of cost, it is expressed as D for the sake of simplicity. The reader should bear in mind that stockout costs are a function of several factors such as demand, type of item, and order quantity.

SHORT-TERM FINANCING

The previous two chapters discussed the management of various current assets. Working capital management also involves decisions about the financing of current assets. The primary purpose of this chapter is to discuss the varied sources of short-term financing and to examine their associated costs. As discussed in Chapter 6, part of the decision regarding the investment in current assets involves a trade-off between the organization's ability to provide service and its ability to pay bills on time. As the not-for-profit organization reduces its investment in current assets, the level of services provided can be increased. The ability of the organization to pay its bills on time, however, is decreased since the pool of funds available to provide for contingencies is reduced. The financing of current assets is a decision which involves a trade-off between the cost of financing and the risk of not being able to pay bills on time.

SOURCES OF SHORT-TERM FINANCING

Short-term financing is a type of financing which generally requires repayment within a year or less. The three major forms of short-term financing for

not-for-profit organizations are accounts payable,
other liabilities, and short-term loans. Each of
these three major sources is discussed in the following sections.

Accounts Payable

When an organization purchases goods or services
from another organization, the seller often allows
the buyer a period of time before cash payment is
required. This short-term source, also know as
trade credit, results in the creation of an account
payable. Accounts payable, which are debt obligations arising from the regular activities of the
organization, are technically a form of short-term
debt.

The majority of trade credit is of the open
account type. The open account credit sale involves
the seller shipping the goods or providing the services to the buyer. The goods or services are
accompanied by an invoice that specifies the goods
or services provided, prices, and terms of the sale.
There is no formal acknowledgment of the debt. The
liability appears on the buyer's books as an accounts payable. Trade credit is extended based on
the seller's evaluation of the credit worthiness of
the buyer. Notes payable and trade acceptances,
types of trade credit in which the debt is formally
acknowledged, are used to a limited extent.

The use of accounts payable to finance working
capital affords flexibility and it is widely and
readily available. Except for organizations with
poor credit ratings, accounts payable is a spontan-
eous, almost automatic, source of short-term financing. Once approved for credit, there are no negotiations or special arrangements required. The
buyer is extended the credit upon delivery of the
goods or services, according to the terms of the
invoice.

Accounts payable affords flexibility in that its
level expands or contracts with the level of purchases. This source expands automatically to meet
increased requirements for funds during periods of
increased purchases. Likewise, the organization can
readily reduce its use during periods of decreased
activity. The use of accounts payable usually involves fewer restrictions on financial activities
than negotiated sources of funds. The major disadvantage of the use of accounts payable is its

cost. Before examining this issue, however, the credit terms usually associated with accounts payable will be explained.

"Credit terms" refer to the conditions under which trade credit is extended. Credit terms define the time for which credit is extended and the discount given for early payment. For example, credit terms are usually stated in the form, 2/10, net 30. This is interpreted as: a 2 percent cash discount is given if the bill is paid within 10 days of the date of the invoice. Otherwise, the full amount of the invoice is due by the 30th day. For a $1,000 invoice with the above terms, the buyer can discharge the obligation by paying $980 through the 10th day. If the discount is not taken, $1,000 is due by the 30th day. Similarly, if the discount is not taken there is no advantage to paying before the 30th day. In effect, $980 is the actual price of the goods or services with 10 days of free credit extended. Credit may be extended an additional 20 days by incurring a cost of $20. Another option is available; the buyer could decide to pay the invoice after the 30th day. Paying after the net date is known as "stretching the accounts payable." In this case a cost equal to the deterioration of the credit rating of the buyer is incurred. This could lead to higher financing charges and, if carried to an extreme, could result in denial of trade credit.

The use of trade credit involves a cost. The selling firm is, in effect, granting a loan. A loan involves some type of cost; it is not provided free of charge. The cost may be explicit or implicit. An explicit cost is a cost whose dollar value can be measured easily while an implicit cost is much more difficult to measure. The selling firm may increase the selling price of its goods or service in order to cover its cost of obtaining funds. To the extent that the selling cost includes financing costs, the buyer is incurring an implicit cost for the loan. Another implicit cost is the cost associated with stretching accounts payable. It is very difficult to measure the cost associated with a deterioration of credit rating.

It is much easier to calculate the cost of trade credit when the customer pays within the credit terms. The cost of accounts payable in this instance is equal to the explicit, or measurable, cost of trade credit. There is an explicit cost of zero if paid within the discount period. If the not-for-profit organization delays payment and foregoes the discount, it incurs a positive explicit cost.

Returning to the example of a $1000 invoice with credit terms of 2/10, net 30, the credit terms state that only $980 must be paid if the bill is paid within 10 days. If not paid until the 30th day, the full amount of the invoice, $1000, is due. The seller is, in essence, charging the buyer $20 to extend trade credit for 20 days. The percentage interest cost of not taking the discount, i_e, can be calculated by Equation 9-1:

$$i_e = \left[\frac{\text{Interest charge in dollars}}{\text{Principal}} \right] \times \left[\frac{365}{\text{Days principal borrowed}} \right] \qquad \text{(Equation 9-1)}$$

The first term expresses the interest expense on a percentage basis, and the second term converts the percentage to an annual basis. In this example the cost of not taking the discount is $20/980 or 2.04 percent. This is the cost for only 20 days of credit and must now be converted to an effective annual interest rate. This is done by multiplying this percentage by the number of twenty-day periods in a year. There are 365/20, or 18.25 twenty-day periods. Consequently, the cost of foregoing the cash discount for 2/10, net 30 terms is:

$$i_e = (2.04\%) \times (18.25) = 37.23\%$$

Equation 9-1 may be modified to calculate the cost of not taking the cash discount when the invoice amount is unknown. Equation 9-2 is the formula which may be used in this case.

$$i_e = \left[\frac{\text{Percent cash discount}}{100 \text{ minus percent cash discount}} \right] \times \left[\frac{365}{\text{Days principal borrowed}} \right]$$

$$\text{(Equation 9-2)}$$

Using our previous example and Equation 9-2, the cost of foregoing the discount equals (2/98) x (365/20) or 37.23 percent, the same value obtained with Equation 9-1.

The not-for-profit organization should compare the cost of foregoing cash discounts with the cost of obtaining funds from the best alternative short-term source. If a bank is willing to extend a short-term loan at a 10 percent annual interest rate, the organization should take the discount as long as the cost of foregoing the discount is above 10 percent. Table 9.1 lists the effective annual rates of not taking various cash discounts as computed by Equation 9-2. It is assumed the invoice is paid on the net due date if the discount is not taken.

TABLE 9.1

Credit Terms and the Effective Cost of Lost Discounts

Credit Terms	Effective Rate (%)
1/10, net 20	36.9
1/10, net 30	18.4
1/10, net 45	10.5
2/10, net 20	74.5
2/10, net 45	21.3

Source: Jerome Osteryoung and Daniel McCarty; Financial Management: Analytical Techniques (Columbus, Ohio: Grid Publishing, Inc., 1980), p. 215.

The not-for-profit organization can elect to reduce the explicit cost of foregoing cash discounts by not paying on the due date. Either Equation (9-1) or (9-2) may be used to determine the interest rate for payment on dates other than the due date. Suppose the organization elects to pay the invoice with 2/10, net 30 terms ten days after the due date. Using Equation 9-2, the explicit cost of paying ten days late is equal to:

$$\underline{i_e} = \left(\frac{2}{100-2}\right) \times \left(\frac{365}{30}\right) = (2.04) \times (12.17) = 24.83\%$$

By paying beyond the due date or "stretching the accounts payable" the not-for-profit organization lowers the effective interest rate, provided there is no penalty for late payment. The longer the accounts payable are stretched, the lower the effective interest rate. Although this practice reduces the explicit cost of foregoing the cash discount, it increases the implicit cost as a result of possible deterioration of the organization's credit rating. A history of slow payment may result in less favorable credit terms or even a discontinuance of credit. These possibilities increase the implicit costs associated with stretching accounts payable.

Other Liabilities

The other-liabilities category includes a variety of sources of short-term funds for not-for-profit organizations. It includes deferred gifts and dues. Gifts are reported as income in full in the year for which the gift is intended. If the recording of the gift is deferred to a future period, the gift is reported as a "deferred credit" on the balance sheet.[1] Grants-paid-in-advance is a similar source. Other sources of short-term funds are advance payments for such items as tuition, housing, and camps. A common characteristic of these sources of short-term financing is that they are generated spontaneously from the daily activities of the organization and have no explicit interest costs associated with them. There may be restrictions, however, on how the funds may be used.

In addition, the not-for-profit organization may utilize payables other than trade accounts payable which are generated by services being received prior to payment being made. These payables include salaries and wages, payroll taxes, deferred compensation, and interest. These short-term liabilities are a source of short-term funds to the organization. If immediate payment were required, instead of deferred payment, funds would have to be located to pay off the liability. These expenses vary with the level of operations and are provided at no cost to the organization.

A liability is incurred at the instant labor is furnished. For convenience and cost savings, employees are paid after the service is provided, usually at a fixed interval such as weekly, biweekly, or monthly. Employees, are, in effect, providing short-term financing during the interval that wages and salaries are deferred. The larger the payment interval the greater the amount of short-term financing provided by employees. The frequency of pay days may be changed to increase or decrease the amount of short-term financing provided in this manner. The effect of such a change is illustrated below.

Wages and Salaries Payable Example: Smith University has a semimonthly payroll of

$800,000. The university is considering changing to a monthly payroll which will reduce check writing and other processing expenses by $200 per payroll. The university normally pays 9 percent interest for short-term financing. What is the annual savings from changing from a biweekly to a monthly payroll?

With an $800,000 semimonthly payroll, the university has an average wages payable of $800,000/2 or $400,000 (assuming a zero level of wages payable at the beginning and $800,000 at the end of the payroll period). Changing to a monthly payroll doubles the average level of wages payable to $800,000. The university in effect will receive an additional $400,000 of interest-free financing. The opportunity cost of this additional financing is $400,000 x 0.09 or $36,000 per year. In addition, the university will save $200 per payroll twelve times during the year for a yearly saving of $2,400. The total benefit is $36,000 + $2,400 or $38,400 for the year. Note that there may be an implicit cost of employee dissatisfaction resulting from the stretched out pay period which must be considered in determining the net benefit of changing to a monthly payroll.

Short-Term Loans

Secured short-term loans, using accounts receivable and/or inventory as collateral, are usually not appropriate sources of financing for not-for-profit organizations. Unsecured loans, however, offered by commercial banks represent the major source of nontrade, short-term financing. Commercial banks receive deposits to checking and savings accounts. These funds are in turn loaned to individuals, business firms, and not-for-profit organizations. Short-term bank loans play a role similar to trade credit in the financing of current assets. The major difference between the two sources is the negotiation effort required to secure bank credit. The not-for-profit organization has to apply for the bank loan and supply information so the bank can evaluate the organization's integrity, intended use of the loan proceeds, and prospects for repayment. If granted, the short-term bank loan will be one of two basic kinds: a transaction loan or a line of credit arrangement.

Transaction Loans

A transaction loan is one that is negotiated and administered for a specific purpose. A promissory note is signed to acknowledge the indebtedness. The principal is usually repaid in one lump sum on the due date of the note. The note is often renewable but this requires additional negotiations and the creation of another transaction loan. This type of loan is used most often by organizations which encounter only an occasional need for short-term bank credit.

The interest on this or other types of loans may be calculated using one of several methods. Interest is the price received for lending money or the price paid to borrow money, depending on the view of the transaction. The lender thinks of the interest rate as a rate of return on the funds loaned, while the person borrowing thinks of the interest rate as a cost of borrowing expressed as a percentage of the funds borrowed.

At one time it was necessary to distinguish between simple interest stated on the loan and the effective, or true, rate of interest. As a result of "truth-in-lending laws," commercial banks and other lending institutions are not required to state the annual percentage rate (APR). The concepts of simple and annual percentage rates of interest are discussed below.

A loan may take either a discounted or nondiscounted form. Interest is paid in advance on the discounted note. The nondiscounted note requires payment of interest at maturity. In a discounted note, the simple interest rate is applied to the face amount of the note and this amount is subtracted from the face amount of the note to determine the proceeds of the loan the borrower actually receives. The dollar interest cost is based on the face amount of the loan but the borrower does not have use of the full face amount during the period of the loan. In contrast, interest on a nondiscounted note is paid at maturity. The dollar amount of interest is determined by applying the simple interest rate to the loan proceeds, which, in this case, is equal to the face amount.   With the same simple interest rate, the annual percentage rate for a discounted note is always higher than for a nondiscounted note since the loan proceeds are always less than the face amount for discounted notes.

To illustrate the calculation of annual percentage rates for discounted and nondis- counted notes: Johnson Research Foundation desires to borrow $10,000 for one year.   The simple interest rate is 10 percent. For a nondiscounted note the annual percentage rate (APR) is determined by dividing the annual dollar interest cost by the loan proceeds or:

$$\underline{APR} = \frac{\text{Annual interest payment}}{\text{Loan proceeds}} \qquad \text{(Equation 9-3)}$$

In this example the annual percentage rate equals

$$\underline{APR} = \frac{(0.10)\ (10,000)}{10,000} = 10\%$$

which is the same as the simple interest rate.

If this is a discounted note, the interest, 10% x $10,000 or $1,000, is subtracted ini- tially, leaving loan proceeds of $9,000, or 90 percent of the amount to be repaid.   The annual percentage rate is equal to

$$\underline{APR} = \frac{\text{Annual interest payment}}{\text{Loan proceeds}} = \frac{\$1,000}{\$9,000} = 11.11\%$$

Banks and other lending institutions typically charge add-on interest when making installment loans (principal and interest repaid in installments rath- er than one lump sum).   With an add-on loan, interest is added to the funds received to determine the face amount of the note.   If the Johnson Research Foundation in the above example   borrowed $10,000 to be repaid in twelve equal monthly installments at 10 percent add-on interest, it would still pay total interest charges of $1,000.   The foundation would sign a note for $11,000 and would make twelve equal monthly installments of $11,000 divided by 12,   or $916.67 per month.   Since the borrower makes periodic payments which reduce the outstanding balance of the loan, on an average the Johnson Research Foundation has use of only about one-half the amount of the loan proceeds received. The average amount of the original loan outstanding during the year is approximately $5,000. The approximate annual percentage rate,[2] AAPR, is:

$$\underline{AAPR} = \frac{\text{Annual interest payment}}{\text{Loan proceeds}/2} \qquad \text{(Equation 9-4)}$$

$$\underline{AAPR} = \frac{1,000}{10,000/2} = 20\%$$

Since the borrower has use of only about one-half of the loan proceeds, the effective annual rate is approximately twice the add-on rate.

Banks often require a compensating balance as a condition of granting a loan. The compensating balance is a minimum checking account balance that has to be maintained. The compensating balance is usually 15 to 20 percent of the amount of the loan outstanding. A compensating balance increases the annual percentage rate as shown in the following example.

Compensating Balance Example: Johnson Research Foundation wishes to borrow $10,000 on a nondiscounted note from First National Bank at a stated interest rate of 10 percent. The First National, however, requires a 20 percent compensating balance. What is the annual percentage rate of the loan?

First, since Johnson Research needs $10,000 to finance its current assets, the amount of the loan, $\underline{L}$, required by the foundation is equal to:

$$\underline{L} = \frac{\text{Funds needed}}{1 - \text{compensating balance required expressed as a decimal}} \qquad \text{(Equation 9-5)}$$

$$\underline{L} = \frac{10,000}{1 - 0.2} = \frac{10,000}{0.8} = \$12,500$$

Next, using the 10 percent stated interest, the annual interest expense is 0.10 x $12,500 or $1,250. Finally, using Equation 9-3, the annual percentage rate ($\underline{APR}$) is:

$$\underline{APR} = \frac{\text{Annual interest payment}}{\text{Loan proceeds}} = \frac{\$1,250}{\$10,000} = 12.5\%$$

The following equation can also be used to calculate the annual percentage rate when a compensating balance is required.

$$\underline{APR} = \frac{\text{Stated interest rate}}{1 - \text{compensating balance expressed as a decimal}} \qquad \text{(Equation 9-6)}$$

In the previous example:

$$\underline{APR} = \frac{10\%}{1 - 0.20} = \frac{10\%}{0.8} = 12.5\%$$

Line of Credit Agreements

The line of credit involves an arrangement between the bank and the organization whereby the bank agrees to loan up to a stipulated amount of unsecured short-term funds to the organization during the year.

The line of credit agreement is an informal arrangement, usually for one year, whereby the bank agrees to loan up to the maximum amount as an automatic line of credit if the bank has the funds available. However, the bank does not have to make the loan if funds are not available. This type of arrangement allows the not-for-profit organization to borrow repeatedly during the year without further negotiations as long as the outstanding balance does not exceed the specified limit.

The line of credit is intended only as a source of short-term financing. To accomplish this, banks generally require the borrower to "clean up" the line of credit annually for a period of 30 days or more. During this clean-up period, the debt balance on the line of credit must be equal to zero.

Most organizations have seasonal variations in their cash inflows and outflows. The line of credit is designed to provide temporary financing by filling the gap between cash inflows and outflows. As discussed in Chapter 4, the cash budget summarizes the organization's expected cash inflows, outflows, and cash balances for different subperiods within the planning horizon. By examining the cash budget, the financial manager can determine whether the borrowing needs are temporary or permanent. The line of credit can then be established at the amount equal to the largest cumulative negative net cash balance during the cash budget period.

The combination of the cash budget and the line of credit provides the financial manager with considerable flexibility in financial planning. By using the cash budget, the financial manager is able to anticipate temporary borrowing needs. Sufficient time is available to shop around and negotiate a line of credit, ensuring the availability of funds when actually needed.

Line of Credit Example: A basic monthly cash budget for Municipal Hospital is shown in Table 9.2. By determining the cumulative investment (borrowing), the bottom line of Table 9.2, the financial manager is able to anticipate the maximum amount of temporary borrowing necessary in year 19X0. Maximum borrowing will occur in May when $95,000 will be needed to cover all cash outflows. The table also allows the financial manager to determine that no borrowed funds will be required before April nor after September.

In January, 19X0, then, the financial manager can negotiate a line of credit with the First National Bank for $100,000 for the coming year. The extra $5,000 is requested as a buffer against the uncertainty associated with a forecasted cash budget. The cash budget itself may also be used in the negotiation process to convince the bank's loan officer that the financing needs are temporary and that the hospital will be able to repay the debt promptly.

As the cash shortage becomes imminent on April 1, the financial manager signs a 180-day promissory note for $95,000. At that time, he has only $60,000 credited to the hospital's checking account to provide for the shortage of funds in April. By doing this, the financial manager has "taken down" $60,000 of the total line of credit.[3] The hospital is still able to borrow an additional $40,000. An additional $35,000 will be taken down in May to provide for that month's cash shortage. The total $95,000 borrowed will then be repaid from the surplus cash generated during June, July, August, and September. The loan balance is reduced to zero by October and the hospital has excess cash to invest during the last quarter of the year.

TABLE 9.2

Monthly Cash Budget for Municipal Hospital for 19X0

	January	February	March	April	May	June
Beginning cash balance	$100,000	$100,000	$100,000	$100,000	$100,000	$100,000
Cash receipts	310,000	250,000	285,000	290,000	305,000	315,000
Total cash available	$410,000	$350,000	$385,000	$390,000	$405,000	$415,000
Cash disbursements	$305,000	$240,000	$300,000	$350,000	$340,000	$310,000
Cash available end of period	105,000	110,000	85,000	40,000	65,000	105,000
Less: Minimum cash balance	100,000	100,000	100,000	100,000	100,000	100,000
Surplus (shortage)	$ 5,000	$ 10,000	($15,000)	($60,000)	($35,000)	$ 5,000
Cumulative investment (borrowing)	$ 5,000	$ 15,000	$ 0	($60,000)	($95,000)	($90,000)

	July	August	September	October	November	December
Beginning cash balance	$100,000	$100,000	$100,000	$100,000	$100,000	$100,000
Cash receipts	325,000	328,000	325,000	342,000	330,000	310,000
Total cash available	$425,000	$428,000	$425,000	$442,000	$430,000	$410,000
Cash disbursements	$300,000	$305,000	$290,000	$285,000	$278,000	$295,000
Cash available end of period	125,000	123,000	135,000	157,000	152,000	115,000
Less: Minimum cash balance	100,000	100,000	100,000	100,000	100,000	100,000
Surplus (shortage)	$ 25,000	$ 23,000	$ 35,000	$ 57,000	$ 52,000	$ 15,000
Cumulative investment (borrowing)	($65,000)	($42,000)	($ 7,000)	$ 50,000	$102,000	$117,000

SUMMARY

In this chapter several sources of short-term financing were identified. The major sources available to the not-for-profit organization are accounts payable (trade credit), other liabilities, and short-term loans. Accounts payable represent the major source of interest-free financing; however, the cost of foregoing cash discounts on accounts payable and paying beyond the due date must be considered. Other liabilities represent another source of interest-free financing but their flexibility is generally quite limited.

Loans from commercial banks represent the major source of unsecured, nontrade, short-term financing. Secured short-term loans, using accounts receivable and inventories as collateral, are usually not appropriate sources of financing for not-for-profit organizations. Bank loans negotiated as needed are known as transaction loans.

Next, the three ways of calculating interest on bank loans, simple interest, discounted interest, and add-on interest, were discussed. Finally, pre-arranged bank loans known as lines of credit were explained. An example was used to illustrate the flexibility of the line of credit as a source of short-term financing.

QUESTIONS

1. What are the sources of short-term financing? Briefly describe each of them.

2. What are credit terms? What is meant by the term 1/15, net 60?

3. What is meant by explicit and implicit costs of trade credit?

4. What types of other liabilities constitute sources of short-term financing?

5. What are the major sources of short-term loans?

6. What is a transaction loan?

7. Explain the difference between a discounted and a nondiscounted loan.

8. What is an add-on installment loan?

9. What is a compensating balance? How does it relate to the effective interest rate of a loan?

10. What is a line of credit?

PROBLEMS

1. Using Equation 9-1, calculate the interest cost of not taking the discount on a $10,000 purchase with terms of 3/10, net 60.

2. Using Equation 9-1, calculate the interest cost

of not taking the discount on a $75,000 purchase with terms of 1-1/2 /15, net 45.

3. Using Equation 9-2, calculate the cost of foregoing the discount on purchase terms of 2/10, net 30.

4. Using Equation 9-2, calculate the cost of foregoing the discount on purchase terms of 1/20, net 45.

5. What is the cost of foregoing the discount on purchase terms of 2/10, net 30? If you can "stretch" payment of the payable to 60 days without any penalty, what is the new cost of foregoing the discount?

6. The Hempstead Hospital currently pays all hourly personnel on a weekly basis. In order to cut costs, it is considering switching to a biweekly payroll. Processing costs are $175 per payroll regardless of whether there are weekly or biweekly pay periods. The weekly payroll is $20,000. The hospital would be able to invest idle funds at 12 percent interest. How much would the hospital save by changing to a biweekly payroll?

7. The city of Anderson wanted to change from a biweekly to monthly payroll to effect cost savings. The employees, however, strongly objected to this move. As an alternative, the city proposed a semimonthly payroll (24 pay periods per year), which the workers accepted. Determine savings if payroll processing costs are $310 per period, the annual payroll is $2,600,000, and idle funds may be invested at 10 percent interest.

8. What is the APR for a bank discount loan of $200,000 at 12 percent interest?

9. What is the APR for a bank discount loan of $750,000 at 14 percent interest?

10. What is the approximate annual percentage rate for an add-on loan of $50,000 at 15 percent interest if repayment is made in 12 equal monthly installments?

11. The Unity Church needs $30,000 for one year to finance some church repairs. It is a simple interest loan with an 11 percent interest rate; the bank, however, requires a compensating balance of $2,000. What is the APR?

12. A local social service agency needs $10,000 for one year. The bank will loan it the money at 12 percent interest under the bank discount note; in addition, the agency must maintain a compensating balance of $1,000. What is the APR for this transaction?

13. Prince county must negotiate a line of credit with the bank for the coming year. Using the following information, prepare a cash budget and determine the amounts and the timing of borrowing using the line of credit. The beginning cash balance is $20,000.

	Cash receipts	Cash disbursements	Minimum cash balance
January	$200,000	$185,000	$20,000
February	300,000	190,000	25,000
March	600,000	200,000	25,000
April	300,000	200,000	25,000
May	150,000	210,000	30,000
June	150,000	210,000	30,000
July	130,000	195,000	30,000
August	130,000	195,000	25,000
September	110,000	180,000	25,000
October	90,000	180,000	25,000
November	120,000	190,000	20,000
December	220,000	190,000	20,000

14. The Kinder Child Center must prepare a cash budget for its first six months of operation and negotiate a line of credit to carry it through these first months. Prepare the basic cash budget; however, in the final determination of the timing and amounts of borrowing using the line of credit, assume that excess funds can be invested or shortages borrowed at the beginning of the month and incorporate the interest, paid at the beginning of the following month, within the budget. Funds may be invested at 10 percent and borrowed at 15 percent. The beginning cash balance is $200,000, representing the initial funding for the center.

	Cash receipts	Cash disbursements	Minimum cash balance
January	2,000	100,000	10,000
February	3,000	70,000	10,000
March	6,000	65,000	10,000
April	20,000	35,000	10,000
May	25,000	30,000	10,000
June	40,000	30,000	10,000

ENDNOTES

1. Malvern J. Gross, Jr. and Stephen F. Jablonsky, _Principles of Accounting and Reporting for Nonprofit Organizations_ (New York: John Wiley & Sons, 1979), p. 204.
2. This is an approximation of the true effective interest rate. The true rate involves solution of the following equation:

$$\$10,000 = \sum_{t=1}^{12} \$916.67 \left[\frac{1}{1 + \underline{R}}\right].$$

   $\underline{R}$ = 1.4997% per month or 17.97% per year.

3. Eugene F. Brigham, _Financial Management Theory and Practice_, 2d ed (Hinsdale, Ill.: The Dryden Press, 1979), p. 325.

10

TIME VALUE OF MONEY

Most not-for-profit organizations make decisions in which benefits or costs occur in different time periods. It is critical to the decision process that these timing differences are neutralized. The time value of money concept allows us to make decisions when benefits and/or costs occur in more than one year.

A dollar available today does not have the same value as a dollar received at some time in the future. The dollar today is worth more than the future dollar because today's dollar can be invested and earn interest; it can then be reclaimed in the future along with this interest. Since the value of money changes over time, we need some method of comparing the value of money available at different points in time. The concept of future value allows us to calculate the future value of sums, including both the principal and interest earned on the investment. This technique is also useful in determining interest and growth rates associated with cash flows. On the other hand, the concept of discounting allows us to determine the present value of cash flows received in the future. Discounting of future cash flows is the inverse of compounding to find the future value of cash flows and involves taking into consideration the opportunity cost of

232

money. This concept is the key to evaluation of future cash flows associated with capital projects. It is also used to determine the prices and yields-to-maturity of bonds.

This chapter examines the concepts, terminology, and calculations of future and present values. The equations, tables, and computations associated with these two essential concepts are explained. The chapter contains two major sections. The first section is devoted to future-value concepts and applications. Present-value concepts and selected applications are discussed in the second section.

COMPOUND INTEREST - FUTURE VALUE CONCEPTS

Compounding involves the process of converting a known value today into some greater value at a later date. This process is most commonly associated with savings institutions. If $1,000 is placed in a bank paying 6 percent annually, the amount of money in the account at the end of the year, two years, or three years can be determined systematically. First, several terms must be defined:

PV = principal sum in dollars at time zero

FV_n = future value at the end of n periods

i = interest rate per period

At the end of year 1, the account would contain the principal sum plus the interest for one period, or a future value determined as follows:

$$FV_1 = PV + (PV)i = PV (1 + i) \qquad \text{(Equation 10-1)}$$

Using Equation 10-1 in the above example yields

$$FV_1 = \$1,000 (1.0 + 0.06) = \$1,000 (1.06) = \$1,060$$

at the end of year 1.

The value at the end of two years, FV_2, is found as follows:

$$FV_2 = FV_1 (1 + i)$$

Substituting the value of FV_1 from Equation 10-1 into this expression results in:

$$FV_2 = PV (1 + i)(1 + i)$$
$$= PV (1 + i)^2$$

(Equation 10-2)

Continuing the example of $1,000 compounded at 6 percent annually yields

$$FV_2 = \$1,000 (1 + 0.06)^2$$
$$= \$1,000 (1.1236)$$
$$= \$1,123.60$$

at the end of year 2. Similarly, FV_3, the balance at the end of the three years is found as follows:

$$FV_3 = FV_2 (1 + i) = PV (1 + i)^3$$

(Equation 10-3)

In the example, then:

$$FV_3 = \$1,000 (1.06)^3$$
$$= \$1,000 (1.1910)$$
$$= \$1,191.00$$

The general equation for determining FV_n, the amount of money at the end of n periods, is:

$$FV_n = PV (1 + i)^n$$

(Equation 10-4)

Equation 10-4 is the basic equation of compound interest. Equations 10-1, 10-2, and 10-3 are just special cases of Equation 10-4, where n equals 1, 2, and 3, respectively.

A simple example illustrates the application of the future value concept:

Future-Value Example: Rodgers University places $500 in a savings account which earns 5 percent interest compounded annually. How much money will there be in the savings account at the end of eight years? Substituting PV = $500, i = 0.05, and n = 8 into Equation 10-4 yields the following value at the end of year 8.

$$FV_8 = \$500 (1.05)^8$$
$$= \$500 (1.4775)$$
$$= \$738.75$$

> The savings account will be worth $738.75 at
> the end of eight years.

Fortunately, future values can be calculated in a less cumbersome fashion than using Equation 10-4. In solving Equation 10-4 in the previous example, 1.05 was raised to the eighth power. Compound interest tables have been compiled which simplify compound interest calculations. These tables contain values for the expression, $(1 + i)^n$, in Equation 10-4 for a wide range of interest rates and periods. The values for $(1 + i)^n$ are known as future-value interest factors. The future-value interest factor for a principal of $1 compounded at i percent for n years is referred to as $FVIF_{i,n}$:

$$FVIF_{i,n} = (1 + i)^n \qquad \text{(Equation 10-5)}$$

Table A.1 in the Appendix contains future-value interest factors. A sample portion of Table A.1 is given in Table 10.1.

The future-value interest factor can now be used to determine the value of $500 invested at 5 percent for eight years by substituting Equation 10-5 into Equation 10-4:

$$FV_n = PV (FVIF_{i,n}) \qquad \text{(Equation 10-6)}$$

Looking in Table 10.1, the interest factor for eight periods and 5 percent interest factor is 1.477. This is the value of $1 compounded at 5 percent for eight years. The value of $500 at the end of eight years can be determined using Equation 10-6.

$$
\begin{aligned}
FV_8 &= PV (FVIF_{5\%,\ 8\ yrs}) \\
&= \$500\ (1.477) \\
&= \$738.50
\end{aligned}
$$

$$\text{(Equation 10-6)}$$

This is the same value obtained using the longer method of Equation 10-4, except for a slight difference due to rounding.

Figure 10.1 illustrates the following relationships between future-value interest factors, the number of periods interest is earned, n, and various interest rates, i: the higher the interest rate, the greater the future-value factor; at any given interest rate, the future value increases as time, n, increases; the future value factor at zero percent interest always equals one.

TABLE 10.1

Future Value Interest Factors for One Dollar, $FVIF_{i,n}$

Period	Interest Rates (%)								
	4	5	6	7	8	9	10	11	12
1	1.0400	1.0500	1.0600	1.0700	1.0800	1.0900	1.1000	1.1100	1.1200
2	1.0816	1.1025	1.1236	1.1449	1.1664	1.1881	1.2100	1.2321	1.2544
3	1.1249	1.1576	1.1910	1.2250	1.2597	1.2950	1.3310	1.3676	1.4049
4	1.1699	1.2155	1.2625	1.3108	1.3605	1.4116	1.4641	1.5181	1.5735
5	1.2167	1.2763	1.3382	1.4026	1.4693	1.5386	1.6105	1.6851	1.7623
6	1.2653	1.3401	1.4185	1.5007	1.5869	1.6771	1.7716	1.8704	1.9738
7	1.3159	1.4071	1.5036	1.6058	1.7138	1.8280	1.9487	2.0762	2.2107
8	1.3686	1.4775	1.5938	1.7182	1.8509	1.9926	2.1436	2.3045	2.4760
9	1.4233	1.5513	1.6895	1.8385	1.9990	2.1719	2.3579	2.5580	2.7731
10	1.4802	1.6289	1.7908	1.9672	2.1589	2.3674	2.5937	2.8394	3.1058

236

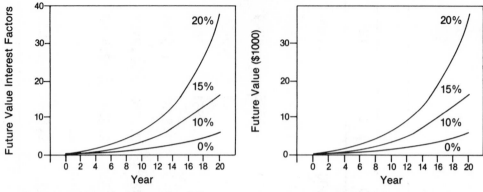

(A) Amount Which $1 Grows After *T* Years
at Various Interest Rates

(B) Amount Which $1000 Grows After *T* Years
at Various Interest Rates

FIGURE 10.1   The relationship between future-value interest factors, time, and interest rates.

Source: J. Fred Weston and Eugene F. Brigham, Essentials of Managerial Finance, 5th ed. (Hinsdale, Ill.:   The Dryden Press, 1979), p. 258.

Intrayear Compounding

Up to this point in the discussion of future values, annual compounding, i.e., interest paid at the end of one-year intervals, has been implied.   In most cases, interest is paid more frequently than once a year.   Interest on bonds is usually paid semiannually.   Financial institutions such as credit unions often pay interest quarterly.   Some savings institutions will pay interest daily or even continuously.   The following material discusses semiannual and quarterly compounding, with a general equation for intrayear compounding presented.

One thousand dollars invested in a bank at an annual rate of 6 percent interest compounded semiannually results in interest credited to the account every six months.   In this case, one-half of the annual interest payment (1/2) ($1,000) (0.06) or $30, is credited to the account at the end of the first six months.   For the second six-month period, however, $1030 earns interest so that (1/2) (1,030) (0.06) or $30.90 in interest is earned during this period.   At the end of one year, $1,030 plus $30.90 or $1,060.90 is in the account.   Note that interest paid with semiannual compounding is 90 cents greater than it would have been under annual compounding.

The future-value factor for $1 invested for one year at an annual rate of 6 percent interest compounded semiannually may be determined in the following manner:

$$FV_1 = \$1 \ (1 + \frac{0.06}{2})^{2 \times 1}$$

$$FV_1 = \$1 \ (1 + 0.03)^2$$

$$FV_1 = 1.0609$$

For \$1,000 invested at an annual rate of 6 percent interest compounded semiannually, the future value is equal to \$1,000 (1.0609) or \$1,060.90, the same value determined previously.

The general equation for intrayear compounding is:

$$FV_n = PV \ (1 + \frac{i}{t})^{tn} \qquad \text{(Equation 10-7)}$$

where t = number of times a year interest is compounded,

i = annual interest rate,

FV_n = future value at end of n annual periods, and

PV = present value.

If \$1 is substituted for PV, this formula can also be used to calculate the future-value factors in Table A.1 of the Appendix.

Intrayear Compounding Example: Equation 10-7 can be used to determine the future value of \$1,000 invested in a bank at 8 percent interest compounded quarterly. The future value at the end of the year is equal to:

$$FV_1 = \$1,000 \ (1 + \frac{0.08}{4})^{(4)(1)}$$

$$= \$1,000 \ (1 + 0.020)^4$$

$$= \$1,000 \ (1.0824)$$

$$FV_1 = \$1,082.40$$

This problem can also be worked using the future-value factors in Table A.1. Since there are four compounding periods per year, we must divide the interest rate by four and multiply the number of periods by four. The future-value factor for 2 percent and 4 periods is 1.082. Using this value in Equation 10-4 yields:

$$\underline{FV}_4 = 1000 \ (1.082) = \$1,082$$

in the account at the end of the year with quarterly compounding.

Future Value of an Annuity

Many times the future value of a series of even annual cash flows must be determined. A series of even cash flows, either received or paid, is known as a fixed annuity. For example, if $1,000 is deposited at the end of each year in a bank, how much will there be in the account at the end of six years if interest is paid at a rate of 6 percent compounded annually? The first $1,000 deposited at the end of year 1 earns interest for five years. The deposit at the end of year 2 earns interest for only four years and so on. The number of years each deposit earns interest is shown in Column 3 of Table 10.2. Column 4 of Table 10.2 gives the future-value factors for single sums left on deposit at 6 percent interest for zero through five years with annual compounding. Multiplying the annual $1000 deposit by the appropriate factor yields its value at the end of year 6. These values are shown in Column 5

Table 10.2

Calculation of the Sum of a $1,000 6-Year Annuity Compounded at 6 Percent

(1) End of year	(2) Payment	(3) Number of years compounded	(4) Compound interest factor	(5) Compound value
1	$1,000	5	1.338	$1,338
2	1,000	4	1.262	1,262
3	1,000	3	1.191	1,191
4	1,000	2	1.124	1,124
5	1,000	1	1.060	1,060
6	1,000	0	1.000	1,000
			6.975	

Total at end of year 6--$6,975

and are $1,338, $1,262, $1,191, $1,124, $1,060, and $1,000 for payments at the end of years 1 through 6, respectively. The total amount available at the end of year 6 is equal to the sum of the value of all six payments or $6,975.

In equation form, Column 5 in Table 10.2 was calculated by:

Amount at end
of year 6 = $1,000 (1.338) + $1,000 (1.262)
+ $1,000 (1.191) + $1,000 (1.124)
+ $1,000 (1.060) + $1,000 (1.000)

Since this is a fixed annuity in which the cash flow is a constant, the calculations can be simplified as follows:

Amount at end
of year 6 = $1,000 (1.338 + 1.191 + 1.124
+ 1.060 + 1.000) = $1,000 (6.975)

In other words, in determining the total value of the annuity, the constant annuity amount can also be multiplied by the sum of the future-value interest factors. A general equation for the sum of an annuity is:

$$S_N = A \left(\sum_{n=1}^{N} FVIF_{i,n} \right)$$ (Equation 10-8)

where S_N = sum of an annuity after N payments, A = amount deposited or received at end of each year, N = number of years annuity is paid or received, and $FVIF_{i,n}$ = future-value interest factor for nth period at i annual interest rate.

Future-value interest factors do not have to be summed in order to solve the previous example. To simplify calculations, sum of annuity tables have been compiled and are presented in Table A.2 of the Appendix. A portion of the sum of an annuity table has been reproduced in Table 10.3. The individual FVIFs for n periods are summed in order to develop the sum of an annuity factor for i percent and n periods, designated as $SAF_{i,n}$. In equation form this is:

$$S_N = A(SAF_{i,n})$$ (Equation 10-9)

where S_N = sum of annuity after N periods and A = amount deposited or received at the end of each year.

To calculate the sum of six annual $1,000 annuity payments compounded annually at 6 percent using the

TABLE 10.3

Sum of an Annuity Factor for One Dollar per Period

Period	4	5	6	7	8	9	10	11	12
1	1.0000	1.0000	1.0000	1.0000	1.0000	1.0000	1.0000	1.0000	1.0000
2	2.0400	2.0500	2.0600	2.0700	2.0800	2.0900	2.1000	2.1100	2.1200
3	3.1216	3.1525	3.1836	3.2149	3.2464	3.2781	3.3100	3.3421	3.3744
4	4.2465	4.3101	4.3746	4.4399	4.5061	4.5731	4.6410	4.7097	4.7793
5	5.4163	5.5256	5.6371	5.7507	5.8666	5.9847	6.1051	6.2278	6.3528
6	6.6330	6.8019	6.9753	7.1533	7.3359	7.5233	7.7156	7.9129	8.1152
7	7.8983	8.1420	8.3938	8.6540	8.9228	9.2004	9.4872	9.7833	10.0890
8	9.2142	9.5491	9.8975	10.2598	10.6366	11.0285	11.4359	11.8594	12.2997
9	10.5828	11.0266	11.4913	11.9780	12.4876	13.0210	13.5795	14.1640	14.7757
10	12.0061	12.5779	13.1808	13.8164	14.4866	15.1929	15.9374	16.7220	17.5487

Interest Rates (%)

factors in Table 10.3, locate the $\underline{SAF}_{6\%,6}$ (6 percent interest and six years) factor which is equal to 6.9753. The sum of a $1,000 annuity is ($1,000)6.975.30 or $6,975.30, which is the same value obtained using the longer method shown in Table 10.2.

Future-Value Applications

The future-value concepts discussed in this chapter have many important applications in financial management. Two major applications are discussed in this section: accumulation of a future sum and determination of growth rates.

Accumulation of a Future Sum

It is often necessary to determine the annual payments required to accumulate a fixed sum at some time in the future.

> For example, a city must have $750,000 available in five years to retire a bond issue. If the city earns 6 percent on its investments, how much must it set aside in equal annual deposits to accumulate $750,000 at the end of five years? In other words, what fixed annuity will result in a sum equal to $750,000 at the end of year 5? This problem, which involves the sum of an annuity, is represented in the time diagram of Figure 10.2.

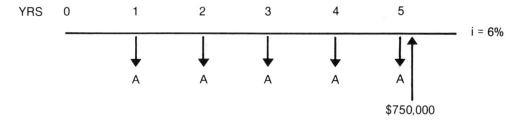

FIGURE 10.2 **Time diagram of accumulation for a future sum problem.**

This problem involves the determination of the size of the annual payments, <u>A</u>. Solving

Equation 10-9 for $\underline{A}$ yields:

$$\underline{A} = \frac{SN}{SAF_{\underline{i},\underline{N}}} \qquad \text{(Equation 10-10)}$$

The size of the payment is equal to the future sum divided by the sum of the annuity factor. Substitution of the future sum of $750,000 and the sum of an annuity factor for 6 percent and five years from Table 10.3 into Equation 10-1 results in

$$\underline{A} = \frac{\$750,000}{5.637} = 133,049.49$$

The city can deposit $133,049.49 per year for 5 years at 6 percent and have $750,000 available for retirement of the bond issue.

Interest and Growth Rates

The finance officer of Alexander City has an opportunity to invest $10,000 today which will yield $14,693 five years from now. Before making a decision about the investment, the finance officer must determine its growth rate, or rate of return. The time diagram of this type of problem is shown in Figure 10.3. The present and future values, along

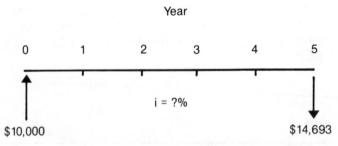

FIGURE 10.3 Time diagram of growth rate problem.

with the number of periods, are known in this problem. However, the interest rate which equates the present value of $10,000 to the future value of $14,693 when compounded for five periods is unknown.
 This type of problem can be solved using the future-value tables by finding in the table the interest rate which equates the $10,000 present value to the $14,693 sum five years from now.[1] Solving Equation 10-6 for the future-value interest

factor, $\underline{FVIF}_{\underline{i},\underline{n}}$ yields:

$$\underline{FVIF}_{\underline{i},\underline{n}} = \frac{\overline{FV}_5}{\overline{PV}} \qquad\qquad \text{(Equation 10-11)}$$

Substituting the present and future values into Equation 10-11 yields a future-value interest factor of:

$$\underline{FVIF}_{\underline{i},\underline{n}} = \frac{\$14,693}{\$10,000} = 1.4693$$

The future-value factor for $\underline{i}$ percent for five years is equal to 1.4693. Using a future-value table, such as Table 10.1 or Table A.1, the interest rate at $\underline{n}$ equal to five years that most closely corresponds to an $\underline{FVIF}$ of 1.4693 is 8 percent. This investment, then, yields 8 percent compounded annually.

The problem of determining the interest rate on a loan is handled in the same manner as finding the growth rate. A loan of $10,000 which requires $14,693 to be repaid at the end of five years is equivalent to the above example. It is still necessary to determine the interest rate which equates the $10,000 present value to the $14,693 sum five years from now. The only difference from the previous example is that loan interest is paid instead of being received.

DISCOUNTING - PRESENT VALUE CONCEPTS

In many instances, the value of a sum of money to be received in the future is known but its value today must be determined. The dollar available today does not have the same value as the dollar received in the future. Today's dollar is worth more than the future dollar since today's dollar can be loaned or invested and reclaimed with interest in the future. The concept of present value, or discounting, allows us to take into consideration the opportunity cost associated with not having the dollar today.

Imagine attending a Dollar Fair where certificates which are redeemable in cash in some future year with absolute certainty are auctioned. The auctioneer puts a certificate up for bid which can be redeemed for $100 in one year. The amount you are willing to pay for the certificate today is its current or present value. The value of the certificate in one year is its future or compound value. If the current rate of interest is 10 percent, what would you be willing to bid for the $100 to be received at the end of one year? Recall that future value is calculated using Equation 10-4:

$$FV_n = PV (1 + i)^n$$

where FV_n = future value in dollars at the end of period n, PV = present value in dollars, i = interest rate in percent, and n = number of periods.

Substituting the above values into Equation 10-4 yields

$$\$100 = PV (1 + 0.10)^1$$

$$PV = \frac{\$100}{1.10} = \$90.91$$

This simple calculation shows that $90.91 invested today at 10 percent interest will yield $100 one year from now. Assuming that 10 percent is the realistic rate of interest available in the economy, you would then be willing to bid an amount not exceeding $90.91 for the $100 certificate. Rearranging the terms of Equation 10-4 yields a general equation for present value:

$$PV = \frac{FV_n}{(1 + i)^n} \qquad \text{(Equation 10-12)}$$

For example, the present value of $1,000 received in three years and discounted at a 6 percent annual rate is:

$$PV = \frac{1000}{(1 + 0.06)^3} = \frac{1000}{1.1910} = \$839.62$$

Profit-oriented firms use these concepts of present and future value in making a number of business decisions such as long-term asset selections. In effect, they see possible projects on an auction block which produce inflows in future years but require current cash investments. In order to bid wisely, they must determine the present value of these future cash inflows so that the current investment does not exceed the present value of the return. Not-for-profit organizations should also use the present and future-value concepts stated in Equation 10-12 in order to take into account that a dollar available today is more valuable than one received in the future.

Since determining the present value of a project can be very time-consuming, present-value tables which contain values for $1/(1 + i)^n$, the present-value interest factors, have been developed. The present-value interest factor for $1 discounted at i percent for n periods is referred to as $PVIF_{i,n}$:

$$PVIF_{i,n} = \frac{1}{(1 + i)^n} \qquad \text{(Equation 10-13)}$$

Table A.3 of the Appendix contains present-value interest factors for $1 received in years 1 through 25, n, at annual interest rates of 1 through 40 percent, i. A portion of Table A.3 is given in Table 10.4.

The present-value interest factors may be used to find the current equivalent value of any future amount by multiplying the factor by that sum:

$$PV = FV_n(PVIF_{i,n}) \qquad \text{(Equation 10-14)}$$

For example, the present value of $1,000 received at the end of six years if the interest rate is 8 percent is equal to the $PVIF_{(8\%, 6)}$ multiplied by $1,000. From Table 10.4, the $PVIF_{(8\%, 6)}$ is 0.6301; $1,000 received in six years at 8 percent is equal to only $630.20 now. One interpretation of this example is that a person would be indifferent to receiving $630.20 today or $1,000 in six years if his/her opportunity cost is 8 percent; i.e. the funds could be invested today to earn 8 percent interest.

Intrayear Discounting

Again, up to this point in the discussion of present values it has been implicitly assumed that interest is paid annually. This assumption must be relaxed since interest is often paid or received more often than once a year. Recall that the general formula for finding the compound or future value with intrayear compounding was expressed in Equation 10-7:

$$FV_n = PV \left(1 + \frac{i}{t}\right)^{tn}$$

TABLE 10.4

Present Value Factors for One Dollar, $\text{PVIF}_{i,n}$

Interest Rates (%)

Period	4	5	6	7	8	9	10	11	12
1	0.96154	0.95238	0.94340	0.93458	0.92593	0.91743	0.90909	0.90090	0.89286
2	0.92456	0.90703	0.89000	0.87344	0.85734	0.84168	0.82645	0.81162	0.79719
3	0.88900	0.86384	0.83962	0.81630	0.79383	0.77218	0.75131	0.73119	0.71178
4	0.85480	0.82270	0.79209	0.76290	0.73503	0.70843	0.68301	0.65873	0.63552
5	0.82193	0.78353	0.74726	0.71299	0.68058	0.64993	0.62092	0.59345	0.56743
6	0.79031	0.74622	0.70496	0.66634	0.63017	0.59627	0.56447	0.53464	0.50663
7	0.75992	0.71068	0.66506	0.62275	0.58349	0.54703	0.51316	0.48166	0.45235
8	0.73069	0.67684	0.62741	0.58201	0.54027	0.50187	0.46651	0.43393	0.40388
9	0.70259	0.64461	0.59190	0.54393	0.50025	0.46043	0.42410	0.39092	0.36061
10	0.67556	0.61391	0.55839	0.50835	0.46319	0.42241	0.38554	0.35218	0.32197

This equation can also be solved for the present value to derive a general formula for finding the present value with interest paid more frequently than once a year:

$$PV = \frac{FV_n}{(1 + i/t)^{tn}} = FV_n \frac{1}{(1 + i/t)^{tn}} \quad \text{(Equation 10-15)}$$

where t = number of times a year interest is compounded, i = annual interest rate, FV_n = future value at end of period n, PV = present value, and n = number of periods.

The present value of \$1,000 received at the end of year 1 discounted at an annual rate of 8 percent compounded quarterly can be calculated using Equation 10-15 as shown:

$$PV = \frac{\$1,000}{(1 + 0.08/4)^{(4)(1)}} = \frac{\$1,000}{(1.02)^4} = \frac{\$1,000}{1.0824} = \$923.85$$

The present value of \$1,000 received at the end of one year at a discount rate of 8 percent with no intrayear compounding is \$925.93. Therefore, intrayear compounding tends to reduce present values of a future sum. This should be evident since intrayear compounding increases the annual discount rate which would, in turn, decrease the present value.

The preceding problem can also be solved using the present-value factors in Table A.3. Since there are four compounding periods per year, the annual interest rate of 8 percent must be divided by four and the number of periods multiplied by four. The present-value factor for i equal to 2 percent and n equal to four periods is 0.9238. The present value of the \$1,000 at the end of the year then, using Equation 10-14 is,

$$PV_4 = \$1,000 \ (0.9238) = \$923.80.$$

This is the same value obtained previously, except for the rounding error.

Present Value of an Annuity

Frequently, an asset produces a constant stream of benefits over a number of years. Here, too, the present-value tables are helpful. What would you be willing to pay for an investment that returns annual cash benefits of \$680 for three years? In other

words, what is the present value of a series of
equal annual cash flows of $680 for three years?

One method of evaluating the present value of
this cash flow is to sum the present values of each
separate annual cash flow. Assuming a 10 percent
discount rate, this would be:

PV = $680(0.909) + $680(0.826) + $680(0.751)

Since the task of discounting each benefit is tedious, it is simpler to factor the $680 producing:

PV = $680(0.909) + 0.826 + 0.751) = $680(2.486)

Notice that this last bracketed expression, the
summation of the relevant present-value factors, is
the present-value factor for a constant amount or
fixed annuity of three years at 10 percent interest.
In the present value of an annuity table, Table A.4
of the Appendix, the present-value factors have
already been summed for various time periods and
discount rates. Part of Table A.4 has been reproduced in Table 10.5. This annuity table aids in the
evaluation of a fixed flow of benefits over a number
of years. Observe that the present value of an
annuity table shows the present-value factor of i =
10 percent and n = three years as 2.4868, the same
factor above except for a slight rounding error.

The general equation for finding the present
value of an annuity is:

$$PVA = A(PVAF_{i,n}) \qquad \text{(Equation 10-16)}$$

where PVA = present value of an annuity, A = amount
deposited or received at end of each period, and
$PVAF_{i,n}$ = present value of an annuity factor for i
percent and n periods.

Some additional examples will help to illustrate
the uses of Table 10.5. What is the present value
of a constant cash flow of $2,000 per year for four
years at a 6 percent discount rate? Using Table
10.5 or Table A.4, the $PVAF_{6\%,4}$ is 3.4651 and the
present value of the annuity is $2,000(3.4651) =
$6.930. This $6,930 can also be interpreted as that
amount which, if deposited today in a bank paying
interest of 6 percent, will yield $2,000 a year for
the next four years.

Flows which vary from year to year can also be
evaluated using the present value of an annuity
table. What is the present value of flow of $600

TABLE 10.5

Present Value of One Dollar Per Year, $\underline{n}$ Years at $i\%$

Interest Rates (%)

Period	4	5	6	7	8	9	10	11	12
1	0.96154	0.95238	0.94340	0.93458	0.92593	0.91743	0.90909	0.90090	0.89286
2	1.88609	1.85941	1.83339	1.80802	1.78326	1.75911	1.73554	1.71252	1.69005
3	2.77509	2.72325	2.67301	2.62432	2.57710	2.53129	2.48685	2.44371	2.40183
4	3.62990	3.54595	3.46511	3.38721	3.31213	3.23972	3.16986	3.10245	3.03735
5	4.45182	4.32948	4.21236	4.10020	3.99271	3.88965	3.79079	3.69590	3.60478
6	5.24214	5.07569	4.91732	4.76654	4.62288	4.48592	4.35526	4.23054	4.11141
7	6.00205	5.78637	5.58238	5.38929	5.20637	5.03295	4.86842	4.71220	4.56376
8	6.73274	6.46321	6.20979	5.97130	5.74664	5.53482	5.33493	5.14612	4.96764
9	7.43533	7.10782	6.80169	6.51523	6.24689	5.99525	5.75902	5.53705	5.32825
10	8.11090	7.72173	7.36009	7.02358	6.71108	6.41766	6.14457	5.88923	5.65022

annually for three years followed by a flow of $900 in years 4 and 5 if the discount rate is currently 12 percent? This combined flow can be factored into two annuities, $600 a year for five years and $300 a year in years 4 and 5. The present value of $600 at 12 percent for five years is:

$$\$600(3.605) = \$2,163$$

The present value of $300 in years 4 and 5 equals the present value of an annuity of $300 for five years minus the present value of an annuity of $300 for the first three years. Numerically, this equals:

$$\$300(3.605) - \$300(2.402)$$

which simplifies to:

$$\$300(3.605 - 2.402) = \$300(1.203) = \$360.90$$

The total present value of the annuity then is:

$$\$2,163 + \$360.90 = \$2,523.90$$

Present-Value Applications

The present-value concept has many important applications in the not-for-profit sector. The concept is applicable any time a known future-dollar amount must be converted to a current value. Three important applications, amortization of a loan, determination of interest rates, and determination of bond values, are demonstrated in the following sections.

Amortization of a Loan

Frequently, a not-for-profit organization is concerned with determining the annual payments necessary to amortize a loan. By amortization is meant the constant payment which will be sufficient to retire the principal over the life of the loan as well as pay the interest on the outstanding balance at any time. For example, Regional Hospital borrows $200,000 for five years from the City State Bank at an 8 percent interest rate. How large must the annual payments be to retire the $200,000 balance by the end of five years and pay the 8 percent interest on the outstanding balance? A time diagram of this problem is shown in Figure 10.4.

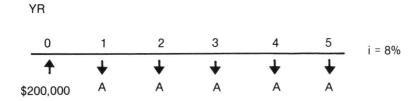

YR

FIGURE 10.4 Time diagram of amortization of a loan problem.

Notice that this type of problem requires equating an unknown stream of future payments to a known present value of an annuity. This loan amortization problem is solved by rearranging Equation 10-16 as shown:

$$\underline{A} = \frac{PVA}{PVAF_{\underline{i,n}}}$$ (Equation 10-17)

The size of the annual payment is the present value of the annuity $\underline{A}$, which equals the loan principal, divided by the present value of an annuity factor for i percent and n periods. From Table 10.5 the $\underline{PVA}$ (8%, 5 years) is equal to 3.993. Substituting into Equation 10-17 yields:

$$\underline{A} = \frac{\$2,000,000}{3.993} = \$50,087.65$$

The hospital can make payments of $50,087.65 per year for five years to repay the $200,000 loan and the 8 percent interest compounded annually on the outstanding principal balance.

Determination of Interest Rates

The determination of interest rates is similar to the determination of growth rates, except the present-value concept is used instead of future value.

To illustrate, the finance officer of the Bierman Rehabilitation Center is considering borrowing $10,000 to provide working capital for a new project. If the bank requires

repayment at an annual rate of $2,570 for
five years, what rate of interest is being
charged? Figure 10.5 depicts a time diagram
for this type of problem.

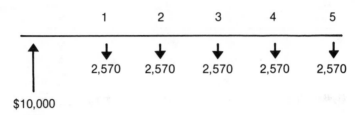

FIGURE 10.5 Time Diagram

This problem involves determining the interest rate that equates a stream of known
future payments to a known present value of
$10,000. Since it requires translating an
annuity into an equivalent present value,
the present value of an annuity table should
be used. Solving Equation 10-16 for the
present value of an annuity factor, $PVAF_{i,n}$,
yields:

$$PVAF_{i,n} = \frac{PVA}{A} \qquad \text{(Equation 10-18)}$$

Substituting the problem values into this
equation:

$$PVAF_{i,n} = \frac{\$10,000}{2.570} = 3.8911$$

Examining Table A.4 for the present value of
annuity factors for n equal to 5 years, it
is found that the interest rate that corresponds closest to 3.8911 is 9 percent. Consequently, the bank would be charging a 9
percent annual interest rate.

Bond Values

A bond is simply a long-term IOU or promise to
pay the face amount of the bond at the maturity
date. A periodic rent, or interest, is paid for the
use of the other person's money. Bonds typically
pay interest semiannually. Frequently, we are concerned with calculating the current price of a bond.

The current price is equal to the present value of the cash flows received by the bond holder. The cash flows are the periodic interest payments and the principal payment at maturity. In equation form:

$$P = \sum_{t=1}^{m} \frac{(F)(C)}{(1+k)^m} + \frac{F}{(1+k)^m} \qquad \text{(Equation 10-19)}$$

where P = current price of the bond, F = face amount of the bond, C = coupon rate of the bond, k = market discount rate = return currently available on bonds of similar risk and maturity, and m = maturity of the bond. By using present-value and present value of annuity factors, Equation 10-19 can be rewritten as:

$$P = FC\ (PVAF_{k\%,m}) + F\ (PVF_{k\%,m})$$

$$\text{(Equation 10-20)}$$

Since interest is usually paid semiannually, factors for one-half the discount rate and twice the number of years to maturity must be found and the interest payment, FC, has to be divided by two.

For example, what is the current price of an Alexander City Electric Revenue Bond? The bond matures in 20 years, pays 7 percent coupon interest semiannually, and the face amount of the bond is $5,000. The market rate currently available on municipal bonds of similar risk and maturity is 6 percent.

The bond holder receives an annuity equal to $(F)(C)/2$ every six months for 40 periods. In addition, the bond holder receives $5,000 at the end of 40 six-month periods. Substituting these values into Equation 10-20 yields:

$$P = \frac{(5000)(0.07)}{2}\ PVAF_{(3\%,40)} + \$5000\ PVF_{(3\%,40)}$$

$$P = 175(23.115) + 5000(0.307)$$

$$= \$4045 + \$1535$$

$$P = \$5,580$$

The present value of the interest payments only is $4,045, while the present value of the $5,000 face value received at the end of 20 years is $1,535. The current selling price of the bond is equal to the sum of these two cash flows or $5,580.

SUMMARY

This chapter has examined the relationship between sums of money received today and sums of money received in the future. Future-value techniques allow us to determine the future value of some known present value of an interest-bearing asset. The inverse of future value, discounting, or the determination of the present value of a known future sum was also examined. These techniques allow us to translate future values into present values and vice versa. This chapter explained the equations, tables, and calculations associated with these two essential concepts.

The chapter also examined the concepts associated with the determination of the present and future values of annuities. An annuity is a fixed payment or receipt of funds for a specified period of time. Selected applications involving accumulation of a future sum, amortization of a loan, determination of interest and growth rates, and determination of bond values were also presented.

The techniques and concepts presented in this chapter provide the basic tools for comparing alternative proposals which have costs and benefits occurring in different time periods. By neutralizing the effect of these timing differences we are able to develop the decision models presented in the following two chapters.

QUESTIONS

1. Explain the meaning of the term <u>time value of money</u>.

2. How are the present value and the future value of a single sum related to one another?

3. What is meant by intrayear compounding?

4. What is an annuity? A fixed annuity?

5. What is meant by the term <u>discounting</u> when considering the time value of money?

6. What is meant by the term <u>loan</u> <u>amortization?</u>

7. How is the future value of an annuity factor related to the future value of a single sum factor?

8. How is the present value of an annuity factor related to the present value factor for a single sum?

9. Explain some examples of the uses of the various present-value and future-value concepts for both single sums and annuities.

PROBLEMS

1. What will the future value of $2,500 invested at 6 percent interest be in 5 years? In 10 years?

2. What will the future value of $12,000 invested at 10 percent interest be in 3 years? In 6 years?

3. St. John's Church has received $30,000 in donations for its building fund. If these funds can be invested at 4 percent, how much will the church have at the end of 6 years? How much will the church have at the end of 6 years if the funds are invested at 12 percent?

4. What will the future value of $5,000 invested at 8 percent annual interest be at the end of 5 years with annual, semiannual, and quarterly compounding?

5. What will the future value of $150,000 invested at 10 percent annual interest be at the end of 5 years with annual and semiannual compounding?

6. What is the future value of a 10-year fixed annuity of $2,000 per year invested at 6 percent?

7. What is the future value of a 5-year fixed annuity of $25,000 per year invested at 12 percent?

8. What is the future value of a 4-year fixed annuity of $100,000 per year, paid in semiannual installments of $50,000 each, invested at 10 percent?

9. The city of Manitou must have $200,000 at the end of 5 years. How much must it set aside annually in equal installments to accumulate the $200,000 if interest rates on investments are 10 percent?

10. What interest rate must the city controller earn of an initial investment of $25,000 if he wants to have $49,975 at the end of 9 years?

11. What interest rate is the local service agency paying on its loan of $15,000 if it must pay $24,157.50 at the end of 5 years?

12. What is the present value of $10,000 received at the end of 10 years if interest rates are 12 percent? 6 percent?

13. What is the present value of $5,000 received at the end of 5 years at an 8 percent interest rate with annual, semiannual, and quarterly compounding?

14. Which alternative should a foundation prefer--to receive $100,000 now or $150,000 at the end of 7 years? Interest rates on investments are 8 percent.

15. What is the present value of a fixed annuity of $500 annually for 10 years if the interest rate is 4 percent?

16. What is the present value of a fixed annuity of $25,000 paid semiannually for 5 years if interest rates are 8 percent?

17. What is the future value of an 8-year fixed annuity of $2000 per year at 10 percent interest?

18. What is the future value of an 8-year fixed annuity of $1000 paid semiannually at 10 percent interest?

19. What will the required annual installment

payments be if a $500,000 loan at 12 percent interest is to be repaid over 8 years?

20. If $25,000 is borrowed for 10 years at 8 percent interest, how much will each installment have to be if payments are made semiannually?

21. If $200,000 is borrowed by the United Agency for 5 years, what rate of interest is being charged if it must make annual payments of $52,760 on the loan?

22. How much would an investor be willing to pay for an investment which yields $100 every 6 months for 10 years with a lump sum payment of $2000 at the end of 10 years, if the annual interest rate is 12 percent?

23. How much will a 10-year, 7 percent $1000 face-value bond sell for currently if interest rates are now 12 percent?

ENDNOTES

1. This type of problem can also be solved using the present-value factors presented in the following section.

APPENDIX–TABLE A-1 FVIF (Future Value Interest Factors)

Interest rate, I, %

Periods, n	1	2	3	4	5	6	7	8	9	10	11	12	13	14	15
1	1.0100	1.0200	1.0300	1.0400	1.0500	1.0600	1.0700	1.0800	1.0900	1.1000	1.1100	1.1200	1.1300	1.1400	1.1500
2	1.0201	1.0404	1.0609	1.0816	1.1025	1.1236	1.1449	1.1664	1.1881	1.2100	1.2321	1.2544	1.2769	1.2996	1.3225
3	1.0303	1.0612	1.0927	1.1249	1.1576	1.1910	1.2250	1.2597	1.2950	1.3310	1.3676	1.4049	1.4429	1.4815	1.5209
4	1.0406	1.0824	1.1255	1.1699	1.2155	1.2625	1.3108	1.3605	1.4116	1.4641	1.5181	1.5735	1.6305	1.6890	1.7490
5	1.0510	1.1041	1.1593	1.2167	1.2763	1.3382	1.4026	1.4693	1.5386	1.6105	1.6851	1.7623	1.8424	1.9254	2.0114
6	1.0615	1.1262	1.1941	1.2653	1.3401	1.4185	1.5007	1.5869	1.6771	1.7716	1.8704	1.9738	2.0820	2.1950	2.3131
7	1.0721	1.1487	1.2299	1.3159	1.4071	1.5036	1.6058	1.7138	1.8280	1.9487	2.0762	2.2107	2.3526	2.5023	2.6600
8	1.0829	1.1717	1.2668	1.3686	1.4775	1.5938	1.7182	1.8509	1.9926	2.1436	2.3045	2.4760	2.6584	2.8526	3.0590
9	1.0937	1.1951	1.3048	1.4233	1.5513	1.6895	1.8385	1.9990	2.1719	2.3579	2.5580	2.7731	3.0040	3.2519	3.5179
10	1.1046	1.2190	1.3439	1.4802	1.6289	1.7908	1.9672	2.1589	2.3674	2.5937	2.8394	3.1058	3.3946	3.7072	4.0456
11	1.1157	1.2434	1.3842	1.5395	1.7103	1.8983	2.1049	2.3316	2.5804	2.8531	3.1518	3.4785	3.8359	4.2262	4.6524
12	1.1268	1.2682	1.4258	1.6010	1.7959	2.0122	2.2522	2.5182	2.8127	3.1384	3.4985	3.8960	4.3345	4.8179	5.3502
13	1.1381	1.2936	1.4685	1.6651	1.8856	2.1329	2.4098	2.7196	3.0658	3.4523	3.8833	4.3635	4.8980	5.4924	6.1528
14	1.1495	1.3195	1.5126	1.7317	1.9799	2.2609	2.5785	2.9372	3.3417	3.7975	4.3104	4.8871	5.5348	6.2613	7.0757
15	1.1610	1.3459	1.5580	1.8009	2.0789	2.3966	2.7590	3.1722	3.6425	4.1772	4.7846	5.4736	6.2543	7.1379	8.1371
16	1.1726	1.3728	1.6047	1.8730	2.1829	2.5404	2.9522	3.4259	3.9703	4.5950	5.3109	6.1304	7.0673	8.1372	9.3576
17	1.1843	1.4002	1.6528	1.9479	2.2920	2.6928	3.1588	3.7000	4.3276	5.0545	5.8951	6.8660	7.9861	9.2765	10.7613
18	1.1961	1.4282	1.7024	2.0258	2.4066	2.8543	3.3799	3.9960	4.7171	5.5599	6.5436	7.6900	9.0243	10.5752	12.3755
19	1.2081	1.4568	1.7535	2.1068	2.5270	3.0256	3.6165	4.3157	5.1417	6.1159	7.2633	8.6128	10.1974	12.0557	14.2318
20	1.2202	1.4859	1.8061	2.1911	2.6533	3.2071	3.8697	4.6610	5.6044	6.7275	8.0623	9.6463	11.5231	13.7435	16.3665
21	1.2324	1.5157	1.8603	2.2788	2.7860	3.3996	4.1406	5.0338	6.1088	7.4002	8.9492	10.8038	13.0211	15.6676	18.8215
22	1.2447	1.5460	1.9161	2.3699	2.9253	3.6035	4.4304	5.4365	6.6586	8.1403	9.9336	12.1003	14.7138	17.8610	21.6447
23	1.2572	1.5769	1.9736	2.4647	3.0715	3.8197	4.7405	5.8715	7.2579	8.9543	11.0263	13.5523	16.6266	20.3616	24.8915
24	1.2697	1.6084	2.0328	2.5633	3.2251	4.0489	5.0724	6.3412	7.9111	9.8497	12.2392	15.1786	18.7881	23.2122	28.6252
25	1.2824	1.6406	2.0938	2.6658	3.3864	4.2919	5.4274	6.8485	8.6231	10.8347	13.5855	17.0001	21.2305	26.4619	32.9189
26	1.2953	1.6734	2.1566	2.7725	3.5557	4.5494	5.8074	7.3964	9.3992	11.9182	15.0799	19.0401	23.9905	30.1666	37.8568
27	1.3082	1.7069	2.2213	2.8834	3.7335	4.8223	6.2139	7.9881	10.2451	13.1100	16.7386	21.3249	27.1093	34.3899	43.5353
28	1.3213	1.7410	2.2879	2.9987	3.9201	5.1117	6.6488	8.6271	11.1671	14.4210	18.5799	23.8839	30.6335	39.2045	50.0656
29	1.3345	1.7758	2.3566	3.1187	4.1161	5.4184	7.1143	9.3173	12.1722	15.8631	20.6237	26.7499	34.6158	44.6931	57.5754
30	1.3478	1.8114	2.4273	3.2434	4.3219	5.7435	7.6123	10.0627	13.2677	17.4494	22.8923	29.9599	39.1159	50.9501	66.2118
31	1.3613	1.8476	2.5001	3.3731	4.5380	6.0881	8.1451	10.8677	14.4618	19.1943	25.4104	33.5551	44.2010	58.0832	76.1435
32	1.3749	1.8845	2.5751	3.5081	4.7649	6.4534	8.7153	11.7371	15.7633	21.1138	28.2056	37.5817	49.9471	66.2148	87.5651
33	1.3887	1.9222	2.6523	3.6484	5.0032	6.8406	9.3253	12.6760	17.1820	23.2252	31.3082	42.0915	56.4402	75.4849	100.6998
34	1.4026	1.9607	2.7319	3.7943	5.2533	7.2510	9.9781	13.6901	18.7284	25.5477	34.7521	47.1425	63.7774	86.0528	115.8048
35	1.4166	1.9999	2.8139	3.9461	5.5160	7.6861	10.6766	14.7853	20.4140	28.1024	38.5748	52.7996	72.0685	98.1002	133.1755

Periods, n	16	17	18	19	20	21	22	23	24	25	26	27	28	29	30
1	1.1600	1.1700	1.1800	1.1900	1.2000	1.2100	1.2200	1.2300	1.2400	1.2500	1.2600	1.2700	1.2800	1.2900	1.3000
2	1.3456	1.3689	1.3924	1.4161	1.4400	1.4641	1.4884	1.5129	1.5376	1.5625	1.5876	1.6129	1.6384	1.6641	1.6900
3	1.5609	1.6016	1.6430	1.6852	1.7280	1.7716	1.8158	1.8609	1.9066	1.9531	2.0004	2.0484	2.0972	2.1467	2.1970
4	1.8106	1.8739	1.9388	2.0053	2.0736	2.1436	2.2153	2.2889	2.3642	2.4414	2.5205	2.6014	2.6844	2.7692	2.8561
5	2.1003	2.1924	2.2878	2.3864	2.4883	2.5937	2.7027	2.8153	2.9316	3.0518	3.1758	3.3038	3.4360	3.5723	3.7129
6	2.4364	2.5652	2.6996	2.8398	2.9860	3.1384	3.2973	3.4628	3.6352	3.8147	4.0015	4.1959	4.3980	4.6083	4.8268
7	2.8262	3.0012	3.1855	3.3793	3.5832	3.7975	4.0227	4.2593	4.5077	4.7684	5.0419	5.3288	5.6295	5.9447	6.2749
8	3.2784	3.5115	3.7589	4.0214	4.2998	4.5950	4.9077	5.2389	5.5895	5.9605	6.3528	6.7675	7.2058	7.6686	8.1573
9	3.8030	4.1084	4.4355	4.7854	5.1598	5.5599	5.9874	6.4439	6.9310	7.4506	8.0045	8.5948	9.2234	9.8925	10.6045
10	4.4114	4.8068	5.2338	5.6947	6.1917	6.7275	7.3046	7.9259	8.5944	9.3132	10.0857	10.9153	11.8059	12.7614	13.7858
11	5.1173	5.6240	6.1759	6.7767	7.4301	8.1403	8.9117	9.7489	10.6571	11.6415	12.7080	13.8625	15.1116	16.4622	17.9216
12	5.9360	6.5801	7.2876	8.0642	8.9161	9.8497	10.8722	11.9912	13.2148	14.5519	16.0120	17.6053	19.3428	21.2362	23.2981
13	6.8858	7.6987	8.5994	9.5964	10.6993	11.9182	13.2641	14.7491	16.3863	18.1899	20.1752	22.3588	24.7588	27.3947	30.2875
14	7.9875	9.0075	10.1472	11.4198	12.8392	14.4210	16.1822	18.1414	20.3191	22.7374	25.4207	28.3957	31.6913	35.3391	39.3738
15	9.2655	10.5387	11.9737	13.5895	15.4070	17.4494	19.7423	22.3140	25.1956	28.4217	32.0301	36.0625	40.5648	45.5875	51.1859
16	10.7480	12.3303	14.1290	16.1715	18.4884	21.1138	24.0856	27.4462	31.2426	35.5271	40.3579	45.7994	51.9230	58.8078	66.5417
17	12.4677	14.4265	16.6722	19.2441	22.1861	25.5477	29.3844	33.7588	38.7408	44.4089	50.8510	58.1652	66.4614	75.8621	86.5042
18	14.4625	16.8790	19.6733	22.9005	26.6233	30.9127	35.8490	41.5233	48.0386	55.5111	64.0722	73.8698	85.0706	97.8622	112.4554
19	16.7765	19.7484	23.2144	27.2516	31.9480	37.4043	43.7358	51.0737	59.5679	69.3889	80.7310	93.8147	108.8904	126.2422	146.1920
20	19.4608	23.1056	27.3930	32.4294	38.3376	45.2593	53.3576	62.8206	73.8641	86.7362	101.7211	119.1446	139.3797	162.8524	190.0496
21	22.5745	27.0336	32.3238	38.5910	46.0051	54.7637	65.0963	77.2694	91.5915	108.4202	128.1685	151.3137	178.4060	210.0796	247.0645
22	26.1864	31.6293	38.1421	45.9233	55.2061	66.2641	79.4175	95.0413	113.5735	135.5253	161.4924	192.1683	228.3596	271.0027	321.1838
23	30.3762	37.0062	45.0076	54.6487	66.2474	80.1795	96.8894	116.9008	140.8311	169.4066	203.4804	244.0538	292.3003	349.5933	417.5388
24	35.2364	43.2973	53.1090	65.0320	79.4968	97.0172	118.2050	143.7880	174.6306	211.7582	256.3853	309.9482	374.1444	450.9756	542.8005
25	40.8742	50.6578	62.6686	77.3881	95.3962	117.3908	144.2101	176.8592	216.5420	264.6978	323.0454	393.6343	478.9048	581.7583	705.6407
26	47.4141	59.2697	73.9490	92.0918	114.4754	142.0429	175.9364	217.5369	268.5121	330.8722	407.0372	499.9156	613.0002	750.4282	917.3329
27	55.0004	69.3455	87.2598	109.5893	137.3706	171.8719	214.6424	267.5704	333.0850	413.5903	512.8669	634.8928	784.6371	968.0525	1192.5333
28	63.8004	81.1342	102.9666	130.4112	164.8447	207.9650	261.8637	329.1115	412.8640	516.9879	646.2122	806.3140	1004.3362	1248.8545	1550.2933
29	74.0085	94.9271	121.5005	155.1893	197.8136	251.6377	319.4736	404.8072	511.9514	646.2349	814.2275	1024.0199	1285.5503	1611.0229	2015.3813
30	85.8499	111.0646	143.3706	184.6753	237.3763	304.4814	389.7578	497.9128	634.8198	807.7935	1025.9265	1300.5037	1645.5044	2078.2188	2619.9956
31	99.5858	129.9456	169.1772	219.7636	284.8516	368.4226	475.5044	612.4326	787.1765	1009.7419	1292.6675	1651.6396	2106.2456	2680.9023	3405.9941
32	115.5196	152.0364	198.6293	261.5186	341.8218	445.7915	580.1155	753.2922	976.0991	1262.1772	1628.7611	2097.5825	2695.9944	3458.3640	4427.7891
33	134.0027	177.8826	234.5625	311.2070	410.1860	539.4077	707.7417	926.5494	1210.5629	1577.7215	2052.2390	2663.8298	3450.8730	4461.0896	5756.1289
34	155.4432	208.1226	276.9638	370.3364	492.2231	652.6833	863.4441	1139.6558	1500.8499	1972.1521	2585.8213	3383.1909	4417.1172	5754.8046	7482.9676
35	180.3141	243.5035	327.9971	440.7004	590.6682	789.7468	1053.4016	1401.7769	1861.0540	2465.1902	3258.1350	4296.6523	5653.9102	7424.0313	9727.8594

APPENDIX–TABLE A-2 SAF (Sum of Annuity Factor)

Interest rate, I, %

Periods, n	1	2	3	4	5	6	7	8	9	10	11	12	13	14	15
1	1.0000	1.0000	1.0000	1.0000	1.0000	1.0000	1.0000	1.0000	1.0000	1.0000	1.0000	1.0000	1.0000	1.0000	1.0000
2	2.0100	2.0200	2.0300	2.0400	2.0500	2.0600	2.0700	2.0800	2.0900	2.1000	2.1100	2.1200	2.1300	2.1400	2.1500
3	3.0301	3.0604	3.0909	3.1216	3.1525	3.1836	3.2149	3.2464	3.2781	3.3100	3.3421	3.3744	3.4069	3.4396	3.4725
4	4.0604	4.1216	4.1836	4.2465	4.3101	4.3746	4.4399	4.5061	4.5731	4.6410	4.7097	4.7793	4.8498	4.9211	4.9934
5	5.1010	5.2040	5.3091	5.4163	5.5256	5.6371	5.7507	5.8666	5.9847	6.1051	6.2278	6.3528	6.4803	6.6101	6.7424
6	6.1520	6.3081	6.4684	6.6330	6.8019	6.9753	7.1533	7.3359	7.5233	7.7156	7.9129	8.1152	8.3227	8.5355	8.7537
7	7.2135	7.4343	7.6625	7.8983	8.1420	8.3938	8.6540	8.9228	9.2004	9.4872	9.7833	10.0890	10.4047	10.7305	11.0668
8	8.2857	8.5830	8.8923	9.2142	9.5491	9.8975	10.2598	10.6366	11.0285	11.4359	11.8594	12.2997	12.7573	13.2328	13.7268
9	9.3685	9.7546	10.1591	10.5828	11.0266	11.4913	11.9780	12.4876	13.0210	13.5795	14.1640	14.7757	15.4157	16.0853	16.7858
10	10.4622	10.9497	11.4639	12.0061	12.5779	13.1808	13.8164	14.4866	15.1929	15.9374	16.7220	17.5487	18.4197	19.3373	20.3037
11	11.5668	12.1687	12.8078	13.4864	14.2068	14.9716	15.7836	16.6455	17.5603	18.5312	19.5614	20.6546	21.8143	23.0445	24.3493
12	12.6825	13.4121	14.1920	15.0258	15.9171	16.8699	17.8884	18.9771	20.1407	21.3843	22.7132	24.1331	25.6502	27.2707	29.0017
13	13.8093	14.6803	15.6178	16.6268	17.7130	18.8821	20.1406	21.4953	22.9534	24.5227	26.2116	28.0291	29.9847	32.0886	34.3519
14	14.9474	15.9739	17.0863	18.2919	19.5986	21.0151	22.5505	24.2149	26.0192	27.9750	30.0949	32.3926	34.8827	37.5811	40.5047
15	16.0969	17.2934	18.5989	20.0236	21.5786	23.2760	25.1290	27.1521	29.3609	31.7725	34.4053	37.2797	40.4174	43.8424	47.5804
16	17.2579	18.6393	20.1569	21.8245	23.6575	25.6725	27.8881	30.3243	33.0034	35.9497	39.1899	42.7533	46.6717	50.9803	55.7175
17	18.4304	20.0121	21.7616	23.6975	25.8404	28.2129	30.8402	33.7502	36.9737	40.5447	44.5008	48.8837	53.7391	59.1176	65.0751
18	19.6147	21.4123	23.4144	25.6454	28.1324	30.9057	33.9990	37.4502	41.3013	45.5992	50.3959	55.7497	61.7251	68.3941	75.8364
19	20.8109	22.8406	25.1169	27.6712	30.5390	33.7600	37.3790	41.4463	46.0185	51.1591	56.9395	63.4397	70.7494	78.9692	88.2118
20	22.0190	24.2974	26.8704	29.7781	33.0659	36.7856	40.9955	45.7620	51.1601	57.2750	64.2028	72.0524	80.9468	91.0249	102.4436
21	23.2392	25.7833	28.6765	31.9692	35.7192	39.9927	44.8652	50.4229	56.7645	64.0025	72.2651	81.6987	92.4699	104.7684	118.8101
22	24.4716	27.2990	30.5368	34.2480	38.5052	43.3923	49.0057	55.4567	62.8733	71.4027	81.2143	92.5026	105.4910	120.4360	137.6316
23	25.7163	28.8450	32.4529	36.6179	41.4305	46.9958	53.4361	60.8933	69.5319	79.5430	91.1479	104.6029	120.2048	138.2970	159.2764
24	26.9734	30.4219	34.4265	39.0826	44.5020	50.8156	58.1767	66.7648	76.7898	88.4973	102.1741	118.1552	136.8315	158.6586	184.1678
25	28.2432	32.0303	36.4593	41.6459	47.7271	54.8645	63.2490	73.1059	84.7009	98.3470	114.4133	133.3339	155.6196	181.8708	213.7793
26	29.5256	33.6709	38.5530	44.3117	51.1134	59.1564	68.6765	79.9544	93.3240	109.1818	127.9988	150.3339	176.8501	208.3327	245.7120
27	30.8209	35.3443	40.7096	47.0842	54.6691	63.7058	74.4838	87.3508	102.7231	121.0999	143.0786	169.3740	200.8406	238.4993	283.5686
28	32.1291	37.0512	42.9309	49.9676	58.4026	68.5281	80.6977	95.3388	112.9682	134.2099	159.8173	190.6989	227.9499	272.8892	327.1040
29	33.4504	38.7922	45.2189	52.9663	62.3227	73.6398	87.3465	103.9659	124.1354	148.6309	178.3972	214.5827	258.5833	312.0935	377.1697
30	34.7849	40.5681	47.5754	56.0849	66.4388	79.0582	94.4608	113.2832	136.3075	164.4940	199.0209	241.3327	293.1990	356.7866	434.7451
31	36.1327	42.3794	50.0027	59.3283	70.7608	84.8017	102.0730	123.3459	149.5752	181.9434	221.9132	271.2925	332.3149	407.7368	500.9569
32	37.4941	44.2270	52.5028	62.7015	75.2988	90.8898	110.2181	134.2135	164.0370	201.1378	247.3236	304.8477	376.5160	465.8200	576.1005
33	38.8690	46.1116	55.0778	66.2095	80.0638	97.3432	118.9334	145.9506	179.8003	222.2515	275.5292	342.4294	426.4631	531.9133	661.6553
34	40.2577	48.0338	57.7302	69.8579	85.0670	104.1838	128.2588	158.6267	196.9823	245.4767	306.8374	384.5208	482.9033	607.5198	765.3652
35	41.6603	49.9945	60.4621	73.6522	90.3203	111.4348	138.2369	172.3168	215.7108	271.0242	341.5894	431.6633	546.6807	693.5725	881.1699

Periods, n	16	17	18	19	20	21	22	23	24	25	26	27	28	29	30
1	1.0000	1.0000	1.0000	1.0000	1.0000	1.0000	1.0000	1.0000	1.0000	1.0000	1.0000	1.0000	1.0000	1.0000	1.0000
2	2.1600	2.1700	2.1800	2.1900	2.2000	2.2100	2.2200	2.2300	2.2400	2.2500	2.2600	2.2700	2.2800	2.2900	2.3000
3	3.5056	3.5389	3.5724	3.6061	3.6400	3.6741	3.7084	3.7429	3.7776	3.8125	3.8476	3.8829	3.9184	3.9541	3.9900
4	5.0665	5.1405	5.2154	5.2913	5.3680	5.4457	5.5242	5.6038	5.6842	5.7656	5.8480	5.9313	6.0156	6.1008	6.1870
5	6.8771	7.0144	7.1542	7.2966	7.4416	7.5892	7.7396	7.8926	8.0484	8.2070	8.3685	8.5327	8.6999	8.8700	9.0431
6	8.9775	9.2068	9.4420	9.6830	9.9299	10.1830	10.4423	10.7079	10.9801	11.2588	11.5442	11.8366	12.1359	12.4423	12.7560
7	11.4139	11.7720	12.1415	12.5227	12.9159	13.3214	13.7396	14.1708	14.6153	15.0735	15.5458	16.0324	16.5339	17.0506	17.5828
8	14.2401	14.7733	15.3270	15.9020	16.4991	17.1189	17.7623	18.4300	19.1229	19.8419	20.5876	21.3612	22.1634	22.9953	23.8577
9	17.5185	18.2847	19.0859	19.9234	20.7989	21.7139	22.6700	23.6689	24.7125	25.8023	26.9404	28.1287	29.3692	30.6639	32.0150
10	21.3215	22.3931	23.5213	24.7089	25.9587	27.2738	28.6574	30.1128	31.6434	33.2529	34.9449	36.7235	38.5925	40.5564	42.6195
11	25.7329	27.1999	28.7551	30.4035	32.1504	34.0013	35.9620	38.0387	40.2379	42.5661	45.0306	47.6388	50.3985	53.3178	56.4053
12	30.8502	32.8239	34.9311	37.1802	39.5805	42.1416	44.8737	47.7877	50.8950	54.2077	57.7386	61.5013	65.5100	69.7799	74.3270
13	36.7862	39.4040	42.2187	45.2445	48.4966	51.9913	55.7459	59.7788	64.1097	68.7596	73.7506	79.1066	84.8529	91.0161	97.6250
14	43.6720	47.1027	50.8180	54.8409	59.1959	63.9095	69.0100	74.5279	80.4961	86.9495	93.9258	101.4654	109.6116	118.4106	127.9125
15	51.6595	56.1101	60.9653	66.2607	72.0351	78.3305	85.1922	92.6694	100.8151	109.6868	119.3465	129.8611	141.3029	153.7500	167.2863
16	60.9250	66.6488	72.9390	79.8502	87.4421	95.7799	104.9345	114.9834	126.0108	138.1085	151.3766	165.9236	181.8677	199.3374	218.4722
17	71.6730	78.9791	87.0680	96.0217	105.9306	116.8937	129.0201	142.4295	157.2533	173.6357	191.7345	211.7230	233.7907	258.1453	285.0137
18	84.1407	93.4056	103.7403	115.2659	128.1167	142.4413	158.4045	176.1883	195.9942	218.0446	242.5855	269.8879	300.2520	334.0073	371.5178
19	98.6032	110.2846	123.4135	138.1664	154.7400	173.3540	194.2535	217.7116	244.0328	273.5557	306.6577	343.7578	385.3225	431.8694	483.9731
20	115.3797	130.0329	146.6280	165.4180	186.6880	210.7584	237.9893	268.7842	303.6006	342.9447	387.4886	437.5625	494.2128	558.1116	630.1651
21	134.8405	153.1385	174.0210	197.8474	225.0256	256.0176	291.3467	331.6057	377.4648	429.6809	489.1096	556.7170	633.5925	720.9641	820.1151
22	157.4150	180.1721	206.3448	236.4384	271.0307	310.7813	356.4431	408.8750	469.0562	538.1011	617.2783	708.0308	811.9985	931.0437	1067.2795
23	183.6014	211.8013	244.4868	282.3616	326.2369	377.0452	435.8606	503.9165	582.6296	673.6262	778.7705	900.1992	1040.3582	1202.0464	1388.4634
24	213.9776	248.8076	289.4944	337.0103	392.4842	457.2249	532.7500	620.8174	723.4609	843.0327	982.2510	1144.2529	1332.6584	1551.6399	1806.0024
25	249.2140	292.1049	342.6034	402.0423	471.9811	554.2419	650.9551	764.6052	898.0916	1054.7910	1238.6362	1454.2012	1706.8030	2002.6155	2348.8032
26	290.0883	342.7627	405.2721	479.4306	567.3773	671.6328	795.1653	941.4646	1114.6336	1319.4888	1561.6816	1847.5356	2185.5879	2584.3342	3054.4443
27	337.5024	402.0323	479.2211	571.5224	681.8528	813.6758	971.1016	1159.0016	1383.1457	1650.3611	1968.7188	2347.2551	2798.7061	3334.4414	3971.7776
28	392.5028	471.3777	566.4808	681.1116	819.2233	985.5479	1185.7439	1426.5718	1716.1006	2063.9514	2481.5859	2982.6443	3583.3438	4302.9453	5164.3086
29	456.3032	552.5120	669.4473	811.5227	984.0679	1193.5129	1447.6074	1755.6833	2128.9648	2580.9392	3127.7983	3788.5683	4587.6797	5551.8008	6714.6016
30	530.3117	647.4390	790.9478	966.7122	1181.8815	1445.1506	1767.0813	2160.4905	2640.9163	3227.1741	3942.0259	4812.9766	5873.2305	7162.8203	8729.9844
31	616.1616	758.5037	934.3186	1151.3875	1419.2579	1749.6321	2156.8391	2658.4033	3275.7361	4034.9676	4967.9692	6113.4805	7518.7344	9241.0430	11349.9805
32	715.7475	888.4492	1103.4960	1371.1511	1704.1094	2118.0549	2632.3438	3270.8362	4062.9128	5044.7070	6260.6172	7765.1102	9624.9805	11921.9453	14755.9727
33	831.2671	1040.4856	1303.1253	1632.6698	2045.9314	2563.0464	3213.2534	4024.1265	5039.0119	6306.8587	7889.3777	9863.1800	12320.9766	15380.3063	19183.7656
34	965.2698	1218.3682	1538.6878	1943.8770	2456.1174	3102.3544	3920.2004	4950.6758	6249.1757	7884.8234	9941.6158	12527.6328	15771.8477	19841.5977	24939.8984
35	1120.7129	1426.4910	1816.6516	2314.2136	2948.3411	3755.9377	4783.6445	6090.3320	7750.2227	9856.7578	12527.4414	15909.8203	20188.9648	25596.6602	32422.8672

259

APPENDIX – TABLE A-3 PVIF (Present Value Interest Factors)

Interest rate, I, %

Periods, n	1	2	3	4	5	6	7	8	9	10	11	12	13	14	15
1	0.99010	0.98039	0.97087	0.96154	0.95238	0.94340	0.93458	0.92593	0.91743	0.90909	0.90090	0.89286	0.88496	0.87719	0.86957
2	0.98030	0.96117	0.94260	0.92456	0.90703	0.89000	0.87344	0.85734	0.84168	0.82645	0.81162	0.79719	0.78315	0.76947	0.75614
3	0.97059	0.94232	0.91514	0.88900	0.86384	0.83962	0.81630	0.79383	0.77218	0.75131	0.73119	0.71178	0.69305	0.67497	0.65752
4	0.96098	0.92385	0.88849	0.85480	0.82270	0.79209	0.76290	0.73503	0.70843	0.68301	0.65873	0.63552	0.61332	0.59208	0.57175
5	0.95147	0.90573	0.86261	0.82193	0.78353	0.74726	0.71299	0.68058	0.64993	0.62092	0.59345	0.56743	0.54276	0.51937	0.49718
6	0.94205	0.88797	0.83748	0.79031	0.74622	0.70496	0.66634	0.63017	0.59627	0.56447	0.53464	0.50663	0.48032	0.45559	0.43233
7	0.93272	0.87056	0.81309	0.75992	0.71068	0.66506	0.62275	0.58349	0.54703	0.51316	0.48166	0.45235	0.42506	0.39964	0.37594
8	0.92348	0.85349	0.78941	0.73069	0.67684	0.62741	0.58201	0.54027	0.50187	0.46651	0.43393	0.40388	0.37616	0.35056	0.32690
9	0.91434	0.83676	0.76642	0.70259	0.64461	0.59190	0.54393	0.50025	0.46043	0.42410	0.39092	0.36061	0.33288	0.30751	0.28426
10	0.90529	0.82035	0.74409	0.67556	0.61391	0.55839	0.50835	0.46319	0.42241	0.38554	0.35218	0.32197	0.29459	0.26974	0.24718
11	0.89632	0.80426	0.72242	0.64958	0.58468	0.52679	0.47509	0.42888	0.38753	0.35049	0.31728	0.28748	0.26070	0.23662	0.21494
12	0.88745	0.78849	0.70138	0.62460	0.55684	0.49697	0.44401	0.39711	0.35553	0.31863	0.28584	0.25668	0.23071	0.20756	0.18691
13	0.87866	0.77303	0.68095	0.60057	0.53032	0.46884	0.41496	0.36770	0.32618	0.28966	0.25751	0.22917	0.20416	0.18207	0.16253
14	0.86996	0.75788	0.66112	0.57748	0.50507	0.44230	0.38782	0.34046	0.29925	0.26333	0.23199	0.20462	0.18068	0.15971	0.14133
15	0.86135	0.74301	0.64186	0.55526	0.48102	0.41727	0.36245	0.31524	0.27454	0.23939	0.20900	0.18270	0.15989	0.14010	0.12289
16	0.85282	0.72845	0.62317	0.53391	0.45811	0.39365	0.33873	0.29189	0.25187	0.21763	0.18829	0.16312	0.14150	0.12289	0.10686
17	0.84438	0.71416	0.60502	0.51337	0.43630	0.37136	0.31657	0.27027	0.23107	0.19784	0.16963	0.14564	0.12522	0.10780	0.09293
18	0.83602	0.70016	0.58739	0.49363	0.41552	0.35034	0.29586	0.25025	0.21199	0.17986	0.15282	0.13004	0.11081	0.09456	0.08081
19	0.82774	0.68643	0.57029	0.47464	0.39573	0.33051	0.27651	0.23171	0.19449	0.16351	0.13768	0.11611	0.09806	0.08295	0.07027
20	0.81954	0.67297	0.55368	0.45639	0.37689	0.31180	0.25842	0.21455	0.17843	0.14864	0.12403	0.10367	0.08678	0.07276	0.06110
21	0.81143	0.65978	0.53755	0.43883	0.35894	0.29416	0.24151	0.19866	0.16370	0.13513	0.11174	0.09256	0.07680	0.06383	0.05313
22	0.80340	0.64684	0.52189	0.42196	0.34185	0.27751	0.22571	0.18394	0.15018	0.12285	0.10067	0.08264	0.06796	0.05599	0.04620
23	0.79544	0.63416	0.50669	0.40573	0.32557	0.26180	0.21095	0.17032	0.13778	0.11168	0.09069	0.07379	0.06014	0.04911	0.04017
24	0.78757	0.62172	0.49193	0.39012	0.31007	0.24698	0.19715	0.15770	0.12640	0.10153	0.08170	0.06588	0.05323	0.04308	0.03493
25	0.77977	0.60953	0.47761	0.37512	0.29530	0.23300	0.18425	0.14602	0.11597	0.09230	0.07361	0.05882	0.04710	0.03779	0.03038
26	0.77205	0.59758	0.46369	0.36069	0.28124	0.21981	0.17220	0.13520	0.10639	0.08391	0.06631	0.05252	0.04168	0.03315	0.02642
27	0.76440	0.58586	0.45019	0.34682	0.26785	0.20737	0.16093	0.12519	0.09761	0.07628	0.05974	0.04689	0.03689	0.02908	0.02297
28	0.75684	0.57437	0.43708	0.33348	0.25509	0.19563	0.15040	0.11591	0.08955	0.06934	0.05382	0.04187	0.03264	0.02551	0.01997
29	0.74934	0.56311	0.42435	0.32065	0.24295	0.18456	0.14056	0.10733	0.08215	0.06304	0.04849	0.03738	0.02889	0.02237	0.01737
30	0.74192	0.55207	0.41199	0.30832	0.23138	0.17411	0.13137	0.09938	0.07537	0.05731	0.04368	0.03338	0.02557	0.01963	0.01510
31	0.73458	0.54125	0.39999	0.29646	0.22036	0.16425	0.12277	0.09202	0.06915	0.05210	0.03935	0.02980	0.02262	0.01722	0.01313
32	0.72730	0.53063	0.38834	0.28506	0.20987	0.15496	0.11474	0.08520	0.06344	0.04736	0.03545	0.02661	0.02002	0.01510	0.01142
33	0.72010	0.52023	0.37703	0.27409	0.19987	0.14619	0.10723	0.07889	0.05820	0.04306	0.03194	0.02376	0.01772	0.01325	0.00993
34	0.71297	0.51003	0.36604	0.26355	0.19035	0.13791	0.10022	0.07305	0.05339	0.03914	0.02878	0.02121	0.01568	0.01162	0.00864
35	0.70591	0.50003	0.35538	0.25342	0.18129	0.13011	0.09366	0.06763	0.04899	0.03558	0.02592	0.01894	0.01388	0.01019	0.00751

Periods, n	16	17	18	19	20	21	22	23	24	25	26	27	28	29	30
1	0.86207	0.85470	0.84746	0.84034	0.83333	0.82645	0.81967	0.81301	0.80645	0.80000	0.79365	0.78740	0.78125	0.77519	0.76923
2	0.74316	0.73051	0.71818	0.70616	0.69444	0.68301	0.67186	0.66098	0.65036	0.64000	0.62988	0.62000	0.61035	0.60093	0.59172
3	0.64066	0.62437	0.60863	0.59342	0.57870	0.56447	0.55071	0.53738	0.52449	0.51200	0.49991	0.48819	0.47684	0.46583	0.45517
4	0.55229	0.53365	0.51579	0.49867	0.48225	0.46651	0.45140	0.43690	0.42297	0.40960	0.39675	0.38440	0.37253	0.36111	0.35013
5	0.47611	0.45611	0.43711	0.41905	0.40188	0.38554	0.37000	0.35520	0.34111	0.32768	0.31488	0.30268	0.29104	0.27993	0.26933
6	0.41044	0.38984	0.37043	0.35214	0.33490	0.31863	0.30328	0.28878	0.27509	0.26214	0.24991	0.23833	0.22737	0.21700	0.20718
7	0.35383	0.33320	0.31393	0.29592	0.27908	0.26333	0.24859	0.23478	0.22184	0.20972	0.19834	0.18766	0.17764	0.16822	0.15937
8	0.30503	0.28478	0.26604	0.24867	0.23257	0.21763	0.20376	0.19088	0.17891	0.16777	0.15741	0.14776	0.13878	0.13040	0.12259
9	0.26295	0.24340	0.22546	0.20897	0.19381	0.17986	0.16702	0.15519	0.14428	0.13422	0.12493	0.11635	0.10842	0.10109	0.09430
10	0.22668	0.20804	0.19106	0.17560	0.16151	0.14864	0.13690	0.12617	0.11635	0.10737	0.09915	0.09161	0.08470	0.07836	0.07254
11	0.19542	0.17781	0.16192	0.14757	0.13459	0.12285	0.11221	0.10258	0.09383	0.08590	0.07869	0.07214	0.06617	0.06075	0.05580
12	0.16846	0.15197	0.13722	0.12400	0.11216	0.10153	0.09198	0.08339	0.07567	0.06872	0.06245	0.05680	0.05170	0.04709	0.04292
13	0.14523	0.12989	0.11629	0.10421	0.09346	0.08391	0.07539	0.06780	0.06103	0.05498	0.04957	0.04473	0.04039	0.03650	0.03302
14	0.12520	0.11102	0.09855	0.08757	0.07789	0.06934	0.06180	0.05512	0.04921	0.04398	0.03934	0.03522	0.03155	0.02830	0.02540
15	0.10793	0.09489	0.08352	0.07359	0.06491	0.05731	0.05065	0.04481	0.03969	0.03518	0.03122	0.02773	0.02465	0.02194	0.01954
16	0.09304	0.08110	0.07078	0.06184	0.05409	0.04736	0.04152	0.03643	0.03201	0.02815	0.02478	0.02183	0.01926	0.01700	0.01503
17	0.08021	0.06932	0.05998	0.05196	0.04507	0.03914	0.03403	0.02962	0.02581	0.02252	0.01967	0.01719	0.01505	0.01318	0.01156
18	0.06914	0.05925	0.05083	0.04367	0.03756	0.03235	0.02789	0.02408	0.02082	0.01801	0.01561	0.01354	0.01175	0.01022	0.00889
19	0.05961	0.05064	0.04308	0.03670	0.03130	0.02673	0.02286	0.01958	0.01679	0.01441	0.01239	0.01066	0.00918	0.00792	0.00684
20	0.05139	0.04328	0.03651	0.03084	0.02608	0.02209	0.01874	0.01592	0.01354	0.01153	0.00983	0.00839	0.00717	0.00614	0.00526
21	0.04430	0.03699	0.03094	0.02591	0.02174	0.01826	0.01536	0.01294	0.01092	0.00922	0.00780	0.00661	0.00561	0.00476	0.00405
22	0.03819	0.03162	0.02622	0.02178	0.01811	0.01509	0.01259	0.01052	0.00880	0.00738	0.00619	0.00520	0.00438	0.00369	0.00311
23	0.03292	0.02702	0.02222	0.01830	0.01509	0.01247	0.01032	0.00855	0.00710	0.00590	0.00491	0.00410	0.00342	0.00286	0.00239
24	0.02838	0.02310	0.01883	0.01538	0.01258	0.01031	0.00846	0.00695	0.00573	0.00472	0.00390	0.00323	0.00267	0.00222	0.00184
25	0.02447	0.01974	0.01596	0.01292	0.01048	0.00852	0.00693	0.00565	0.00462	0.00378	0.00310	0.00254	0.00209	0.00172	0.00142
26	0.02109	0.01687	0.01352	0.01086	0.00874	0.00704	0.00568	0.00460	0.00372	0.00302	0.00246	0.00200	0.00163	0.00133	0.00109
27	0.01818	0.01442	0.01146	0.00912	0.00728	0.00582	0.00466	0.00374	0.00300	0.00242	0.00195	0.00158	0.00127	0.00103	0.00084
28	0.01567	0.01233	0.00971	0.00767	0.00607	0.00481	0.00382	0.00304	0.00242	0.00193	0.00155	0.00124	0.00100	0.00080	0.00065
29	0.01351	0.01053	0.00823	0.00644	0.00506	0.00397	0.00313	0.00247	0.00195	0.00155	0.00123	0.00098	0.00078	0.00062	0.00050
30	0.01165	0.00900	0.00697	0.00541	0.00421	0.00328	0.00257	0.00201	0.00158	0.00124	0.00098	0.00077	0.00061	0.00048	0.00038
31	0.01004	0.00770	0.00591	0.00455	0.00351	0.00271	0.00210	0.00163	0.00127	0.00099	0.00077	0.00061	0.00047	0.00037	0.00029
32	0.00866	0.00658	0.00501	0.00382	0.00293	0.00224	0.00172	0.00133	0.00102	0.00079	0.00061	0.00048	0.00037	0.00029	0.00023
33	0.00746	0.00562	0.00425	0.00321	0.00244	0.00185	0.00141	0.00108	0.00083	0.00063	0.00049	0.00038	0.00029	0.00022	0.00017
34	0.00643	0.00480	0.00360	0.00270	0.00203	0.00153	0.00116	0.00088	0.00067	0.00051	0.00039	0.00030	0.00023	0.00017	0.00013
35	0.00555	0.00411	0.00305	0.00227	0.00169	0.00127	0.00095	0.00071	0.00054	0.00041	0.00031	0.00023	0.00018	0.00013	0.00010

APPENDIX–TABLE A-4   PVAF (Present Value of Annuity Factor)

Interest rate, I, %

Periods, n	1	2	3	4	5	6	7	8	9	10	11	12	13	14	15
1	0.99010	0.98039	0.97087	0.96154	0.95238	0.94340	0.93458	0.92593	0.91743	0.90909	0.90090	0.89286	0.88496	0.87719	0.86957
2	1.97039	1.94156	1.91347	1.88609	1.85941	1.83339	1.80802	1.78326	1.75911	1.73554	1.71252	1.69005	1.66810	1.64666	1.62571
3	2.94098	2.88388	2.82861	2.77509	2.72325	2.67301	2.62432	2.57710	2.53129	2.48685	2.44371	2.40183	2.36115	2.32163	2.28323
4	3.90197	3.80773	3.71710	3.62990	3.54595	3.46511	3.38721	3.31213	3.23972	3.16987	3.10245	3.03735	2.97447	2.91371	2.85498
5	4.85343	4.71346	4.57971	4.45182	4.32948	4.21236	4.10020	3.99271	3.88965	3.79079	3.69590	3.60478	3.51723	3.43308	3.35215
6	5.79548	5.60143	5.41719	5.24214	5.07569	4.91732	4.76654	4.62288	4.48592	4.35526	4.23054	4.11141	3.99755	3.88867	3.78448
7	6.72819	6.47199	6.23028	6.00205	5.78637	5.58238	5.38929	5.20637	5.03295	4.86842	4.71220	4.56376	4.42261	4.28830	4.16042
8	7.65168	7.32548	7.01969	6.73274	6.46321	6.20979	5.97130	5.74664	5.53482	5.33493	5.14612	4.96764	4.79877	4.63886	4.48732
9	8.56602	8.16224	7.78611	7.43533	7.10782	6.80169	6.51523	6.24689	5.99525	5.75902	5.53705	5.32825	5.13166	4.94637	4.77158
10	9.47130	8.98259	8.53020	8.11090	7.72173	7.36009	7.02358	6.71008	6.41766	6.14457	5.88923	5.65022	5.42624	5.21612	5.01877
11	10.36763	9.78685	9.25262	8.76048	8.30641	7.88687	7.49867	7.13896	6.80519	6.49506	6.20652	5.93770	5.68694	5.45273	5.23371
12	11.25508	10.57534	9.95400	9.38507	8.86325	8.38384	7.94269	7.53608	7.16073	6.81369	6.49236	6.19437	5.91765	5.66029	5.42062
13	12.13374	11.34837	10.63495	9.98565	9.39357	8.85268	8.35765	7.90378	7.48690	7.10336	6.74987	6.42355	6.12181	5.84236	5.58315
14	13.00370	12.10625	11.29607	10.56312	9.89864	9.29498	8.74547	8.24424	7.78615	7.36669	6.98187	6.62817	6.30238	6.00207	5.72448
15	13.86505	12.84926	11.93793	11.11839	10.37966	9.71225	9.10791	8.55948	8.06069	7.60608	7.19087	6.81086	6.46238	6.14217	5.84737
16	14.71787	13.57771	12.56110	11.65230	10.83777	10.10590	9.44665	8.85137	8.31256	7.82371	7.37916	6.97399	6.60388	6.26506	5.95423
17	15.56225	14.29187	13.16612	12.16567	11.27407	10.47726	9.76322	9.12164	8.54363	8.02155	7.54879	7.11963	6.72909	6.37286	6.04716
18	16.39825	14.99203	13.75351	12.65930	11.68959	10.82760	10.05909	9.37189	8.75562	8.20141	7.70162	7.24967	6.83990	6.46742	6.12797
19	17.22600	15.67846	14.32380	13.13394	12.08532	11.15812	10.33560	9.60360	8.95011	8.36492	7.83929	7.36578	6.93797	6.55037	6.19823
20	18.04555	16.35143	14.87747	13.59033	12.46221	11.46992	10.59401	9.81815	9.12854	8.51356	7.96333	7.46944	7.02475	6.62313	6.25933
21	18.85698	17.01121	15.41502	14.02916	12.82115	11.76408	10.83553	10.01680	9.29224	8.64869	8.07507	7.56200	7.10155	6.68696	6.31246
22	19.66037	17.65804	15.93692	14.45111	13.16300	12.04158	11.06124	10.20074	9.44242	8.77154	8.17574	7.64465	7.16951	6.74294	6.35866
23	20.45581	18.29220	16.44360	14.85684	13.48857	12.30338	11.27219	10.37106	9.58021	8.88322	8.26643	7.71843	7.22966	6.79206	6.39884
24	21.24338	18.91393	16.93554	15.24696	13.79864	12.55036	11.46933	10.52876	9.70661	8.98474	8.34814	7.78432	7.28288	6.83514	6.43377
25	22.02315	19.52346	17.41315	15.62208	14.09394	12.78336	11.65358	10.67478	9.82258	9.07704	8.42174	7.84314	7.32998	6.87293	6.46415
26	22.79520	20.12104	17.87683	15.98277	14.37519	13.00317	11.82578	10.80998	9.92897	9.16094	8.48806	7.89566	7.37167	6.90608	6.49056
27	23.55960	20.70689	18.32703	16.32959	14.64303	13.21053	11.98671	10.93516	10.02658	9.23722	8.54780	7.94255	7.40856	6.93515	6.51353
28	24.31644	21.28127	18.76410	16.66306	14.89813	13.40616	12.13711	11.05108	10.11613	9.30657	8.60162	7.98442	7.44120	6.96066	6.53351
29	25.06578	21.84438	19.18845	16.98370	15.14107	13.59072	12.27767	11.15841	10.19828	9.36961	8.65011	8.02181	7.47009	6.98304	6.55088
30	25.80770	22.39646	19.60044	17.29203	15.37245	13.76483	12.40904	11.25778	10.27365	9.42691	8.69379	8.05518	7.49565	7.00266	6.56598
31	26.54228	22.93770	20.00043	17.58849	15.59281	13.92909	12.53181	11.34980	10.34280	9.47901	8.73315	8.08499	7.51828	7.01988	6.57911
32	27.26958	23.46832	20.38876	17.87355	15.80268	14.08404	12.64656	11.43500	10.40624	9.52637	8.76860	8.11159	7.53830	7.03498	6.59053
33	27.98968	23.98856	20.76578	18.14764	16.00255	14.23023	12.75379	11.51389	10.46444	9.56943	8.80054	8.13535	7.55602	7.04823	6.60046
34	28.70265	24.49858	21.13184	18.41119	16.19290	14.36814	12.85401	11.58693	10.51783	9.60857	8.82932	8.15656	7.57170	7.05985	6.60910
35	29.40857	24.99861	21.48721	18.66461	16.37419	14.49825	12.94767	11.65457	10.56682	9.64416	8.85524	8.17550	7.58557	7.07004	6.61661

Periods, n	16	17	18	19	20	21	22	23	24	25	26	27	28	29	30
1	0.86207	0.85470	0.84746	0.84034	0.83333	0.82645	0.81967	0.81301	0.80645	0.80000	0.79365	0.78740	0.78125	0.77519	0.76923
2	1.60523	1.58521	1.56564	1.54650	1.52778	1.50946	1.49153	1.47399	1.45682	1.44000	1.42353	1.40740	1.39160	1.37612	1.36095
3	2.24589	2.20958	2.17427	2.13992	2.10648	2.07393	2.04224	2.01137	1.98130	1.95200	1.92344	1.89559	1.86844	1.84195	1.81611
4	2.79818	2.74324	2.69006	2.63859	2.58873	2.54044	2.49364	2.44827	2.40428	2.36160	2.32019	2.27999	2.24097	2.20306	2.16624
5	3.27429	3.19935	3.12717	3.05763	2.99061	2.92598	2.86364	2.80347	2.74538	2.68928	2.63507	2.58267	2.53201	2.48300	2.43557
6	3.68474	3.58918	3.49760	3.40978	3.32551	3.24461	3.16692	3.09225	3.02047	2.95142	2.88498	2.82100	2.75938	2.70000	2.64275
7	4.03856	3.92238	3.81153	3.70570	3.60459	3.50795	3.41551	3.32704	3.24232	3.16114	3.08332	3.00866	2.93702	2.86822	2.80211
8	4.34359	4.20716	4.07757	3.95436	3.83716	3.72558	3.61927	3.51791	3.42122	3.32891	3.24073	3.15643	3.07579	2.99862	2.92470
9	4.60654	4.45057	4.30302	4.16333	4.03097	3.90543	3.78628	3.67310	3.56550	3.46313	3.36566	3.27278	3.18421	3.09971	3.01900
10	4.83323	4.65860	4.49409	4.33893	4.19247	4.05408	3.92318	3.79927	3.68186	3.57050	3.46481	3.36439	3.26892	3.17807	3.09154
11	5.02864	4.83641	4.65601	4.48650	4.32706	4.17692	4.03540	3.90184	3.77569	3.65640	3.54350	3.43653	3.33509	3.23881	3.14734
12	5.19711	4.98839	4.79322	4.61050	4.43922	4.27845	4.12737	3.98524	3.85136	3.72512	3.60595	3.49333	3.38679	3.28590	3.19026
13	5.34233	5.11828	4.90951	4.71471	4.53268	4.36235	4.20277	4.05304	3.91239	3.78010	3.65552	3.53805	3.42718	3.32241	3.22328
14	5.46753	5.22930	5.00806	4.80228	4.61057	4.43170	4.26456	4.10816	3.96160	3.82408	3.69486	3.57327	3.45874	3.35070	3.24867
15	5.57546	5.32419	5.09158	4.87586	4.67547	4.48901	4.31521	4.15297	4.00129	3.85926	3.72608	3.60100	3.48339	3.37264	3.26821
16	5.66850	5.40529	5.16235	4.93770	4.72956	4.53637	4.35673	4.18941	4.03330	3.88741	3.75086	3.62283	3.50265	3.38964	3.28324
17	5.74870	5.47461	5.22233	4.98966	4.77463	4.57551	4.39077	4.21904	4.05911	3.90993	3.77052	3.64002	3.51769	3.40283	3.29480
18	5.81785	5.53385	5.27316	5.03333	4.81219	4.60786	4.41866	4.24312	4.07993	3.92794	3.78613	3.65356	3.52945	3.41305	3.30369
19	5.87746	5.58449	5.31624	5.07003	4.84350	4.63460	4.44152	4.26270	4.09672	3.94235	3.79851	3.66422	3.53863	3.42097	3.31053
20	5.92884	5.62777	5.35275	5.10086	4.86958	4.65669	4.46027	4.27862	4.11026	3.95388	3.80834	3.67261	3.54581	3.42711	3.31579
21	5.97314	5.66476	5.38368	5.12677	4.89132	4.67495	4.47563	4.29156	4.12117	3.96311	3.81615	3.67922	3.55141	3.43187	3.31984
22	6.01133	5.69637	5.40990	5.14855	4.90943	4.69004	4.48822	4.30208	4.12998	3.97048	3.82234	3.68443	3.55579	3.43556	3.32295
23	6.04425	5.72340	5.43212	5.16685	4.92453	4.70251	4.49854	4.31063	4.13708	3.97639	3.82725	3.68852	3.55921	3.43842	3.32535
24	6.07263	5.74649	5.45095	5.18223	4.93710	4.71282	4.50700	4.31758	4.14281	3.98111	3.83115	3.69175	3.56189	3.44064	3.32719
25	6.09709	5.76623	5.46691	5.19515	4.94759	4.72134	4.51393	4.32324	4.14742	3.98489	3.83425	3.69429	3.56397	3.44236	3.32861
26	6.11818	5.78310	5.48043	5.20601	4.95632	4.72838	4.51962	4.32784	4.15115	3.98791	3.83670	3.69629	3.56560	3.44369	3.32970
27	6.13636	5.79753	5.49189	5.21513	4.96360	4.73420	4.52428	4.33158	4.15415	3.99033	3.83865	3.69787	3.56688	3.44472	3.33054
28	6.15204	5.80985	5.50160	5.22280	4.96967	4.73901	4.52810	4.33462	4.15657	3.99226	3.84020	3.69911	3.56788	3.44552	3.33118
29	6.16555	5.82039	5.50983	5.22924	4.97472	4.74298	4.53123	4.33709	4.15853	3.99381	3.84143	3.70008	3.56865	3.44614	3.33168
30	6.17720	5.82939	5.51681	5.23466	4.97894	4.74626	4.53379	4.33910	4.16010	3.99505	3.84240	3.70085	3.56926	3.44662	3.33206
31	6.18724	5.83709	5.52272	5.23921	4.98245	4.74898	4.53589	4.34073	4.16137	3.99604	3.84318	3.70146	3.56974	3.44700	3.33236
32	6.19590	5.84366	5.52773	5.24303	4.98537	4.75122	4.53762	4.34205	4.16239	3.99683	3.84379	3.70194	3.57011	3.44729	3.33258
33	6.20336	5.84928	5.53197	5.24625	4.98781	4.75308	4.53903	4.34313	4.16322	3.99746	3.84428	3.70231	3.57040	3.44751	3.33275
34	6.20979	5.85409	5.53557	5.24895	4.98984	4.75461	4.54019	4.34401	4.16389	3.99797	3.84467	3.70261	3.57062	3.44768	3.33289
35	6.21534	5.85820	5.53862	5.25121	4.99153	4.75587	4.54114	4.34472	4.16443	3.99838	3.84497	3.70284	3.57080	3.44782	3.33299

11

THE CAPITAL BUDGETING DECISION

Not-for-profit organizations are finding it increasingly difficult to cover the gap between current costs and revenues and at the same time provide for their capital needs. These difficulties are a result of "an increase in the demand for the organization's services, inflation-related cost pressures, and the increasing reluctance of both lenders and donors to provide needed long-term capital for asset replacement and growth."[1] This has placed more pressure on not-for-profit organizations to justify their capital acquisitions. Emphasis has to be placed on the development of new methodologies and practical tools to aid the decision maker in the area of capital asset selection.

In this chapter the capital expenditure is first discussed. Next, methods of estimating costs and benefits are analyzed. Although many of the benefits associated with capital expenditures by not-for-profit organizations are difficult to quantify, there are techniques which can be used when benefits are quantifiable with a reasonable degree of accuracy. This chapter presents those techniques for analysis of capital expenditure decisions when benefits are quantifiable. The next chapter, cost-benefit analysis, covers methods to use when the benefits are difficult to quantify.

THE CAPITAL BUDGETING DECISION

A capital expenditure can be defined as a current outlay or series of outlays of cash resources which provide an anticipated flow of future benefits in return. A capital expenditure decision has three distinguishing elements: anticipated benefits, a time dimension, and an element of risk involved in the realization of these benefits. The magnitude of these elements distinguishes the capital expenditure decision from other types of investment decisions. In other words, the typical capital expenditure is characterized by potentially large anticipated benefits, a relatively high degree of risk, and a relatively long time between the initial outlay and the anticipated return.

The unique characteristics of capital expenditure decisions have brought about the development of special decision tools for use in their resolution. The process of selecting the capital expenditure projects to be implemented is known as capital budgeting. The desirability and necessity for such tools lies in the relative importance of capital budgeting decisions compared to other investment decisions. To understand the importance of capital budgeting decisions, it is necessary to examine the context in which the decisions are made.

First, capital expenditures demand a commitment of relatively large amounts of the organization's resources at a given point or points in time. Capital investments include expenditures for land, buildings, equipment, and other assets which have a significant value and long lives. Not many organizations can survive an inopportune capital investment decision. Second, the consequences of the organization's selection of capital assets extend well into the future. For example, the capital expenditure decisions of a city affect land use, traffic circulation, the density of population, and the future physical look of the municipality.[2]

Third, in addition to determining future conditions, capital expenditure decisions, once made, are not easily reversible. In contrast, current operating decisions can often be reversed in whole, or in part, during the current budget period. Consequently, capital expenditure mistakes are apt to be more costly and have longer-lasting effects than current operating mistakes. These three factors impinge to varying degrees on the capital expenditure decision. The overall effect is to increase the importance of the capital budgeting decision and to emphasize the element of risk to the organization.

Choices among alternative capital investments create difficulties for the decision maker for several reasons. First, benefits from investments are received in some future period. Since the future can never be known with certainty, the element of risk is involved. Second, problems arise because both costs and benefits incurred in different time periods are not truly comparable. In other words, a dollar received now does not have the same value as a dollar received at some future date because of the interest phenomenon. This is a major reason why capital expenditures should be perceived and evaluated by the financial analyst in terms of cash flows adjusted to a base year. Third, not all the benefits or the costs of a particular course of action can be measured in strictly quantitative terms.

A discussion of the initial costs and anticipated benefits relevant to the capital budgeting decision for not-for-profit organizations is contained in the next section. This is followed by the presentation of various investment evaluation techniques.

ESTIMATION OF COSTS AND BENEFITS

The term "project," as used in this text, describes any activity or group of related activities which elicit the conditions set forth in the definition of a capital expenditure; specifically, a current outlay of resources in return for future benefits. The term refers to both simple and complex activities. For example, both the replacement of a single machine and the construction of a complex of buildings to house the elderly would be considered capital expenditure projects. Thus, the term project refers to a very broad range of undertakings.

The sources of data for evaluation of particular projects vary with the nature of the project. Tools such as marginal analysis are useful in locating and isolating the pertinent data for a specific investment decision. As project proposals develop beyond the initial idea stage, all benefits and costs associated with each proposal must be analyzed. From an abundance of available information, the organization must determine what is relevant to that particular capital expenditure decision.

The collection and organization of data in support of specific projects is perhaps the most tedious aspect of capital budgeting. The problem of what and how much data to collect is complicated by several factors. First, the technological expertise required to evaluate the project may be beyond the capability of the organization. A charitable organization investing in a computer to handle billing and payroll may need to hire an independent consultant to determine which line of equipment and software is most suitable. Often, the vendor of such specialized equipment can be helpful in making this determination but he can also be self-serving. Second, if new projects or processes are involved, little information may be available beyond that which the organization can obtain through its own research. Third, since each project proposal has its own distinct data base, the guidelines for data collection are often vague. Much depends on the nature of the particular project the organization has in mind and the type and amount of resources at its disposal.

The information sought when developing project proposals generally falls into one of two broad categories. The first category of data collection deals with the size of the outlays necessary to produce future benefits--the costs or cash outflows associated with acceptance of the project. Depending on the nature of the project, the organization may or may not require specialized outside help to determine these costs. If the equipment required for a capital expenditure is available in standard units from a number of manufacturers, e.g., stainless steel pipe, copper tubing, and electric motors, the problem is merely one of competitive shopping, taking into account the user's needs and the quality of the various lines offered by the manufacturers. If more sophisticated equipment is required, e.g., the sophisticated electronic controls for the stage equipment of an auditorium, the purchaser needs specialized knowledge to analyze the requirements and the relative merits of alternative equipment. The pricing of such specialized equipment also presents difficulties, particularly where items must be custom built to the organization's specifications. Sometimes an estimate may be made by considering the known prices of similar equipment. At other times, competitive bidding may be used as a way of determining costs. Many times, the scientific and engineering expertise needed to conduct a thorough evaluation is lacking and outside consultants will have to be employed.

The second category of data collection is concerned with the measurement of future benefits. For example, a city is considering establishing a children's day care facility. Benefits will be received from user fees (tuition paid by parents) but tax revenues may also increase because of the greater number of parents who will now be able to work. In addition, industry may now locate near the facility to take advantage of this new labor supply. For some other capital expenditures, however, the benefits would be measured in terms of cost savings. A charity contemplating installation of a computer system to handle the collection of pledges would receive its benefits in the form of lower per unit fund-raising costs.

Initial Costs

The data on the initial costs of the proposed project must be compiled from the various sources and analyzed. The compilation of the data may come under headings such as material or equipment purchases, shipping and transportation expenses, labor and administrative costs, working capital requirements, installation expenditures, and salvage value of old equipment.

Regardless of the headings used to compile data on the proposed initial cost of the project, the analyst must first determine which items of data are relevant and which are not relevant to the asset-selection decision. Marginal analysis is a useful technique for determining the relevancy of information. In marginal analysis, only information which is altered or changed by the acceptance of the project is considered pertinent to the decision. Other information, such as overhead costs, which remain the same whether or not the project is accepted or rejected, is not considered.

In determining the initial cost of a proposed project only <u>current</u> cash outflows are relevant. For example, a machine which is already owned by the organization but has some remaining economic life will be transferred to the new project if the old project is terminated. No remaining value for this machinery would be included as part of the initial cost of the project since there is no cash outflow from the organization. However, the cost of all

newly acquired machinery or equipment, which includes the purchase or invoice price, shipping and
transportation charges, and installation costs,
would have to be included in the calculations to
determine the initial cost of the project.

> **For example**, Municipal Hospital is consider-
> ing the purchase of a new computerized scan-
> ning X-ray machine which costs $226,400.
> Shipping and transportation charges are
> estimated to be 5 percent of the purchase
> price. Once the equipment is on the site,
> electrical wiring and plumbing costs to
> place the equipment into operation are ex-
> pected to be $13,100 and $9,850 for labor
> and materials, respectively. The initial
> cost of procuring any future benefits is
> computed in Table 11.1.

A major element in asset selection is the amount
of net working capital necessary to support a project. Net working capital is defined as current
assets minus current liabilities. If the hospital
purchases new equipment, there may be an increase in
current assets in the form of increased inventory
and/or an increase in the number of accounts receivable. Part of this buildup of current assets, however, will be offset by an increase in current
liabilities in the form of increased accounts payable and other payables. The difference between the
increases in current assets and current liabilities
is the amount of working capital that will be needed
to support this new investment.

> **For example**, assume the equipment purchased
> in the preceding example requires a $35,000
> increase in supplies inventory and a $65,000
> increase in accounts receivable (current
> assets). Forty thousand dollars of this
> increase in current assets is offset by
> increases in current liabilities to trade
> creditors (accounts payable). The remaining
> $60,000 difference is the net working capi-
> tal requirement for the project and would be
> included as part of the initial cost of
> accepting the project. Table 11.2, which
> includes cost data of Table 11.1, illus-
> trates the influence of net working capital
> on the initial cost of the equipment.

TABLE 11.1

Project Partial Initial Cost Computations
For New X-Ray Equipment

Equipment purchase price	$226,400
Add: Shipping and transportation charges	11,320
Labor installation expenses	13,100
Material installation costs	$ 9,850
Equals: Total cash outlay or initial cost	$260,670

TABLE 11.2

Project Total Initial Cost Calculations
For New X-Ray Equipment

Equipment purchase price	$226,400
Add: Shipping and transportation charges	11,320
Labor installation expenses	13,100
Material installation costs	9,850
Increase in accounts receivables	65,000
Increase in suplies inventory	35,000
Total	360,670
Less: Increase in accounts payable	40,000
Equals: Total cash outlay or or initial cost	320,670

Capital projects will not always require an in-crease in working capital, however. If the project increases the organization's efficiency in such a way that the amount of inventory on hand or accounts receivable is reduced, then working capital would be reduced and the initial cost of the project lowered. Examples of the latter would be improved inventory control systems or billing and collection procedures.

It is also important to remember that all or a portion of the increased net working capital will be returned to the organization at the end of the project's life. When this happens, the working capital returned in the last period should be treated as a cash inflow of that time in evaluating the project.

Annual Benefits

The previous section discussed in detail the items which must be considered in computing the initial cost of a capital expenditure. The second category of information needed to evaluate a project proposal is the stream of annual benefits resulting from the initial investment cost. Many of the annual benefits realized by not-for-profit organizations are difficult to measure in dollars. This chapter presents those evaluation techniques applicable when project benefits can readily be quantified. The techniques available to evaluate projects whose benefits are more difficult to measure are discussed in the next chapter.

The methods for evaluating capital expenditure projects are based on the cash flows that result from each project. Cash flows are the funds received or paid out by the organization as a result of undertaking the project. The cash flow for any period can be expressed in terms of the relevant costs and benefits associated with the project for the period[3]:

Net cash flow = cash inflows from the project
minus cash outflows from the project

(Equation 11-1)

If, during the period, cash inflows exceed cash outflows, we have a positive net cash flow. When cash outflows exceed cash inflows, we have a negative net cash flow for the period. The entire stream of net cash flows generated by the project represents the benefit stream of the investment.

Measurement of the benefits in terms of cash flows allows us to account for the reinvestment potential of the benefits, since cash flows represent the amount of funds available either for reinvestment or for other operating needs.

Project revenues in Equation 11-1 include all cash inflows to the organization which result from the acquisition of the asset or project. This includes additional revenues as a result of the project as well as any cash realized when the asset is sold or scrapped. Labor, material, and other cash outlays required by the use of the asset are included in the expense category. However, this category does not include depreciation or interest on any debt used to finance the capital expenditure. Interest expense is the cost of financing the capital expenditure and will be treated later when the opportunity cost of funds tied up in the capital project are considered. It is not, however, considered a cash outflow for capital budgeting when the interest is paid.

A not-for-profit organization may utilize depreciation accounting to measure the cost of using a fixed asset or to be in accordance with "generally accepted accounting principles." Depreciation is a method of spreading the cost of a capital expenditure over the life of a capital project; it does not require a cash outlay, however. From a cash flow viewpoint, the capital expenditure is treated as a cash outflow at the time the fixed asset is acquired. The tax effect of depreciation enters into the net cash flow equation for profit-oriented firms. Since depreciation is deductible for tax purposes, the firms experience a reduction in their tax liability, thereby increasing their cash flow. Depreciation, however, is not relevant for the not-for-profit organization since it pays no federal income tax.

Capital expenditures are also included in Equation 11-1 since not all cash outlays occur initially. Acquisition expenditures may be spread over several years. For example, acquisition of a large civic center may involve cash outlays for several years while the building is being constructed. In addition, repairs, maintenance, and remodeling as well as labor costs and increases in working capital may require cash outflows beyond the initial acquisition year.

Continuing the Memorial Hospital example,
the new X-ray equipment has an estimated
salvage value of $10,000 at the end of its
5-year useful life. Straight-line depreciation is used by the hospital to account for
wear, tear, and obsolescence of the X-ray
machine. Consequently, the depreciation
expense is its initial cost of $260,670
(from Table 11.1) divided by five, or
$52,134 per year. It is estimated that fees
charged for the use of the new machine will
generate $480,000 per year. Salaries for
technicians, X-ray film, and other materials
are estimated at $350,000 per year.

Table 11.3 shows the calculation of the net
cash flows using Equation 11-1 for each of
the five years of the life of the project.
For the sake of simplicity, it is assumed
the cash flows occur at the end of the year.
The project revenues are $480,000 per year
for years 1 to 4. The project revenue for
year 5 is increased by $10,000 because of
the salvage value of the X-ray equipment at
the end of year 5. The cash outlays each
year are $350,000. There are no additional
capital expenditures, so net cash flows are
$130,000 per year in years 1 to 4 and
$140,000 in year 5. Note that the deprecia-
tion expense of $52,134 per year is not
included since it does not require a cash
outlay. Again, the reader is cautioned that
intangible benefits such as the reduction of
pain and suffering as a result of earlier
detection of diseases are ignored in this
chapter. Such intangible benefits will be
considered in the next chapter.

Generally, the future cash flows are not known
with certainty but must be estimated. The cash flow
values for future years are an "educated guess"
based on the best information available. It is
usually some reasonable or middle value which lies
somewhere between high and low estimates.[4]
After calculation of the initial cash investment
and the net cash flows over the life of the project,
it is necessary to determine whether the capital
expenditure should be made. The major methods of
evaluating capital budgeting projects are examined
in the following section.

TABLE 11.3

Calculation of Net Cash Flows for New X-Ray Equipment

	Year				
	1	2	3	4	5
Project revenues	$ 480,000	$ 480,000	$ 480,000	$ 480,000	$ 480,000
Expenses other than depreciation	(350,000)	(350,000)	(350,000)	(350,000)	(350,000)
Capital expenditures	0	0	0	0	0
Net cash flows	$ 130,000	$ 130,000	$ 130,000	$ 130,000	$ 130,000

EVALUATION TECHNIQUES

Four evaluation techniques frequently utilized by commercial enterprises are: (1) payback, (2) net present value, (3) internal rate of return, and (4) profitability index. Each of these four methods is also appropriately used by the not-for-profit organization and will be examined in turn.

Payback

The payback period is defined as the number of years of cash flow required to recapture the original cost of an investment. There are two methods of calculating payback. The first method, the average payback, can be used when a project's cash flows are approximately equal in each year of the project's life. The second method, the actual payback, must be used when the project's cash flows vary from year to year.

Table 11.4 summarizes the net cash flows and the initial cash outlay from Tables 11.2 and 11.3 for new X-ray equipment for Municipal Hospital. The average payback is calculated by dividing the inital cash outlay by the average net cash flow per year. The average payback then, for the X-ray equipment is 2.43 years, $320,670 divided by the average net cash flow of $132,000 ($660,000 divided by 5 years).

When annual cash flows vary, payback is calculated by analyzing the cumulative cash flow. Table 11.5 shows the unequal annual cash flows and cumulative cash flows for a project with a $15,000 initial cost and a 5-year useful life. The cumulative cash flows are the summation of the project's annual cash

TABLE 11.4

Cash Flows for X-Ray Equipment

Year	Net Cash Flow
1	$130,000
2	$130,000
3	$130,000
4	$130,000
5	140,000
Total	$660,000

$\underline{I}_0$ = Initial cash outlay = $320,670

TABLE 11.5

Annual and Cumulative Cash-Flows for a Project

Year	Annual cash flow	Cumulative cash flow
1	$2,000	$ 2,000
2	4,000	6,000
3	6,000	12,000
4	7,000	19,000
5	3,000	22,000

Initial cost = $15,000

flow from its inception to that specific year. In year 3, the cumulative cash flow for the project is:

Year 1	Year 2	Year 3	
$2,000 +	$4,000 +	$6,000 =	$12,000

The cumulative cash flow at the beginning of the fourth year ($19,000) exceeds the initial cost of the investment ($15,000). Since the recovery of the investment falls between the third and fourth year, the payback period is 3 and a fraction years. To calculate the fraction, the amount of funds needed to recover the investment in year 4 is divided by the amount of cash flow in that year. Since the cumulative cash flow in year 3 is $12,000, we need another $3,000 to recover the total initial cost of $15,000. The annual cash flow in year 4 is $7,000; thus, the payback fraction is $3,000/$7,000 or 0.43.

The payback period for the project, therefore, is 3.43 years.

The acceptance criterion for payback for a commercial enterprise is usually determined by company policy and is normally a function of the cost and availability of funds. The acceptance payback criterion is usually decreased during times of funds shortages. The payback acceptance criterion would not normally constitute the only determining factor in the accept/reject decision for the not-for-profit organization since it is concerned with providing a service, rather than making a profit. A hospital is not going to reject a project which will reduce pain and suffering simply because the maximum payback period criterion has been violated. Payback, however, would be helpful for the hospital considering several mutually exclusive projects. Mutually exclusive projects are alternative ways of accomplishing the same task. Acceptance of one project precludes acceptance of any of the other mutually exclusive projects. A ranking by payback of the mutually exclusive projects would provide the decision maker with additional information regarding their relative desirability.

While the payback period method of project evaluation is relatively simple both in its theory and required calculations, it has several drawbacks. First, it disregards all cash flow beyond the payback period. Table 11.6 shows alternative projects with payback periods of two years. The projects differ, however, in the amount of cash flow generated after the second year. The cash flow for Project A stops at the end of year 2, while the cash flow for Project B continues into year 5. Most organizations would prefer Project B because of the continuing cash flow after the payback period. The payback method fails to take this into consideration.

Another deficiency is that payback does not differentiate between projects in terms of the timing of the cash flows. While some projects have high cash flows in their early years which then decrease, other projects start with lower cash flows that increase throughout their lives. Table 11.7 is a comparison of the annual cash flows of two such projects. While both projects have the same $600 initial cost, the cash flows in years 1 and 3 differ by $200. The payback period for both projects is 3 years but Project B has the obvious advantage of supplying the firm with cash for reinvestment at an earlier time than Project A.

TABLE 11.6

Initial Costs, Cash Flows, and Payback Periods for Two Projects

Initial cost	$3,000	$3,000
Cash flow in year		
1	1,000	1,000
2	2,000	2,000
3	-0-	1,000
4	-0-	1,000
5	-0-	1,000
Payback period	2	2

TABLE 11.7

Initial Costs and Cash Flows for Two Projects

	Project A	Project
Initial cost	$600	$600
Cash flow in year		
1	100	300
2	200	200
3	300	100

Net Present Value

The net present value (NPV) capital budgeting technique incorporates the needed time factor when evaluating the costs and benefits of a project. NPV is defined as the summation of the present value of the annual net cash flows minus the present value of the initial cost. For example, a project with an initial cost of $10,000 with annual cash flows as indicated in Table 11.8 has an NPV of $363. The annual cash flows must be converted to present values by discounting them to the present using a discount factor which is, in this example, 14 percent. As explained in Chapter 10, discounting future cash flows is necessary because of the time value of money. The present value of the three net cash flows is $10,363 at 14 percent. The NPV of the project is thus, $10,363 minus $10,000 or $363.

The decision rule for a project under NPV is to accept the project as long as the NPV is zero or positive. An NPV of zero implies that the original investment is recovered and that a return equal to the discount rate is earned on funds employed. Therefore, any project with a zero or positive NPV should be accepted.

TABLE 11-8

Project Annual Cash Flows

Year	Cash flow	Discount rate @ 14%*	Present Value
1	$6,000	0.877	$ 5,262
2	4,000	0.769	3,076
3	3,000	0.675	2,025
		Total	$10,363

*From Appendix Table A-3

A mathematical model of the NPV is given in Equation 11-2.

$$NPV = \frac{A_1}{(1 + i)^1} + \frac{A_2}{(1 + i)^2} + \ldots + \frac{A_n}{(1 + i)^n} - I_0$$

(Equation 11-2)

A is the cashflow in periods 1 to n, I_0 the initial cost of the investment, and i the discount rate. All cashflows are in a summation series except the initial cost and therefore Equation 11-2 can be simplified as shown in Equation 11-3.

$$NPV = \sum_{t=1}^{n} \frac{A_t}{(1 + i)^t} - I_0$$

(Equation 11-3)

The discount rate used in the NPV calculation is the opportunity cost of funds to the not-for-profit organization. The determination of the appropriate opportunity cost reduces to the following question: If, in a given period, cash flows are increased by $1, what return, with the same level of risk, will be earned or imputed on this $1 if it is invested elsewhere? Or, stated in a different manner: If the funds were not invested in the capital project, what rate of return or yield would be earned if the funds were invested in the best alternative at the same level of risk?

The discount rate used in NPV calculations by profit-oriented firms is the marginal cost of capital to the firm. The marginal cost of capital is the cost of raising the last $1 of long-term funds. Unfortunately, there is no general agreement on the appropriate opportunity cost for a governmental unit or a nonprofit organization.

An extended discussion of the issues involved in the selection of a discount rate for not-for-profit organizations and a suggested methodology are included in Chapter 12. One point, however, needs elaboration at this time. Since the discount rate already incorporates a charge for all funds being used to finance projects, it is unnecessary to reduce the annual cash flows by any finance charges. To do so would, in effect, double count the finance costs.

The NPV technique will now be used to evaluate the cash flows associated with the X-ray machine being considered by Municipal Hospital. It is assumed that the hospital's discount rate is 10 percent. Calculation of the NPV for this project is shown in Table 11.9. The net cash flows in the second column are multiplied by the present value factors for 10 percent shown in Column 3. Their product is the present value of the cash flows for each of the periods shown in Column 4. Summing the values in Column 4 yields the total present value of the cash flows of $499,010.60. Subtracting the initial cash outlay of $320,670 results in a net present value of $178,340.60 for the X-ray machine project. The X-ray machine should be purchased since the net worth of the hospital will be increased by $178,340.60 by its purchase.

TABLE 11.9

**Calculation of NPV for X-Ray Machine
Municipal Hospital**

Year (1)	Net cash flow In period t (A_t) (2)	PV factor @ 10% (3)	Present value (4)
1	$130,000	0.90909	$118,181.70
2	130,000	0.82645	107,438.50
3	130,000	0.75131	97,670.30
4	130,000	0.68301	88,791.30
5	140,000	0.62092	86,928.80
		Total PV =	$499,010.60

$$NPV = \sum_{t=1}^{n} \frac{A_t}{(1 + k)^t} - I_o = \$499,010.60 - \$320,670$$

NPV = $178,340.60

I_o = initial cash outlay = $320,670,
K_o = discount rate = 10 percent,
A_t = net cash flow in period t.

Table 11.9 illustrates the calculation techniques for uneven cash flows. The net cash flow for each year must be multiplied by the present value factor for the appropriate year and then summed to yield the total present value of the cash inflows. The cash flows in Table 11.9, however, also represent a annuity of $130,000 per year plus a lump sum cash flow of $140,000 in year 5. The present value of the cash flows is easier to calculate for the annuity as shown below:

PV of cash = PV of 4-year annuity + PV of year 5 cash flow
inflows

$\qquad$ = $130,000 [PVAF: 10%, 4 years] +
$\qquad$ $140,000 [PVF: 10%, 5 years]

$\qquad$ = $130,000 [3.1699] + $140,000 [0.62092]

$\qquad$ = $412,087 + $86,928.80

$\qquad$ = $499,015.80

the <u>NPV</u> is:

NPV = \$499,015.80 - \$320,670

      = \$178,345.80

This is the same value obtained in Table 11.9, except for a rounding error.

<u>NPV</u> has three characteristics which make it a very attractive technique to use in evaluating new assets. First, it considers the time value of money; second, it focuses on the marginal cash flow of projects; third, a changing discount rate can be built into <u>NPV</u> calculations by altering the denominator of Equation 11-2. However, the <u>NPV</u> technique suffers from a drawback. The use of <u>NPV</u> necessitates calculating the opportunity cost of funds used by not-for-profit organizations. This calculation is complex and there is no agreement by experts as to the exact method to be used.

Internal Rate of Return

The internal rate of return of a project (sometimes referred to as the discounted rate of return) is the discount rate ($\underline{r}$) which equates the present value of the net cash inflows with the initial cost of the project as shown in the following equation:

$$\sum_{\underline{t=1}}^{n} \frac{A_{\underline{t}}}{(1 + \underline{r})^{\underline{t}}} = I_O$$

(Equation 11-4)

Note that this equation is similar to Equation 11-3. The calculation of the internal rate of return is usually a trial and error process. That is, different discount rates must be tried until one is found that makes the <u>NPV</u> equal to zero. For example, a project with an initial cost of \$1,000 has net cash flows of \$700 and \$500 in years 1 and 2, respectively. If a 20 percent discount rate is assumed for the first trial, a negative \$70 <u>NPV</u> results. A negative <u>NPV</u> means that the present value of the cash flows is less than the initial project cost and the discount rate must be lowered to raise the present value of the net cash flows to zero. If an 8 percent discount rate is tried, the <u>NPV</u> is \$77.

This positive NPV occurred because the present value of the net cash flows is in excess of the initial cost. To reduce this excess, the discount rate must be increased. If a 14 percent discount rate is used, the NPV is -$1. Since this is very close to an NPV of zero, the IRR of this project is just under 14 percent. The acceptance criteria for the IRR method is simply to accept any project having an IRR equal to or greater than a desired cut-off rate. normally, this cut-off rate is the opportunity cost of funds to the organization. It is important to note, however, that the IRR of a project is determined completely independently of the opportunity cost. In this illustration, if the opportunity cost were 10 percent, the project would be accepted.

The IRR criterion has advantages similar to those of the NPV technique in that it too considers the time value of money and focuses on the marginal cash flows of a project. In addition, it is distinguished from the NPV technique since it produces a return on a project expressed as a percent rather than a dollar amount. Most practitioners prefer this method of expressing a return. However, the IRR does have some disadvantages. First, it is relatively difficult to compute by hand due to the large number of trial and error procedures required. This is not a major problem since most organizations have access to computers which can compute the IRR very quickly. A second disadvantage is that if the annual net cashflows for a project are both positive and negative over the project's life, multiple IRRs may be produced. These sign reversals and multiple rates of return can be confusing.[5] For this reason, the NPV is frequently preferred over the IRR method.

Continuing the previous example, Municipal Hospital uses the IRR technique to evaluate the purchase of the X-ray machine. The calculation of the IRR is contained in Table 11.10. To solve for the project's IRR, the interest rate that equates the present value of net cash flows to the net investment must be determined. A trial and error method must be used. First, a discount rate of 25 percent is assumed. Since the present value of the net cash flows is greater than the initial cash outlay when discounted at 25 percent, a higher discount rate should be used to decrease the present value. Using a discount rate of 35 percent, the present value of the net cash flows is less than the initial cash outlay. Therefore, the IRR lies somewhere between 25 and 35 percent. When evaluated at a discount rate of 30 percent, the present value of the net cash flows, $319,319, is approximately equal to the initial cash outlay of $320,670. Consequently, the IRR of the X-ray machine project is approximately 30 percent. (It is actually equal to 29.78 percent.) The project would be accepted if the opportunity cost of the hospital is less than 30 percent.

TABLE 11.10

Calculations of IRR for X-Ray Machine

Year	Net cash flow in period t A_t	PV factor @ 25%	PV of cash flows @ 25%	PV factor @ 35%	PV of cash flows @ 35%	PV factor @ 30%	PV of cash flows @ 30%
1	$130,000	0.80000	$104,000	0.74074	$ 96,296	0.76923	$100,000
2	130,000	.64000	83,200	.54870	71,331	.59172	76,924
3	130,000	.51200	66,560	.40644	52,837	.45517	59,172
4	130,000	.40960	53,248	.30107	39,139	.35013	45,517
5	140,000	.32768	45,875	.22301	31,221	.26933	-37,706
		Total	$352,883		$290,824		$319,319

I_o = initial cash outlay = $320,670
A_t = net cash flows in period t.

If a project has equal annual net cash flows the IRR of a project can be calculated more directly. If the net cash flows for the X-ray machine are assumed to be $130,000 per year for years 1 to 5, while the initial cash outlay remains $320,670, the initial cash outlay can be divided by the annual net cash flows to obtain the present value of annuity factor for the project. For the X-ray machine project,

$$\text{PVAF } (0.X\%, \ 5 \text{ years}) = \frac{320,000}{130,000} = 2.4669$$

Next, scan the five-year row of a present value of annuity table until the interest rate closest to the calculated present value of an annuity factor is found. Scanning the 5-year row of Appendix Table A-4, the discount rate closest to a present value of annuity factor of 2.4669 is 29 percent which is the approximate IRR for this project.

Profitability Index

Both the NPV and IRR evaluation techniques compare a project's total benefits with its initial cost in absolute amounts. The profitability index (PI) evaluates a project in terms of its relative magnitude as indicated in the following equation:

$$PI = \frac{NPV}{I_o}$$

(Equation 11-5)

The decision rule for the PI technique is to accept a project with a positive PI and reject it if the PI is negative. Note that if a project's IRR is below its opportunity cost it will have a negative NPV and its PI will also be negative. The converse is also true. The PI has the same advantages and disadvantages as the NPV and IRR techniques. In most cases all three evaluation techniques will produce the same rankings for various investment proposals.

Table 11.11 provides the NPV and initial cost of four projects. The PI for each project is shown in the last column. Projects A and B have PIs greater than zero while Projects C and D have negative PIs. Projects A and B would be accepted while Projects C and D would be rejected.

TABLE 11.11

Computations and Ranking by the PI

Project	NPV	I_o	PI
A	$ 900	$1,000	0.9
B	2,100	3,000	0.7
C	-200	2,000	-0.1
D	-400	2,000	-0.2

While the above discussion addresses the qualitative techniques available to the decision maker for making capital budgeting decisions, it is of critical importance that any capital budgeting project considered by the decision maker be congruent with the long-range plans of the organization. For example, a municipal government should not consider the possible acquisition of a new warehouse if its long-term plans are to utilize state facilities at no cost. Similarly, a school principal should not seek significant improvements in the physical facilities of his school if the school board is planning to abandon that particular school in the near future because of population shifts. In summary, a not-for-profit organization MUST be sure that its capital budgeting projects are consistent with its long-term objectives.

QUALITATIVE FACTORS

While the quantitative aspects of capital budgeting are extremely important, it is of equal importance to consider the qualitative aspects in detail. Frequently, decisions will be made on the basis of qualitative factors if the objective criterion ranks the projects approximately equal. Also, political consequences of specific actions need to be ascertained.

Frequently in capital budgeting decisions, heroic assumptions must be made regarding an asset's life, cost savings, etc. In these cases, the quantitative analysis may be of little value because of the highly uncertain nature of the assumptions. As a consequence, the qualitative analysis may take on more importance than the quantitative analysis.

If two proposed projects are equivalent quantitatively, then the qualitative factors should become the deciding considerations. Suppose a hospital is evaluating two X-ray machines, which are comparable, and whose differences in acquisition and operating costs are below 5 percent. In this case, the qualitative factors, such as patient comfort, safety, and staff preference, should be the deciding factors.

The political considerations also frequently outweigh objective quantitative decision criteria since the political environment frequently mandates a decision which is either politically expedient or popular. For example, a local government knows that the ideal location for its new sewage treatment plant is in the center of an affluent neighborhood. However, political realities force the local government to move this sewage treatment plant to another location.

SUMMARY

This chapter provided an introduction to the capital expenditure decision and presented four capital budgeting evaluation techniques. The payback, net present value, internal rate of return, and profitability index techniques were developed, numerical examples were presented, and the advantages and disadvantages of each method were discussed.

A capital expenditure decision has three distinguishing elements: anticipated benefits, a time dimension, and an element of risk. An expenditure is made today in return for a series of future benefits. Two broad categories of information are needed to evaluate capital projects. The first category is the size of the outlays needed to produce future benefits. The second category is the measurement of future flows in the form of net cash flows.

The payback period is calculated by determining the number of years of net flows required to recoup the original investment. This method is simple to calculate; however, it ignores the time value of money and the net cash flows which occur beyond the payback period. The net present value technique involves finding the present value of the net cash flows by discounting them at the organization's opportunity cost. It considers all of the cash flows and it takes into consideration the time value of money. The internal rate of return technique involves determining the discount rate which equates the present value of the net cash flows to the net investment. This method also considers the time value of money and all the cash flows. For uneven cash flows, however, a trial and error solution is required. The profitability index is the present value of the net cash flows divided by the net cash outlay. It is a measure of the present value of the benefits per dollar of net cash outlays. It has advantages and disadvantages similar to those of net present value, except it evaluates projects on a relative rather than an absolute basis.

Finally, there was a discussion of the need to consider some of the qualitative factors in the decision process. In not-for-profit organizations, qualitative factors often play important roles in capital decisions. In addition, political considerations often override other quantitative factors.

QUESTIONS

1. What is a capital expenditure? What are its characteritics?

2. What are some examples of capital expenditures?

3. In order to make a capital expenditure decision, what information must be gathered?

4. What costs are included in the determination of initial cost for a capital expenditure?

5. What basis of measurement is commonly used for the analysis of costs and benefits for a capital expenditure? Why?

6. Explain why depreciation is an irrelevant factor in the capital budgeting decision for a not-for-profit firm but must be explicitly considered in profit-oriented firms?

7. What are four capital budgeting evaluation techniques? Evaluate each.

8. What is the decision rule for project acceptance using the NPV technique?

9. What is the decision rule for project acceptance using the IRR technique?

10. Does the PI provide any advantages over the NPV or IRR techniques?

11. What is meant by qualitative factors and how do they affect capital expenditure decisions?

PROBLEMS

1. The Premier Hospital is considering the purchase of an automated medicine delivery system from

the pharmacy to each nurses' station. What initial cost would be used for the capital budgeting decision from the following data?

System purchase price, f.o.b. factory	$20,000
Shipping costs	750
Installation costs	9,500
Annual depreciation charges	5,000
Salvage value at end of life	2,250

2. The local rehabilitation workshop is considering investing in several projects. Determine the initial cost that would be used for each project from the following data.

	Project			
	A	B	C	D
Purchase price (f.o.b. factory)	$43,000	$125,000	$95,000	$180,000
Transportation	7,000	5,000	3,000	10,000
Installation	500	7,000	4,000	8,000
Employee retraining	0	2,000	1,000	4,000
Increase in accounts rec.	0	30,000	10,000	50,000
Increase in inventory	10,000	20,000	20,000	40,000
Increase in accounts pay.	0	20,000	20,000	40,000

3. Determine the net cash flows for years 1 through 6 for a project with an initial cost of $50,000, maintenance costs of $2,000 in year 1 which will increase by 10 percent each year for years 2 through 6; cash inflows of $15,000 in year 1; cash inflows will increase by 8 percent each year in years 2 through 6; and a salvage value of $2,000 in year 6.

4. What is the payback period for a project which has an initial cost of $50,000; cash flows in years 1 through 3 of $5,000, $7,500, and $10,000, respectively; and cash flows of $12,000 in the 4th and all subsequent years.

5. What is the payback period for a project which requires a $14,000 initial cash investment and has successive net cash inflows of $3,000, $4,500, $6,000, $8,500, and $3,000 in years 1 through 5?

6. Calculate the payback period for two projects with the following characteristics:

	Project	
	A	B
Initial cash outflow	$12,000	$16,000
Salvage value	-0-	-0-
Estimated life	8 years	8 years
Annual net cash Benefits		
Years 1-4	$ 2,500	$ 3,000
Years 5-8	2,000	3,000

7. The City of Allenton is considering two alternative recreation facilities. Facility X has an initial cost of $125,000, and a life of eight years and no salvage value. Facility Y costs $200,000 initially, has a life of eight years, and an estimated salvage of $25,000. Cash flows anticipated for each of the projects are:

	X	Y
1-4 years	$25,000/yr	$45,000/yr
5-8 years	20,000/yr	45,000/yr

Determine the net present value of each of the projects using a 10 percent discount rate.

8. If Panama City purchased a piece of property seven years ago for $20,000 and sold it today for $45,000, what would its internal rate of return be?

9. Evaluate the following two proposals using the IRR and NPV techniques. Use a 9 percent discount rate for NPV evaluation.

	A	B
Initial cost	$20,000	$15,000
Net cash flows:		
Year 1	2,000	10,000
Year 2	7,000	8,000
Year 3	8,000	4,000
Year 4	9,000	2,000

10. What is the IRR of a project which has a 10-year life, a $25,000 initial cost, and an annual cash flow of $5,000?

11. Determine the profitability index for the following projects:

Project	Initial cost	NPV
A	$40,000	$5,900
B	25,000	-3,600
C	50,000	3,200
D	30,000	2,000
E	35,000	-1,900

12. What are the NPV and PI for the following projects?

	Investment A	Investment B
Initial cost	$20,000	$30,000
Annual cash flows		
Year 1	6,000	-5,000
Year 2	8,000	5,000
Year 3	8,000	10,000
Year 4	-2,000	15,000
Year 5	6,000	15,000
Discount rate	8%	8%

ENDNOTES

1. Richard F. Wacht, "A Long-Range Financial Planning Technique for Nonprofit Organizations," Atlanta Economic Review (September/October 1976), p. 2.
2. Lennox L. Moak and Albert M. Hillhouse, Concepts and Practices in Local Government Finance (Chicago: Municipal Finance Officers Association, 1975), p. 98.
3. Lawrence D. Schall and Charles W. Haley, Introduction to Financial Management (New York: McGraw-Hill Book Company, 1977), p. 207.
4. Ibid., p. 210.
5. For an in-depth treatment of these topics see: Jerome S. Osteryoung, Capital Budgeting: Long-Term Asset Selection, 2nd ed., (Columbus, Ohio, Grid Publishing, Inc., 1979), Chapter 3.

12

DETERMINATION OF DISCOUNT RATE AND COST-BENEFIT ANALYSIS

In making capital budgeting decisions in the not-for-profit sector, certain modifications must be made to the previously developed models for certain asset selection applications. Due to the nature of the not-for-profit organization, two major problems arise. The first is the measurement of the benefits to be derived from project acceptance and second is the determination of the specific discount rate to be employed in the capital budgeting decision.

This chapter first presents cost-benefit analysis, a capital budgeting technique especially suitable to the not-for-profit sector. Next, an extensive example of cost-benefit analysis is presented. Finally, the appropriate discount rate to be used by not-for-profit and governmental agencies in making capital budgeting decisions is discussed.

COST-BENEFIT ANALYSIS

Cost-benefit analysis is the public sector counterpart of the capital budgeting techniques used by profit-oriented firms. Cost-benefit analysis is a method "for assessing the desirability of projects, when it is necessary to take both a long and a wide view of the repercussions of a particular program

expenditure or policy change."[1] Cost-benefit analysis represents a systematic approach to the examination of benefits and costs associated with a particular public program.

It is important to note that appropriate capital
budgeting techniques such as cost-benefit analysis
are as critical to the public and not-for-profit
sector as to the private sector. That is, if we are
to have a growing and sound economy, the public
sector must use funds (culled through taxes, donations, or user fees from the private sector in an
economical and prudent manner. Only through the
optimal allocation of resources in the public sector
can the private sector exist efficiently. While
cost-benefit analysis has been thought of as unique-
ly applicable to governmental use, it is also of
value in the not-for-profit sector as well. In
addition, it is also being applied to more complicated business decisions where the benefits cannot
be completely quantified, i.e., installation of
pollution control equipment or the evaluation of
hiring minority workers.

The basic objective of cost-benefit analysis (as
in other capital evaluation techniques) is to compare the costs of a project to the benefits. Obviously, the benefits and costs of proposed projects
extend over many years so that present-value concepts must be used. Cost-benefit analysis is usually accomplished which one of three techniques. The
first cost-benefit evaluation technique solves for
the discount rate which equates the benefits of a
project with its costs. This technique is the internal-rate-of-return cost-benefit method. Using
this technique, a project is accepted if it has a
higher rate of return than the discount rate or
opportunity cost of the organization.

In mathematical terms this first technique is
defined:

$$\sum_{t=1}^{n} \frac{B_t}{(1+r)^t} = \sum_{t=1}^{n} \frac{C_t}{(1+r)^t} \qquad \text{(Equation 12.1)}$$

where B_t = benefits in year t, C_t = costs in year t,
and r = internal rate of return for cost-benefit
analysis.

The second cost-benefit analysis technique is a
derivative of the NPV methodology. With this technique, the present value of the net costs of the
project are subtracted from the present value of the

benefits using the appropriate discount rate to determine present values. If the benefits exceed the costs (adjusted for present value), the project should be accepted. In mathematical terms, this model is:

$$CB_{NPV} = \sum_{t=1}^{n} \frac{B_t}{(1 + r_t)^t} - \sum_{t=1}^{n} \frac{C_t}{(1 + r_t)^t}$$

(Equation 12-2)

where CB_{NPV} = cost-benefit analysis in NPV dollars, r_t = the appropriate rate of discount in period t, B_t = benefits in year t, and C_t = costs in year t.
   The third and most common format for the cost-benefit analysis is the cost-benefit ratio, an adaptation of the profitability index. In mathematical terms this ratio is:

$$CB_R = \frac{\sum_{t=1}^{n} \frac{B_t}{(1+r_t)^t}}{\sum_{t=1}^{n} \frac{C_t}{(1+r_t)^t}}$$

(Equation 12-3)

where CB_R = cost-benefit ratio and all other terms are as defined previously.
   The cost-benefit ratio is the ratio of the present value of the benefits divided by the present value of the costs, both discounted at the opportunity cost. If a proposed project has a cost-benefit ratio greater than one, the project should be accepted; otherwise, it should be rejected.

Determining Benefits and Costs

   The costs of governmental and other not-for-profit programs are generally easier to measure in dollar terms than are its benefits. The relevant costs to be measured include: direct capital outlays for project construction or equipment, salaries for project administration, supplies, labor, and overhead. These costs are the primary or measurable costs of a project. There may also be intangible or social costs associated with a project which may be more difficult to quantify. For example, it is difficult to identify and measure the costs of pollution resulting from a coal-fired power plant. Whether social costs are directly measurable or not, an attempt should be made to estimate their value because of their impact on the decision process.

The measurement of specific benefits resulting from a public project presents an even greater problem for the planners in the not-for-profit sector. Very few services of government and not-for-profit agencies are sold at a market-determined price. Much of their service output is intangible and not directly measurable. As a result, the value of benefits received must, for the most part, be measured by the use of a surrogate. For example, the direct benefit from a visiting nurse program for senior citizens is the value to them of being able to stay in their own homes or with family members rather than being placed in hospitals or nursing homes. The cost savings of not having to provide full-time care could be a surrogate measure of the value of staying at home.

While the measurement of benefits in many cases is fairly straightforward, either directly or through readily available surrogates, the valuation of benefits from the many public projects which exist for the purpose of saving or extending human lives or relieving suffering and hardship, presents a much greater problem. How much is a human life worth? Society does place an implicit value on the saving of human lives when it makes everyday decisions ranging from how many policemen to put on a beat to how many intensive-care units to install in a hospital. In an article in Business Week, Walter Oi of the University of Rochester proposed the idea that the value of a human life is a function of a person's expected earnings over his lifetime. This estimate is then discounted at a substantial rate (around 10 percent) to determine its present value.[2]

Oi's proposal yields some pretty awesome conclusions. For example, the economic value of the old and retired is almost zero. In addition, saving the life of a child yields a relatively small benefit because a child will not become a productive member of society until adulthood. E. J. Mishan of the London School of Economics argues against Oi's measure, and says the relevant measure is the amount that potential victims, their families, and society as a whole would be willing to pay to minimize the risk of death. In another study, the amount an individual would pay to reduce his risk of death was quantitatively estimated. By measuring wage differentials in 37 risky occupations, it was found that a worker would increase his risk of dying by 0.001 if he were paid $300 per year. Thus, eliminating one death in a thousand is worth $300,000 to the potential victims. The value of life as determined by workers in nonrisky occupations (the majority of the world) was estimated to be more than $500,000. These figures conflict with governmental figures (using Oi's approach) which show that a human life is worth no more than $250,000. Similar valuation problems also occur when trying to measure the benefits of programs that "improve the quality of life," or have purely aesthetic value.

In addition to measuring the primary benefits of a public project, directly or by surrogates, it is necessary to include secondary, or indirect, effects in the cost-benefit analysis. For example, a glaucoma detection campaign which reduces the number of people who go blind would also reduce the need for future government disability payments. A thorough cost-benefit analysis requires that both the value of all direct and possible indirect benefits be included in the estimates. Consider the analysis of the benefits of a rapid rail and bus transit system for the metropolitan Atlanta, Georgia area.[3] The estimated values of the quantifiable benefits for the new system are listed in Table 12.1. The benefits were estimated for the period from 1971 through 2020 and discounted to 1971 at a 6 percent rate. More than one-quarter of the value of the benefits is in the form of expected time savings by highway users making no direct use of the rapid transit system. Due to reduced congestion on the highways, the expected decrease in costs of highway accidents is the second largest category of benefits. This example illustrates the major role that indirect benefits may have in a cost-benefit study.

Uses of Cost-Benefit Analysis

As was brought out in the preceding discussion, the purpose of cost-benefit analysis is to bring to decisions concerning government and not-for-profit organization programs the same kind of quantitative analysis that is used for making business decisions. To decide whether a prospective investment is sound, the business executive sums the costs and compares

TABLE 12.1

Monetary Values of the Quantifiable Benefits of the Proposed Marta System (Cumulative Benefits by 2020, Discounted to Constant 1971 Dollars)

Constant transient commuters	$ 321,650,000
Diverted motorists (total)	
Time savings	219,770,000
Operating cost savings	217,930,000
Insurance cost savings	22,540,000
Additional vehicle savings	160,170,000
Parking cost savings	103,840,000
Nondiverted commuters	1,052,990,000
Business community	
Time savings to trucking industry	685,040,000
Parking facilities savings to employers	7,990,000
Other benefits	
Termination of present bus system savings	58,000,000
Highway accident savings	745,410,000
Total	$3,595,330,000

Source: Development Research Associates, "Benefits to the Atlanta Metropolitan Area from the Proposed Regional Transportation Program," (Metropolitan Atlanta Rapid Transit Authority, 1971), p. 36, as appeared in: William R. Henry and W. Warren Haynes, Managerial Economics: Analysis and Cases, 4th ed. (Dallas, Texas: Business Publications, Inc., 1978), p. 661.

them to the expected return. If the return exceeds the costs, then the investment is worthwhile. The financial manager in the not-for-profit sector should make the same comparisons. However, as brought out in Chapter 11, qualitative variables are especially critical for not-for-profit organizations to consider.

Another use for cost-benefit analysis is to guide resource-allocation decisions both within and between such major program areas as health, defense, education, and welfare. The objective of such a comprehensive system would be to maximize the discounted benefits minus the cost of all government programs; however, a number of serious flaws arise here. First, measurement techniques have not been sufficiently refined or standardized to permit meaningful comparisons between such diverse areas as cancer research and the space shuttle program, for example. Second, incompatible goals frequently make cost-benefit analysis extremely difficult to accomplish. A new health care facility may appear to be very beneficial since additional health care can now be provided to individuals who were unable to utilize the existing facilities. However, this new facility will place greater demands on the city's entire medical service function which is already operating at capacity. Consequently, the two goals of additional medical facilities must be examined and balanced against the city's overall goal of reducing the workload on its existing medical personnel and resources.

When there is a limitation on available funds, such as those imposed by governmental budgets, cost-benefit analysis can be used to rank prospective projects according to their respective rates of return. As in conventional capital budgeting, the projects with higher rates of return should be chosen over projects with lower rates of return until the budget constraint is reached. A note of caution is in order, however, when working with any of these quantitative techniques. The planner must guard against becoming so enamored with quantification in terms of the rates of return or cost-benefit ratios that he forgets about the public welfare function, which forms the basis for public investment. In other words, he may fail to include the social side effects of his decision. In addition, it may be very difficult to make accurate comparisons of incompatible projects even when all facets of the projects are considered.

In spite of its drawbacks, cost-benefit analysis provides a systematic framework within which to make decisions. In addition, it has its greatest use in comparing projects which are designed to achieve the same or similar objectives and in focusing on the "optimal" level of expenditures for a particular program or project. Note, too, that these techniques may be applied to a whole spectrum of projects or programs. With careful application, cost-benefit analysis cannot only guide major governmental outlays but is useful in analyzing such things as proposed law changes and new price guidelines. For example, the law requiring seat belts in all cars necessitated a very small governmental outlay. The law, however, can still be evaluated by comparing the costs of seat belt installations with the value of the expected reduction in deaths and injuries due to automobile accidents.

Cost-Benefit Analysis: **An Example** At present, most buildings on the campus of Florence State University are air conditioned by individual refrigeration units installed in each building. Several types of refrigeration units are used, such as absorption liquid chillers, hermetic centrifugal liquid chillers, and reciprocating liquid chillers. Design refrigeration requirements for campus buildings under the existing system are 7,367 tons. Additional design requirements for buildings with planned renovations, new buildings, and buildings without central cooling systems are 6,450 tons. Thus, total campus design refrigeration requirements will exceed 13,800 tons within the next eight to ten years.

The university is considering replacing the present decentralized air conditioning system with a central refrigeration plant. The central system initially would include one 1,500-ton and two 3,000-ton refrigeration machines. The refrigeration machines would provide water at 38°F to the buildings on campus by means of a new underground piping system installed between the central plant and various campus buildings. The chilled water would provide cooling instead of individual air conditioning units located in each of the campus buildings.

The central refrigeration system is advocated as a means to provide more economical
and reliable air conditioning services to
buildings on the Florence State University
campus. Cost savings should be realized not
only in capital construction but in operating costs as well. Far fewer refrigeration
machines of larger size will be more economical to operate and maintain than hundreds
of package and window units. Reliability is
enhanced by a central plant since each
building will in fact be served by all central units; if one central unit is off-line
for preventive maintenance or repairs, the
others provide service to all buildings.

An energy consulting firm conducted a study
to define the advantages and disadvantages
of a central thermal energy system for the
campus. This report considered plant concept and design, the distribution system,
construction costs, projected thermal energy
production requirements, and annual operating costs. The physical planning division
of Florence State University then prepared a
comprehensive analysis to determine if the
central refrigeration system would be feasible and economical to meet current and future air conditioning requirements.

The annual operating expenses of the existing decentralized system are compared to
those estimated for the central plant system
in Table 12.2. The central system is more
economical to operate because equipment
maintenance costs are lower for fewer pieces
of equipment and economies of scale are
realized since the central system machines
operate at or near full capacity, their most
efficient operating point. As indicated by
the data in Table 12.2, annual operating
costs should be reduced by $381,850 with a
central heating and refrigeration plant
versus the current decentralized refrigeration system and central heating plant.

The construction costs for the central refrigeration plant and chilled water distribution system are estimated at $4,500,000 as
shown in Table 12.3. The central plant cost

is $2,430,000; the distribution system cost
is $1,483,000; and $587,000 is budgeted for
fees and contingencies.

If the central refrigeration plant is not
built, it will be necessary to meet new
building air conditioning requirements with
additional individual refrigeration systems.
In addition, replacement equipment for some
of the existing building refrigeration systems will be required. Thus, it is important to project and analyze the costs of
continuing with a decentralized refrigeration system. Refrigeration requirements for
new buildings, renovation requirements, and
probable replacement requirements were forecasted for the next several years. Since
these costs will not be incurred until some-
time in the future, they must be discounted
to their present value. Since Florence
State University is supported by tax funds,
a 10 percent discount rate is used by the
university to reflect the opportunity cost
of these funds to society. (Determination

TABLE 12.2

Annual Operating Expenses of Decentralized Versus Central Air Conditioning Systems

	Decentralized (existing system) (1)	Central system (2)	Incremental difference (2) - (2) (3)
Labor and benefits	$ 178,900	$ 178,900	$ 0
Maintenance	347,800	104,600	243,200
Supplies	25,500	29,200	3,700
Electricity	419,000	172,300	246,700
Fuel oil and gas	958,000	1,062,350	104,350
Water	11,000	11,000	0
Insurance	10,000	10,000	0
General and administrative (expense)	23,600	23,600	0
Total annual operating expense	$1,973,800	$1,591,950	$381,850

TABLE 12.3

Central Refrigeration Plant Construction

The construction costs for the central refrigeration plant and chilled water distribution system are estimated at $4,500,000. An analysis of these costs are as follows:

Central plant

Refrigeration machines	$650,000
Boilers	250,000
Chilled-condenser water pumps	100,000
Well water system	300,000
BTU metering and controls	39,000
Water treatment	6,000
Expansion and storage tanks	12,000
Miscellaneous equipment	11,000
Electrical service	174,000
Plant piping and labor	290,000
Insulation	42,000
Building & renovation	350,000
Painting	10,000
Contractor overhead & administration	196,000
Subtotal	$2,430,000

Distribution System

Chilled water mains	$ 995,000
Chilled water branches to buildings with refrigeration systems	206,000
Chilled water branches to new and certain buildings without refrigeration systems	90,000
Chilled water piping modifications inside buildings	192,000
Subtotal	$1,483,000
Contingency and Fees	587,000
Total	$4,500,000

of appropriate discount rates is discussed more fully in the next section of this chapter.) Table 12.4 presents the projected data for both new equipment costs and equipment replacement costs on a present-value basis by discounting at the 10 percent rate. The present-value cost of installing new individual refrigeration systems is estimated at $1,342,727 while the present value of the replacement costs are estimated at $696,436. The present value of the total costs for the decentralized refrigeration system are forecasted at $2,039,163.

Florence State University elects to use the present-value cost-benefit evaluation technique. The internal-rate-of-return technique (Equation 12.1) involves determining the internal rate of return for a 25-year uneven stream of cash flows. A tedious trial and error solution is required for this type of analysis.

The appropriate data from Tables 12.2 through 12.4 are summarized in Table 12.5. The future quantifiable benefits from this project are the incremental cost savings between the two types of air conditioning and heating systems. As shown in Table 12.5, the central system results in annual incremental cost savings of $381,850 per year for 25 years. The incremental cost of the central system is $2,460,837 expressed in current dollars. Equation 12-2 is used to make the cost-benefit analysis in terms of NPV dollars:

$$CB_{NBV} = \sum_{t=1}^{n} \frac{B_t}{(1+r_t)^t} - \sum_{t=1}^{n} \frac{C_t}{(1+r_t)^t}$$

(Equation 12-2)

TABLE 12.4

Estimated Costs of Refrigeration Equipment For a Decentralized System

New projects

Building	Refrig. (tons)	Estimated year of construction	Estimated cost*	Present Value at 10%
Tully gym	460	1	$117,500	$ 106,818
Physics labs & classrooms	60	2	32,500	26,860
Diffenbaugh	250	2	78,000	64,463
Smith Hall	300	2	88,700	73,306
Education complex	570	2	145,000	119,835
Relocated ROTC facility	70	3	38,200	28,700
Medical sciences	150	3	65,200	48,986
Library expansion	240	3	79,900	60,030
Seminole/Suwannee building	370	3	106,900	80,316
Office Ser./Post Office	100	3	59,600	44,778
University Union expansion	300	4	95,900	65,501
Dodd Hall	150	4	67,900	46,377
Music/Arts	400	4	121,700	83,123
Central Information Center	200	4	77,200	52,729
DeGraff Hall	120	5	62,000	38,497
Kellum Hall	300	5	99,800	61,968
New science building	320	6	108,800	61,415
Other buildings	1,630	10	723,720	279,025
Total	5,990			$1,342,727

Replacement of Existing Equipment

A. Installed equipment (design tons)
    Major system   7,125 Tons
    Pkg. & window units   1,400
    Total   8,525
B. Replacement @ 4% per year   340 Tons
C. Replacement cost/ton $225/Ton
D. Replacement cost per year $76,725
E. Period of years   25
F. Total replacement cost
    Discounted to present at 10% $696,436

Present Value of Total Cost for Refrigeration
Equipment for a Decentralized System

New equipment	$1,342,727
Replacement equipment	696,436
Total	$2,039,163

TABLE 12.5

Central Refrigeration Plant Economic Analysis of Quantitative Factors

---

Annual Operating Expenses [over 25-year life]:

Decentralized system	$1,973,800
Central system	1,591,950

Annual incremental savings $381,850

Capital Construction Costs [expressed in present dollars]:

Central system	$4,500,000
Decentralized system	2,039,163

Incremental investment $2,460,837

$$\underline{CB}_{NBV} = \sum_{t=1}^{25} \frac{381,850}{(1+0.10)^{t}} - \$2,460,837^{*}$$

$$= (381,850)\,(\underline{PVAF}(10\%,25 \text{ yr})) - \$2,460,837$$

$$\underline{CB}_{NBV} = \$1,005,231$$

*No further discounting is necessary since these costs were stated in current dollars.

Based on an analysis of quantitative factors, the central air conditioning system should be installed since it results in a net benefit of $1,005,231.

The cost-benefit ratio can also be applied to the data in Table 12.5 as shown below:

Since the central air conditioning project has a cost-benefit ratio greater than one,

$$CB_R = \frac{\displaystyle\sum_{t=1}^{n} \frac{B_t}{(1+r_t)^t}}{\displaystyle\sum_{t=1}^{n} \frac{C_t}{(1+r_t)^t}} \qquad \text{(Equation 12-3)}$$

$$CB_R = \frac{\$3,466,068}{\$2,460,837}$$

$$CB_R = 1.408$$

it should be accepted based on the quantitative factors.

The qualitative factors, however, also need to be examined before a final decision is made. To these favorable cost comparisons should be added the indirect costs to university academic and research programs which occur because of failures of the individual building systems. The unseen costs in terms of damaged and destroyed research projects, endless wasted days, months, and even years of effort by research scientists, doctoral students, postdoctoral associates, technicians, and staff members adds substantially to the cost of air conditioning equipment breakdowns. Examples of these costs are:

Love Building: The absorption machine has deteriorated to the point where it is totally unreliable and repeatedly malfunctions. The daily costs of these shutdowns in the Meteorology Department alone are:

Salaries	$ 823
Equipment	
Computer repairs	$ 240
Computer loss of use	170
Copying machine, paper replacement	105
Copying machine, loss of use	85
Total	$1,423
	(per day)

Chemistry Unit I Building: This facility houses approximately 37 professors, 75 full-time staff, numerous student assistants, 129 graduate students, and 36 postdoctoral associates. This totals approximately 300 man-hours per hour valued at $1,738 per hour. It is estimated that 90 percent of these manhour costs are lost during air conditioning system shutdowns. Many long-term experiments must be redone or abandoned when controlled environmental conditions fail. Laboratory animals, insects, and fish life are rendered useless for their intended purposes and many die or must be destroyed. The glass blowing shop, with its oxygen-burning torches, becomes unbearable and dangerous. Experiments employing toxic gases must be terminated when air conditioning failure interrupts the flow of ventilating air. It is estimated that the many air conditioning shutdowns cost this department approximately $2,300 per hour not including loss of staff and faculty time, based solely on contract and grant activities. While the quantifiable factors in this case led to the accept decision, the qualitative variables were also very important. It is important to analyze both the quantitative and qualitative factors when making a cost-benefit analysis.

THE APPROPRIATE DISCOUNT RATE[4]

This section examines the consensus views of the appropriate discount rates for private, profit-oriented firms, and governmental bodies. The underlying rationales for determining the discount rates for the profit-oriented and governmental cases are first presented. Then an argument is developed that neither rationale is appropriate for the nongovernmental, not-for-profit organization. Finally, a rationale for selecting the appropriate discount rate for these not-for-profit organizations is presented along with an example of its determination.

The Discount Rate for Profit-Seeking Firms

Conceptually, there appears to be general agreement on the appropriate discount rate to be used by private profit-seeking firms in the evaluation of capital expenditures. The firm's cost of capital, or cost of long-term funds, is the appropriate rate. This is the minimum rate that has to be earned on an investment in order for the firm's stock price to remain unchanged.

There is some disagreement, however, on how the cost of capital should be calculated, though the underlying rationale appears to be the same regardless of the point of view. The discount rate is the return expected by the providers of the funds. The firm has to earn a sufficient return on capital expenditures to pay the interest required on a new debt, the current yield on preferred stock, and the required rate of return on common stock. The firm is competing for funds so the focus is on the return required by providers at the margin. Otherwise, the value of the firm would be reduced by an inadequate return, resulting in a reduction in stockholders' wealth.

The Discount Rate for Government Expenditures

In contrast to the profit-oriented firm, there is no consensus on the appropriate discount rate for governmental expenditures. Two major reasons are given, however, for the need to use a discount rate for government expenditures: "(1) to reflect the opportunity cost associated with the funds used in public investment and (2) to reflect a social preference for current rather than future benefits."[5] The rationale for choosing the discount rate hence rests on the concept of opportunity cost. It is not clear, however, whether the opportunity cost is foregone consumption, foregone private investment, or a combination of the two.

Some people argue that the rate of discount should be the long-term interest rate at which government can finance its debt to support the project. Presently, the federal government can finance long-term debt at about 8 percent, while local governments can finance debt at approximately 6 to 7 percent. While these rates are easily established, Baumol argues that:

> ...the correct discount rate for the evaluation of a governmental project is the percentage rate of return that the resources utilized would otherwise provide in the

private sector. The correct discount rate
for a project will be of a weighted average
of the opportunity cost rate for the various
sectors from which the project would draw
its resources, and the weight for each such
sector in this average is the proportion of
the total resources that would come from
that sector.[6]

Unlike the cost of capital for the business firm,
the social discount rate advocated by Baumol and
others focuses on the weighted average pretax cost
of funds, not the weighted average cost of funds at
the margin. "The underlying rationale is that public investment decisions should turn on returns to
the society as a whole, not on the returns of the
providers of funds at the margin as in the case of
the private, profit-oriented firms."[7] In calculating
the opportunity cost of funds withdrawn from the
private sector, it is important to recognize that
funds withdrawn from corporate investment generally
incur a higher opportunity cost than funds taken
from personal consumption. (The opportunity cost
for personal consumption is usually assumed to be
the personal savings rate.) For example, if the
funds utilized by a firm generally yield a 15 percent rate of return before taxes, then this 15
percent is the opportunity cost of those funds to
society.

The choice of a particular discount rate will
have a profound effect on the types of projects
accepted. A low rate favors investments with long
lives--dams, parks, buildings, etc., whereas a high
rate favors projects whose benefits begin to accrue
soon after the initial investment. In practice,
there has been a long history of public agencies
favoring low discount rates, because they tend to
result in the acceptance of more projects. There
has also been considerable variation between agencies in their use of discount rates. As a matter of
fact, in 1969 thirteen agencies reported that they
did not use any discount rate at all in evaluating
proposed projects--among these agencies were the
Department of Housing and Urban Development, the
Department of the Treasury, and the Department of
Labor. At that time, the Department of Agriculture
was using a 4.875 percent discount rate and the Job
Corps program was evaluated using two rates--3 and 5
percent. The Department of Defense used a 10 percent rate, while the Atomic Energy Commission used a

5 percent rate for some programs, 7.5 percent for others, 9 percent for others, and 15 percent for still others.[8] It is obvious that such a wide variation in rates is difficult to justify and could lead to an inefficient allocation of resources. As a result, in the early 1970s all agencies were ordered to use a rate of at least 10 percent in discounting program costs and benefits, except water-resource agencies, which are still allowed to use 4.875 percent.

While government cannot ignore or haphazardly select a discount rate, care must be used in the selection of the appropriate discount rate. The most logical rate to use is the opportunity cost of funds withdrawn from the private sector.

Determination of Appropriate Discount Rate for Nonprofit Organizations

The consensus view of the appropriate discount rates for governmental and business firms is some form of weighted costs. The difference between the rates for these two types of organizations centers around three key interrelated issues: (1) the use of a marginal versus a weighted average cost, (2) pre-tax versus after-tax costs, and (3) the source of the funds. Specifically, the consensus discount rate for government bodies is a pre-tax average opportunity cost based on the average cost of funds that would have been used for investments weighted by the proportion of total funds taken from that source. Business firms, however, use after-tax weighted average marginal costs, with these costs defined as the after-tax cost to the firm of raising funds at the margin weighted by the composition of the capital structure.

Neither of the above approaches is directly applicable for private, nonprofit organizations. Although a nonprofit organization resembles a governmental body in that its mission is to benefit society as a whole, it lacks the power of taxation as a source of funds and as a basis for borrowing funds. The nonprofit organization must raise its funds in an environment in which it competes with other organizations for funds. The approach used by profit-seeking firms is not applicable for several reasons. Business firms use an after-tax rate while the not-for-profit organization should use a pre-tax rate since, like the governmental body, the resources could earn that rate elsewhere. It is extremely difficult, if not impossible, however, to determine the cost of funds at the margin for a not-for-profit organization raising funds through donations. The concept of capital structure cannot be used to determine the weights for a not-for-profit organization since it lacks an equity, or residual ownership, component as found in the business firm.

As a result, the approach suggested to determine the appropriate discount rate for a private not-for-profit organization incorporates some of the features of each of the methodologies used to determine the discount rate for governmental units and profit-seeking firms. It also includes some features that are unique to this type of organization.

The discount rate used by the nonprofit organization should reflect the weighted opportunity cost associated with the funds utilized. This requires three steps: (1) identification of the sources of funds, (2) determination of the cost of each source, and (3) assignment of the appropriate weight to each source. To accomplish the first step, the organization must determine the source of funds for capital expenditures, such as donations, borrowing, endowment income, and grants from public agencies. Next, the appropriate cost of each source must be determined; conceptually it is the opportunity cost for the sector of the economy from which the funds are raised. The costs of two sources, debt and endowment income, are easily calculated. Debt funds should earn a rate of interest at least equal to the interest rate paid to borrow the funds. Endowment funds can always be investigated elsewhere, if not used by the organization. Consequently, their opportunity cost is the rate earned by invested funds under current policy.

Calculation of the opportunity costs of donations and grants is not as straightforward. The appropriate cost for donations is the alternative investment rate for the sector of the economy from which the funds are raised. The private, not-for-profit organization should generate at least this minimum return or the funds should be employed elsewhere. There is a separate cost for each sector of the economy from which the funds are drawn. Since determination of the costs at the margin is impossible, average cost must be used. These costs must also be adjusted for the fund-raising costs associated with the source. The cost of donations, then, is equal to:

$$K_D = \frac{\sum\limits_{i=1}^{P} (K_{oi}) w_i}{(1-FR)} \qquad \text{(Equation 12.4)}$$

where K_D is equal to the cost of donation; K_{oi} is equal to the opportunity cost of funds for sector i, FR are the fund-raising costs expressed as a percentage of total funds raised by the nonprofit organization, w_i is the donation from sector i as a percentage of all donations, and p is the number of sources of donations.

An approximation is used to determine the opportunity cost of grants. The cost of grants is the discount rate used by the granting agency. This is a minimum of 10 percent for a federal grant, since all federal agencies, except water-resource agencies, use this minimum rate. The not-for-profit organization should generate at least a 10 percent return or the grant should be used elsewhere.

The third step is to weight the costs of the various sources of funds. A problem arises because the not-for-profit organization has no equivalent capital structure such as is found in the business sector. If the weights used are determined by the mix of funds financing a particular capital project, then project acceptance will vary with the funding mix. To minimize this consistency problem, a weighted average funding mix determined for a long time period, such as ten years, is used. Once the weights and costs are determined, they are then combined to obtain a weighted average cost of funds to be used as the discount rate. The calculation of the weighted average cost of funds for a not-for-profit organization is illustrated with the following example.

Illustration of Determination of Discount Rate for a Nonprofit Organization: Johnson Charity receives funds from four sources: donations, borrowing, endowment earnings, and federal grants. Over a ten-year period the average mix has been 50, 20, 20, and 10 percent, respectively, from these sources. Sixty percent of the donations are from individual donors with an average opportunity cost of 8 percent, while the remainder come from corporations with an estimated opportunity cost of 18 percent. Fundraising costs consume 25 percent of each dollar raised. The charity can borrow funds at a 10 percent rate and it earns 9 percent on any invested endowment earnings.

Equation 12-4 is used to calculate the component cost of donations:

$$K_D = \frac{(8.0\%) (0.6) + (18.0\%) (0.4)}{1-0.25}$$

$$= \frac{4.8\% + 7.2\%}{0.75} = 16\%$$

The overall discount rate can then be calculated as shown in Table 12.6. The cost of each source of funds is multiplied by the appropriate component of the ten-year average mix to obtain the weighted cost for each source of funds. Summing the weighted cost of each source results in an overall discount rate of 12.8 percent. Two things should be noted in this example. First, this illustrates how the discount rate varies with the mix of funds and the cost of each source of funds and, second, the cost of raising funds has a major impact on the overall discount rate.

TABLE 12.6

Calculation of Discount Rate for a Nonprofit Organization

Source	10-year average mix	Component cost(%)	Weighted cost(%)
Donations	0.50	16	8.00
Borrowing	0.20	10	2.00
Endowment earnings	0.20	9	1.80
Federal grants	0.10	10	1.80
Totals	1.00		12.80

SUMMARY

This chapter presented two major topics--cost-benefit analysis and the appropriate discount rate for nonprofit and governmental organizations. Cost-benefit analysis is a systematic method of evaluating the benefits and costs of a particular capital investment project. It is especially appropriate in situations in which the benefits cannot be completely quantified.

Cost-benefit analysis can be accomplished by one of three methods. The first method uses an internal-rate-of-return model which solves for the discount rate which equates the benefits of a project with its costs. A project is accepted if the calculated return rate is higher than the organization's opportunity cost. The second cost-benefit analysis technique is a derivative of the net present value methodology discussed in Chapter 11. The present values of the costs are subtracted from the present value of the benefits. If the benefits exceed the cost, the project is accepted. The third format is an adaptation of the profitability index. The present value of the benefits is divided by the present value of the costs. The project should be accepted if it has a cost-benefit ratio greater than one.

An example involving a centralized air conditioning system for a university is used to illustrate an application of cost-benefit analysis. The factors which can be quantified are evaluated using the net present value and cost-benefit ratio models. The factors which cannot be easily quantified are also examined. The qualitative analysis supports the quantitative analysis in this particular example.

There is no consensus on the appropriate discount rate to be used for governmental agencies. Some people argue that the rate of discount should be the long-term interest rate at which the government can finance its debt to support the project. Other people argue that the most logical rate is the opportunity cost of funds withdrawn from the private sector. An approach, incorporating some of the features of the methodology for both governmental units and profit-seeking firms, is suggested for nonprofit organizations. The discount rate used by nonprofit organizations should reflect the opportunity costs associated with the funds used. The opportunity costs from the major sources--donations, borrowing, endowment, and federal grants--are weighted by the percentage each source provides.

QUESTIONS

1. What is cost-benefit analysis? How is it related to the capital budgeting techniques discussed in Chapter 11?

2. What cost-benefit techniques are discussed in this chapter? Briefly describe each.

3. What major difficulties are encountered when using cost-benefit techniques?

4. What is the major advantage of using cost-benefit analysis for decision purposes?

5. What discount rate(s) are generally used in the private sector for capital budgeting decisions?

6. What discount rates have been proposed for not-for-profit organizations when making capital budgeting decisions? Briefly state the rationale for their use.

7. How does the discount rate affect the selection of projects?

8. Why do not-for-profit organizations use pre-tax discount rates?

PROBLEMS

1. Metropolitan College is going to construct three footbridges over three heavily traveled streets. They can use two alternative types of bridge construction: steel or concrete. Steel bridges require annual painting and other maintenance which is expected to cost $7,000 per year. If reinforced concrete is used, annual maintenance is negligible but the initial cost is $100,000 higher than for steel. Both bridges have a 20-year life. Using a 10 percent discount rate and cost-benefit analysis in NPV dollars, which type bridge should be built?

2. Homes along the Prince River sustain an average of $1,800,000 per year in losses and damages

from flooding due to inadequate storm sewers. New storm sewers can be built for $15,000,000 with annual maintenance costs of $160,000. Using a 15-year time horizon for evaluation, what is the internal rate of return for the cost-benefit analysis?

3. The city of Wyomissing Hills has three intersections, controlled by stop signs, which account for 40 percent of all traffic accidents within the city limits. It can install traffic lights at each intersection at a cost of $20,000 per intersection. The lights have a 10-year life and maintenance costs of $2,000 per year per light. If the average cost of each accident is $1,000 and a total of 40 accidents occurs annually at these intersections, should the lights be installed if they will reduce the number of accidents by 50 percent? Use the internal-rate-of-return cost-benefit technique for evaluation.

4. A local school district is considering the installation of microcomputers for instructional purposes in the junior high classes. The initial cost is $300,000 and annual maintenance is $5,000. Three specialized teacher positions will be eliminated at an annual savings of $45,000. The computers have a 10-year life, and the school district uses a 10 percent discount rate for evaluation. Does the cost-benefit analysis in NPV dollars support the installation of the computer?

5. Using the data in problem 4, determine the cost-benefit ratio for the installation of the microcomputers.

6. The government railroad system is planning on extending service to the northwest to either Plains City or Mountain View. If they extend the railroad all the way to Mountain View, construction will be $2,000,000 more initially than the cost of the track ending at Plains City. Maintenance costs will also be $80,000 more each year. Annual revenue from passenger and freight service will be $100,000 and $200,000 greater, respectively, however. If the railroad uses a 5 percent discount rate, should it construct the extension to Mountain View? (Use the CB-NPV technique over a 30 year period.)

7. Using the data in problem 6, determine the cost-benefit ratio for the track extension to Mountain View.

8. The University Hospital must decide to undertake extensive remodeling of its present facilities or build an entirely new medical complex. Data on the two alternatives are:

	Remodel	New
Initial cost	$3,000,000	$8,000,000
Annual maintenance	500,000	200,000
Annual net cash inflow (excluding maintenance)		
Years 1-3	600,000	400,000
Years 4-15	600,000	800,000

In addition, the new facility is expected to attract highly qualified medical personnel and have a major positive effect on the morale of both patients and nurses. Using a time horizon of 15 years for evaluation, a discount rate of 4 percent, and the CB-NPV technique, which alternative should be selected? What is the cost-benefit ratio?

9. Highland Fundamental College has an endowment of $3,000,000 which can be used to build dormitories. The school plans to build two new dormitories. They are expected to cost a total of $7 million. If the endowment is currently earning 12 percent and additional funds can be borrowed at 14 percent, what cost of funds should be used for further project analysis?

10. The United Charities receives money from four sources--private donations, corporate donations, federal grants, and borrowing. Determine the weighted average cost of funds using the following:

40 percent of total funds come from private donations which have an average opportunity cost of 7 percent and fund-raising consumes 20 percent of each dollar.

20 percent of total funds come from corporate donations which have an average opportunity cost of 14 percent; fund-raising consumes only 5 percent of each dollar, however.

20 percent of its funds are borrowed at an average interest rate of 14 percent.

The balance of the funds come from federal grants which carry a 10 percent opportunity cost.

ENDNOTES

1. James R. McGuigan and R. Charles Moyer, _Managerial Economics: Private and Public Sector Decision Analysis_ (Hinsdale, Ill.: The Dryden Press, 1975), p. 542.
2. Walter Oi, "Are Government Programs Worth the Price?" _Business Week_ (June 30, 1975), p. 116.
3. This example is from: William R. Henry and W. Warren Haynes, _Managerial Economics: Analysis and Cases_, 4th ed. (Dallas, Texas: Business Publications, Inc., 1978), pp. 659-661.
4. This section is based on the following paper: Michael C. Walker, "On the Appropriate Discount Rate for Private, Not-for-Profit Organizations," a paper presented at the 1976 annual meeting of the Southern Finance Association in Atlanta, Georgia.
5. Ibid., p. 5.
6. William J. Baumol, "On the Social Rate of Discount," _American Economic Review_ (September 1968), pp. 778-79.
7. Walker, p. 7.
8. N. C. Terre, D. W. Warnke, and A. P. Ameiss, "Cost/Benefit Analysis of Public Projects," _Management Accounting_ (January 1973), p. 37.

13

FINANCING OF CAPITAL PROJECTS: AN OVERVIEW

There are numerous ways a not-for-profit organization can finance its capital projects. The method of financing used by the organization will depend upon several factors, such as the financial position of the organization, type of organization, nature of the project being financed, and cash flow stability. Some of the common methods of financing are discussed in this chapter, along with an overview of the tax-free bond market, commonly called the municipal bond market. The role of the underwriter in the bond market is also explained. The use of bonds and leasing for financing, plus methods of improving debt management, are discussed in the following two chapters.

METHODS OF FINANCING

Numerous methods are available to finance capital improvement projects, and a careful study should be made of these various alternatives prior to undertaking the capital project. Some not-for-profit organizations obtain a major portion of their funds from revenues realized from the sale of goods or services. For example, tuition is a major source of revenue for many colleges and universities; many hospitals are financed primarily by patient charges; mutual insurance companies, transit authorities, and other similar governmental units are financed by user charges.[1] Many other not-for-profit organizations must obtain their funds from other sources such as appropriation from other organizations, taxes, contributions, grants, and other nonrevenue sources. Either type of organization may finance a certain portion of its capital projects on a "pay-as-you-go" basis, i.e., projects are financed out of current revenues. The pay-as-you-go approach is more feasible when capital expenditures are recurrent as to purpose or amount, such as the paving of streets.[2]

Other types of projects may be more appropriately financed by short-term loans. For example, some cities have used short-term borrowing initially to finance the construction of a series of smaller capital improvements rather than issuing separate amounts of long-term bond issues to finance each individual improvement. The projects can then be refinanced with a long-term bond issue once the size of the consolidated projects warrants it.[3]

A major alternative to pay-as-you-go and short-term borrowing is to issue bonds to finance the capital project. Still other funding options are federal or state assistance or gifts. Governmental agencies can elect to use special assessments or taxes to finance capital projects. Leasing is another method of financing, in which the not-for-profit organization pays an annual or monthly rental fee for the use of the facility on a long-term basis. Advantages and disadvantages of each of the major alternative methods of financing are discussed in the following sections. Bond financing and lease financing are also discussed in more detail in subsequent chapters.

Pay-As-You-Go

The pay-as-you-go method involves the payment of cash for the project instead of borrowing against future revenues. The method is limited to those organizations which collect revenues in excess of what is needed for current operating expenses and the establishment of reserves for contingencies. To illustrate this method, consider the street maintenance department of the city of Rosemont. The department presently has $100,000 in reserve for contingencies. As a matter of policy, the department maintains a minimum of $25,000 in its contingency reserve. The department is budgeted to receive $250,000 in tax revenues during the coming fiscal year and its operating expenses are forecasted at $50,000. The department uses the pay-as-you-go method to finance the resurfacing of the city's streets and desires to know how much can be spent to resurface streets during the next year.

Equation 13-1 states the relationship between cash revenues, cash expenditures, and reserves for contingencies for the pay-as-you-go method.

$$\underline{B}_0 + \underline{R} - \underline{E} - \underline{P} = \underline{B}_1 \qquad \text{(Equation 13-1)}$$

where $\underline{B}_0$ is the reserve level at the beginning of the year, $\underline{R}$ is the cash revenue received during the year, E represents the cash expenditures during the year, $\underline{P}$ is the capital expenditure for the year, and $\underline{B}_1$ is the desired cash reserve level at the end of the year. Rearranging Equation 13-1 results in Equation 13-2, which expresses the relationship in terms of $\underline{P}$, the capital expenditures for the period.

$$\underline{P} = (\underline{B}_0 - \underline{B}_1) + (\underline{R} - \underline{E}) \qquad \text{(Equation 13-2)}$$

As we can see from Equation 13-2, the amount of funds available for capital expenditures using the pay-as-you-go method is the sum of the differences between the beginning reserve level and desired reserve level at the end of the year and between the cash revenues and cash expenditures for the year. The pay-as-you-go method works best for organizations in which cash revenues and cash expenditures are predictable with a reasonable degree of accuracy. The capital needs of the organization should be relatively constant and adequate reserves need to be established.

Using Equation 13-2, the funds available to the street maintenance department in the example can be determined:

$$\underline{P} = (\underline{B}_0 - \underline{B}_1) + (\underline{R} - \underline{E}) \qquad \text{(Equation 13-2)}$$

$$\underline{P} = (\$100,000 - \$25,000) + (\$250,000 - \$50,000)$$

$$\underline{P} = \$75,000 + \$200,000$$

$$\underline{P} = \$275,000$$

The department has $75,000 available from reserves and $200,000 from the difference between cash revenues and cash expenditures, or a total of $275,000 available for resurfacing.

There are two possible major advantages to the pay-as-you-go method. First, it can result in cost savings. Since borrowed funds are not being used, there are no interest payments. At a 9 percent interest rate and no intervening principal payments, the interest would double the original capital cost in a little over eight years.[4] This method also avoids any expense involved with marketing long-term debt such as fees for the financial advisor, legal counsel, underwriter, and printing costs. Second, the pay-as-you-go method preserves the organization's borrowing capacity for future capital projects. The steady completion of capital projects on a pay-as-you-go basis may even increase the borrowing capacity of the not-for-profit organization by enhancing its bond rating.

The pay-as-you-go method, despite its two favorable characteristics, has several disadvantages.[5] First, the ability of most organizations to pay from current revenues is extremely limited. Second, the method places a heavy financial burden on the organization when a capital project is undertaken. The use of long-term financing smooths this awkward, fluctuating expenditure cycle for capital projects. Third, financing a project with a long life is more equitable than financing by users who may not enjoy the benefits of the project over its full life.[6] For example, an increase in municipal rates in order to pay for a project in a short time period is not equitable to those citizens who leave after a brief residence. Finally, with the inflationary increases in construction costs experienced during the last decade, it may be less expensive to borrow funds now and pay today's prices rather then postpone the project until adequate cash is available. A project which costs $100,000 today will cost $125,970 three years from now if construction costs increase at an 8 percent rate.[7] Also, by borrowing during an inflationary period, today's dollars are received but are repaid with cheaper dollars in the future. When the annual inflation rate is 6 percent, $1,000 borrowed today can be repaid with only $558.39 in ten years in terms of today's dollars.[8]

Short- and Intermediate-Term Debt

Not-for-profit organizations can use short- and/or intermediate-term notes issued by commercial banks or other financial sources for capital projects which do not lend themselves to the pay-as-you-go method. Short-term debt usually has a maturity of one year or less, while intermediate-term debt matures in two to five years. The addition of short- or intermediate-term debt to Equation 13-2 results in the following relationship:

$$\underline{P} = (\underline{B}_0 - \underline{B}_1) + (\underline{R} - \underline{E}) + (\underline{S} - \underline{O}) \quad \text{(Equation 13-3)}$$

where $\underline{S}$ is the amount of new borrowing during the year and $\underline{O}$ is the amount of any principal or interest payments. The undertaking of added debt increases the sum available for investment by the difference between new short-term loan principal and any payments of principal and interest on outstanding short-term loans.

The use of short- or intermediate-term loans for financing capital projects affords several advantages.[9] First, it offers an additional source for the financing of capital projects when funds provided by the pay-as-you-go method are not sufficient. Second, a lump sum can be borrowed and repaid in installments over the next few years, resulting in a smoothing of the expenditure pattern. Third, the use of short- or intermediate-term debt usually results in interest savings over long-term debt, since the principal is repaid sooner, thereby reducing the interest expense. The use of shorter-term debt, in most cases, avoids the marketing costs associated with the issuance of long-term debt. During inflationary periods, the use of shorter-term debt allows construction at today's lower prices.

There are, however, several significant disadvantages to the use of short- or intermediate-term debt to finance capital projects. First, there is the risk associated with the refinancing of the debt, if this becomes necessary. The life of most capital projects will usually extend beyond the maturity date of shorter-term loans. If the not-for-profit organization, for some unforeseen reason, is unable to repay the loan when it becomes due, it must refinance all or part of the loan. If the organization has suffered financial setbacks, it may be unable to obtain a new loan. Even if the loan can be renewed, it may be renewed at a much higher interest rate.

Another disadvantage of using shorter-term loans is that the borrowing capacity of the organization is reduced. Thus, the organization has less flexibility in obtaining financing for future capital projects. The use of shorter-term debt to finance capital projects results in a less stable expenditure cycle than with long-term financing, although the fluctuations are not as severe as with the pay-as-you-go method. In inflationary periods, the use of shorter-term debt also affords some advantages over the pay-as-you-go method, though the benefit is not as great as with long-term financing. Finally, the cost of the project may exceed the bank's capacity to grant a short-term loan. The size of a loan is limited by the bank's available capital.

Long-Term Debt

The use of long-term debt, usually through the issuance of bonds, is a major alternative to the pay-as-you-go and short-term debt methods for financing capital projects. Long-term bonds issued by state and local governments are known as municipal bonds. These bonds are used to finance capital projects such as schools, highways, hospitals, airports, sewage treatment plants, and civic centers. Similarly, long-term bonds can be used by other not-for-profit organizations to finance capital projects. Most not-for-profit organizations would be hard-pressed to expand, improve, or in some cases, to continue services without long-term borrowing. Capital projects usually make large, infrequent demands on the resources of the not-for-profit organization which cannot be met by current resources or short-term debt.

The use of long-term debt to finance capital projects has several advantages and, like the other methods, it also has several limitations. The use of long-term debt allows a not-for-profit organization to obtain for current use a capital facility that would be beyond its capacity to finance on a pay-as-you-go basis. It avoids the increased construction costs associated with delayed construction in an inflationary period. It allows the organization to repay its obligations in dollars that have lost some of their value because of increased prices. In addition, the not-for-profit organization is able to smooth out its expenditure pattern over a period of several years.

The use of long-term debt, however, increases the not-for-profit organization's exposure to financial risk. The organization assumes an obligation to make a series of principal and interest payments. A combination of poor planning for debt administration and/or unforeseen events may result in cash revenues below expectations. If severe, these revenue short-falls may mean the organization will be unable to meet principal and/or interest payments. At best, the organization will suffer financial embarrass-ment; at worst, the organization could be forced into bankruptcy. Long-term debt also reduces the borrowing capacity of the not-for-profit organiza-tion, thereby limiting its flexibility to finance future capital projects or requiring increased in-terest costs for future debt issues. Because of the complex nature of municipal bonds and their impor-tance as a source of financing capital projects, the next chapter contains a more detailed discussion of the characteristics of municipal bonds.

Gifts or Grants From Third Parties

Federal and/or state assistance is often avail-able to local governments and other types of not-for-profit organizations through grant programs. These grant programs, however, may place con-straints on the operating budgets and flexibility of the recipients. Often, this type of funding re-quires matching funding by the recipient organiza-tions. Charities, hospitals, museums, and similar types of not-for-profit organizations often receive gifts or bequests for capital projects. Again, strings are often attached to these gifts, and their acceptance should not be automatic. The organiza-tion should analyze the effect on overall operations before accepting gifts which contain limiting provi-sions.

Leasing

An alternative to direct acquisition of capital assets is to acquire their use through leasing. The not-for-profit organization need not own the asset, as long as it has use of it. A wide variety of assets, including automobiles, trucks, office equip-ment, and buildings are available through lease arrangements.

Lease arrangements are long-term contracts for the use of an asset. The lessor maintains ownership of the asset and receives periodic rental payments for its use over the life of the contract. The lessee, in this case a not-for-profit organization, makes periodic rental payments and enjoys the use of the asset over the life of the contract. Because of the unique features of leases and the effects of the not-for-profit organization's tax-exempt status on the benefits of leasing, lease contracts are explored in more detail in Chapter 15.

THE MUNICIPAL BOND MARKET

A bond is simply a long-term IOU or promise to pay. It is a promise to repay a specified amount of money (the face amount of the bond) on a particular date (the maturity date). A periodic rent (or interest) is paid for the use of the other person's money. Bonds issued by state or local governments are known as municipal bonds, even though they may be issued by states, counties, or special governmental authorities. Municipal bonds are issued by state and local governments primarily to finance capital outlays, which usually account for about 20 to 25 percent of state and local government spending.

Municipal bonds are being increasingly used to finance health care facility construction. Prior to 1960, hospital financing was generally a small, localized operation. Until then, local gifts and charity, income from operations, funded depreciation, and small federal grants provided the financing for capital improvements.[10] Since 1960, however, new trends have completely changed the nature of hospital financing in this country. An increased rate of obsolescence for capital expenditures resulting from new medical technology has forced the upgrading of all medical facilities. Medicare has caused a dramatic increase in the use of health services. In addition, inflation has had a severe impact on both operating and capital costs. "Hospital construction costs alone have shot up from less than $1 billion to close to $10 billion in 1979."[11]

These trends and others have forced hospitals to seek capital from outside their areas by entering the municipal bond market. As a result, by 1977 nearly 90 percent of the total new capital required to finance hospital expansion came from the issuance of some form of long-term debt, with nearly 88 percent of this debt financed by the issuance of tax-exempt bonds.[12] In late 1980, tax-exempt bonds issued for hospital and medical facility construction accounted for approximately 8 percent of all new long-term municipal bond issues.[13]

Types of Municipal Bonds

One way to classify municipal bonds is by the claim the holder has on revenues and/or assets for repayment of the bonds. There are two general types of claims for municipal bonds--general obligation bonds and revenue bonds. General obligation bonds are backed by the full faith, credit, and taxing power of the issuing government. Revenue bonds are backed only by the revenues from a specific project--such as a hospital, dormitory, or toll road. Since general obligation bonds are backed by an inclusive pledge from the issuing authority and revenue bonds are not, revenue bonds are considered to be riskier than the general obligation bonds. The credit quality of the revenue bond is directly related to the ability of the issuer to collect revenues from the project financed. Everything else being equal, revenue bonds carry yields which are 15 to 20 basis points[14] higher than that of general obligation bonds.[15]

Municipal and Corporate Bond Differences

Municipal and corporate bonds generally have the same characteristics and attributes with two major exceptions. The interest income from municipal bonds is exempt from all federal income tax. In most cases, the interest income is also exempt from state and local income taxes in the issuing locality. The tax-exempt feature results in a lower borrowing cost for the issuing government; this, in turn, enables them to offer investors a lower yield but one that is competitive with the after-tax yield available on corporate bonds. The yields on tax-exempt bonds have usually been between two-thirds and three-quarters of those on similar taxable bonds.[16]

The other major difference is that most corporate bonds are sold as term bonds while most municipal bonds are sold as serial bonds. A term bond matures at a single point in time with the full amount of the bond due at maturity. For example, a $10 million, ten-year term bond issue would have the entire $10 million face amount due at the end of ten years. A serial bond issue is a bundle of terms. The issue is divided into a series of individual term bonds that mature at different times. A $10 million, ten-year serial bond issue might contain ten different $1 million term bonds which mature sequentially in years 1 through 10.

The Supply of Municipal Bonds

The volume of outstanding municipal bonds has grown tremendously over the past twenty years. As can be seen in Table 13.1, the volume of municipal bonds issued per year has increased from $7.5 billion in 1960 to approximately $45.0 billion in the late 1970s, an annual compound growth rate of approximately 9 percent. This growth in sales of new municipal bonds has caused an increase in outstanding municipal bonds from $67 billion at the end of 1960 to over $263 billion at the end of 1978.

Another striking trend has been the increase in the issuance of revenue bonds compared to general obligation bonds. Since 1970, the sale of new general obligation bonds has fluctuated between $12 billion and $18 billion per year. The sale of new revenue bonds, however, has steadily increased from $6 billion to $31 billion per year, an annual compound growth rate of almost 20 percent. This dramatic increase in revenue bonds has caused a shift in the composition of municipal bond sales. In 1970, almost 65 percent of the sales were general obligation bonds and 34 percent were revenue bonds. (The other 1 percent represented U.S. Government Loans and Housing Assistance Administration issues). During 1979, approximately 28 percent of the new sales were general obligation bonds, while almost 72 percent of the new bonds were revenue bonds.

Several factors have contributed to this general increase in borrowing and the increased reliance on revenue bonds. First, local governments have faced an increased demand for their services. This increase in demand for services has resulted in a strong growth in demand for public facilities. "The housing boom, increasing urbanization, and the rapid redistribution of population lifted demands for supporting public services and utilities to unprecedented levels."[17] Second, the concept of charging users of services rather than the entire population of the locality has contributed to the increased use of revenue bonds. Many new facilities, such as bridges, toll roads, civic centers, and museums, which have been constructed lend themselves to the imposition of user charges.

TABLE 13.1

Selected Data on State and Local Government Debt Issues, 1955–1979 (Billions of Dollars)

YEAR	New long-term issues			Amount outstanding		
	(1) Total*	(2) General obligation	(3) Revenue	(4) Total	(5) Long-term	(6) Short-term
1960	7.5	4.6	2.1	70.8	67.3	3.4
1965	11.3	7.2	3.5	100.3	94.3	5.5
1970	18.2	11.8	6.1	144.4	131.1	13.3
1971	25.0	15.2	8.7	161.8	146.1	15.7
1972	23.6	14.3	9.3	176.6	160.9	15.8
1973	24.0	12.3	10.6	191.2	175.1	16.1
1974	24.3	13.6	10.2	209.1	190.5	18.6
1975	30.6	16.0	14.5	217.2	198.6	18.6
1976	35.3	18.0	17.1	230.3	215.9	14.5
1977	46.8	18.0	28.7	250.5	238.6	11.9
1978	48.6	17.9	30.7	275.6	263.2	12.4
1979	43.5	12.1	31.3	NA	NA	NA

Source: Columns (1) - (3); Various issues of Federal Reserve Bulletin, "New Issues of State and Local Governments Securities." Columns (4) - (6); Federal Reserve Board, Flow of Funds Accounts.

*Total includes United States Government Loans and Housing Assistance Administration issues.

Next, in most localities, the issuance of new general obligation bonds requires approval of the electorate. Public officials have recognized the increasing reluctance of the public to approve new debt issues, particularly since the 1975 financial crisis in New York City. When the city defaulted on a note after rapidly increasing its debt outstanding for over a decade, doubts were cast on the viability of various municipal issues throughout the country. The general public became wary of approving any new debt issues. As a result, the use of revenue bonds which usually do not require voter approval has increased greatly.

The dramatic increase in the issuance of tax-exempt bonds by hospitals has also contributed to both this increased borrowing and the use of revenue bonds. State, municipal, and other types of not-for-profit hospitals have been authorized by state legislatures to issue tax-exempt bonds for capital improvements. (Note that nearly 50 percent of all hospital beds in the United States are controlled by voluntary or religiously affiliated not-for-profit organizations which are permitted to finance capital expenditures with municipal revenue bonds.[18] This debt is usually secured by first claims on the revenues of the hospitals. Hospital financing is now a major component of the municipal bond market. In 1979, there were 289 bond issues with a total value of over $3.47 billion sold in the bond market.[19]

The Demand for Municipal Bonds

Because of their tax-exempt feature, municipal bonds are especially attractive to individuals and corporations in the higher tax brackets. A not-for-profit organization, which pays no income tax, would have little incentive to invest in municipal bonds. The not-for-profit organization could earn a higher yield by investing in a Treasury security and would not be faced with a risk of default. Life insurance companies, which are subject to limited taxes, also cannot take full advantage of municipal bonds. Consequently, the demand for municipal securities is segmented. Table 13.2 presents the demand for municipal securities by major sources. At the end of 1978, commercial banks and fire and casualty companies held over 68 percent of the municipal securities outstanding. Over 27 percent were held by individuals. The remaining 4 percent of municipal securities were held by life insurance companies, pension funds, and similar institutions.

The 1960s saw a dramatic increase in demand for municipal securities by commercial banks. The

TABLE 13.2

Ownership of State and Local Securities, 1950–1978
(Billions)

Investor Group	Dollar amount (billions) for selected years				
	1950	1960	1970	1975	1978
Banks	8.2	17.7	70.2	102.9	126.2
Individuals	10.0	30.8	45.2	68.1	75.0
Fire & casualty ins. co.	1.1	8.1	17.8	33.3	62.5
Others	5.9	14.2	11.2	12.9	11.9
Total	25.2	70.8	144.4	217.2	275.6

Percentage ownership for selected years

Investor group	Year				
	1950	1960	1970	1975	1978
Banks	32.6%	25.0%	48.6%	47.4%	45.8%
Individuals	39.6	43.5	31.3	31.4	27.2
Fire & casualty ins. co.	4.4	11.5	12.3	15.3	22.7
Others	23.4	20.0	7.8	5.9	4.3
Total	100.0%	100.0%	100.0%	100.0%	100.0%

Source: Federal Reserve Board, Flow of Funds Accounts

amount of municipal securities held by banks increased from $17.7 billion at the end of 1960 to $70.2 billion at the end of 1970. The percentage of total municipal securities held by commercial banks increased from 25.0 percent to 48.6 percent during the decade. The 1970s have been characterized by an increase in demand by fire and casualty insurance companies. Their holdings of municipal securities have increased from $17.8 billion at the end of 1970 to $62.5 billion at the end of 1978. The percentage of total municipal securities held by fire and casualty companies increased from 12.3 percent to 22.7 percent during the same time period.

The demand for municipal securities has varied considerably from year to year as can be seen from Table 13.3. During periods of tight money such as in 1966, 1969, 1971, and 1975, commercial banks increased their holdings only slightly.[20] During these same periods, however, individuals greatly expanded their holdings. During other periods such as 1962, 1965, 1967-1968, 1970-1971, banks substantially increased their net purchases of muncipal securities while individuals reduced theirs.

Fire and casualty companies purchase tax-exempt bonds when they want to shelter profits that other-

TABLE 13.3

Net Changes in Holdings of Municipal Securities, 1960-1976 (in billions)

Year	Banks	Individuals	Fire & Casualty Companies	Other	Total Change
1960	$ 0.7	$ 3.5	$0.8	$ 3.0	$ 5.3
1961	2.8	1.2	1.0	1.0	5.1
1962	5.7	−1.0	0.8	−0.1	5.4
1963	3.9	1.0	0.7	0.1	5.7
1964	3.6	2.6	0.4	−0.6	6.0
1965	5.2	1.7	0.4	0	7.3
1966	2.3	3.6	1.3	−1.6	5.6
1967	9.1	−2.2	1.4	−1.5	7.8
1968	8.6	−0.8	1.0	0.7	9.5
1969	0.2	9.6	1.2	−1.1	9.9
1970	10.7	−0.8	1.5	−0.1	11.3
1971	12.6	−0.2	3.9	1.3	17.6
1972	7.2	2.2	4.8	1.2	15.4
1973	5.7	7.2	3.6	−0.2	16.3
1974	5.5	11.2	2.5	0.4	19.6
1975	1.7	8.7	1.8	5.1	17.3
1976	2.9	6.4	3.6	4.3	17.2

Source: Federal Reserve Board, Flow of Funds Accounts

wise would be taxable at the highest marginal corporate tax rate. Consequently, their demand depends on the availability of investment funds and their desire for tax shelters.[21] During the period from 1971-1973, fire and casualty companies were extremely active in the municipal bond market, acquiring nearly 30 percent of the net new issues. The industry experienced record underwriting losses in 1974 and their losses soared by 70 percent in 1975 to an estimated $4.5 billion. As a result, their purchases of municipal bonds dropped significantly.[22]

The increase in the "other" sector in 1975 and 1976 was largely due to purchases of New York City obligations by the Municipal Assistance Corporation for the City of New York (dubbed "Big Mac"). These purchases resulted from the near bankruptcy of New York City in 1975. The Municipal Assistance Corporation for the City of New York was created to rescue New York City from its fiscal crisis. This corporation, a governmental agency of New York State was created by legislation in June 1975 to provide financial assistance and oversee fiscal matters for the City of New York. It was given the authority to issue debt, to pay or lend funds to New York, and to exchange its obligations for those of the city. Eventually the financial crisis in New York City was abated, with the assistance of seasonal loans by the federal government and long-term loans from certain city pension funds and the Municipal Assistance Corporation.

ROLE OF UNDERWRITER

The issuers of tax-exempt bonds rarely deal directly with the investors that ultimately purchase their bonds. Rather, there is an intermediary, or buffer, between the issuer and the final investor. This intermediary is called an underwriter and the primary function of the underwriter is to guarantee that issuers of municipal bonds receive their funds without encountering any marketing difficulties. To do this, the underwriter actually purchases an entire bond issue from the issuer, providing the funds immediately. The underwriter, in turn, reoffers the issue to individual investors as a series of smaller investments, which enhances the marketability of the issue.

In reality, an underwriter is usually not a single individual or bond dealer, but rather a syndicate of financial institutions specializing in bond investments, headed by one or several managers who organize the group into selling units. Each unit then is responsible for the sale of a specific allocation or portion of the bond issue. The syndicate makes a profit by selling the smaller-denomination bonds to individual investors at a price higher than the price paid to the issuer. This mark-up in price, known as the "spread," is intended to compensate the underwriter for (1) distributing the bonds, (2) assuming the risk of changes in market value of the bonds from the date of purchase until the final distribution, and (3) advising and counseling the issuer if the bonds are sold on a negotiated basis, rather than by competitive bidding.

Municipal bond underwriters may be either commercial banks and/or securities dealers. Banks, however, are prohibited by law (except for a few special cases) from underwriting revenue bonds. Consequently, the majority of general obligation bonds are underwritten by banks and the majority of revenue bonds are underwritten by securities dealers. With the strong shift from general obligation to revenue bonds there has been mounting pressure applied to allow banks to underwrite revenue issues.

SUMMARY

This chapter has discussed some of the common methods of financing capital projects in the not-for-profit organization. Projects may be financed on a "pay-as-you-go" basis from current revenues. This method can result in cost savings since the interest charges are avoided and the borrowing capacity of the organization is also preserved. This method, however, places a heavy financial burden on the organization when a capital project is undertaken. The use of short-term debt offers an additional source of financing for capital projects with interest expense incurred for only short periods of time. This method has several disadvantages, such as the risk of not being able to refinance the project and the decrease in overall borrowing capacity.

The use of long-term debt is a major alternative to the pay-as-you-go and short-term debt methods for financing capital expenditures. Long-term bonds issued by state and local governments are known as municipal bonds. The advantages and disadvantages

of using municipal bonds were discussed. Other sources of financing such as gifts or grants from third
parties and the use of leases were introduced.

The volume of new municipal bonds issued has
grown from $7.5 billion in 1960 to around $45 billion in late 1970, an annual increase of around 9
percent a year. Most striking has been the increase
in revenue bonds compared to general obligation
bonds. The revenues from a specific project are
pledged as security for a revenue bond. The general
obligation bond carries a pledge of the full faith
and taxing power of the issuer.

Because of their tax-exempt feature, municipal
bonds are especially attractive to individuals and
organizations in high marginal tax brackets. Two
types of financial institutions, commercial banks
and fire and casualty companies, hold over 68 percent of the total municipal securities outstanding.
Over 27 percent of the securities are held by individuals.

Finally, the role of the underwriter in the sale
of municipal bonds was discussed. The underwriter
is an intermediary between the issuer and final
investor. The major function of the underwriter is
to ensure that issuers receive their funds without
encountering any marketing difficulties.

QUESTIONS

1. How are capital projects financed by not-for-
   profit organizations? Briefly explain each.

2. Evaluate the pay-as-you go method of financing
   capital projects.

3. Evaluate the use of short- or intermediate-term
   debt to finance capital projects.

4. Evaluate the use of long-term debt to finance
   capital projects.

5. Distinguish general obligation from revenue
   bonds.

6. Explain the effect of the income tax structure
   on interest rates of municipal bonds.

7. What is the difference between a term bond and a
   serial bond?

8. What advantages do revenue bonds have over general obligation bonds?

9. What is "Big Mac?" Why was it created?

10. Briefly describe the role of the underwriter in a municipal bond issue.

PROBLEMS

1. The local recreation department must pay for all capital expenditures on a pay-as-you-go basis. It currently has a reserve fund of $8,000; expects tax revenue for operating and capital expenditures of $223,000; estimates operating expenses at $65,000 per month for each of the three summer months it operates; and desires a reserve of $5,000 for the coming year. How much may the recreation department spend on capital improvements?

2. The Little Theater Group, because of its small sustaining endowment, must pay for all capital improvements as they are made; in addition, it has a $7,000 deficit which must be offset prior to any other expenditures. The group has sold $35,000 in advance season tickets and estimates that single-performance ticket sales will be $40,000. Expenses incurred during the season are estimated at $8,000 for rent; $2,000 for utilities; $8,000 for costumes; $6,000 for scenery; $15,000 for the salary of the director; $10,000 for administrative services; and $3,000 for miscellaneous expenses. How much could the group spend for additional acoustics and a new curtain if it desires a $2,000 reserve at year-end?

3. The local hospital badly needs updated emergency room facilities, but it has limited borrowing power. How much must it borrow to finance a $600,000 renovation under the following circumstances?

Current reserve	$ 12,000
Estimated revenue	2,685,000
Cash expenses	
Wages & salaries	1,300,000
Drugs & supplies	400,000

Utilities	200,000
Maintenance	250,000
Administrative	200,000
Housekeeping	150,000
Miscellaneous	50,000

4. The local Lutheran church wants to build an education building. It can borrow one-half the cost from its synod at very reasonable interest rates. How much can the church spend on the building under the following assumptions?

Current reserve	$ 32,000
Estimated Sunday revenue	230,000
Estimated pledges for bldg. program (40% due currently, the balance used to retire any debt)	300,000
Cash expenses:	
Wages & salaries	45,000
Utilities	20,000
Maintenance of parsonage	15,000
Program expenses	10,000
Expenses for services, hymnals, robes	9,000
Debt payment	60,000
Miscellaneous	10,000

5. What is the difference in total interest cost between a $10,000 loan for 1 year at 12 percent or a $10,000 loan for 5 years at 10 percent repaid in equal annual installments?

6. What is the difference in total interest cost per bond between 10-year, 8 percent bonds and 20-year, 7 percent bonds, both with $1,000 face value?

7. What would you recommend to the administration of Central City in the following situation? They can construct a swimming pool today for $200,000 by paying $50,000 down and borrowing the balance at 12 percent interest over 5 years with repayment in equal annual installments; or, they can wait five years and construct the facility at a new estimated cost, due to inflation, of $300,000. (Operating revenues equal expenses and are not a factor in the decision.)

8. Hansen Nursing Home wants to add a physical therapy unit at a cost of $75,000. It has a

338

$25,000 reserve for this purpose and can borrow the balance at 15 percent interest for 3 years with repayment in equal annual installments. It can wait 3 years to construct the unit, paying cash, at an estimated cost of $110,000. In the meantime, however, it would forego the added revenue from the unit's operation of $6,000 per year. What action do you recommend?

ENDNOTES

1. Robert N. Anthony, Financial Accounting in Non-business Organizations: An Exploratory Study of Conceptual Issues (Stamford, Connecticut: Financial Accounting Standards Board, 1978), p. 9.
2. Alan Walter Steiss, Local Government Finance: Capital Facilities Planning and Debt Administration (Lexington, Mass.: Lexington Books, 1975), p. 109.
3. Ibid.
4. This is simply a future-value problem. The FV factor for 9 percent and 8 years is 1.993, so $100,000 borrowed for construction at 9 percent would require a $199,300 payment if the debt is retired at the end of 8 years with one payment.
5. C. Wayne Stallings, A Capital Improvement Programming Handbook for Small Cities and Other Government Projects (Chicago, Ill.: Municipal Financial Officers Association, 1978), p. 20.
6. Ibid.
7. The future value of $100,000, three years from now at an 8 percent rate is equal to: $FV_3 = PV(FVIF(8\%, 3yr)) = 100,000 (1.2597) = \$125,970$.
8. The present value of $1,000, ten years from now, at a 6 percent discount rate is equal to: $PV = FV_5(PVIF(6\%, 10yr)) = 1,000(0.55839) = \$558.39$.
9. Stalling, pp. 71-72.
10. Robert Lamb and Stephen P. Rappaport, Municipal Bonds: The Comprehensive Review of Tax-Exempt Securities and Public Finance (New York: McGraw-Hill Book Company, 1980), p. 185.
11. Ibid.
12. Ibid, pp. 185-186.
13. Leon J. Karvelis, Jr. and Richard M. Gerwitz, "Hospital Bond Analysis: A Primer"; Merrill, Lynch, Pierce, Feaner, & Smith Inc.; Fixed Income Research-Tax-Exempt Hospital Report; October 1980, p. 1.
14. A basis point is 1/100 of 1 percent.

15. John E. Peterson, The Rating Game (New York: The Twentieth Century Fund, 1974), p. 29.
16. Ibid., p. 35.
17. Ibid., p. 26.
18. Lamb and Rappaport, p. 188.
19. Karvelis and Gerwitz, p. 1.
20. This section is based on: James C. Van Horne, Financial Market Rates and Flows (Englewood Cliffs, N.J.: Prentice-Hall, Inc., 1978), pp. 191-192.
21. Ronald W. Forbes and John E. Peterson, Building a Broader Market (New York: Twentieth Century Fund, Inc., 1976), p. 83.
22. Ibid., p. 84.

BASIC CHARACTERISTICS
OF MUNICIPAL BONDS

The first part of this chapter presents the various characteristics that municipal bonds may possess and their effect on interest rates and selling prices. The latter part discusses the methods available to market municipal bonds and ways to improve their marketability. The succeeding chapter provides a detailed discussion of ways to improve the efficiency and effectiveness of debt management by evaluating municipal bond bids, determining the optimal size of bond issues, analyzing the bond refunding decision, evaluating the use of municipal bond insurance, and making the lease versus buy decision.

TYPES OF MUNICIPAL BOND ISSUES

As discussed in the previous chapter, there are two basic types of municipal bonds--general obligation and revenue bonds. The general obligation or "full faith and credit" bonds are based on the legal pledge of the taxing power of a local government to cover the bonds, principal and interest payments by levying taxes, if necessary. Revenue bonds, or limited liability bonds, generally do not constitute an obligation backed by the taxing power of the local government. Funds for interest and principal payments come from rents or fees earned by operation of the projects for which the funds are being raised. There are advantages and disadvantages to both types of bonds from the viewpoint of the issuer. General revenue bonds, because of their all-inclusive pledge, historically have been considered a less risky investment. Consequently, the interest rates on general obligation bonds are lower than the rates on similar revenue bonds.

Revenue bonds, however, are growing increasingly popular. Revenue bonds are a more equitable way of paying for projects which benefit only specific segments of a community since only the project users pay for the cost of the project. Revenue bonds are also the only alternative for communities which reach their legal debt ceiling or are reluctant to seek voter approval for new debt issues. Revenue bonds do not constitute debt in the legal manner used in measuring debt limits and voter approval is not required before issuance.

SERIAL VERSUS TERM MATURITY

Before 1920, most municipal bonds issued were term bonds. This meant that the full bond debt principal remained outstanding for the entire term of the bonds and interest payments were computed on the entire face value of the original issue. At the same time, most state laws required bond issuers to make sinking fund payments.[1] Serial bonds grew in acceptance as bond issuers began to realize that the total dollar amount of interest could be reduced by using serial bonds instead of term bonds.

The major advantage of serial bond issues compared to term bonds is that serial issues may be more marketable. The serial bond issue, with the diversity of maturity dates, may attract a wider range of investors interested in bonds with various terms to maturity. A term bond issue relies completely on a single maturity preference.

Term bonds are frequently issued when a project is financed by estimated future revenues for which a reliable pattern has not been established. Projects for which term bonds are frequently used are toll roads, turnpikes, and bridges.[2] Interest payments are made from current revenues with additional funds set aside periodically in a sinking fund for repayment of principal. In this manner, the repayment of the principal is deferred until the project is well established or, in many cases, until full maturity of the bonds. If revenues exceed project projections, the bonds can be retired prior to maturity.

It should be noted, however, that there is no one "correct" maturity structure. The correct choice depends on the particular project and future expectations. In addition, other factors such as alternative opportunities for the reinvestment of sinking funds, flexibility, and debt service ability must be considered before the decision is made for any particular issue.

SINKING FUNDS

A sinking fund, also called a debt service fund, is the mechanism designed to ensure that sufficient funds are available for repayment of debt at its maturity, and that unusual demands are not made on a local government's annual revenues. Proper management of a sinking fund requires periodic contributions to a separate sinking fund account, which, along with the compounded earnings from the investment of these funds, will provide a sufficient amount to repay the debt obligation at maturity. While this appears to be a simple task, the investment of sinking fund assets in reality presents a major problem to municipal management. Many communities, especially smaller ones, frequently lack the expertise to efficiently oversee such investments. No specific models (studies) are currently available to aid local units in sinking fund investment practices, but the two general principles that should dictate sinking funds administration are (1) make high-quality investments, and (2) keep funds relatively liquid in case early debt retirement is necessary.

Proper sinking fund management allows the government to lower the net cost of a bond issue through the return from investing the funds in the sinking fund. At the same time the uncertainty that bond buyers associate with future debt repayment is reduced, ensuring that adequate funds will be available at maturity. In addition, the expected return from the sinking fund investments affects the size of the bond issue. If the funds in the sinking fund earn a high return, a smaller amount must be set aside in the sinking fund, freeing the funds for current operations and permitting a reduction in the required debt.

Call Provisions

Bond retirement and refinancing represent an important part of debt management. Bond contracts often contain a provision allowing local governments the legal right to redeem, or "call," bonds prior to their maturity date. Without this feature, bondholder consent would have to be obtained for early redemption of bonds. This means that bondholders, rather than local governments, would be in a position to dictate the price at which bonds are redeemed prior to maturity.

Call provisions offer several advantages to bond issuers. First, they provide local governments with future flexibility by allowing them to reduce outstanding debt through early retirement if circumstances warrant. Early redemption can always be achieved by purchasing bonds in the open market, but this requires the bond issuer to be a price-taker. The call option, on the other hand, establishes a maximum fixed price for early repayment. Another advantage of the call feature is that it allows the borrowers to remove undesirable restrictions contained in the bond indenture by calling the issue. Finally, and perhaps most important, the call provision allows local units to achieve interest savings either through repurchase or refunding. If the general market interest rate on new municipal bonds is lower than the interest rate on the outstanding bonds, the call provision provides a means by which the local government can lower its annual interest payments. The issuer can repurchase the outstanding bonds, retire them, and issue new bonds at lower interest rates. The mathematics of the refunding decision are discussed in Chapter 15.

A disadvantage of the call provision must also be noted, however. Investors who purchase callable bonds face the possibility of financial injury through lower interest income, i.e., investors may be forced to reinvest at lower interest rates when bonds are recalled. In addition, investors are also faced with the uncertainty of when, or if, their bonds will be called. Although a call provision generally cannot be exercised until a specific date, from that point in time until maturity it is the local government's option as to when, or if, early redemption will occur.

Note then that most of the advantages of a call provision accrue to the bond issuer, while the disadvantages are borne by the bondholder. Therefore, one would expect that new municipal bond issues with call provisions would require higher interest rates than the same noncallable issue in order to compensate the investor for the additional uncertainty undertaken. In an empirical study, it was discovered that this relationship was not necessarily true.[3] In fact, there was no additional borrowing cost attributable to callable revenue bond issues compared to similar noncallable issues. On the other hand, the inclusion of a call provision in general obligation bonds did have some effect on the cost of borrowing. When the call features were analyzed, however, only the call deferment (years to first call) had any significant effect on new issue borrowing cost. In particular, the shorter the period to the first call date, the higher the interest cost; e.g., on a 20-year bond issue, callable in 10 years, the interest cost was 20 basis points higher than a similar noncallable bond.[4]

The assertion that local governments increase the use of call provisions as interest rates increase was also tested for municipal bond issues. During the period tested, 24 percent to 40 percent of the general obligation issues and 88 percent to 97 percent of the revenue issues contained call provisions.[5] Considering the interest rate variability during the period, it does not appear that interest rate levels have any statistically significant effect on a government's decision to include a call provision in new bond issues. Similarly, state and local governments also do not alter the call deferment date as interest rates change. These two results would imply, then, that local governments do not consider current or prior interest rate levels in their decisions to include call provisions in new bond issues.

Additional evidence did support the belief that call provisions were exercised more frequently in periods of lower interest rates. This relationship, however, was not as strong as expected. It was also found that the call provisions of revenue bonds were exercised more frequently than the call provisions of general obligation bonds.

Finally, the results of the study indicated that the magnitude of the call premium, the excess of the redemption price over the face value, had no significant effect on the interest rate of general obligation bond issues. There was a positive relationship, however, for revenue bonds. That is, a higher interest cost was associated with a higher call

346

premium. "No rationale can be offered for the per-
verse results."[6]
The above study indicates that in-depth consideration is needed into whether to include a call
feature in new bond issues. Callability is neither
costless nor a "cure-all," and should not be included automatically in new bond issues. Consideration must be given to the level of interest rates.
If rates are low at issuance, then the probability
of a future call is remote since rates will probably
not be lower in the future. In addition, the time
period to the first call should be made as long as
possible while still maintaining the desired level
of flexibility.

BOND RATINGS

Until recently, decisions to extend credit were
often based on the close personal relationship between the borrower and the lender, regardless of
whether the borrower was an individual, a corporation, or local government. Today, however, the
sheer size of the public market for corporate and
municipal debt has made some sort of impersonal
credit judgment necessary.[7] Bond ratings provide
investors with a symbol of credit quality that is
easily recognized. Ratings are intended to evaluate
the credit risk of a bond. These ratings, however,
must be credible if they are to be useful to investors. To ensure this credibility, rating agencies
must maintain an independent, objective, and dis-
interested attitude toward issuers. Rating agencies
are neither mandated nor regulated by any government
entity. They exist because they perform an essential service in the world of finance.
Bond ratings are designed to reflect the credit
worthiness of a particular bond issue. Rating agencies do not recommend that investors purchase, sell,
or hold a particular bond nor are the ratings intended as a general purpose evaluation of the
issuer. A financially sound local government may
have a bond issue with a mediocre rating because of
the financial security backing that particular bond.
The security underlying a bond is of major importance to a rating agency.
The rating of a particular bond issue is also
affected by the general economic climate and financial position of a local government. Rating agencies request annual audited financial statements and

budget documents to perform their ongoing evaluation of a bond. Failure of local governments to provide adequate information to the rating agency will result in a suspension or withdrawal of the rating. Ratings must be based on complete and up-to-date information in order to be reliable.

There are three primary rating agencies which provide bond ratings--Moody, Standard and Poor, and Fitch. All three assign credible and respected ratings for use by investors.

The rating of a municipal bond issue can definitely influence how the issue trades with respect to other local government obligations. Table 14.1 lists Moody's and Standard and Poor's ratings and their meanings. Bond ratings have become very important influences on bond interest rates and whether a particular bond issue may be invested in by certain types of institutions. Figure 14.1 graphs the difference in interest rates between Baa- and Aaa-rated municipal bonds during the period from 1955-1975. During that period, the yields of Aaa-rated bonds were between 40 and 110 basis points less than that of Baa-rated bonds.

Though the bond rating is important, not all bonds are rated. Rating agencies charge for their services and some local governments believe a rating is unnecessary. Borrowing costs, however, vary significantly between bonds of different ratings; the higher the rating, the lower the cost regardless of the economic stability of the investment market. For example, the following average interest cost differences for various quality bonds were reported for the period 1963 to 1971[8]:

Differential between grades	Average increased interest cost (basic points)
A - Aaa	30
Baa - A	30
Ba - A	70
Ba - Aaa	more than 100

The importance of bond ratings in reducing the interest cost of the local government is readily apparent. At the same time, ratings are important to the investor because they increase comparability.

Consequently, the decision-making process is acutely sensitive to the rating agencies' opinions.

Regardless of the rating agency chosen, specific information must be provided to that agency. The

TABLE 14.1

Comparison of Municipal Bond Rating Systems

Moody's Investors Service	Symbol	Symbol	Standard and Poor's Corporation
Best quality, carrying smallest degree of investment risk; referred to as "gilt edge"	Aaa	AAA	Prime: obligation of highest quality and lowest probability of default; quality management and low debt structure
High quality; rated lower than Aaa because margins of protection not as large	Aa	AA	High grade: only slightly less secure than prime; second lowest probability of default
Higher medium grade, many favorable investment attributes; some element of future risk evident	A	A	Upper medium grade: safe investment; weakness in local economic base, debt burden, or fiscal balance
Lower medium grade; neither highly protected nor poorly secured; may be unreliable over any great length of time	Baa	BBB	Medium grade: lowest investment security rating; may show more than one fundamental weakness; higher default probability
Judged to have speculative elements; not well safeguarded as to interest and principal	Ba	BB	Lower medium grade; speculative noninvestment grade obligation; relatively high risk and uncertainty
Lacks characteristics of desirable investment	B	B	Low grade; investment characteristics virtually nonexistent
Poor standing; issues may be in default	Caa	CCC	
Speculative in high degree; marked shortcomings	Ca	CC	Defaults
Lowest-rated class; extremely poor prospects of ever attaining any real investment standing	C	C	

Source: John E. Petersen, ed. The Rating Game (New York: The Twentieth Century Fund, 1974).

more complete the information, the easier it is for the rating agency to evaluate the bonds. If an agency is completely familiar with an issuer's financial position, it is in a better position to assign a respectable rating. Of course this is true only if the local government is financially healthy.

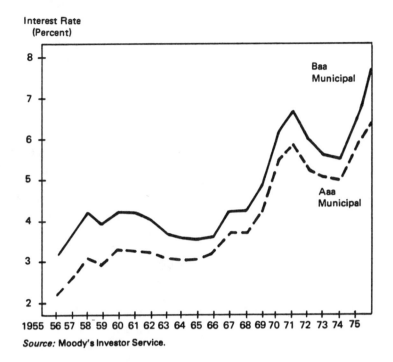

Interest Rate
(Percent)

Source: Moody's Investor Service.

FIGURE 14.1.   Average annual interest rates on municipal bonds rated Aaa and Baa

Source: Ronald W. Forbes and John E. Peterson, Building a Broader Market (New York: The Twentieth Century Fund, 1976), p. 117.

The information needed by the rating agency is generally the same information required for proper disclosure relative to the bond issue.   The information requirements include the current debt structure of the issuer, its financial practices, current and historical results from operations, and current or pending litigation which may affect the local government's position.   Economic and demographic information affecting the local government are also essential for bond rating.

Moody's Investor Services lists several areas in which most local governments fail to adequately provide information.   These areas are long-term indebtedness, overlapping debt involving several tiers of local government, short-term and floating debt such as current tax debt and outstanding and accrued payrolls which have not been expensed, and the provisions for debt retirement.   Local government must provide adequate information to receive the highest bond rating consistent with its overall financial condition. Since the bond rating has a significant effect on the borrowing costs of a local government, the manager must make every effort to maximize the bond rating.

DISCLOSURE OF BOND ISSUES

Until recently, financial statements of local governments were prepared with a lackadaisical attitude and did not provide adequate and complete information to underwriters and investors. Municipal bonds, especially general obligation bonds, were considered financially impeccable. Common sense told investors that a municipal entity could raise taxes if circumstances dictated. Underwriters and investors relied almost exclusively on ratings generated by private rating agencies such as Moody's or Standard and Poor's. They reasoned that since these agencies analyzed each issue, they did not need to do their homework. A general description of the bond issue sufficed for many investors and this system worked fine for many years. Then the 1975 New York City financial crisis hit, sending the entire tax-exempt bond market into a tailspin. Lenders suddenly realized that they did not know their borrowers. The ensuing loss of confidence affected all municipalities, regardless of whether they had been properly run, maintaining balanced budgets, or had severe problems.[9] With the information or rather, lack of information, available at the time, it was not easy to distinguish between the two.

The New York City debacle provides a good example of what can go wrong in municipal finance, especially when the municipalities are aided by complacent credit markets. Throughout the late 1960s and early 1970s, New York City's aggregate operating expenditures continually exceeded its aggregate operating revenues; credit was used to make up the difference. Each year the mounting city budget deficits were funded by short-term seasonal notes or by incorporating recurring expense items into the capital budget for financing through long-term debt. Seasonal notes were continually rolled over, and the costs of debt service were paid with new debt. Finally, the spiraling costs became such a crushing burden that the city could no longer borrow its way out. When the capital markets closed to it, default and eventual bankruptcy seemed imminent.[10]

Surprisingly, the large New York City banks which served as underwriters for the city's debt finally blew the whistle, rather than the bond rating services. (New York City received an 'A' rating from Moody's the year preceding the disaster.) If bond ratings no longer provided a guarantee, the once magical phrase "full faith and credit" fell equally into disrepute. A municipality such as New York City on the brink of default most probably was already overtaxed; its citizenry simply would not or could not pay any more. Faced with a multitude of internal problems, authorities would choose to pay their police, teachers, and fireman, leaving their creditors holding the bag. Investors soon realized that municipal bonds were not the riskless investment they were once thought to be.

The months following the New York City financial crisis brought revolutionary changes to the municipal bond market. Investors began to demand the same disclosure required of corporate debt issues. Those municipalities either unwilling or unable to divulge their financial condition found themselves shut out of the capital markets.[11] Investors and underwriters became increasingly wary. During that same year, the State of Rhode Island was unable to attract bidders for its bonds until 17 pages of financial information were added to the original four-page tender offer. Richmond, Virginia found no buyers for its December 1975 issue because of inadequate disclosure in the 30-page descriptive circular. The issue finally sold only when additional bond counsel opinions, statements by the city auditor, and descriptions of impending litigation were added to the prospectus. Issues with full and adequate disclosure faced significantly lower coupon rates than those that required either additional disclosure or were tainted by proximity to New York City.[12]

When the capital markets placed new constraints on municipal bond offerings, they also provided new incentives. Certainly, New York City was not the only city facing the spiraling costs of union contracts, bloated and inefficient administration, eroding tax bases, and rising welfare costs. The important point is that perhaps now the private credit markets can force a certain discipline on the cities' financial actions that these same cities were previously unable or unwilling to exercise. The detailed, relevant disclosure the market now requires has led to more-informed investment decisions with increased pressure for fiscal responsibility on the part of the issuer.

When municipalities submit financial information to rating agencies it must be both comprehensive and well organized before the agency will agree to assign a rating. This same information makes up a substantial pat of the information legally required to be provided to investors. However, some issuers are unwilling or unable to transfer this information from document form into a form understandable by investors.

The Municipal Finance Officers Association has drawn up recommended disclosure guidelines for state and local governments to follow.[13] These guidelines are designed to assist local governments in disclosing financial information only, not to dictate legal directives to government entities. A majority of local governments have attempted to conform to these guidelines, though many still fall short through lack of knowledge or experience.

The MFOA guidelines basically specify that the official statement prepared by the issuer contains detailed security and financial information pertinent to the issue. "The overriding consideration is to provide a complete, accurate, and objective description of those factors that relate to the securities being offered and that are necessary to make an informed investment decision."[14]

The cover page of the official statement usually contains a summary of the terms, conditions, and features of the isue. The MFOA recommends the following details appear on the cover page:

1. The total principal amount of the securities
2. The name of the issuer (with appropriate identification
3. The type or title of issue being offered (e.g., general obligation, water revenue, etc.)
4. The date of the obligations, interest payment dates, and the date from which interest is paid
5. The denominations in which the securities are offered
6. Registration and exchange privileges
7. Trustee and paying agents
8. Redemption features, if any, including sinking fund provisions
9. Maturity dates and principal amounts by maturity in columnar form
10. A statement of the tax status of interest on the securities being offered[15]

Additional information sometimes given on the cover page includes:

11. Ratings by the various agencies
12. Designation of new issues
13. Brief statement of the authority for issuance
14. Anticipated date and place of delivery
15. Summary statement of the security or source of payment[16]

Figure 14.2 contains a sample cover page from an official statement, keyed to the above suggested items.

The MFOA guidelines also suggest that the issuer divide the information within the official statement into the following four categories and subcategories:

Financial Report Information

1. Current and detailed operating statement
2. Operating statement for prior years
3. Basic method of accounting used
4. Audited financial statement
5. Current "pro forma" or budget statement
6. Detailed balance sheet
7. Balance sheet for prior years
8. Contingent liabilities (or lack thereof)

Revenue Information

1. Current-year assessed property value
2. Assessed value for prior years
3. Current market value of property
4. Market value for prior years
5. Composition of assessed property
6. Method of assessment discussed
7. Current real property tax rate
8. Tax rates for prior years
9. Tax collection (or delinquency) rate
10. Tax collection rate for prior years
11. Policy toward tax collections
12. List of "top 10" taxpayers
13. Discussion of intergovernmental programs
14. Property tax limits (or lack thereof)

Debt Information

1. Current direct bonded debt
2. Direct debt for prior years

(10) *In the opinion of Bond Counsel, the interest on the Bonds is, under existing laws, regulations and judicial decisions, exempt from all Federal income taxation and the Bonds and the income thereon are exempt from taxation under the laws of the State of Florida, except as to estate taxes and taxes imposed by Chapter 220, Florida Statutes, on interest, income or profits on debt obligations owned by corporations.*

(12) NEW ISSUE

Ratings:
(11) Standard & Poor's:
AAA (MBIA insured)

(1) $1,670,000

(2) Leon County, Florida

(3) Capital Improvement, Series 1977, Revenue Bonds

Dated: July 1, 1978   Due: October 1, as shown below

The Capital Improvement, Series 1977, Revenue Bonds (the "Bonds") are being issued by the Board of County Commissioners of Leon County, Florida (the "Board") to finance the cost of acquiring and constructing a solid waste disposal system.

The Bonds shall be secured by a prior lien on and pledge of the Non-Ad Valorem Funds of the County, as more fully described herein.

(7) (5) (6) (4) (8) The Bonds are to be issued in coupon form, in the denomination of $5,000 each, payable as to principal and interest at Capital City First National Bank, Tallahassee, Florida, and registrable as to principal only. The interest on the Bonds is payable semi-annually on April 1 and October 1 of each year. The Bonds maturing in the year 1988 and thereafter are subject to redemption prior to maturity at the option of the County on or after October 1, 1987 at par plus a premium of 3% initially.

(9) MATURITIES, AMOUNTS, COUPON RATES and PRICES or YIELDS

Amount	Due	Coupon Rate	Yield or Price	Amount	Due	Coupon Rate	Yield or Price
$25,000	1979	5.00%	4.40%	$ 55,000	1994	6.25%	6.05%
30,000	1980	5.00	4.60	60,000	1995	6.25	6.10
30,000	1981	5.00	4.75	60,000	1996	6.25	6.15
30,000	1982	5.00	4.90	65,000	1997	6.25	6.20
30,000	1983	5.50	5.00	70,000	1998	6.30	6.25
35,000	1984	5.50	5.10	75,000	1999	6.35	6.30
35,000	1985	5.50	5.20	75,000	2000	6.40	6.35
35,000	1986	5.50	5.30	80,000	2001	6.45	6.40
40,000	1987	5.50	5.40	85,000	2002	6.50	6.45
40,000	1988	6.00	5.50	90,000	2003	6.50	6.50
45,000	1989	6.00	5.60	90,000	2004	6.55	6.50
45,000	1990	6.00	5.70	100,000	2005	6.55	6.55
45,000	1991	6.00	5.80	100,000	2006	6.55	6.55
50,000	1992	6.00	5.90	100,000	2007	6.55	6.55
50,000	1993	6.25	6.00				

(Plus Accrued Interest)

The Bonds are offered subject to prior sale, when, as and if issued, subject to the unqualified approval of legality by Messrs. Bryant, Miller and Olive, Tallahassee, Florida, Bond Counsel. Certain legal matters are being passed on for the County by F.E. Steinmeyer, III, Attorney for the Board.

William R. Hough & Co.

August 25, 1978

FIGURE 14.2. Sample cover page of an official statement

Debit Information (Cont.)

3. Authorized but unissued debt
4. Future debt service requirements
5. Current overlapping debt
6. Discussion of debt limitations
7. Calculation of unused debt capacity
8. Nature of short-term debt (or lack thereof)
9. Legal rights of bondholders
10. Description of employee pension plan

Demographic, Economic, and Governmental Information

1. Population of issuer
2. Population trends
3. Per capita or other income data
4. Unemployment rate
5. Description of economic base and activity
6. List of principal firms or employers
7. Information on building permits
8. Discussion of governing body and key officials
9. Discussion of governmental services[17]

MUNICIPAL BOND INSURANCE

Many cities and counties are now following a new trend in municipal bonds by buying municipal bond insurance from companies such as the Municipal Bond Insurance Association (MBIA), or other insurance companies which insure bonds. Bond insurance assures investors that they will receive the scheduled coupon and principal payments from the insurer of the bond in the event of default by the issuer. This trend has increased due to the New York City fiscal crisis; for example, insured bonds accounted for 2 percent of the tax-exempt bonds sold in 1978.

There were no direct financial benefits received from the insurer by the issuer, but there may be substantial indirect benefits. Rating agencies take into consideration the security underlying municipal bonds. Bond insurance provides almost foolproof security and the rating agencies generally assign high ratings to insured bonds. Recently the bond insurance obtained by Dade County, Florida, changed its Standard and Poor bond rating from BBB to AAA. The higher rating is expected to save the county an estimated $1 million dollars over the next 20 years. The cost of the insurance premium is more than offset by a $4.3 million interest rate reduction.

Some additional benefits that can be derived from
bond insurance are higher proceeds from underwriters, and/or improved marketability since the
bonds will appeal to a wider audience. Thus, the
decision to purchase bond insurance requires a cost-
benefit evaluation by the issuer.

Municipal bond insurance is not for every local
government, however. If a small government unit has
already obtained a high-grade or premium bond rating
then the insurance would be worthless. The interest
difference between being insured and uninsured would
not offset the insurance fee. A decision model for
making the municipal bond insurance decision is presented in the next chapter.

Note that no states or large cities are among
those insured by the MBIA. The MBIA feels that to
concentrate in these areas would concentrate risk,
something the association prefers not to do. MBIA
will not insure an issue of more than $20 million in
principal. In 1978 more than twice as many appli-
cants were rejected as accepted by the MBIA.

Note also that Moody's does not recognize municipal bond insurance. They feel it would confuse the
public by departing from its established rating
methods. As a result, local governments which have
obtained bond insurance rarely apply for a rating
from Moody's.

NEGOTIATED VERSUS COMPETITIVE BIDDING

Many local governments are questioning the continued use of their traditional method of obtaining
underwriters for a bond issue. This question is
important because either of the traditional methods,
negotiation or competitive bidding, has cost-saving
features and disadvantages associated with it. What
is each method and which is the best method are
questions that must be answered.

Negotiation involves the use of one or several
cooperating underwriters who negotiate a price between themselves and the issuer. The underwriter
generally prepares the prospectus, secures a credit
rating, designs bond features such as call provisions and maturity structure, selects sale dates,
and in general markets the bond for the local
government. A majority of issuers feel that the
underwriter provides an invaluable service in
readying the bond for issuance. Of major importance
is the interest rate the underwriters attach to the

bonds. This is usually negotiated after the underwriter conducts his presale distribution efforts.
Presale distribution provides both parties with
information relative to the demand for the bonds.
The underwriter may actually sell a substantial
number of the bonds during this presale period.
After continued negotiation a purchase contract is
signed by both parties. Sometimes the negotiation
period is rather lengthy before the parties agree on
the terms of the purchase contract.

There are certain potential benefits in this
negotiation process for the issuer. When an issue is
risky or faces demand uncertainties, the negotiation
process can help the underwriter improve the flow of
information, reducing underwriting risk and enhancing the underwriter's ability to sell bonds at lower
yields relative to competitive bidding underwriting.
The resulting decrease in spread causes a corresponding decrease in interest cost to the issuer.[18]
On the negative side, however, negotiating underwriters are placed in a position of almost monopoly
power. They may use this power to increase an
issuer's interest cost.

State governments have historically used competitive bidding as the method of securing underwriters.
Competitive bidding involves advertising for bids
and selecting the underwriter who submits the lowest
bid based on some established criterion. Most
states have laws which require issues be open to
public bidding. There has been a trend in recent
years, however, for municipal governments to switch
to the negotiated method. This may appear counter-
productive at first since some studies have shown
that negotiated issues cost more than issues underwritten by competitive bids. In comparing certain
low-grade bonds, however, the interest rates are
virtually equal. This is probably due to the expertise of underwriters in marketing these types of
bonds. The higher costs for negotiated issues may
be attributable to the additional services that
underwriters provide in this type of arrangement.
The monopoly power of the underwriter may also be a
significant factor. There is no doubt, however,
that the trend toward negotiated underwriting is
partly due to local governments seeking expertise in
the handling of their bond issues.

Categorical generalizations are difficult to make
regarding the preference of either method of underwriting. The demand for a particular issue may dictate the most efficient method. Issues having low

ratings and/or complex issues which are not easily understood by investors should probably use the negotiation method. Large issuers who feel that demand will be high for their bonds and the underwriting risks low will probably find the competitive bidding method more suitable due to its lower cost.

BOND COUNSEL

Bond counsels, also called bond lawyers, emerged as important participants in the municipal bond issuing process about a century ago. Local governments often placed unrealistically high valuations on community assets and overestimated financial capabilities in attempts to issue bonds to finance railroad facilities. At that time, these inflated asset valuations allowed the communities to issue more bonds and entice railroads into communities because of this available financing. Widespread defaults subsequently occurred, however, when the estimated financial expectations failed to materialize. The courts ruled that many of the bonds had been issued illegally, fortunes were lost, and municipal debt became very unpopular and difficult to sell. Thus, bond counsels, whose function was to assure investors that government bonds were legally issued, emerged.

Each new bond issue must be approved by an attorney whose reputation for integrity and legal expertise can establish investors' confidence in the issue to be sold; the marketability of the issue is at stake. Although there is no special certification requirement for bond lawyers, most bond counsel firms specialize in this particular area and are considered experts. This is necessary if the opinion of the bond counsel is to be accepted by the investing public. The importance of a bond counsel opinion is evident--without a respected legal certification, even the most valid issue may not be marketable.

The investigations conducted by bond counsel law firms vary, but some of the areas frequently reviewed are:

1. The powers of the issuing government;
2. The specific authorization for the bond issue;
3. The procedures which have been followed in the authorization, advertising, and sale of the bonds;

4. The presence of a quorum of the issuing body and the necessary votes in favor of the various resolutions and other actions;
5. The approval by required majorities in cases where approval of the electorate is required;
6. The right to impose the taxes, or to levy the necessary charges in case of a revenue bond to pay for the interest and principal on the bond issue;
7. The validity of leases, if any, which are executed in relation to the bonds;
8. The form and content of the bonds themselves.

In effect, the bond counsel acts as a legal advisor to the ultimate investor in municipal bonds. Again, his primary function is investor assurance.

In the early development of bond counsel opinions, an attorney was employed by the prospective bond purchaser; in most cases this was the underwriter. As time passed, however, controversy arose over the degree of responsibility of the local government in the legal verification process. Today it is common practice for the issuing government to select and pay the bond counsel. No matter which party hires the bond attorney, purchaser or seller, more independence is being exercised by these counsels in an attempt to uphold the integrity of their opinions. Municipal bond attorneys can be influential in reducing borrowing cost. The opinion of a highly reputable bond counsel can reduce interest costs. Thus, the importance of the integrity and opinion of the bond counsel cannot be overstated.

The fee charged by a law firm for issuing an opinion is now generally negotiated by the issuing government. This amount is influenced greatly by the complexity of the work involved and, to a lesser degree, by the issue size.

ROLE OF THE TRUSTEE

A bank or trust company is usually appointed as trustee for the bond issue to receive the proceeds of the bond sale and to supervise their use according to the covenants of the bond contract. The trustee is responsible for ensuring that all debt obligations are met; i.e., that funds are available for present and future contractual payments. One of the primary functions of the trustee is to maintain any sinking funds or reserve accounts required by the bond contract. The trustee acts as a guardian, constantly protecting the financial position of outstanding bond issues.

The trustee is the representative of both the issuer and the bondholders from the inception of the bond issue until its ultimate maturity. Some of the specific services performed by the trustee are:

1. To act for the issuing government in making settlement for the bonds at the time of their delivery;
2. To maintain necessary records concerning interest payments and debt repayment;
3. To oversee all payments;
4. To oversee and manage the payments and investment operation of any required reserve accounts (i.e., sinking funds);
5. To cancel paid bonds and coupons with proper financial adjustments;
6. To provide safekeeping for records, duplicate bonds, and coupons (in case bonds are stolen);
7. To handle routine correspondence on other matters arising with respect to bonds;
8. To arrange for and supervise, in the presence of appropriate governmental officers, the burning of cancelled bonds and coupons;
9. To act as an agent for bond issuers;
10. To institute legal action on behalf of bondholders should the issuer fail to comply with terms of the bond contract.

The trustee, then, is in charge of the overall management of any operations concerning a municipal bond issue.

One of the most important aspects of governmental debt is the payment of principal and interest when due. As noted above, the trustee is responsible for ensuring that adequate funds are available to meet these obligations and to oversee their payment. The actual payment transaction, however, may be carried out by a paying agent, whose sole purpose is to make the required payments as they become due. It is the paying agent who distributes cash to the appropriate bondholders for periodic interest and debt retirement. Therefore the paying agent can be considered an "employee" of the trustee with the following specific functions:

1. To make payment of interest on bonds as due and to pay the bonds at maturity or call them in advance of maturity;
2. To provide replacement bonds in case of lost or destroyed original bonds;
3. To determine the specific investors who will legally be paid the interest and/or maturity.

MARKET CHARACTERISTICS

Once a local government issues a bond which will be repaid over a period of years, it becomes involved in a highly complex financial market. This market consists of a variety of investors, each with distinct preferences for maximizing returns while minimizing the risks undertaken. At the same time, a variety of instruments compete for the investment dollars circulating in the financial markets. Therefore, it is important for municipalities to understand the factors which influence the selling price of bonds if they are to borrow wisely. Although bond prices in both the primary (new securities) and secondary (existing securities) markets are significantly influenced by market interest rates, local governments must be concerned primarily with conditions in the primary market as this is where the issuers themselves receive their funds.

The primary market is greatly affected by the monetary and fiscal policies of the federal government. The policies of the federal government affect interest rates in the primary market through the strain each creates on credit. An easy credit market means lower interest rates and lowers borrowing costs for local governments; a tighter credit market leads to higher borrowing costs. Any action by the federal government which increases the demand for borrowed funds will increase the borrowing costs of local governments. Consequently, bond market operations are ultimately a supply and demand function (specifically the supply of and demand for credit) like other goods. Municipal bond issuers often delay financing when conditions are unfavorable but they increase their participation in the funds market when conditions improve.

The secondary market can also affect the price local governments receive for their issues. Bond price movements in the secondary market are inversely related to interest-rate movements. That is, as interest rates decline, the bond prices increase.

New bonds have to sell at a yield competitive with existing issues. Since the periodic interest payment on a bond is tied to its face value, both of which remain constant throughout the life of the issue, only market price modifications can vary the bond's actual yield. For example, if a local government issues a $1 million dollar perpetual bond at a 7 percent coupon rate while the yield on similar investment instruments is 10 percent, not many investors would be willing to purchase the perpetual bonds at this lower yield. In order to be competitive, its market price would have to be lowered to $700,000[19] to ensure investors a return similar to that of comparable investments.

The supply and demand for municipal bonds in the secondary market can also influence bond yields and their prices. A large new issue could create significant shocks in the general market on the date of the issue. However, there are examples that indicate the market's reaction to any changes in supply are anticipated long before the actual change. Since municipal bonds are registered months in advance of their issue the market has an opportunity to adjust appropriately.

SUMMARY

This chapter examined the basic characteristics of municipal bonds. There are basically two types of bonds: General obligation bonds are backed by an all-inclusive pledge of the full-faith, credit, and taxing power of the issuer; revenue bonds are retired with the revenue from specific projects pledged for this purpose. The correct choice in maturity structures between serial bonds and term bonds depends on the municipality's particular situation and future expectations. Factors such as alternative investment opportunities, flexibility, and stability of revenue patterns should be considered before deciding on the maturity structure of a particular issue.

A sinking fund is a reserve established to ensure that sufficient funds will be available for retirement of bonds at maturity. Proper sinking fund management lowers the cost of the bond issue through the returns earned from the investment of sinking fund assets. The call provision allows the issuer to redeem bonds prior to their maturity date by the payment of a call premium. The call provision provides flexibility to the issuing government by allowing it to reduce outstanding debt through early retirement if circumstances warrant. The investor, on the other hand, is subjected to the risk of having his bonds retired early and could suffer financial injury through lower interest income and/or future capital gains.

Bond ratings, which are an attempt by the rating agencies to evaluate credit risk, are a major factor in the determination of interest costs. The higher the rating, the lower the interest costs regardless of the economic stability of the investment market. Adequate financial disclosure is a necessity in today's municipal bond market. It assists in obtaining a higher bond rating and it enhances the marketability of the issue. Adequate disclosure includes a complete description of the bond issue, debt structure, financial practices, current and historical results of operations, and pending and current legal proceedings.

Bond insurance, which guarantees that investors will receive prompt payment of principal and interest in the event of issuer default, can result in substantial interest savings. Bonds insured by the Municipal Bond Insurance Association automatically receive Standard & Poor's AAA rating. The interest savings resulting from the insurance must be compared, however, to the cost of the insurance premium.

It is difficult to make generalizations regarding the issuance of bonds through an underwriter by negotiated versus competitive biddings. Negotiated bidding involves selecting an underwriter and establishing a mutually agreed upon price for his services. Competitive bidding involves awarding the issue to the underwriter submitting the lowest bid based upon some established criterion. Negotiated bidding is probably more advantageous for complex issues with low credit ratings. Large issues with little underwriting risk will probably find competitive bidding more suitable and less expensive.

The important roles of the bond counsel and the trustee were also discussed. The bond counsel acts as a legal advisor to the ultimate investor, providing certification that the bond issue is legally valid. The opinion and reputation of the bond counsel can greatly affect interest costs. The trustee is responsible for receiving the proceeds from the issue and supervising their use according to the terms of the bond contract.

It is important for muncipalities to become familiar with the general factors affecting the primary and secondary markets for their bonds. The primary market is the market for new bonds, while the secondary market is the market for existing bonds. Monetary and fiscal policy greatly affect interest rates in the primary market. Attitudes in the secondary market also affect the price that local governments receive for their issues.

QUESTIONS

1. What advantages do serial bonds have over term bonds?

2. Define and explain the purpose of sinking funds.

3. What is a call provision? How does it affect a bond's interest rate?

4. What are the advantages and disadvantages of a call premium?

5. What is the purpose of a bond rating? What factors affect a bond's rating?

6. What are the three principal municipal bond rating agencies?

7. What adjustments occurred in the financial bond markets following the New York City financial crisis?

8. What is the purpose of municipal bond insurance? What are the benefits of municipal bond insurance?

9. Explain the difference between negotiated and competitive bidding for underwriting a bond issue?

10. What is the function of bond counsels? How do they affect a bond issue?

11. What role does a trustee play in the issuance of bonds? What is a paying agent?

12. What is the relationship between bond prices and interest rates? Explain.

ENDNOTES

1. Sinking fund payments are periodic contributions to a fund to ensure that a sufficient amount of cash is available to repay the debt at maturity. Sinking funds are discussed in more detail in the next section.
2. Alan Walter Steiss, Local Government Finance (Lexington, Mass.: Lexington Books, 1975), p. 164.
3. David S. Kidwell, "Call Provisions and Their Effect on Municipal Bond Issues," Governmental Finance (August 1975), pp. 28-32.
4. Ibid.
5. The averages were 31 percent and 94 percent, respectively, for the period tested.
6. Ibid., p. 32.
7. Standard & Poor's Corporation, Municipal and International Bond Ratings: An Overview, (New York: Standard & Poor's Corp.), p. 5.
8. John Peterson, ed. The Rating Game, (New York: The Twentieth Century Fund, 1974), p. 44.
9. Banking, February, 1977, pp. 87-89.
10. Financial World, May 15, 1978, p. 12.
11. Forbes, March 1, 1976, pp. 22-23.
12. Ibid.
13. Municipal Finance Officers Association. Disclosure Guidelines for Offerings of Securities by State and Local Governments, (Chicago: Municipal Finance Officers Association, December 1976).
14. Ibid, p. 1.
15. Ibid, p. 3.
16. Ibid, p. 4.
17. Robert Lamb and Stephen P. Rappaport, Municipal Bonds: The Comprehensive Review of Tax-Exempt Securities and Public Finance, (New York: McGraw-Hill Book Company, 1980), pp. 284-285.
18. Eric H. Sorensen, "Negotiated vs. Competitive Issues: In Most Cases, Costs are About the Same," The Daily Bond Buyer, October 1977.
19. For a perpetual issue:

$$\frac{\text{interest income}}{\text{market price}} = \text{rate of return}$$

so:

$$\frac{\$70,000}{price} = 10\%$$

price = $700,000.

IMPROVING THE EFFICIENCY AND EFFECTIVENESS OF DEBT MANAGEMENT

Many advances have been made in financial management policies and procedures regarding the issuance and administration of municipal bonds. These advances, however, generally have been made in the context of large governmental units. Small local governments and other not-for-profit organizations are often unaware of the analytical methods available. This chapter describes the latest techniques available for evaluating alternatives available in the issuance of long-term debt. Determination of the size of the issue, the evaluation of competitive bids, the decision to purchase private municipal bond insurance, and the bond refunding decision are discussed. In addition, the lease versus purchase decision is examined.

The issuance of long-term debt involves a fixed obligation for a long period of time. Consequently, careful planning is required to avoid placing an undue strain on future revenues. The practices, procedures, and techniques described in this chapter can be used to improve the efficiency and effectiveness of the issuance and administration of long-term debt.

DETERMINING THE OPTIMAL
SIZE OF THE BOND ISSUE

In periods of record high interest and inflation rates, as have been experienced recently, it is vital that the not-for-profit organization correctly determines the size of its bond issue. If the bond issue is too small, the issuer will be forced to obtain expensive additional financing in order to complete the capital project. The project may even suffer long and expensive delays because of inadequate funding. If the issue size is too large, then the issuer pays high interest charges on unneeded funds.

A present-value method developed by Philip M. Law, Jr.[1] is a fast, simple, and accurate way to determine the optimum bond size. The principal amount of the bonds issued is equal to the cost and expenses paid from the net proceeds of the issue less any earnings on the investment of the net proceeds from the date of the issue to the date expended. This method is conceptually sound and involves the following three steps:

1. Determination of the costs and expenses associated with the issue and the estimated dates of occurrence. The fixed costs are expressed in dollars and the variable costs are expressed as a percentage of the bond issue.
2. Calculation of the present value of the costs and expenses.
3. Construction and solution of an equation for the bond size.

The method of determining the optimal bond size is illustrated by the following example.

> Revenue bonds will be used to finance a $50,000,000 civic center, which will take three years to construct. The bonds will be dated and issued January 1, 1981. Amortization is on a level debt service basis with the first maturity on January 1, 1986, two years after beginning operation of the center. The last maturity is January 1, 2010, making 25 equal payments of principal and interest.
>
> The annual interest rate is 8 percent and is payable semiannually on January 1 and July

1.   The following costs and expenses are incurred on the <u>date of issue</u>, January 1, 1981:   bond discount of $15 per $1,000 of principal amount of bonds; fixed financing expenses of $300,000; and prior construction costs of $1,500,000.   The estimated construction costs are given in Table 15.1.   A contingencies fund of $500,000 and a reserve fund equal to the maximum annual debt service are to be funded on the date of issue from the net proceeds of the bond issue. Investments earn 10 percent per year and mature each January 1 and July 1 in the exact amounts required.   Interest is paid semiannually.

TABLE 15.1

Costs and Expenses Expressed in Thousands of Dollars for Civic Center

Date (1)	Construction cost (2)	Financing cost (3)	Contingencies fund (4)	Total (5)
1-1-81	$1,500	$300		$1,800
7-1-81	3,000			3,000
1-1-82	6,000			6,000
7-1-82	12,000			12,000
1-1-83	10,000			10,000
7-1-83	10,000			10,000
1-1-84	7,500		$500	8,000
Total	$50,000	$300	$500	$50,800

The first step in determining the bond size is to determine the fixed costs and expenses of construction to be financed by the bond issue, along with the dates of occurrence. Table 15.1 shows the amounts and dates of the fixed costs and expenses expressed in dollars.   Column 1 shows the estimated dates of occurrence.   The construction costs, totaling $50 million, are shown in Column 2. The construction costs include $1,500,000 on the date of issue and semiannual expenditures to January 1, 1984, the estimated date of operation.   Column 3 shows the $300,000 financing expenses incurred on January 1, 1981, the date of issue.   The contingencies fund of $500,000 is shown on January 1, 1984.   This $500,000 will be invested from the date of the bond issue to the estimated date of operation of the center, with the investment earnings offsetting other expenditures during the period.

The next step is to express the variable costs and expenses as a percentage of this unknown principal amount, P, as shown in Table 15.2. Again the estimated dates of the expenditures are shown in Column 1. The

TABLE 15.2

Costs and Expenses Expressed as Percentage of P

Date (1)	Bond Discount (2)	Capitalized interest (3)	Reserve fund (4)	Total (5)
1-1-81	0.015P			0.01500P
7-1-81		0.04P		0.04000P
1-1-82		0.04P		0.04000P
7-1-82		0.04P		0.04000P
1-1-83		0.04P		0.04000P
7-1-83		0.04P		0.04000P
1-1-84		0.04P		0.13368P
7-1-84		0.04P	0.09368P	0.04000P
Total	0.015P	0.28P	0.09368P	0.38868P

bond discount is $15 per $1,000 of bonds or 1.5 percent of P as shown in Column 2, which occurs on the date of issue, January 1, 1981. The annual interest rate on the outstanding bonds is 8 percent which is equivalent to a 4 percent semiannual rate. The capitalized interest of 0.04P, payable each January 1 and July 1 from July 1, 1981 to July 1, 1984, is shown in Column 3. A reserve fund must also be established which is equal to the maximum annual debt service. The bonds are to be amortized with level principal and interest payments over 25 years. The present value of an annuity factor for 25 periods at 8 percent is 10.6748. Taking the reciprocal of the PVAF of 10.6748 and multiplying by P yields a factor of 0.09368P. The factor of 0.0936P for the reserve fund is shown in Column 4 on January 1, 1984. The last column in Table 15.2 shows the total expenditures for each period.

The next step in determining the optimal bond size is to calculate the present value of the costs and expenses. The total expenditures in dollars from Table 15.1 and the total expenditures expressed as a percentage of P from Table 15.2 are multiplied by the present-value factors for each semiannual period. The present values of both fixed and variable costs and expenses are calculated in Table 15.3.

The issuer earns a 10 percent annual rate on its investments, or a 5 percent semiannual rate. The 5 percent semiannual rate represents the issuer's discount rate or opportunity cost. Column 1 of Table 15.3 shows the estimated dates of expenditures. The present value factors at a semiannual rate are shown in Column 2. The costs and expenses in dollars from Table 15.1 are shown in Column 3. The present values of the costs and expenses in dollars, obtained by multiplying Column 2 by Column 3, are shown in Column 4. Similarly, the costs and expenses in terms of P are taken from Table 15.2 and are shown in Column 5. The present values of the costs expressed in terms of P are shown in Column 6. These figures were obtained by multiplying Column 2 by Column 5.

The third step is to construct and solve an equation in which P is equal to the present value of both the fixed and variable costs and expenses. The fixed expenses are expressed in dollars while the variable costs and expenses are expressed in terms of P. The following results:

$$P = PV \text{ of costs in dollars}$$
$$+ PV \text{ of costs in terms of } P$$
$$(\text{Equation } 15\text{-}1)$$

Substituting the appropriate values from Table 15.3:

$$P = \$42,497,000 + 0.31636P$$
$$P - 0.31636P = \$42,497,000$$
$$0.68364P = \$42,497,000$$
$$P = \frac{\$42,497,000}{0.68364} = \$62,162,834$$

TABLE 15.3

Present Value of Costs and Expenses

Date (1)	PV factor at 5% (2)	Expressed in Dollars (1,000s)		Expressed in Terms of P	
		Total (3)	Present value (4)	Total (5)	Present value (6)
1-1-81	1.0000	$ 1,800	$ 1,800	0.01500P	0.01500P
7-1-81	0.9524	3,000	2,857	0.04000P	0.03810P
1-1-82	0.9070	6,000	5,442	0.04000P	0.03628P
7-1-82	0.8638	12,000	10,366	0.04000P	0.03455P
1-1-83	0.8227	10,000	8,227	0.04000P	0.03291P
7-1-83	0.7835	10,000	7,835	0.04000P	0.03134P
1-1-84	0.7462	8,000	5,970	0.13368P	0.99750P
7-1-84	0.7107	0	0	0.04000P	0.02843P
Totals		50,800	42,497	0.38868P	0.31636P

Solution of Equation 15-1 results in a principal amount of $62,162,834. In practice, this would be rounded up to at least $62,165,000 since municipal bonds are sold in denominations of $5,000.

It is important to double check the results of this analysis. This can be done by expressing all costs and expenses in dollars and demonstrating that the cash flow from investments and bond proceeds are sufficient to cover all costs and expenses.[2] Table 15.4 shows all costs and expenses expressed in thousands of dollars. The financing expense, construction costs, and contingencies fund were originally expressed in dollars and are shown in Columns 2, 5, and 6, respectively. The bond discount, capitalized interest, and reserve funds in Columns 3, 4, and 7, respectively, were originally expressed in terms of $\underline{P}$. They have been converted to dollars by multiplying the appropriate decimal factor by the principal amount of $62,165. For example, the reserve fund of $5,824 was obtained by multiplying $62,165 by 0.09368.

The cash flows on the investments are shown in Table 15.5. The $62,165,000 bond issue is sold on January 1, 1981 and the financing expense of $300,000, bond discount of $932,000, and prior construction costs of $1,500,000 are subtracted, leaving a balance of $59,433,000 for investment. This is invested at a 5 percent semiannual rate, resulting in $2,972,000 of interest income on July 1, 1981. This interest income plus $2,515,000 of maturing investments is used to cover the $5,487,000 in expenses for that period. This leaves a total of $56,918,000 invested, which generates $2,846,000 of interest income on January 1, 1982. The remaining funds needed to cover the $8,487,000 in total expenses for the period come from maturing investments. The remaining portion of Table 15.5 is completed in a similar fashion.

Tables 15.4 and 15.5 serve as a double check on the results. The total interest income

TABLE 15.4

Total Costs and Expenses
(Dollars in Thousands)

Date (1)	Financing expense (2)	Bond discount (3)	Capitalized interest (4)	Construction costs (5)	Contingencies fund (6)	Reserve fund (7)	Total (8)
1-1-81	300	932		1,500			2,732
7-1-81			2,487	3,000			5,487
1-1-82			2,487	6,000			8,487
7-1-82			2,487	12,000			14,487
1-1-83			2,487	10,000			12,487
7-1-83			2,487	10,000			12,487
1-1-84			2,487	7,500	500	5,824	16,311
7-1-84			2,487				2,487
	300	932	17,409	50,000	500	5,824	74,965

TABLE 15.5

Cash Flows on Investments
(Dollars in Thousands)

Date	Outstanding principal	Seminannual interest @ 5%	Maturing principal	Total costs & expenses
1-1-81	62,165	-	2,732	2,732
7-1-81	59,433	2,972	2,515	5,487
1-1-82	56,918	2,846	5,641	8,487
7-1-82	51,277	2,564	11,923	14,487
1-1-83	39,354	1,968	10,519	12,487
7-1-83	28,835	1,442	11,045	12,487
1-1-84	17,789	889	15,422	16,311
7-1-84	2,368	118	2,368	2,487
		$12,799*	$62,165*	$74,965*

*The totals of $12,799 and $62,165 do not quite equal
$74,965 due to slight rounding errors.

of $12,799,000 plus the bond issue of
$62,165,000 are sufficient to cover the
total costs and expenses of $74,965,000
(except for rounding error). The user of
this model should be cautioned that these
results assume certainty. Of course, expenses and/or interest rates different from
the estimated values may occur. In practice, the issuer will probably want to issue
more than $62,165,000 in bonds in order to
have a buffer for uncertainty.

EVALUATION OF COMPETITIVE BIDS[3]

Most municipal bonds are issued in serial form, a
single issue which contains bonds with different
maturities and coupon rates. Generally, a portion
of the full series matures each of several years,
usually on an anniversary of the date of the bonds.
Unlike other bonds, the coupon rates on municipal
bonds are usually determined by the underwriters
within limits set by the issuing government. The
steps involved in the preparation of a bid for the
municipal bond have been summarized as follows:

. . . An underwriting syndicate generally
makes four types of decisions, explicitly or
implicitly. First, it decides on the actual
schedule of yields at which it believes the
entire issue of bonds can be sold to the
public.

Second the syndicate decides on the total spread for expenses, risk, and profits that it will try to obtain on the issue. Third, the syndicate decides on the restrictions which must be placed on the issuer's coupon schedule to insure its ready marketability. Placing an interest coupon which is either unconventionally high or unconventionally low on a given maturity will reduce the extent to which some investors will be willing to purchase the bonds. Fourth, and finally, the syndicate must determine the schedule of coupons to be placed on the issue.[4]

The method of evaluating bids has little, if any, influence on the first three decisions of the underwriting syndicate. "The rates at which various serial maturities can be sold to the public, for example, are primarily determined by overall conditions in the money and capital markets; spreads tend to vary with such factors as issue quality and average term to maturity; while constraints on the potential size of coupon are due to tax laws, investor preferences and portfolio regulations."[5] The method of awarding the bid is important in making the fourth decision. The underwriting syndicate will vary its strategy in establishing the coupon schedule depending on the method selected for the evaluation of bids.

An issuer using an underwriter should attempt to minimize its cost and should not be concerned with the reoffering yield. The reoffering yield is that return the underwriter receives based on the price paid by the investor. The underwriter's spread is the percentage of that price taken by the underwriter to cover costs of origination, underwriting, and distribution. The cost to the local government depends on both yield and spread.

There are three bid evaluation techniques available for selecting the lowest cost bid. The net interest cost (NIC), the true interest cost (TIC) and the present value of interest (PIC). The PIC technique is theoretically superior to the NIC and TIC methods and can be applied readily to practical situations. The following sections examine the three methods.

NIC Method

Because of the complex form of serial issues, most underwriter bids are evaluated on the basis of a simple computation called Net Interest Cost (NIC), also known as the Investment Bankers Association method. NIC is calculated using the following formula:

$$\text{NIC} = \frac{\left[\sum_{n=s}^{m} n A_n C_n\right] - P}{\sum_{n=s}^{m} n A_n}$$

(Equation 15-2)

where A_n = aggregate par value measured in dollar of bonds maturing in n periods,

c_n = coupon rates of bonds maturing in n periods,

n = number of years to maturity,

s = number of years to first maturity,

m = number of years to last maturity, and

P = premium bid measured in dollars over aggregate par value for all maturities.

The underwriter submitting the lowest NIC bid is awarded the issue.

Although Equation 15-2 looks complicated, the calculation involves the following simple steps:

1. Sum the total interest payments to be made (minus any bond premium).
2. Compute the number of bond years (number of bonds maturing a certain year times the years to maturity).
3. Compute the interest cost per year (divide result from step 1 by result from step 2).
4. Divide by 50 (assuming a $5,000 bond) to place the cost on a percentage basis or divide by $5,000 to place the cost on a per dollar basis.

The following example illustrates the calculation of NIC. A municipality is considering a $3,000,000 bond issue which has $1,000,000 of bonds maturing each year for the next three years. The face amount or principal of each bond is $5,000; thus, 200 bonds mature each year. Two underwriter bids are received: Underwriter A's bid has

coupon rates of 4.59 percent in each of the
next 3 years, while Underwriter B's bid
specifies coupon rates of 20 percent, 2
percent, and 1 percent in years 1, 2, and 3
respectively. Both underwriters offer to
pay face amount for the bond issue.

The calculation of the <u>NIC</u> for each of the
bids is shown in Table 15.6. The interest

TABLE 15.6

Calculation of <u>NIC</u> for Two Bids

NIC for bid A:

(1) Term to maturity	(2) Coupon rate (%)	(3) Interest/Bond	(4) Number of bonds maturing	(5) Total interest (1x3x4)	(6) Bond years (1x4)
1	4.59	$229.50	200	$ 45,900	200
2	4.59	229.50	200	$ 91,800	400
3	4.59	229.50	200	$137,700	600
		Totals	600	$275,400	1200

$$\text{Interest cost per year} = \frac{\$275,400}{1200} = \$229.50$$

$$\text{NIC} = \frac{\$229.50}{50} = 4.59\%$$

NIC for Bid B:

(1) Term to maturity	(2) Coupon rate (%)	(3) Interest/Bond	(4) Number of bonds maturing	(5) Total interest (1x3x4)	(6) Bond years (1x4)
1	20	$1,000	200	$200,000	200
2	2	100	200	40,000	400
3	1	50	200	30,000	600
		Totals	600	$270,000	1200

$$\text{Interest cost per year} = \frac{\$270,000}{1200} = \$225.00$$

$$\text{NIC} = \frac{\$225.00}{50} = 4.50\%$$

per bond in Column 3 is calculated by multiplying the coupon rate in Column 2 times
$5,000. Since $1,000,000 of bonds with a

face amount of $5,000 mature each year, there are 200 bonds maturing each year as shown in Column 4. The total interest paid for each maturity is shown in Column 5 and is derived by multiplying the term to maturity times the interest per bond times the number of bonds maturing each year. The bond years in Column 6 is the product of the term to maturity (Column 1) and the number of bonds of each maturity (Column 4). The interest cost per year for each bond is simply the total interest divided by bond years or $229.50 for bid A and $225.00 for bid B. This represents the average dollars of interest paid for each bond. The NIC value is calculated by dividing the interest cost per year by 50 for the $5,000 face value bonds. The NIC value is the average simple interest rate paid on each bond. Using the NIC, the issuer would select bid B since its NIC value of 4.50 percent is lower than the 4.59 percent value for bid A.

Unfortunately, the simplicity of the NIC method may lead to interest rates higher than necessary. As can be seen from the above example, the NIC completely ignores the time value of money. Funds paid out during the first year are valued equally with funds paid out in later years. Investors, however, place a higher value on dollars received during the earlier years. Consequently, underwriters can sell shorter-term bonds at a higher price than long-term bonds even though they both generate the same aggregate coupon payment. In order to generate a low NIC bid, underwriters assign lower coupon rates to later maturities. This type of high-low pattern can give rise then to inefficient bonds when compared to a method which discourages this pattern. Many studies and texts have documented that the awarding of serial bond issues on the basis of the NIC has resulted in interest rates higher than necessary.[6] To be consistent, the issuer should evaluate alternative underwriter bids based on a method which takes the time value of money into consideration since both underwriters and investors consider the time value of money in determining their strategies.

TIC Method

The True Interest Cost (TIC) method,[7] includes the time value of money and has been advocated as superior to NIC for the evaluation of underwriter bids. The formula for computing the TIC, with interest paid semiannually, is as follows:

$$B = \sum_{j=1}^{2n} \frac{C_n A_{n/2}}{(1 + \frac{TIC}{2})^j} + \sum_{n=s}^{m} \frac{A_n}{(1 + \frac{TIC}{2})^{2n}}$$

(Equation 15-3)

where B = aggregate dollar amount bid for bonds,
   A_n = total par value of bonds maturing in n periods.
   C_n = coupon rate on bonds maturing in n periods.
   n = number of years to maturity,
   s = years to first maturity,
   m = years to last maturity, and
   j = number of semiannual coupon periods.

With the aggregate dollar amount bid for the bonds, coupon rates, and par values of bonds maturing in each of the periods given, the TIC is obtained by a method of successive approximations. Since this is an IRR model, it must be solved using a trial and error methodology. The TIC is the rate which equates the present value of the principal and interest payments to the aggregate dollar amount bid for the bonds. Without a computer, the calculations are time-consuming and costly.

Using the same data for the bond issue in the NIC example, the TIC can be calculated for Underwriters A and B. To simplify the calculations, annual principal and interest payments are assumed. With annual coupons and compounding, the TIC equation becomes:

$$B = \sum_{n=s}^{m} \left[\frac{A_n}{(1 + TIC)^n} + \frac{C_n A_n}{(1 + TIC)^n} \right]$$

(Equation 15-4)

Computationally, the TIC is the rate which equates the present value of the principal and interest payments to the bond proceeds and involves the following steps:

Step 1: Calculate the total principal and interest payments for each year.

Step 2: Assume a value for the TIC and calculate the present value of the principal and interest payments.

Step 3: Compare the present value of the principal and interest payments (PV) with the bond proceeds (B). If the PV is greater than B, try a higher rate for the TIC. IF the PV is less than B, try a lower rate for the TIC.

Step 4: Repeat steps 2 and 3 until the PV is equal to B.

The calculations for the total principal and interest payments are shown in Table 15.7 for both bids. Step 2 involves the calcula-

TABLE 15.7

Calculation of Cash Flows for Two Bids

Bid A:

Term to maturity	Principal payment	Coupon rate (%)	Interest payment	Total principal and interest
1	1,000,000	4.59	137,700	1,137,700
2	1,000,000	4.59	91,800	1,091,800
3	1,000,000	4.59	45,900	1,045,900

Bid B:

Term to maturity	Principal payment	Coupon rate (%)	Interest payment	Total principal and interest
1	1,000,000	20	230,000	1,230,000
2	1,000,000	2	30,000	1,030,000
3	1,000,000	1	10,000	1,010,000

tion of the present value of the principal and interest payments based on an assumed TIC rate. Assuming a TIC rate of 4 percent for bid A results in:

$$\$3,000,000 = \$1,137,700 \ [PVF(4\%, \ 1 \ yr)]$$
$$+ \ 1,091,800 \ [PVF(4\%, \ 2 \ yr)]$$
$$+ \ 1,045,900 \ [PVF(4\%, \ 3 \ yr)]$$

$3,000,000 = 1,137,700 (0.96154)
            + 1,091,800 (0.92456)
            + 1,045,900 (0.88900)

$3,000,000 = $1,093,944 + $1,009,435
            + $929,805

$3,000,000 ≠ $3,033,184

Since the present value of the principal and interest payments is greater than the bond proceeds, a higher rate for the <u>TIC</u> must be used.

Next, assume a <u>TIC</u> of 5 percent for bid A:

$3,000,000 = $1,137,700 [PVF(5%, 1 yr)]
            + 1,091,800 [P̅V̅F̅(5%, 2 yr)]
            + 1,045,900 [P̅V̅F̅(5%, 3 yr)]

$3,000,000 = $1,137,700(0.95238)
            + 1,091,800(0.90703)
            + 1,045,900(0.86384)

$3,000,000 = $1,083,523 + 990,295
            + $903,490

$3,000,000 ≠ $2,977,308

Since the present value of the principal and interest payments is less than the bond proceeds, the <u>TIC</u> rate for bid A must be between 4 percent and 5 percent.

The present-value tables shown in this text are for integer interest rates only. To proceed further with tables we must gain access to tables with fractional values. This is not necessary, however, since hand-held financial calculators are readily available at a low cost which are programmed with this data. An alternative is interpolation; however, this method is subject to slight error. Using a Texas Instruments Business Analyst Calculator and a discount rate of 4.590% we find:

$3,000,000 = $1,137,700[PVF(4.59%, 1 yr)]
            + 1,091,800[P̅V̅F̅(4.59%, 2 yr)]
            + 1,045,900[P̅V̅F̅(4.59%, 3 yr)]

$3,000,000 = $1,087,771 + 998,074 + 914,155

$3,000,000 = $3,000,000

The present value of the principal and interest payments is equal to the bond proceeds. Consequently, the TIC for bid A is 4.59 percent. Using the same procedure, the TIC for bid B is found to be 4.597 percent.

Using the NIC, underwriter B would be selected, because the NIC for A is 4.59 percent, while the NIC for bid B is 4.50 percent. The TIC recognizes the actual timing of the cash flows and reverses the decision.

The TIC, however, does not consider the actual discount rates for each year. The TIC method discounts the cash flows at a constant TIC rate and ignores the yield curve. It is highly unlikely that the yield curve will be constant and equal to the TIC rate. Moreover, the evaluation of several bids using the TIC assumes an opportunity cost for each bid equal to its TIC rate. The opportunity cost assumption of the TIC method appears unrealistic in the case of serial tax-exempt bond issues. A present-value technique which allows the user to specify the discount rates, or opportunity costs, is a more appropriate methodology for the evaluation of bids for municipal issues. This technique, the present value of interest cost methods, or PIC, is discussed in the following section.

PIC Method

The PIC method recognizes that rates are not the same for bonds of different maturities. Because the issuing government specifies the maturity schedule for serial bond issues, the discounted value of the principal payments will be the same for all bids. In addition, the aggregate proceeds will be equal except for any discount or premium. The difference between bids manifests itself only in the bond coupons; this, then, is all that needs to be considered when determining the best bid. The PIC formulation for evaluating underwriters' bids is:

$$PIC = \sum_{n=1}^{m} \left[\frac{I_n}{\sum_{j=1}^{n}(1+k_j)} \right] - P+D$$

(Equation 15-5)

where PIC = present number of interest cost measured in dollars,

n = number of years to maturity,

m = number of years to maturity of the bond with last maturity,

I_n = aggregate interest or coupon payment in period n,

k_j = the expected borrowing rate for period j,

P = premium bid in dollars over aggregate par value for all maturities, and

D = discount bid in dollars over aggregate par value for all maturities.

No principal payments are included in Equation 15-5 since the timing and the magnitude of principal payments must be the same for each bid. The only variation in the bids is in coupon payment and any premium or discount. Using the PIC method, the issue would be awarded to the underwriter submitting the coupon rate schedule which results in the lowest present value of interest cost.

To illustrate: the same $3,000,000 bond issue with $1,000,000 principal payments in each year for the first three years used in the NIC and TIC examples is used for determination of the PIC. Two bidders offer to purchase the issue at par. Bidder A specifies 4.59 percent coupon rates for all three maturities while bidder B specifies rates of 20 percent, 2 percent, and 1 percent for years 1, 2, and 3, respectively. The calculation of the PIC for each of the two bids is shown in Table 15.8.

The calculation of the PIC requires yield-curve information prior to the bidding so that underwriters know the criteria to evaluate the bids. Ideally, the appropriate discount rates are the forward borrowing rates for the issuer. For example, the relevant discount rate for year four is the

Table 15.8

Calculation of the PIC for Bids A and B

(1)	(2)	(3)	Underwriter A		Underwriter B	
	Discount rate for the year	Present value of $1	(4)	(5) PV of coupon	(6)	(7) PV of coupon
Year	(%)	in year	Coupon payment	payment	Coupon payment	payment
1	3.8	0.9633	$137,700	$132,646	$230,000	$221,559
2	4.1	0.9254	91,800	84,952	30,000	27,762
3	4.4	0.8864	45,900	40,686	10,000	8,864
PIC				$258,284		$258,185

interest rate for funds borrowed in three years, repaid in four years, with the contract made now. Unfortunately, forward rates are not directly observable. Good approximations of the forward rates, however, are the yields-to-maturity of just-issued bonds of approximately the same size and rating. The reoffering yields of just-issued bonds of similar size and rating are shown in Column 2 of Table 15.8. These yields are used to approximate the borrowing cost of funds for each year.

The present value factors for each year are shown in Column 3. The factor is derived by taking the reciprocal of the product of one plus the discount rate for each year. For example, the present value factor for year 3 is equal to:

$$\frac{1}{(1+0.038)(1+0.041)(1+0.044)} = \frac{1}{1.1281} = 0.8864$$

The coupon payments are shown in Columns 4 and 6 for bid A and bid B, respectively. Multiplying the coupon payments by the present-value factors yields the present value of the coupon payment shown in columns 5 and 7. The PIC is equal to the sum of the present values of the individual coupon payments. Using the PIC, B would be selected since the PIC of $258,185 is lower than the PIC of $258,284 for bid A. Notice that this represents a reversal of the TIC rankings. The TIC for bid A was 4.59 percent and 4.597 percent for bid B.

In this example, a municipal issuer would make a mistake if the offer of Underwriter A was chosen using the TIC. Given the yield curve with the higher rates in later years, the issuer has obligations with a lower present cost by selecting Underwriter B. This is the information provided by PIC.

The differences in rankings that occur when using the TIC and PIC are due to the different assumptions about borrowing rates. The PIC method deals explicitly with the borrowing rate in each year of the cash flows. The TIC method, however, uses a borrowing rate completely determined by the cash flows of the municipal bond issue and this is not necessarily related to market yields. The TIC method assumes a constant borrowing rate equal to the TIC rate, and the issuer cannot vary these rates. The PIC allows the issuer to specify different borrowing rates for the different maturities in the issue. The greater the difference between the TIC rate and the issuer's actual borrowing rate, the greater the likelihood of a ranking error in using the TIC. The PIC method, then, is a theoretically superior method for evaluation of underwriters' bids, in much the same manner as the net present value method is superior to the internal rate of return method in capital budgeting decisions. Issuers of municipal bonds should consider the use of PIC instead of TIC or NIC for the evaluation of bids since the PIC is not subject to ranking errors.

THE MUNICIPAL BOND INSURANCE DECISION

Municipal bond insurance protects against default risk by guaranteeing investors prompt payment of scheduled coupon and principal payments. The use of municipal bond insurance has increased dramatically since 1975, partly due to changes in attitude by investors as a result of the New York City fiscal crisis. The creation of the Municipal Bond Insurance Association (MBIA), a consortium of four large fire and casualty companies, in 1974 was also a major factor in the increased use of municipal bond insurance.

Presently three carriers offer municipal bond insurance--Municipal Bond Insurance Association (MBIA); the American Municipal Bond Assurance Corporation (AMBAC), a subsidiary of MGIC Investment Corporation; and MGIC Indemnity Corporation, also a subsidiary of MGIC Investment Corporation. MBIA, a joint venture of Aetna Casualty and Surety, Aetna Insurance (of Connecticut General), St. Paul Fire and Marine, and United States Fire, is the most widely used carrier. Since 1974 MBIA has insured approximately 785 issues having a par value of approximately $3.9 billion,[8] confined primarily to new-issue general obligations and utility revenue bonds. AMBAC provides insurance to both new and outstanding municipal issues and portfolios. Over 60 percent of the risk exposure of AMBAC is in nonutility revenue bonds.[9] MGIC Indemnity Corporation provides insurance for the more risky issues that AMBAC will not insure.

Selected features of the three municipal bond insurance programs are shown in Table 15.9. The basic eligibility requirements are fairly uniform for all three. The insurance premium for new bond issues ranges from 0.5 percent to 2.0 percent of total debt service (both principal and interest) for MBIA and from 0.25 percent to 4.5 percent of total debt service for AMBAC. MGIC Indemnity Corporation charges an annual rate of 0.095 percent to 0.92 percent of principal or par value for each issue insured. The actual insurance fee charged varies according to the size of the issue and the credit worthiness of the issuer. The size of the issues which will be insured by each of the insuring agencies ranges from $20 million and $35 million principal and interest for MGIC Indemnity Corporation and AMBAC, respectively, to $60 million principal for MBIA.

Issues insured by MBIA automatically receive a Standard and Poor's rating of AAA while AMBAC-insured bonds receive a Standard and Poor's rating of AA. Standard and Poor's does not, however, consider MGIC Indemnity Corporation insurance when assigning ratings to new issues. Moody's takes the position that it rates bond issues, not insurance carriers, and ignores municipal bond insurance in the rating process.

There are several reasons that municipal bond insurance may be attractive to issuers. MBIA-insured issues receive a Standard and Poor's AAA rating, the highest possible. As discussed in Chapter 13, the bond rating is a major determinant of interest costs. A recent study found that bond insurance reduced average interest costs significantly. In fact, the less credit worthy the municipality, the more it seems to benefit from bond insurance.[10] In addition, the increased quality and

TABLE 15.9

Selected Features of Municipal Bond Insurance

Program	Coverage	Size of issue (in millions)	Quality limitations	Cost of guarantee
MBIA	New G.O.s, utility rev. bonds & selected other revenue bonds	0.275-60* (par value)	Readily salable in public market without insurance	0.5-2% of total debt service (interest & princ.)
AMBAC	New G.O.s & most types of revenue bonds	0.5-35, G.O.s & utility rev. bonds; 0.5-25, nonutility rev. (par value)	None	0.25-4.5% total principal & interest, computed to maturity
MGIC Indemnity	Investment portfolios, tax-exempt mutual funds, unit investment trusts	0.5-20	None	0.095-0.92% par value annually

Source: AMBA, MBIA, and MGIC Investment Corporation.

*Limits subject to continual revue.

the appeal of a nationally recognized guarantee enhances the marketability of the insured issue. The greater the marketability, the lower the borrowing cost. This is one reason why the smaller, less well-known issues may benefit the most from bond insurance.

Special circumstances may also be mitigated by municipal bond insurance. Pending legal action may prevent a municipality from obtaining an unqualified opinion from bond counsel. Municipal bond insurance, which provides security, may make it possible to sell a bond issue which otherwise could not be sold.

Offsetting these benefits are the costs of obtaining municipal bond insurance. The major cost is the cash outlay for the insurance premium. This cost, as shown in Table 15.9, varies with the size of the issue. The cost also varies with quality ratings normally assigned to the obligation and the specific insurance program.[11] There may be other miscellaneous costs such as the expense of additional analytical or consulting work as well. These costs, however, are usually small given the ease and simplicity of obtaining the insurance.

The process of obtaining bond insurance is simple but involves two separate decisions. The first is the carrier's decision on whether or not to insure the issue, and, if so, at what insurance premium. The second is the issuer's decision on whether or not to purchase the insurance. The decision whether to insure an issue is made in a similar manner for all three carriers. The procedure used by MBIA will be presented, but the same general process would apply to the two smaller carriers.

The request for an MBIA qualification for an issue comes from the issuer, the issuer's financial advisor, or the underwriter. MBIA also qualifies certain competitive bid issues without an outside request. There are three ways of purchasing MBIA insurance. In the "optional bidding" program, an announcement is made prior to the bond sale date that MBIA will insure the bonds if anyone is willing to pay the announced insurance premium. With the "direct purchase" method, the issuer purchases the insurance policy outright, and in the "alternative bidding" method, the issuer takes bids on the bonds as insured or uninsured obligations.

In competitive sale using the direct purchase method, the issuer purchases the MBIA insurance and offers the bonds to all bidders as insured bonds

with a Standard and Poor's rating of AAA. The
issuer pays the insurance premium from the general
fund or from the bond proceeds at the time the bonds
are issued. The "market" does not participate
directly in this decision as the issuer solicits
bids only for the insured bonds. The issuer may,
however, postpone the decision to purchase the
insurance by using either the alternative bidding
program or the optional bidding program. Using the
alternative bidding program, the issuer advertises
for two bids--one with and one without MBIA
insurance. Each underwriter bids on insured and
uninsured bonds at the same time. The issuer then
selects the best bid after a cost-benefit comparison. If the bid for the insured bonds is better,
taking the cost of insurance into consideration, the
issuer selects the insured bid and pays the
insurance premium. If the costs of the insurance
equal or exceed the benefits, the issuer may select
the best uninsured bid. This latter method often
limits the presale marketing efforts by underwriters
since they are not sure whether the bonds ultimately
will be offered with or without insurance. Without
the insurance guarantee, the bonds would not be sold
with the AAA rating.

The optional bidding program is similar to the
alternative bidding program except each underwriter
submits only one bid. Potential bidders examine the
market for insured and uninsured bonds. Based on
direct market input, each underwriter then determines whether the increased market value of insured
bonds will cover the premium expense. If so, the
underwriter submits a bid for insured bonds and pays
the premium if awarded the issue. If not, the
underwriter submits a bid on uninsured bonds. Using
this method, the decision to purchase municipal bond
insurance is left to the underwriters. The issuer
does not care whether the issue is insured or not;
he is concerned with the lowest bid.

Decision Model

If the direct purchase or alternative bidding
methods are used, the issuer must make a direct
comparison of the benefits and costs of insurance.
Since the major benefit is a reduction in interest
payments over the life of the issue, the time value
of money must be considered. The decision involves
a comparison of the bonds with insurance to bonds

without insurance. A comparison should be made of the new present value of the differential cash flows of the two alternatives over time. The net-present-value model below compares the differential benefits (cash flows) and costs (cash outflows) associated with municipal bond insurance.[12]

Assuming semiannual compounding, the $\underline{NPV}$ model for deciding whether to purchase municipal bond insurance is:

$$\underline{NPV} = \underline{U}_0 - \underline{M}_0 - \underline{G}_0 + \sum_{t-1}^{2n} (\underline{S}_t)/(1 + \underline{i}/2)^{\underline{t}}$$

$$= \underline{U}_0 - \underline{M}_0 - \underline{G}_0 + \text{present value of } (\underline{S}_t)$$

(Equation 15-6)

where $\underline{U}_0$ = the amount of proceeds realized by the issuer at the time of sale for a guaranteed bond issue minus the amount realized for a nonguaranteed issue,

$\underline{M}_0$ = the amount of miscellaneous expenses incurred by the issuer for a guaranteed bond issue minus the amount spent for a nonguaranteed issue,

$\underline{G}_0$ = insurance premium paid from the general fund at the time of the sale,[13]

$\underline{S}_t$ = the coupon payment required with the nonguaranteed option minus the coupon payment required with the guaranteed bond alternative in a given time period $\underline{t}$,

$\underline{i}$ = annual opportunity cost rate, and

$\underline{n}$ = years to final maturity.

If $\underline{NPV}$ is positive using this model, the insurance should be purchased since the present value of the benefits exceeds the present value of these costs. If the $\underline{NPV}$ is negative, the municipality should not purchase the insurance.

Application of the Model

This model is fairly easy to apply in practice, although it appears otherwise in equation form. To illustrate the use and simplicity of the $\underline{NPV}$ model, consider the following example used by Michael Joehnk and David Kidwell.[14]

A local government intends to issue a $1.5 million serial general obligation bond issue to finance public projects. The issue has a final maturity of 11.5 years, semiannual coupon payments, and annual principal payments with the first principal payment beginning 2.5 years after the date of issue. The principal is amortized in increasing amounts over the life of the issue (this pattern is popular in the municipal bond industry because it allows fairly level debt service payments). The local government's bonds have been A-rated in the past, and if the bond issue is guaranteed, the rating agency would revise its assessment to AAA. The bond insurance premium is $45,000 (approximately 1-1/4 percent of principal and interest). The local government has decided to pay this premium from the general fund. The local government expects the use of the guarantee to result in increased underwriter proceeds of $5,500 and additional miscellaneous expenses of $2,500.

Table 15.10 contains the values used in this example and the analysis of whether to purchase the insurance or not.

Application of the model requires estimating the benefits and costs associated with the guaranteed bond option versus those that might occur with the nonguaranteed alternative. This requires estimating (1) the bond issue's coupon structure without the guarantee, (2) the bond issue's coupon structure with the guarantee, (3) the annual opportunity cost rate or discount rate, and (4) the difference in issuer proceeds and miscellaneous costs between the two alternatives.

The coupon structure without the guarantee can be established by analyzing the yield curves and coupon patterns of similar bonds. This involves locating information on bonds sold by other local governments near the proposed date of sale of the new issue. Issue and issuer characteristics such as bond rating, maturity schedule, issue size, and type of bond should be matched as closely as possible. For this example, the local

TABLE 15.10

Details of Applying the Present Value Model to the Analysis of a
Municipal Bond Guarantee Purchase

| (1) | Issue without guarantee | | | Issue with guarantee | | | Present-value computation | | |
Time period (years)	(2) Principal payment (dollars)	(3) Coupon rate (percent)	(4) Interest payment (dollars)	(5) Principal payment (dollars)	(6) Revised coupon rate (percent)	(7) Revised interest payment (dollars)	(8) Interest saving: S_t (4) − (7) (dollars)	(9) Discount factor (3% semi-annual)	(10) Present value (8) x (9) (dollars)
0	0		0	0		0	0	1.000	0
0.5	0		70,250	0		64,300	5,950	0.971	5,777
1.0	0		70,250	0		64,300	5,950	0.943	5,611
1.5	0		70,250	0		64,300	5,950	0.915	5,444
2.0	0		70,250	0		64,300	5,950	0.889	5,290
2.5	100,000	7.00	70,250	100,000	6.10	64,300	5,950	0.863	5,135
3.0	0		66,750	0		61,250	5,500	0.838	4,609
3.5	100,000	7.00	66,750	100,000	6.20	61,250	5,500	0.813	4,472
4.0	0		63,250	0		58,150	5,100	0.789	4,024
4.5	100,000	6.50	63,250	100,000	5.70	58,150	5,100	0.766	3,907
5.0	0		60,000	0		55,300	4,700	0.744	3,497
5.5	200,000	6.50	60,000	200,000	5.90	55,300	4,700	0.722	3,393
6.0	0		53,500	0		49,400	4,100	0.701	2,874
6.5	200,000	6.00	53,500	200,000	5.40	49,400	4,100	0.681	2,792
7.0	0		47,500	0		44,000	3,500	0.661	2,314
7.5	200,000	6.00	47,500	200,000	5.50	44,000	3,500	0.642	2,247
8.0	0		41,500	0		38,500	3,000	0.623	1,869
8.5	300,000	5.50	41,500	300,000	5.00	38,500	3,000	0.605	1,815
9.0	0		33,250	0		31,000	2,250	0.587	1,321
9.5	300,000	5.50	33,250	300,000	5.10	31,000	2,250	0.570	1,283
10.0	0		25,000	0		23,350	1,650	0.554	914
10.5	300,000	5.00	25,000	300,000	4.60	23,350	1,650	0.536	884
11.0	0		17,500	0		16,450	1,050	0.523	549
11.5	700,000	5.00	17,500	700,000	4.70	16,450	1,050	0.507	532
TOTAL	$2,500,000		$1,167,750	$2,500,000		$1,076,300	$91,450		$70,533

Source: Michael D. Joehnk and David S. Kidwell, "Determining the Advantages and Disadvantages of Private Municipal Bond Guarantees," Governmental Finance (February 1978), p. 34.

government's best estimate of the new issue's coupon structure without the guarantee is shown in Column 3 of Table 15.10. The coupon rate schedule for the guaranteed option is estimated in a similar manner. This latter coupon rate will be lower because of the improved credit rating with the guarantee. The estimate of the coupon structure with the guarantee is shown in Column 6.

Once the coupon rate schedules have been determined, the size of the interest payments can be calculated. The semiannual interest payments for the guaranteed and nonguaranteed alternatives are shown in Columns 4 and 7 of Table 15.10, respectively. The difference between the two semiannual interest payments represents the periodic interest cost savings ($\underline{S}_t$) and is shown in Column 8.

The opportunity cost is the return that could be earned from the best available investment opportunity of the issuer at the same level of risk. The appropriate discount rate used in this example is the U.S. Government's borrowing rate--the yield on Treasury bonds for maturities similar to the proposed issue's average maturity. In this example, the current yield on Treasuries is assumed to be approximately 6 percent. Since semiannual cash flows are involved, a semiannual discount rate of 3 percent is used. The present value factors for a 3 percent semiannual discount rate are shown in Column 9. Multiplication of the differential interest savings in Column 8 by the present-value factors in Column 9 generates the present value of the interest payments shown in Column 10. The total present value of the future interest savings is equal to $70,553.

The final step is to substitute all the estimated cash flow values into Equation 15-6 to determine the net present value. In this example, the $\underline{NPV}$ is:

$$\underline{NPV} = \underline{U}_0 - \underline{M}_0 - \underline{G}_0 + \text{present value of } (\underline{S}_t)$$

$$\underline{NPV} = \$5,500 - \$2,500 - \$45,000 + \$70,553$$

$$= \$28,553$$

Since the $\underline{NPV}$ is positive, the insurance should be purchased. The present value of the interest savings to the issuer is $28,553. If the $\underline{NPV}$ had been negative, the insurance should have been rejected.

This section presented the concept of municipal bond insurance, the different methods of purchasing insurance, and a comparison of benefits and costs for making the municipal bond insurance decision using a net present value model, along with an illustration of its application. A municipality may also be faced with the decision of whether to replace one bond issue with another. The next section contains a net-present-value method for making this bond refunding decision.

THE BOND REFUNDING DECISION

The call provision on the bond issue provides the issuer flexibility in financing. If interest rates decline significantly, it may be advantageous for the issuer to call the old bonds and refinance with new bonds at a lower rate. In this way the issuer does not have to wait until the last serial bond is retired to take advantage of lower interest rates. A second reason for refunding is to eliminate restrictive covenants in the bond resolution. These restrictions can be removed by refinancing with bonds without the restrictive covenants.

The refunding decision takes the form of a capital budgeting decision. There is an initial cash outlay to call the existing bonds and to issue new bonds followed by a series of future interest savings. The annual interest savings are the difference between the cash outflows required under the old bonds and the cash outflows required under the new issue. This section presents a present-value framework for evaluating the direct form of bond refunding, in which the proceeds from the new issue are used directly and immediately to refund the older, higher-cost obligation. Advance refunding, the other basic form, involves selling new bonds well before the old issue is called, and investing the proceeds in an escrow account in the interim period. Recent Internal Revenue Service regulations have severely limited advance refundings.

Direct refunding is the most common form since other types are prohibited by many state and local laws.[15] Direct refunding results in a net benefit to the municipality if the present value of the cash savings from refunding exceeds the cost of refunding. The refunding decision involves three steps: (1) determining the initial cash flow resulting from refunding (C), (2) determining the periodic cash flow differentials of the new versus old issues over their lives (S_t), and (3) determining the appropriate discount rate for evaluating the cash flows (i).

The initial cash flow (C) from refunding has three elements: the cash inflow from the net proceeds of the new bonds (P), the cash outflow to call the old bonds (O), and the cash outflow for miscellaneous costs associated with refunding, such as legal, printing, and clerical costs (M). Thus, the initial cash flow is:

$$C = P - O - M \qquad \text{(Equation 15-7)}$$

The differential cash flow (S_t) is the difference between the periodic principal and interest payments associated with the old bonds (E_t) and the new bonds (N_t). This periodic differential cash flow is:

$$S_t = E_t - N_t \qquad \text{(Equation 15-8)}$$

In direct refunding, S_t will normally be positive for all periods.

The third step is the determination of the appropriate discount rate. Since the net proceeds from the new issue (P) are used to extinguish the old issue, the interest cost associated with issuing the new bonds is a realistic measure of the time value of money (i). This borrowing rate is appropriate since the municipality is solely concerned with evaluating a specific debt management alternative. Since interest usually is paid semiannually on municipal bonds, the discount rate, i, may be expressed in equation form as:

$$P = \sum_{t=1}^{2m} \frac{S_t}{(1 + i/2)^t} \qquad \text{(Equation 15-9)}$$

where m denotes the years to maturity on the refunding issue. The interest rate, i, then is the rate that equates the present value of the principal and interest payments of the new issue to its net proceeds, or the TIC rate of the new issue.

The decision model for direct refunding of municipal bonds may now be expressed as:

$$PVS = C + \sum_{t=1}^{2m} \frac{S_t}{(1 + i/2)^t} \qquad \text{(Equation 15-10)}$$

Equation 15-10 is compatible with the serial nature of municipal issues and the computational procedure is straightforward. If the PVS is positive, the refunding operation should be given serious consideration. A negative PVS implies that the present value of costs exceeds the present value of the savings from refunding.

An example of the use of this direct refunding decision model follows.

Twenty million dollars of 20-year obligation bonds were originally issued in serial form ten years ago. The bonds carried a straight-line principal amortization schedule of $1 million per year and carried a call provision which provided that the bonds were callable in full on or after ten years at a constant call price of 103; the coupon rate was 7.0 percent for all maturities with interest paid semiannually. The new bonds are also to be issued in serial form with the same principal and interest dates as those of the remaining original issue; they will carry a straight-line amortization schedule and have a coupon rate of 6.0 percent for all maturities; the total miscellaneous issuance costs and call premium of the old issue is $33.00 for every $1,000 of principal; the net proceeds of the new issue of $10 million are realized the same day as the original issue is retired.

The net proceeds (P) from the sale of the new bonds are equal to $10 million. On December 31 of year 10, the earliest date that the original issue is freely callable, $1,385,000 in principal and interest ($11 million x 0.035 interest + $1 million principal) are due. In addition, the $10 million in principal to be refunded (i.e., the year 11 to 20 maturities) and the $300,000 call premium ($3 per $100 times $10 million) must be paid. Consequently, the cash outflow required to call the old bonds, $\underline{O}$, is equal to $11,685,000. The miscellaneous costs of refunding are equal to $3 per $1,000 or $30,000. The initial cash flow for this example using Equation 15.7 is:

$$\underline{C} = \underline{P} - \underline{O} - \underline{M}$$

$$\underline{C} = \$10,000,000 - \$11,685,000 - \$30,000$$

$$\underline{C} = -\$1,715,000$$

The discount rate to use in the bond refunding decision is the $\underline{TIC}$ rate of the new bonds. Since the net proceeds of the new bonds equal their face amount, the $\underline{TIC}$ rate equals the coupon rate of 6 percent per year. If this had not been the case, the $\underline{TIC}$ would have to have been calculated using the trial-and-error procedure presented earlier in this chapter.

The present value of the periodic differential cash flows are calculated as shown in Table 15.11. Column 1 shows the 20 semiannual periods remaining to maturity of the old issue (maturities in years 11 to 20). The principal payments of the old and new issues are equal and are shown in Column 2. The total debt service payments of the old issue are shown in Column 3. Interest on the outstanding principal is paid semiannually at a rate of 3.5 percent with the $1,000,000 principal payment made annually. The debt service payments for the new issue, shown in Column 4, are calculated in a similar manner, except the semiannual interest rate is 3 percent. The total savings per year is simply the difference between the debt service payments of the old and new issues as shown in Column 5. Since payments are made semiannually, they must be discounted at one-half the annual $\underline{TIC}$ rate, or 3 percent. The present value factors for a 3 percent semiannual discount rate are shown

TABLE 15.11

Calculation of Present Value of Interest Savings
Direct Refunding Example
(Thousands of Dollars)

(1) Semiannual period	(2) Principal payment	(3) Debt service old issue (7% coupon)	(4) Debt service new issue (6% coupon)	(5) Total savings (col 3 − col 4)	(6) PV factor (3% semi-annual)	(7) PV of savings (Col 5 x Col 6)
1		350	300	50	0.97007	48.50
2 (Yr 11)	1,000	1,350	1,300	50	0.94260	47.13
3		315	270	45	0.91514	41.18
4 (Yr 12)	1,000	1,315	1,270	45	0.88849	39.98
5		280	240	40	0.86261	34.50
6 (Yr 13)	1,000	1,280	1,240	40	0.83748	33.50
7		245	210	35	0.81309	28.46
8 (Yr 14)	1,000	1,245	1,210	35	0.78941	27.63
9		210	180	30	0.76642	22.99
10 (Yr 15)	1,000	1,210	1,180	30	0.74409	22.32
11		175	150	25	0.72242	18.06
12 (Yr 16)	1,000	1,175	1,150	25	0.70138	17.53
13		140	120	20	0.68095	13.62
14 (Yr 17)	1,000	1,140	1,120	20	0.66112	13.22
15		105	90	15	0.64186	9.63
16 (Yr 18)	1,000	1,105	1,090	15	0.62317	9.35
17		70	60	10	0.60502	6.05
18 (Yr 19)	1,000	1,070	1,060	10	0.58739	5.87
19		35	30	5	0.57029	2.85
20 (Yr 20)	1,000	1,035	1,030	5	0.55367	2.77
						445.14

in Column 6. The present value factors are multiplied by the total annual savings yielding the present value of total savings shown in Column 7. The sum of the present value of the annual savings is $445,140.

Substituting these values into Equation 15-10, the PVS of this direct bond refunding example is:

$$PVS = C + \sum_{t=1}^{2n} \frac{S_t}{(1 + i/2)^t}$$

$$PVS = -\$1,715,000 + \$445,140$$

$$PVS = -\$1,269,860$$

This particular refunding alternative is not attractive, since it results in a present value loss of $1,269,860.

The decision to undertake an advance refunding would be analyzed in much the same manner as the direct refunding decision except the investment proceeds of the escrow account need to be taken into consideration. Section 103(c) of the Internal Revenue Code greatly restricts the use of arbitrage bonds and the number of advance refundings has dropped significantly. Essentially, the IRS eliminated the possibility of making any significant arbitrage profits by borrowing funds at low tax-free rates offered on default-free U.S. Government securities which are normally taxable. The possibility of arbitrage profits was a major incentive for advance refundings. Having examined a decision model that local governments can use to determine the desirability of a direct funding operations, the next alternative to be examined is the lease versus buy decision.

THE LEASE VERSUS PURCHASE DECISION

The final section of this chapter examines the leasing decision as an alternative to purchasing a capital asset by financing it with long-term debt. The financial lease is a viable alternative for not-for-profit organizations but it is rarely used.

Evidently, not-for-profit organizations believe leasing is inherently more expensive than other sources of financing or that leasing is not widely available.

It is important to distinguish between two distinctly different kinds of lease. The _operating lease_ is similar to a rental agreement. The lessee acquires the right to use the asset in return for a periodic fee to the lessor, the owner of the asset. This arrangement can be canceled by the lessor or lessee with due notice. Maintenance and other services are usually included as part of the lease. The use of vehicles, computers, copiers, amusement equipment, display fixtures, and furniture are often acquired by operating leases. Operating leases are usually written for periods less than the life of the leased asset. The lessor ultimately depends on the subsequent sale of the used asset to recover any unrecovered costs at the end of the lease period.

The _financial lease_ is a commitment by the lessor and lessee whereby the lessee agrees to make lease payments over a specified period of time in exchange for use of the asset. The lease cannot be cancelled unless _both_ the lessor and lessee agree. The financial lease requires a much larger financial commitment on the part of the lessee than the operating lease. The lessee agrees to make a series of payments, which in total generally equal or exceed the purchase price of the leased asset. The lessee is contractually obligated to make these payments over the life of the lease contract, even if the service of the leased asset is no longer required.

The noncancelable long-term nature of the financial lease makes it similar to long-term debt. Fixed payments must be paid at predetermined dates over long periods of time, similar to the principal and interest payments associated with municipal bonds. Failure to make the contractual payments on a financial lease may result in insolvency and bankruptcy court action. The lessor is entitled to repossess the leased asset and to receive at least partial payment of the lease fees applicable to the remainder of the contract. In spite of these contractual obligations, the financial lease is often a viable alternative to the use of long-term debt.

The small interest in leasing by not-for-profit organizations appears to be a function of a lack of understanding of the use of a financial lease as an alternative to long-term debt.[16] The financial lease, however, may afford several benefits to the not-for-profit organization in need of capital asset financing. Edward Dyl and Michael Joehnk have enumerated several possible advantages to the municipality of using financial leases. The following advantages apply to other types of not-for-profit organizations as well[17]:

1. Leasing may provide an opportunity to raise needed capital in situations where local laws or restrictions prevent direct bank borrowing.

2. Leasing may provide a means of financing for equipment and facilities to not-for-profit organizations with little or no access to traditional capital markets.

3. Leasing may be a convenient means of obtaining equipment that costs too little to warrant a bond issue yet costs too much to finance out of current revenues.

4. Leasing may provide municipalities with a means of avoiding cumbersome and costly voter approval on financing actions and other legal constraints placed on the capital raising function.

5. Leasing frees up cash and debt capacity for other needs without having to defer the acquisition of capital assets.

In addition to these qualitative reasons for leasing, there may be instances in which leasing is the least-expensive means of long-term financing. The following section concentrates on the quantitative aspects of financial leases. A straightforward approach to lease evaluation for use by financial managers of not-for-profit organizations is presented.

The primary economic reason for the existence of the financial lease is related to income taxes. When a profit-oriented firm leases an asset, the entire amount of lease expense is deductible for tax purposes. If the firm were to purchase the asset instead, only the depreciation charges and the interest payments would be deductible for tax purposes. The profit-oriented firm would also be entitled to an investment tax credit on the purchase of the asset. The not-for-profit organization, as a tax-exempt entity, has no use for depreciation tax deductions and investment tax credits. The following example considers the tax consequences of leasing.

An investor is considering a $1,000 investment in either of two assets. Asset A is a security which pays $150 per year to maturity in 4 years and has a maturity value of $1,000. Asset B is an asset that is fully depreciable over 4 years at $250 per year and earns an annual profit before depreciation and taxes of $350.27. These alternate investments will be examined for two types of investors: a not-for-profit organization which pays no taxes, and a profit-oriented firm with a 50 percent tax rate.

The cash flows for the two types of assets and the two investors are shown in Table 15.12:

TABLE 15.12

Tax Consequences of Leasing

Alternative A: Security

(1) Year	(2) Cash flow before taxes	(3) Not-for-profit organization (0% tax rate) cash flow after taxes	(4) Profit-oriented firm (50% tax rate) cash flow after taxes
0	-$1,000.00	-$1,000.00	-$1,000.00
1	150.00	150.00	75.00
2	150.00	150.00	75.00
3	150.00	150.00	75.00
4	1,150.00	1,150.00	1,075.00
		IRR = 15%	IRR = 7.5%

Alternative B: Depreciable Asset

(1) Year	(2) Profit before taxes	(3) Not-for-profit organization (0% tax rate) cash flow after taxes	(4) Profit after taxes	(5) Profit-oriented firm (50% tax rate) Cash flow after taxes
0		-$1,000.00		-$1,000.00
1	$100.27	350.27	$50.14	300.14
2	100.27	350.27	50.14	300.14
3	100.27	350.27	50.14	300.14
4	100.27	350.27	50.14	300.14
		IRR = 15%		IRR = 7.73%

Security A pays $150 per year and the investor receives $1,000 at maturity. The cash flows for the not-for-profit organization after taxes are the same as the cash flows before taxes. The profit-oriented firm, however, has to pay $75 in tax on its $150 per year income; the cash flows after taxes for the profit-oriented firm are shown in Column 4 of alternative A. The internal rate of return for the not-for-profit organization and the profit-oriented firm are 15 percent and 7.5 percent, respectively, for security A.

Investment in the depreciable asset results in a profit before taxes of $100.27 per year in years 1 to 4 after deducting the $250.00 per year depreciation charge from the $350.27 annual return. The cash flows for the not-for-profit organization are equal to the $100.27 per year plus the $250.00 per year depreciation charge (a noncash expenditure) or $350.27 per year in years 1 to 4. The profit-oriented firm, again, has to pay taxes at a 50 percent rate, resulting in $50.14 per year after-tax profit in years 1 to 4. Adding depreciation to after-tax profit results in $300.14 annual cash flows in years 1 to 4 for the profit-oriented firm. The internal rates of return for the investment in the depreciable asset are now 15 percent and 7.73 percent for the not-for-profit organization and profit-oriented firms, respectively.

The not-for-profit organization is indifferent between investing in the security or the depreciable asset since both have an internal rate of return of 15 percent. The profit-oriented firm, however, prefers investing in the depreciable asset since its internal rate of return is 7.73 percent compared to the 7.50 percent internal rate of return of the security. Other things being equal, the profit-seeking firm prefers investments in depreciable assets since depreciation shields part of the firm's cash flows from taxes. The value of the annual depreciation tax shield to the asset owner is:

$$\underline{V} = \underline{TD} \qquad\qquad \text{(Equation 15-11)}$$

where $\underline{V}$ = the value of the tax shield from
   depreciation,
   $\underline{T}$ = the marginal tax rate, and
   $\underline{D}$ = the annual depreciation charge.

Looking at Equation 15-11, it is obvious that the value of the tax shield depends on the tax situation of the asset owner. If the asset is owned by a not-for-profit organization, the tax shield is worthless since the marginal tax rate is zero. Similarly, the tax shield is more valuable to an organization in the 50 percent bracket than it is to one in the 20 percent bracket. The same situation arises with the investment tax credit. The value of the investment tax credit depends on the organization's tax bracket, the cost of the asset, the life of the asset, and the organization's total credits for the year relative to income.

The financial lease in the profit sector provides a means of transferring income tax deductions for depreciation and investment tax credits from lessee firms, unable to fully utilize the benefits, to lessor firms which can fully utilize the benefits. The potential for such a transfer is even greater in the not-for-profit sector. If the lessor firm can capture the tax shield of depreciation and the investment tax credit, which are worthless to the not-for-profit organization, and share these benefits with the lessee, both parties gain. The losers are other taxpayers, since tax revenues are reduced.
The economic rationale for financial leasing by the not-for-profit organization provides a basis for bargaining in lease negotiations, but it does not provide the financial officer with a procedure to assess the economic desirability of a financial lease. The lease decision model and an illustration of its application will now be presented. The financial lease decision involves a present-value, cost-benefit analysis of three items.

1. The annual lease payments to be made over the life of the lease ($\underline{L}$).
2. The estimated salvage value of the capital asset ($\underline{SV}_{\underline{n}}$).

3. The purchase price and installation costs of the capital asset (C).

The cost-benefit analysis first involves discounting the real and opportunity costs of leasing (items 1 and 2 above) to determine their present value. This result is compared to the benefits of leasing, which are the costs of purchasing the asset which are foregone (item 3).

The present value cost (PVC) of the lease option may be specified as[18]:

$$PVC = L + L \sum_{t=0}^{n-1} \frac{1}{(1+i)^t} + \frac{SV_n}{(1+i)^n}$$

(Equation 15-12)

where i = the discount rate, and
n = the term of the lease.

Equation 15-12 states that the present value cost of the lease is equal to the present value of the annual lease payments plus the present value of the estimated salvage value of the asset (an opportunity cost). Note that the annual lease payments in this model are assumed to be made at the beginning of each year. The appropriate discount rate, i, is the not-for-profit organization's borrowing rate. This is the appropriate rate since the debt management alternative of leasing versus borrowing the funds is being evaluated. The appropriate decision rule for the not-for-profit organization is to use the financial lease if PVC is less than the cost of purchasing the asset (C). Otherwise, the organization would purchase the asset, financing it with debt.

> **The following example illustrates the application of the lease evaluation procedure.** A local government can lease a $3,000,000 computer for five years at an annual rate of $550,000, payable one year in advance. If the local government's borrowing rate is 6 percent and the asset's estimated salvage value in year 5 is $500,000, should the local government lease or purchase the asset?
>
> Equation 15-12 is used to evaluate this decision by substituting the annual lease

payment (L) of $550,000 paid in years t=0 to 4; the estimated salvage value of $500,000; and a borrowing rate of 6 percent. Consequently,

$$\underline{PVC} = \$550,000 + \$550,000[\underline{PVAF}(6\%,4 \text{ yr})]$$
$$+ \ 500,000 \ [\underline{PVF}(6\%,5 \text{ yr})]$$

$$\underline{PVC} = \$550,000 + 550,000(3.4651)$$
$$+ \ 500,000(0.74726)$$

$$= \$550,000 + 1,905,805 + 373,630$$

$$\underline{PVC} = \$2,829,435$$

Since the PVC of $2,829,435 is less than the $3,000,000 cost of purchasing the asset, there is economic justification for leasing. By using the financial lease, the local government has a present value savings of $170,565 compared to the purchase alternative. This savings results from the local government's ability to transfer ownership benefits to the lessor, which leads to a difference in the effective costs of leasing versus borrowing.

SUMMARY

Several alternatives for improving the efficiency and effectiveness of debt management were presented in this chapter. Specifically, the determination of the optimal size of a bond issue, the evaluation of competitive bids, the municipal bond insurance decision, the bond refunding decision, and the lease versus purchase decision, were examined. The decision models included present-value analyses of the appropriate cash flows for each alternative.

QUESTIONS

1. Why is it important to determine the optimal size of a bond issue prior to issuance?

2. What techniques are available to select the lowest bid by an underwriter on a bond issue?

3. Evaluate the NIC method.

4. Evaluate the <u>TIC</u> method.

5. Evaluate the <u>PIC</u> method.

6. What is the difference between an optimal bidding program, direct purchase, and alternative bidding program for municipal bond insurance?

7. What decision model is the basis for the municipal bond insurance decision?

8. What is meant by the bond refunding decision? When would bond refunding be appropriate?

9. What is the difference between an operating and a financial lease?

10. What are the advantages to a municipality in using leasing as a method of financing capital expenditures?

PROBLEMS

1. Determine the optimum serial bond issue size to finance road construction using the method developed by Philip Law from the following information:

Costs of construction	$14,000,000
Time to complete	2 years
Date of bond issuance	1/1/X1
(issue at face value)	
Date of first maturity	1/1/X6
Date of last maturity	1/1/Y5
(10 equal principal and	
and interest payments)	
Annual interest rate	10%
(interest paid annually)	
Costs of issuance	$420,000
(paid on date of issue)	
Available funds can be invested at	12%
Timing of construction costs:	
1/1/X1	$ 1,000,000
1/1/X2	7,000,000
1/1/X3	6,000,000
	$14,000,000

2. Determine the optimum serial bond issue size to finance a new high school using the method developed by Philip Law from the following information:

Costs of construction	
1/1/X1	$ 500,000
1/7/X1	1,000,000
1/1/X2	1,000,000
1/7/X2	1,250,000
1/1/X3	1,500,000
1/7/X3	1,250,000
1/1/X4	1,000,000
Total	$7,500,000

Date of bond issue	1/1/X1
Date of first maturity	1/1/X6
Date of last maturity (10 equal semiannual interest and principal payments)	1/1/Y1
Annual interest rate (interest paid semiannually)	8%
Cost of issuance	$200,000
Discount on bonds at issuance	2%
Available funds can be invested at	10%

3. For problem 1, complete tables similar to 15.4 and 15.5 to prove the accuracy of the results obtained.

4. For problem 2, complete tables similar to 15.4 and 15.5 to prove the accuracy of the results obtained.

5. Using the net interest cost method, evaluate the following underwriters' bids on serial bonds.

	Coupon rate	
	Underwriter A (%)	Underwriter B (%)
Yr 1	10	8
Yr 2	10	8
Yr 3	10	10
Yr 4	10	12
Yr 5	10	12

Both underwriters will pay face amount for the $1,000,000 bond issue. One-fifth or $200,000 of the bonds will mature each year. Each bond has a face value of $1,000.

6. Using the net interest cost method of evaluation, which underwriter's bid is preferred on a serial bond issue of 1000 $10,000 face-value bonds? $2,500,000 of the bonds mature in years 5 through 8. Both underwriters will pay face value for the bonds, and coupon rates specified are:

Year	Underwriter A (%)	Underwriter B (%)
5	12.0	10.0
6	11.0	10.0
7	10.0	9.5
8	9.0	9.5

7. Using the data from problem 5 and the true interest cost method, determine which is the preferable underwriter's bid. Interest is paid annually.

8. Using the data from problem 6 and the true interest method, determine which is the preferable underwriter's bid. Interest is paid annually.

9. Using the data from problem 5 and the present-value interest cost method, determine which underwriter is preferred. Discount rates are as follows:

Year	Rate (%)
1	8.0
2	8.5
3	9.0
4	9.0
5	8.5

10. Using the data from problem 6 and the present-value interest cost method, determine which underwriter is preferred. Discount rates are as follows:

Year	Rate (%)
1	7.0
2	7.5
3	7.5
4	8.0
5	8.0

6	8.0
7	8.5
8	8.5

11. The county hospital plans to issue $10,000,000 in serial bonds to finance construction of a new wing. One-fifth of the principal amount matures every two years from year 7 through 15. Insurance is expected to cost $100,000. Should the county hospital purchase the bond insurance if the interest rates on the various maturities with and without insurance are estimated at:

| | Coupon rate | |
Year of maturity	Without insurance(%)	With insurance(%)
7	9.0	8.4
9	8.5	8.1
11	8.0	7.9
13	8.0	7.7
15	8.0	7.5

12. The city of Antonio must issue $5,000,000 in general obligations bonds to construct a freeway around the city. The bonds are to be term bonds due in 10 years. Interest is to be paid semi-annually, and the current discount is 10 percent. Should the city purchase bond insurance? The premium will cost $60,000 but underwriting expenses will increase $10,000 without it. The coupon rates with and without insurance are 11 percent and 12 percent, respectively.

13. Beta city is considering refunding $5,000,000 of 9 percent debentures. The $1,000 par value bonds can be recalled for $1030. New bonds can be sold for $1,000 par value but have selling costs of 4 percent of par value plus $80,000 in other issuing expenses. What is the marginal cost of issuing the new bonds? Should the issue be refunded?

14. The city of Okeane is considering refunding an $8,000,000 bond issue which matures in 10 years and has a coupon rate of 8 percent. The new issue would bear a 6 percent coupon rate and can be sold for $975.61 ($1000 par value). The old issue can be called at 102. The cost of issuing the new bonds is 3 percent of the selling price plus $60,000. Should the issue be refunded?

15. A local hospital can purchase an automated meal delivery system for patients at a cost of $3,000,000 or it can lease the system for 10 years at $350,000 per year. If it purchases the system, the hospital would have to finance it at the current rate of 10 percent interest and the system would have a salvage value of $250,000. If it is leased, payments must be made annually at the beginning of each year. Should the system be purchased or leased?

16. The city of Pere must decide whether to lease or buy five trucks for garbage collection and snow removal. Each truck has a cost of $65,000, an estimated life of 8 years, and a salvage value of $5,000. The city would have to borrow funds at 12 percent to finance the purchase. The lease alternative requires annual lease payments of $9,000 per year per truck paid at the beginning of the year for 8 years. Should the city lease or buy the trucks?

ENDNOTES

1. Philip M. Law, Jr. "How to Calculate the Size of Your Bond Issue," Special Bulletin 1976B, (Chicago: Municipal Finance Officers Association, June 1, 1976).
2. Ibid, p. 3.
3. This section is primarily from: Jerome S. Osteryoung, Ronald C. Braswell, and Dallas R. Blevins. "PIC: An Alternative Approach to Accepting Bids on Local and State Government Bonds," Financial Management (Summer 1979), pp. 36-41.
4. Kalman J. Cohen and Frederick S. Hammer. "Optimal Coupon Structures for Municipal Bonds," Management Science (September 1965), pp. 68-82.
5. Richard R. West. "Net Interest Cost Method of Issuing Tax-Exempt Bonds: Is it Rational?" Public Finance (Fall 1968), pp. 346-354.
6. For examples see:
   i. Michael H. Hopewell and George G. Kaufman. "Cost to Municipalities of Selling Bonds by NIC," National Tax Journal (December 1974), pp. 531-541.
   ii. Lennox L. Moak. Administration of Local Government Debt (Chicago: Municipal Fi-

nance Officers Association, 1970).

   iii. Alan Rabinowitz. Municipal Bond Finance and Administration (New York: Wiley - Interscience, 1969).

   iv. Roland I. Robinson. Postwar Market for State and Local Securities (Princeton: National Bureau of Economic Research, 1960).

7. The TIC method is also referred to as the internal rate of return, bond basis, or Canadian method.

8. Charles Cole and Dennis T. Officer, "The Interest Cost Effect of Private Municipal Bond Insurance"; Paper presented at the Sixteenth Annual Meeting of the Eastern Finance Association, April 17-19, 1980, Savannah, Georgia, p. 2.

9. Ibid.

10. Ibid, pp. 13-14.

11. Michael D. Joehnk and Davis S. Kidwell. "Determining the Advantages and Disadvantages of Private Municipal Bond Guarantees," Governmental Finance (February 1978), p. 32.

12. See Joehnk and Kidwell, pp. 32-35.

13. As Joehnk and Kidwell pointed out in their article, the insurance premium could be added to the principal amount of the issue. In this case, its differential cash outflow would have to be amoritized over the life of the bond issue. For example, the amount of the premium could be added to each of the principal payments in equal installments. The Joehnk and Kidwell model assumes a lump sum payment of the premium at the time of sale.

14. Joehnk and Kidwell, pp. 33-35.

15. The framework that follows is based on: Edward A. Dyl and Michael D. Joehnk. "Refunding Tax Exempt Bonds," Financial Management (Summer 1976), pp. 59-66.

16. This section is based on: Edward A. Dyl and Michael D. Joehnk, "Leasing as a Municipal Finance Alternative," Research Paper No. 182, University of Wyoming, March, 1977.

17. Ibid, pp. 2-3.

18. Ibid, p. 10.

INDEX

415